T0356950

Get the eBook FREE!

(PDF, ePub, Kindle, and liveBook all included)

We believe that once you buy a book from us, you should be able to read it in any format we have available. To get electronic versions of this book at no additional cost to you, purchase and then register this book at the Manning website.

Go to https://www.manning.com/freebook and follow the instructions to complete your pBook registration.

That's it!
Thanks from Manning!

Graph Neural Networks in Action

KEITA BROADWATER
NAMID STILLMAN
FOREWORD BY MATTHIAS FEY

MANNING
SHELTER ISLAND

For online information and ordering of this and other Manning books, please visit
www.manning.com. The publisher offers discounts on this book when ordered in quantity.
For more information, please contact

> Special Sales Department
> Manning Publications Co.
> 20 Baldwin Road
> PO Box 761
> Shelter Island, NY 11964
> Email: orders@manning.com

Manning Publications Co.	Development editor: Frances Lefkowitz
20 Baldwin Road	Technical development editor: Frances Buontempo
PO Box 761	Review editors: Radmila Ercegovac and
Shelter Island, NY 11964	Aleksandar Dragosavljević
	Production editor: Keri Hales
	Copy editor: Julie McNamee
	Proofreader: Jason Everett
	Technical proofreader: Kerry Koitzsch
	Typesetter: Dennis Dalinnik
	Cover designer: Marija Tudor

ISBN: 9781617299056
Printed in the United States of America

This book is dedicated to my son, Akin.

—Keita Broadwater

This book is dedicated to my wife, for her patience as I worked through the night, and to my dog, who kept me company during those same hours.

—Namid Stillman

brief contents

contents

foreword

Our world is highly rich in structure, comprising objects, their relations, and hierarchies. Sentences can be represented as sequences of words, maps can be broken down into streets and intersections, the world wide web connects websites via hyperlinks, and chemical compounds can be described by a set of atoms and their interactions. Despite the prevalence of graph structures in our world, both traditional and even modern machine learning methods struggle to properly handle such rich structural information: machine learning conventionally expects fixed-sized vectors as inputs and is thus only applicable to simpler structures such as sequences or grids. Consequently, graph machine learning has long relied on labor-intensive and error-prone handcrafted feature engineering techniques. Graph neural networks (GNNs) finally revolutionize this paradigm by breaking up with the regularity restriction of conventional deep learning techniques. They unlock the ability to learn representations from raw graph data with exceptional performance and allow us to view deep learning as a much broader technique that can seamlessly generalize to complex and rich topological structures.

When I began to dive into the field of graph machine learning, deep learning on graphs was still in its early stages. Over time, dozens to hundreds of different methods were developed, contributing incremental insights and refreshing ideas. Tools like our own PyTorch Geometric library have expanded significantly, offering cutting-edge graph-based building blocks, models, examples, and scalability solutions. Reflecting on this growth, it's clear how overwhelming it can be for newcomers to navigate the essentials and best practices that have emerged over time, as valuable information is scattered across theoretical research papers or buried in implementations in GitHub repositories.

Now that the power of GNNs has been widely understood, this timely book provides a well-structured and easy-to-follow overview of the field, providing answers to many pain points of graph machine learning practitioners. The hands-on approach, with practical code examples embedded directly within each chapter, invaluably demystifies the complexities, making the concepts tangible and actionable. Despite the success of GNNs across all kinds of domains in research, adoption in real-world applications remains limited to companies that have enough resources to acquire the necessary knowledge for applying GNNs in practice. I'm confident that this book will serve as an invaluable resource to empower practitioners to overcome that gap and unlock the full potential of GNNs.

—MATTHIAS FEY, creator of PyTorch Geometric and founding engineer, Kumo.AI

preface

My journey into the world of graphs began unexpectedly, during an interview at LinkedIn. As the session wrapped up, I was shown a visualization of my network—a mesmerizing structure that told stories without a single word. Organizations I had been part of appeared clustered, like constellations against a dark canvas. What surprised me most was that this structure was not built using metadata LinkedIn held about my connections; rather, it emerged organically from the relationships between nodes and edges.

Years later, driven by curiosity, I recreated that visualization. I marveled once again at how the underlying connections alone could map out an intricate picture of my professional life. This deepened my appreciation for the power inherent in graphs—a fascination that only grew when I joined Cloudera and encountered graph neural networks (GNNs). Their potential for solving complex problems was captivating, but diving into them was like trying to navigate an uncharted forest without a map. There were no comprehensive resources tailored for nonacademics; progress was slow, often cobbled together from fragments and trial and error.

This book is the guide I wish I had during those early days. It aims to provide a clear and accessible path for practitioners, enthusiasts, and anyone looking to understand and apply GNNs without wading through endless academic papers or fragmented online searches. My hope is that it serves as a one-stop resource for you to learn the fundamentals and paves the way for deeper exploration.

Whether you're here out of professional necessity, sheer curiosity, or the same kind of amazement that first drew me in, I invite you to embark on this journey. Together, let's bring the potential of GNNs to life.

—KEITA BROADWATER

acknowledgments

Many people brought this book to life. Thanks to the development and editorial staff at Manning, especially Frances Lefkowitz (development editor) and Frances Buontempo (technical development editor). In addition, thanks to the production staff for all the hard work behind the scenes to shepherd this book into its final format.

Thanks to all the reviewers whose suggestions helped make this a better book: Abe Taha, Adi Shavit, Aditya Visweswaran, Alain Couniot, Allan Makura, Amaresh Rajasekharan, Andrew Mooney, Ariel Gamino, Atilla Ozgur, Atul Saurav, Ayush Bihani, Cosimo Attanasi, Daniel Berecz, Davide Cadamuro, Fernando García Sedano, Gautham K., George Loweree Gaines, Giampiero Granatella, Gourav Sengupta, Igor Vieira, Ioannis Atsonios, John Powell, Karrtik Iyer, Keith Kim, Maciej Szymkiewicz, Maxime Dehaut, Maxim Volgin, Mikael Dautrey, Ninoslav Čerkez, Noah Flynn, Or Golan, Peter Henstock, Richard Tobias, Rodolfo Allendes, Rohit Agarwal, Sadhana Ganapathiraju, Sanjeev Kilarapu, Sergio Govoni, Simona Russo, Simone Sguazza, Sowmya Vajjala, Sri Ram Macharla, Thomas Joseph Heiman, Tymoteusz Wołodźko, Vidhya Vinay, Viton Vitanis, Vojta Tuma, and Wei Luo.

KEITA BROADWATER: I thank my mother and father for instilling within me a love of books and learning. I thank my friends Jaz and Mindy for their encouragement. I thank the team at Cloudera and Fast Forward Labs where the seed of this book began. I thank Jeremy Howard for changing my perspective about deep learning. Many thanks to Frances Lefkowitz who was a steady guide in creating this book. And I thank my co-author, Namid, for sharing this journey with me.

NAMID STILLMAN: I thank my family for fostering my desire to learn about the world and encouraging my inclination to bring others with me as I do. I thank my academic mentors, especially Ollie, Martin, Roberto, and Gilles, who gave me the tools to think technically and the encouragement to go out and use them. And I thank my co-author, Keita, for bringing me on this journey.

about this book

Graph Neural Networks in Action is a book designed for people to jump quickly into this new field and start building applications. At the same time, we try to strike a balance by including just enough critical theory to make this book as standalone as possible. We also fill in implementation details that may not be obvious or are left unexplained in the currently available online tutorials and documents. In particular, information about new and emerging topics is very likely to be fragmented. This fragmentation adds friction when implementing and testing new technologies.

With *Graph Neural Networks in Action*, we offer a book that can reduce that friction by filling in the gaps and answering key questions whose answers are likely scattered over the internet or not covered at all. We've done so in a way that emphasizes approachability rather than high rigor.

Who should read this book

This book is designed for machine learning engineers and data scientists familiar with neural networks but new to graph learning. If you have experience in object-oriented programming, you'll find the concepts particularly accessible and applicable.

How this book is organized: A road map

In part 1 of this book, we provide a motivation for exploring GNNs, as well as cover fundamental concepts of graphs and graph-based machine learning. In chapter 1, we introduce the concepts of graphs and graph machine learning, providing guidelines for their use and applications. Chapter 2 covers graph representations up to and including node embeddings. This will be the first programmatic exposure to graph neural networks (GNNs), which are used to create such embeddings.

In part 2, the core of the book, we introduce the major types of GNNs, including graph convolutional networks (GCNs) and GraphSAGE in chapter 3, graph attention networks (GATs) in chapter 4, and graph autoencoders (GAEs) in chapter 5. These methods are the bread and butter for most GNN applications and also cover a range of other deep learning concepts such as convolution, attention, and autoencoders.

In part 3, we'll look at more advanced topics. We describe GNNs for dynamic graphs (spatio-temporal GNNs) in chapter 6 and give methods to train GNNs at scale in chapter 7. Finally, we end with some consideration for project and system planning for graph learning projects in chapter 8.

About the code

Python is the coding language of choice throughout this book. There are now several GNN libraries in the Python ecosystem, including PyTorch Geometric (PyG), Deep Graph Library (DGL), GraphScope, and Jraph. We focus on PyG, which is one of the most popular and easy-to-use frameworks, written on top of PyTorch. We want this book to be approachable by an audience with a wide set of hardware constraints, so with the exception of some individual sections and chapter 7 on scalability, distributed systems and GPU systems aren't required, although they can be used for some of the coded examples.

The book provides a survey of the most relevant implementations of GNNs, including graph convolutional networks (GCNs), graph autoencoders (GAEs), graph attention networks (GATs), and graph long short-term memory (LSTM). The aim is to cover the GNN tasks mentioned earlier. In addition, we'll touch on different types of graphs, including knowledge graphs.

This book contains many examples of source code both in numbered listings and in line with normal text. In both cases, source code is formatted in a `fixed-width font like this` to separate it from ordinary text. Sometimes code is also **in bold** to highlight code that has changed from previous steps in the chapter, such as when a new feature adds to an existing line of code.

In many cases, the original source code has been reformatted; we've added line breaks and reworked indentation to accommodate the available page space in the book. In rare cases, even this was not enough, and listings include line-continuation markers (➥). Additionally, comments in the source code have often been removed from the listings when the code is described in the text. Code annotations accompany many of the listings, highlighting important concepts.

You can get executable snippets of code from the liveBook (online) version of this book at https://livebook.manning.com/book/graph-neural-networks-in-action. The complete code for the examples in the book is available for download from the Manning website at www.manning.com/books/graph-neural-networks-in-action and from GitHub at https://github.com/keitabroadwater/gnns_in_action.

liveBook discussion forum

Purchase of *Graph Neural Networks in Action* includes free access to liveBook, Manning's online reading platform. Using liveBook's exclusive discussion features, you can attach comments to the book globally or to specific sections or paragraphs. It's a snap to make notes for yourself, ask and answer technical questions, and receive help from the authors and other users. To access the forum, go to https://livebook.manning.com/book/graph-neural-networks-in-action/discussion. You can also learn more about Manning's forums and the rules of conduct at https://livebook.manning.com/discussion.

Manning's commitment to our readers is to provide a venue where a meaningful dialogue between individual readers and between readers and the authors can take place. It is not a commitment to any specific amount of participation on the part of the authors, whose contribution to the forum remains voluntary (and unpaid). We suggest you try asking the authors some challenging questions lest their interest stray! The forum and the archives of previous discussions will be accessible from the publisher's website as long as the book is in print.

about the authors

KEITA BROADWATER, PhD, MBA (https://bsky.app/profile/keitabr.bsky.social), is a data science and machine learning engineering leader with more than two decades of experience shaping data and AI-driven value and innovation. As the Director of Machine Learning Engineering at Hewani Data, he uses his expertise in developing production-ready solutions to complex business challenges. Keita's career spans roles at LinkedIn, Intel, Cloudera, and Disney Streaming. He is a sought-after speaker who regularly shares insights on leadership, technology, and the emerging machine learning space in Africa. As a passionate tech investor, he is dedicated to empowering and inspiring the next generation of technology leaders. When not immersed in code or mentoring aspiring engineers, you can find him exploring California history or running in local races from his home in the San Francisco Bay area.

NAMID STILLMAN, PhD (https://x.com/nrstillman), is an applied research scientist focused on integrating AI methods into scientific research. As an active researcher who has worked on problems in nanoscience, drug discovery, cell biology, and complex systems, he has written more than 20 peer-reviewed articles in top academic journals, and has received generous funding support while conducting research at the University of Bristol, University College, London, and the Alan Turing Institute. He is currently the head of AI at Simudyne, where he helps develop complex models for industry. In his free time, he enjoys spending time in London or going for hikes outside the city. You can learn more at https://nrstillman.github.io.

about the cover illustration

The figure on the cover of *Graph Neural Networks in Action* is "Matelot provençal," or "Sailor from Provence," taken from a collection by Jacques Grasset de Saint-Sauveur, published in 1788. Each illustration is finely drawn and colored by hand.

In those days, it was easy to identify where people lived and what their trade or station in life was just by their dress. Manning celebrates the inventiveness and initiative of the computer business with book covers based on the rich diversity of regional culture centuries ago, brought back to life by pictures from collections such as this one.

Part 1

First steps

Graphs are one of the most versatile and powerful ways to represent complex, interconnected data. This first part introduces the fundamental concepts of graph theory, explaining what graphs are, why they matter as a data type, and how their structure captures relationships that traditional data formats miss. You'll explore the building blocks of graphs and different graph types.

Then, we'll explore foundational concepts about graph neural networks (GNNs), beginning with what they are and how they differ from traditional neural networks. With this foundation, we study graph embeddings, uncovering how to represent graphs in a way that makes them useful for machine learning. These concepts set the stage for mastering GNNs and their transformative capabilities in later chapters. By the end of this part of the book, you'll have a solid understanding of the basics, preparing you to dive deeper into the mechanics of GNNs.

Discovering graph
neural networks

This chapter covers

- Defining graphs and graph neural networks
- Understanding why people are excited about graph neural networks
- Recognizing when to use graph neural networks
- Taking a big picture look at solving a problem with a graph neural network

For data practitioners, the fields of machine learning and data science initially excite us because of the potential to draw nonintuitive and useful insights from data. In particular, the insights from machine learning and deep learning promise to enhance our understanding of the world. For the working engineer, these tools promise to deliver business value in unprecedented ways.

Experience deviates from this ideal. Real-world data is usually messy, dirty and biased. Furthermore, statistical methods and learning systems come with their own set of limitations. An essential role of the practitioner is to comprehend these limitations and bridge the gap between real data and a feasible solution. For example, we may want to predict fraudulent activity in a bank, but we first need to make sure that our training data has been correctly labeled. Even more importantly, we'll need to check that our models won't incorrectly assign fraudulent activity to normal behaviors, possibly due to some hidden confounders in the data.

For graph data, until recently, bridging this gap has been particularly challenging. Graphs are a data structure that is rich with information and especially adept at capturing the intricacies of data where relationships play a crucial role. Graphs are omnipresent, with relational data appearing in different forms such as atoms in molecules (nature), social networks (society), and even models the connection of web pages on the internet (technology) [1]. It's important to note that the term *relational* here doesn't refer to *relational databases*, but rather to data where relationships are of significance.

Previously, if you wanted to incorporate relational features from a graph into a deep learning model, it had to be done in an indirect way, with different models used to process, analyze, and then use the graph data. These separate models often couldn't be easily scaled and had trouble taking into account all the node and edge properties of graph data. To make the best use of this rich and ubiquitous data type for machine learning, we needed a specialized machine learning technique specifically designed for the distinct qualities of graphs and relational data. This is the gap that graph neural networks (GNNs) fill.

The deep learning field often contains a lot of hype around new technologies and methods. However, GNNs are widely recognized as a genuine leap forward for graph-based learning [2]. This doesn't mean that GNNs are a silver bullet. Careful comparisons should be done between predictive results derived from GNNs and other machine learning and deep learning methods.

The key thing to remember is that if your data science problem involves data that can be structured as a graph—that is, the data is connected or relational—then GNNs could offer a valuable approach, even if you weren't aware that something was missing in your approach. GNNs can be designed to handle very large data, to scale, and to adapt to graphs of different sizes and shapes. This can make working with relationship-centric data easier and more efficient, as well as yield richer results.

The standout advantages of GNNs are why data scientists and engineers are increasingly recognizing the importance of mastering them. GNNs have the ability to unveil unique insights from relational data—from identifying new drug candidates to optimizing ETA prediction accuracy in your Google Maps app—acting as a catalyst for discovery and innovation, and empowering professionals to push the boundaries of conventional data analysis. Their diverse applicability spans various fields, offering professionals a versatile tool that is as relevant in e-commerce (e.g., recommendation engines) as it is in bioinformatics (e.g., drug toxicity prediction). Proficiency in GNNs equips data professionals with a multifaceted tool for enhanced, accurate, and innovative data analysis of graphs.

For all these reasons, GNNs are now the popular choice for recommender engines, analyzing social networks, detecting fraud, understanding how biomolecules behave, and many other practical examples that we'll meet over the course of this book.

1.1 Goals of this book

Graph Neural Networks in Action is aimed at practitioners who want to begin to deploy GNNs to solve real problems. This could be a machine learning engineer not familiar with graph data structures, a data scientist who hasn't yet tried GNNs, or even a software engineer who may be unfamiliar with either. Throughout this book, we'll be covering topics from the basics of graphs all the way to more complex GNN models. We'll be building up the architecture of a GNN, step-by-step. This includes the overall architecture of a GNN and the critical aspect of message passing. We then go on to add different features and extensions to these basic aspects, such as introducing convolution and sampling, attention mechanisms, a generative model, and operating on dynamic graphs. When building our GNNs, we'll be working in Python and using some standard libraries. GNN libraries are either standalone or use TensorFlow or PyTorch as a backend. In this text, the focus will be on PyTorch Geometric (PyG). Other popular libraries include Deep Graph Library (DGL, a standalone library) and Spektral (which uses Keras and TensorFlow as a backend). There is also Jraph for JAX users.

Our aim throughout this book is to enable you to

- assess the suitability of a GNN solution for your problem.
- understand when traditional neural networks won't perform as well as a GNN for graph structured data and when GNNs may not be the best tool for tabular data.
- design and implement a GNN architecture to solve problems specific to you.
- make clear the limitations of GNNs.

This book is weighted toward implementation using programming. We also devote some time on essential theory and concepts, so that the techniques covered can be sufficiently understood. These are covered in an "Under the Hood" section at the end of most chapters to separate the technical reasons from the actual implementation. There are many different models and packages that build on the key concepts we introduce in this book. So, this book shouldn't be seen as a comprehensive review of all GNN methods and models, which could run to several thousands of pages, but rather the starting point for the curious and eager-to-learn practitioner.

The book is divided into three parts. Part 1 covers the basics of GNNs, especially the ways in which they differ from other neural networks, such as *message passing* and *embeddings*, which have specific meaning for GNNs. Part 2, the heart of the book, goes over the models themselves, where we cover a handful of key model types. Then, in part 3, we'll go into more detail with some of the harder models and concepts, including how to scale graphs and deal with temporal data.

Graph Neural Networks in Action is designed for people to jump quickly into this new field and start building applications. Our aim for this book is to reduce the friction of implementing new technologies by filling in the gaps and answering key development questions whose answers may not be easy to find or may not be covered elsewhere at all. Each method is introduced through an example application so you can understand how GNNs are applied in practice. We strongly advise you to try out the code for yourself along the way.

1.1.1   Catching up on graph fundamentals

Yes, you do need to understand the basics of graphs before you can understand GNNs. Yet our goal for this book is to teach GNNs to deep learning practitioners and builders of traditional neural networks who may not know much about graphs. At the same time, we also recognize that readers of this book may vary enormously in their knowledge of graphs. How to address these differences and make sure everyone has what they need to make the most of this book? In this chapter, we provide an introduction to the fundamental graph concepts that are most essential to understanding GNNs. If you're well-versed in graphs, you may choose to skip this section, although we recommend skimming through as we cover some specific terminology and use-cases that will be helpful to understand for the remainder of the book. For those of you who have more questions about graphs, we've also included a full tutorial on basic graph concepts and terminology in appendix A. This primer should also serve as a reference for looking up specific concepts.

After the refresher on key concepts in graphs and graph learning, we'll look into some case studies in several fields where GNNs are being successfully applied. Then, we'll break down those specific cases to see what makes a good case for using a GNN, as well as how to know if you have a GNN problem on your hands. At the end of the chapter, we introduce the mechanics of GNNs, the barebone skeleton that the rest of the book will add to.

1.2   Graph-based learning

This section defines graphs, graph-based learning, and some fundamentals of GNNs, including the basic structure of a graph and a taxonomy of different types of graphs. Then, we'll review graph-based learning, putting GNNs in context with other learning methods. Finally, we'll explain the value of graphs, ending with an example of data derived from the Titanic dataset.

1.2.1   What are graphs?

Graphs are data structures with elements, expressed as *nodes or vertices*, and relationships between elements, expressed as *edges or links*, as shown in figure 1.1. All nodes in the graph will have additional *feature data*. This is node-specific data, relating to things such as the names or ages of individuals in a social network. The links are key to the power of relational data, as they allow us to learn more about the system, give new tools for analyzing data, and predict new properties from it. This is in contrast to tabular data such as a database table, dataframe, or spreadsheet, where the data is fixed in rows and columns.

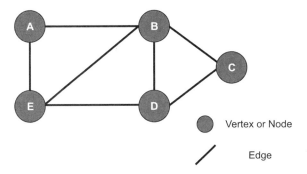

Figure 1.1 A graph. Individual elements, represented here by letters A through E, are nodes, also called vertices, and their relationships are described by edges, also known as links.

To describe and learn from the edges between the nodes, we need a way to write them down. This can be done explicitly, stating that the A node is connected to B and E, and that the B node is connected to A, C, D, and E. Quickly, we can see that describing things in this way becomes unwieldy and that we might be repeating redundant information (that A is connected to B and that B is connected to A). Luckily, there are many mathematical formalisms for describing relations in graphs. One of the most common is to describe the *adjacency matrix*, which we write out in table 1.1. Notice that the adjacency matrix is symmetric across the diagonal and that all values are ones or zero.

Table 1.1 The adjacency matrix for the simple graph in figure 1.1

	A	B	C	D	E
A	0	1	0	0	1
B	1	0	1	1	1
C	0	1	0	1	0
D	0	1	1	0	1
E	1	1	0	1	0

The adjacency matrix of a graph is an important concept that makes it easy to observe all the connections of a graph in a single table [3]. Here, we assumed that there is no directionality in our graph; that is, if 0 is connected to 1, then 1 is also connected to 0. This is known as an *undirected graph*. Undirected graphs can be easily inferred from an adjacency matrix because, in this case, the matrix is symmetric across the diagonal (e.g., in table 1.1, the upper-right triangle is reflected onto the bottom left).

We also assume here that all the relations between nodes are identical. If we wanted the relation of nodes B–E to mean more than the relation of nodes B–A, then we could increase the weight of this edge. This translates to increasing the value in the adjacency matrix, making the entry for the B–A edge in table 1.1 equal to 10 instead of 1, for example.

Graphs where all relations are of equal importance are known as *unweighted graphs* and can also be easily observed from the adjacency matrix because all graph entries are either 1s or 0s. Graphs where edges have multiple values are known as *weighted.*

If any of the nodes in the graph don't have an edge that connects to itself, then the nodes will also have 0s at their own value in the adjacency matrix (0s along the diagonal). This means a graph doesn't have self-loops. A *self-loop* occurs when a node has an edge that connects to that same node. To add a self-loop, we just make the value for that node nonzero at its position in the diagonal.

In practice, an adjacency matrix is only one of many ways to describe relations in a graph. Others include adjacency lists, edge lists, or an incidence matrix. Understanding these types of data structures well is vital to graph-based learning. If you're unfamiliar with these terms, or need a refresher, we recommend looking through appendix A, which has additional details and explanations.

1.2.2   *Different types of graphs*

Understanding the many different types of graphs can help us work out what methods to use to analyze and transform the graph, and what machine learning methods to apply. In the following, we give a very quick overview of some of the most common properties for graphs to have. As before, we recommend you look through appendix A for further information.

HOMOGENEOUS AND HETEROGENEOUS GRAPHS

The most basic graphs are *homogenous graphs,* which are made up of one type of node and one type of edge. Consider a homogeneous graph that describes a recruitment network. In this type of graph, the nodes would represent job candidates, and the edges would represent relationships between the candidates.

If we want to expand the power of our graph to describe our recruitment network, we could give it more types of nodes and edges, making it a *heterogeneous graph.* With this expansion, some nodes may be candidates and others may be companies. Edges could now consist of relationships between candidates and current or past employment of job candidates at the companies. See figure 1.2 for a comparison of a homogeneous

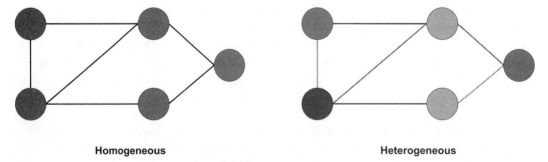

        Homogeneous   Heterogeneous

Figure 1.2   A homogeneous graph and a heterogeneous graph. Here, the shade of a node or edge represents its type or class. For the homogeneous graph, all nodes are of the same type, and all edges are of the same type. For the heterogeneous graph, nodes and edges have multiple types.

graph (all nodes or edges have the same shade) with a heterogeneous graph (nodes and edges have a variety of shades).

BIPARTITE GRAPHS

Similar to heterogeneous graphs, *bipartite graphs* also can be separated or partitioned into different subsets. However, bipartite graphs (figure 1.3) have a very specific network structure such that nodes in each subset connect to nodes outside of their subset and not inside. Later, we'll be discussing recommendation systems and the Pinterest graph. This graph is bipartite because one set of nodes (pins) connects another set of nodes (boards) but not to nodes within their set (pins).

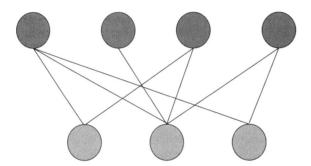

Figure 1.3   **A bipartite graph. There are two types of nodes (two shades of circles). In a bipartite graph, nodes can't be connected to nodes of the same type. This is also an example of a heterogeneous graph.**

CYCLIC GRAPHS, ACYCLIC GRAPHS, AND DIRECTED ACYCLIC GRAPHS

A graph is *cyclic* if it allows you to start at a node, travel along its edges, and return to the starting node without retracing any steps, creating a circular path within the graph. In contrast, in an *acyclic* graph, no matter which path you take from any starting node, you can't return to the starting point without backtracking. These graphs, as shown in figure 1.4, often resemble tree-like structures or paths that don't loop back on themselves.

While both cyclic and acyclic graphs can be either undirected or directed, a *directed acyclic graph (DAG)* is a specific type of acyclic graph that is exclusively directed. In a DAG, all edges have a direction, and no cycles are allowed. DAGs represent one-way relationships where you can't follow the arrows and end up back at the starting point. This characteristic makes DAGs essential in causal analysis, as they reflect causal structures where causality is assumed to be unidirectional. For example, A can cause B, but B can't simultaneously cause A. This unidirectional nature aligns perfectly with the structure of DAGs, making them ideal for modeling workflow processes, dependency chains, and causal relationships in various fields.

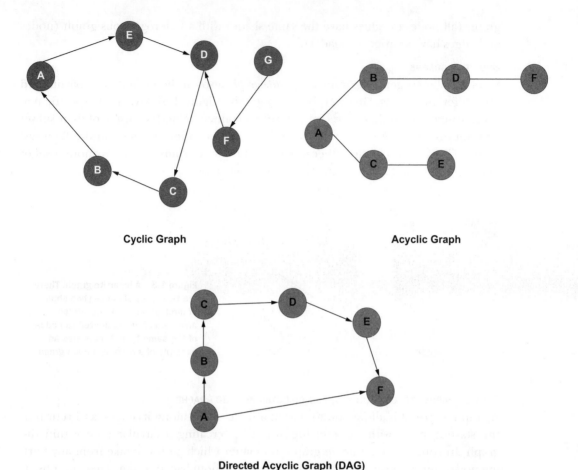

Cyclic Graph

Acyclic Graph

Directed Acyclic Graph (DAG)

Figure 1.4   A cyclic graph (left), an acyclic graph (right), and a DAG (bottom). In the cyclic graph, the cycle is shown by the arrows (directed edges) connecting nodes A-E-D-C-B-A. Note that two nodes, G and F are part of the graph, but not part of its defining cycle. The acyclic graph is composed of undirected edges, and no cycle is possible. In the DAG, all directed edges flow in one direction, from A to F.

KNOWLEDGE GRAPHS

A *knowledge graph* is a specialized type of heterogeneous graph that represents data with enriched semantic meaning, capturing not only the relationships between different entities but also the context and nature of these relationships. Unlike conventional graphs, which primarily emphasize structure and connectivity, a knowledge graph incorporates metadata and follows specific schemas to provide deeper contextual information. This allows for advanced reasoning and querying capabilities, such as identifying patterns, uncovering specific types of connections, or inferring new relationships.

In the example of an academic research network at a university, a knowledge graph might represent various entities such as Professors, Students, Papers, and Research

Topics, and explicitly define the relationships between them. For instance, Professors and Students could be associated with Papers through an Authorship relationship, while Professors might also Supervise Students. Furthermore, the graph would reflect hierarchical structures, such as Professors and Students being categorized under Departments. You can see this knowledge graph depicted in figure 1.5.

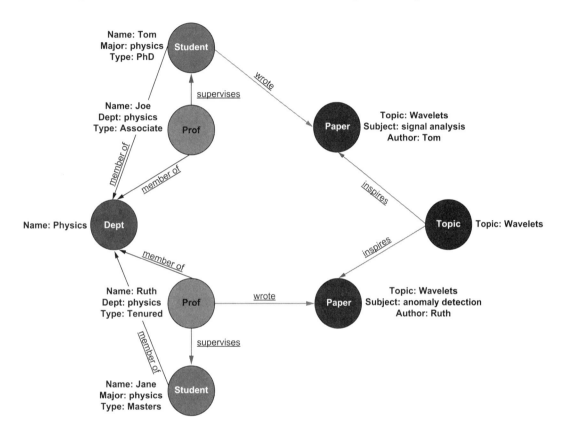

Figure 1.5   A knowledge graph representing an academic research network within a university's physics department. The graph illustrates both hierarchical relationships, such as professors and students as members of the department, and behavioral relationships, such as professors supervising students and authoring papers. Entities such as Professors, Students, Papers, and Topics are connected through semantically meaningful relationships (Supervises, Wrote, Inspires). Entities also have detailed features (Name, Department, Type) providing further context. The semantic connections and features enable advanced querying and analysis of complex academic interactions.

A key feature of knowledge graphs is their ability to provide explicit context. Unlike conventional heterogeneous graphs, which display different types of entities and their basic connections without detailed semantic meaning, knowledge graphs go further by defining the specific types and meanings of relationships. For example, while a traditional graph might show that Professors are connected to Departments or that Students are linked to Papers, a knowledge graph would specify that Professors supervise

Students or that Students and Professors Wrote Papers. This added layer of meaning enables more powerful querying and analysis, making knowledge graphs particularly valuable in fields such as natural language processing, recommendation systems, and academic research analysis.

HYPERGRAPHS

One of the more complex and difficult graphs to work with is the hypergraph. *Hypergraphs* are those where a single edge can be connected to multiple different nodes. For graphs that aren't hypergraphs, edges are used to connect exactly two nodes (or a node to itself for self-loops). As shown in figure 1.6, edges in a hypergraph can connect between any number of nodes. The complexity of a hypergraph is reflected in its adjacency data. For typical graphs, network connectivity is represented by a two-dimensional adjacency matrix. For hypergraphs, the adjacency matrix extends to a higher dimensional tensor, referred to as an *incidence tensor*. This tensor is N-dimensional, where N is the maximum number of nodes connected by a single edge. An example of a hypergraph might be a communication platform that allows for group chats as well as single person conversations. In an ordinary graph, edges would only connect

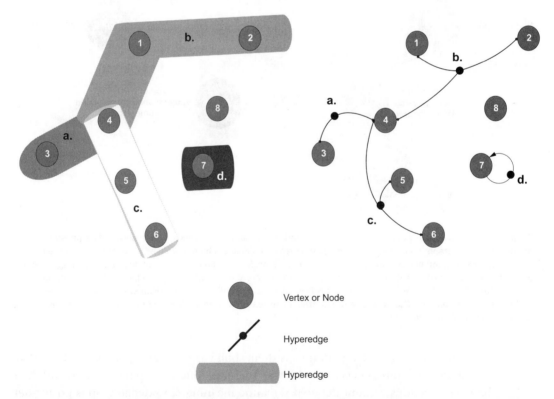

Figure 1.6   One undirected hypergraph, illustrated in two ways. On the left, we have a graph whose edges are represented by shaded areas, marked by letters, and whose vertices are dots, marked by numbers. On the right, we have a graph whose edge lines (marked by letters) connect up to 3 nodes (circles marked by numbers). Node 8 has no edge. Node 7 has a self-loop.

two people. In a hypergraph, one hyperedge could connect multiple people, representing a group chat.

1.2.3 *Graph-based learning*

As we'll see in the rest of this chapter, graphs are ubiquitous in our everyday life. *Graph-based learning* takes graphs as input data to build models that give insight into questions about this data. Later in this chapter, we look at different examples of graph data as well as at the sort of questions and tasks we can use graph-based learning to answer.

Graph-based learning uses a variety of machine learning methods to build *representations* of graphs. These representations are then used for downstream tasks such as node or link prediction or graph classification. In chapter 2, you'll learn about one of the essential tools in graph-based learning, building embeddings. Briefly, embeddings are *low-dimensional* vector representations. We can build an embedding of different nodes, edges, or entire graphs, and there are a number of different ways to do this such as the Node2Vec (N2V) or DeepWalk algorithms.

Methods for analysis on graph data have been around for a long time, at least as early as the 1950s when *clique methods* used certain features of a graph to identify subsets or communities in the graph data [4].

One of the most famous graph-based algorithms is PageRank, which was developed by Larry Page and Sergey Brin in 1996 and formed the basis for Google's search algorithms. Some believe that this algorithm was a key element in the company's meteoric rise in the following years. This highlights that a successful graph-based learning algorithm can have a huge effect.

These methods are only a small subset of graph-based learning and analysis techniques. Others include belief propagation [5], graph kernel methods [6], label propagation [7], and isomaps [8]. However, in this book, we'll focus on one of the newest and most exciting additions to the family of graph-based learning techniques: GNNs.

1.2.4 *What is a GNN?*

GNNs combine graph-based learning with deep learning. This means that neural networks are used to build embeddings and process the relational data. An overview of the inner workings of a GNN is shown in figure 1.7.

GNNs allows you to represent and learn from graphs, including their constituent nodes, edges, and features. In particular, many methods of GNNs are built specifically to scale effectively with the size and complexity of a graph. This means that GNNs can operate on huge graphs, as we'll discuss. In this sense, GNNs provide analogous advantages to relational data as convolutional neural networks have given for image-based data and computer vision.

Historically, applying traditional machine learning methods to graph data structures has been challenging because graph data, when represented in grid-like formats and data structures, can lead to massive repetitions of data. To address this, graph-based learning focuses on approaches that are *permutation invariant*. This means that

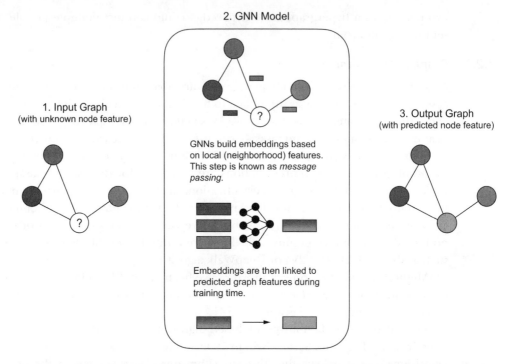

Figure 1.7 An overview of how GNNs work. An input graph is passed to a GNN. The GNN then uses neural networks to transform graph features such as nodes or edges into nonlinear embeddings through a process known as message passing. These embeddings are then tuned to specific unknown properties using training data. After the GNN is trained, it can predict unknown features of a graph.

the machine learning method is uninfluenced by the ordering of the graph representation. In concrete terms, it means that we can shuffle the rows and columns of the adjacency matrix without affecting our algorithm's performance. Whenever we're working with data that contains relational data, that is, has an adjacency matrix, then we want to use a machine learning method that is permutation invariant to make our method more general and efficient. Although GNNs can be applied to all graph data, GNNs are especially useful because they can deal with huge graph datasets and typically perform better than other machine learning methods.

Permutation invariances are a type of *inductive bias*, or an algorithm's learning bias, and are powerful tools for designing machine learning algorithms [1]. The need for permutation-invariant approaches is one of the central reasons that graph-based learning has increased in popularity in recent years.

Being designed for permutation-invariant data comes with some drawbacks along with its advantages. GNNs aren't as well suited for other data, such as images or tables. While this might seem obvious, images and tables are *not* permutation invariant and therefore not a good fit for GNNs. If we shuffle the rows and columns of an image, then we scramble the input. Instead, machine learning algorithms for images seek *translational invariance*, which means that we can translate (shift) the object in an image, and it won't affect the performance of the algorithm. Other neural networks, such as convolutional neural networks (CNNs) typically perform much better on images.

1.2.5   Differences between tabular and graph data

Graph data includes all data with some relational content, making it a powerful way to represent complex connections. While graph data might initially seem distinct from traditional tabular data, many datasets that are typically represented in tables can be re-created as graphs with some data engineering and imagination. Let's take a closer look at the Titanic dataset, a classic example in machine learning, and explore how it can be transformed from a table format to a graph format.

The Titanic dataset describes passengers on the Titanic, a ship that famously met an untimely end when it collided with an iceberg. Historically, this dataset has been analyzed in tabular format, containing rows for each passenger with columns representing features such as age, gender, fare, class, and survival status. However, the dataset also contains rich, unexplored relationships that aren't immediately visible in a table format, as shown in figure 1.8.

	survived	pclass	sex	age	sibsp	parch	fare	embarked	class	who	adult_male	deck	embark_town	alive	alone
0	0	3	male	22.0	1	0	7.2500	S	Third	man	True	NaN	Southampton	no	False
1	1	1	female	38.0	1	0	71.2833	C	First	woman	False	C	Cherbourg	yes	False
2	1	3	female	26.0	0	0	7.9250	S	Third	woman	False	NaN	Southampton	yes	True
3	1	1	female	35.0	1	0	53.1000	S	First	woman	False	C	Southampton	yes	False
4	0	3	male	35.0	0	0	8.0500	S	Third	man	True	NaN	Southampton	no	True

Figure 1.8   The Titanic Dataset is usually displayed and analyzed using a table format.

RECASTING THE TITANIC DATASET AS A GRAPH

To transform the Titanic dataset into a graph, we need to consider how to represent the underlying relationships between passengers as nodes and edges:

- *Nodes*—In the graph, each passenger can be represented as a node. We can also introduce nodes for other entities, such as cabins, families, or even groups such as "third-class passengers."
- *Edges*—Edges represent the relationships or connections between these nodes. For example:
  - Passengers who are family members (siblings, spouses, parents, or children) based on the available data
  - Passengers who share a cabin or were traveling together
  - Social or business relationships that might be inferred from shared ticket numbers, last names, or other identifying features

To construct this graph, we need to use the existing information in the table and potentially enrich it with secondary data sources or assumptions (e.g., linking last names to create family groups). This process converts the tabular data into a graph-based structure, shown in figure 1.9, where each edge and node encapsulates meaningful relational data.

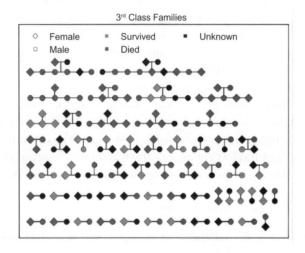

Figure 1.9   The Titanic dataset, showing the family relationships of the people on the Titanic visualized as a graph (Source: Matt Hagy). Here, we can see that there was a rich social network as well as many passengers with unknown family ties.

HOW GRAPH DATA ADDS DEPTH AND MEANING

Once the dataset is represented as a graph, it provides a much deeper view of the social and familial connections between the passengers. For example:

- *Family relationships*—The graph clearly shows how certain passengers were related (e.g., as parents, children, or siblings). This could help us understand survival patterns, as family members might have behaved differently in a crisis than individuals traveling alone.
- *Social networks*—Beyond families, the graph could reveal broader social networks (e.g., friendships or business connections), which could be important factors in analyzing behavior and outcomes.
- *Community insights*—The graph structure also allows for community detection algorithms to identify clusters of related or connected passengers, which may reveal new insights into survival rates, rescue patterns, or other behaviors.

Graph representations add depth by specifying connections that might not be obvious in a tabular format. For example, understanding who traveled together, who shared a cabin, or who had social or family ties can provide more context on survival rates and passenger behavior. This is crucial for tasks such as node prediction, where we want to predict attributes or outcomes based on the relationships represented in the graph.

By creating an adjacency matrix or defining graph edges and nodes based on the relationships in the dataset, we can transition from simple data analysis to more sophisticated graph-based learning methods.

1.3 GNN applications: Case studies

As we've seen, GNNs are neural networks designed to work on relational data. They give new ways for relational data to be transformed and manipulated, by being easier to scale and more accurate than previous graph-based learning methods. In the following, we discuss some exciting applications of GNNs, to see, at a high level, how this class of models are solving real-world problems. Links to source papers are listed at the end of the book if you want to learn more about these particular projects.

1.3.1 Recommendation engines

Enterprise graphs can exceed billions of nodes and many billions of edges. On the other hand, many GNNs are benchmarked on datasets that consist of fewer than a million nodes. When applying GNNs to large graphs, adjustments of the training and inference algorithms and storage techniques all have to be made. (You can learn more about the specifics of scaling GNNs in chapter 7.)

One of the most well-known industry examples of GNNs is their use as recommendation engines. For instance, Pinterest is a social media platform for finding and sharing images and ideas. There are two major concepts to Pinterest's users: collections or categories of ideas, called *boards* (like a bulletin board); and objects a user wants to bookmark called *pins*. Pins include images, videos, and website URLs. A user board focused on dogs might then include pins of pet photos, puppy videos, or dog-related website links. A board's pins aren't exclusive to it; a pet drawing that was pinned to the Dogs board could also be pinned to a Puppies board, as shown in figure 1.10.

As of this writing, Pinterest has 400 million active users who have likely pinned tens if not hundreds of items per user. One imperative of Pinterest is to help their users find content of interest via recommendations. Such recommendations should not only take into account image data and user tags but also draw insights from the relationships between pins and boards.

One way to interpret the relationships between pins and boards is as a *bipartite graph*, which we discussed earlier. For the Pinterest graph, all the pins are connected to boards, but no pin is connected to another pin, and no board is connected to another board. Pins and boards are two classes of nodes. Members of these classes can be linked to members of the other class, but not to members of the same class. The Pinterest graph was reported to have 3 billion nodes and 18 billion edges.

PinSage, a graph convolutional network (GCN), was one of the first documented highly scaled GNNs used in an enterprise system [9]. This was used in Pinterest's recommendation systems to overcome past challenges of applying graph-learning models to massive graphs. Compared to baseline methods, tests on this system showed it improved user engagement by 30%. Specifically, PinSage was used to predict which

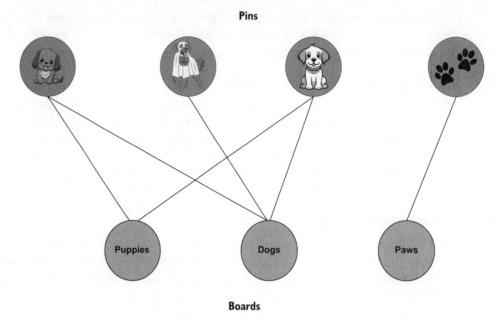

Figure 1.10   A bipartite graph that is like the Pinterest graph. Nodes in this case are the pins and boards.

objects should be recommended to be included in a user's graph. However, GNNs can also be used to predict what an object is, such as whether it contains a dog or mountain, based on the rest of the nodes in the graph and how they are connected. We'll be doing a deep dive on GCNs, of which PinSage is an extension, in chapter 3.

1.3.2   *Drug discovery and molecular science*

In chemistry and molecular sciences, a prominent problem has been representing molecules in a general, application-agnostic way, and inferring possible interfaces between molecules, such as proteins. For molecule representation, we can see that the drawings of molecules that are common in high school chemistry classes bear resemblance to a graph structure, consisting of nodes (atoms) and edges (atomic bonds), as shown in figure 1.11.

Applying GNNs to these structures can, in certain circumstances, outperform traditional "fingerprint" methods for determining the properties of a molecule. These traditional methods involve the creation of features by domain experts to capture a molecule's properties, such as interpreting the presence or absence of certain molecules or atoms [10]. GNNs learn new data-driven features that can be used to group certain molecules together in new and unexpected ways or even to propose new molecules for synthesis. This is extremely important for predicting whether a chemical is toxic or safe for use or whether it has some downstream effects that can affect

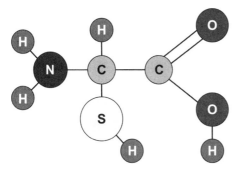

Figure 1.11   **In this molecule, we can see individual atoms as nodes and the atomic bonds as edges.**

disease progression. Therefore, GNNs have shown themselves to be incredibly useful in the field of drug discovery.

Drug discovery, especially for GNNs, can be understood as a graph prediction problem. *Graph prediction* tasks are those that require learning and predicting properties about the entire graph. For drug discovery, the aim is to predict properties such as toxicity or treatment effectiveness (discriminative) or to suggest entirely new graphs that should be synthesized and tested (generative). To suggest these new graphs, drug discovery methods often combine GNNs with other generative models such as variational graph autoencoders (VGAEs), as shown, for example, in figure 1.12. We'll describe VGAEs in more detail in chapter 5 and show how we can use these to predict molecules.

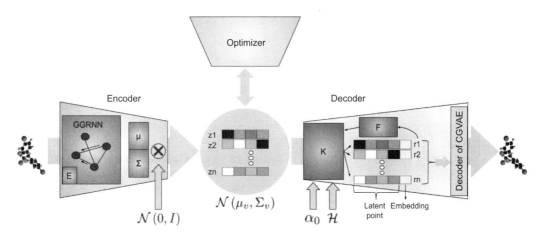

Figure 1.12   **A GNN system used to predict new molecules [11]. The workflow here starts on the left with a representation of a molecule as a graph. In the middle parts of the figure, this graph representation is transformed via a GNN into a latent representation. The latent representation is then transformed back to the molecule to ensure that the latent space can be decoded (right).**

1.3.3   *Mechanical reasoning*

We develop rudimentary intuition about mechanics and physics of the world around us at a remarkably young age and without any formal training in the subject. We don't need to write down a set of equations to know how to catch a bouncing ball. We don't even have to be in the presence of a physical ball. Given a series of snapshots of a bouncing ball, we can predict reasonably well where the ball is going to end up.

While these problems might seem trivial for us, they are critical for many physical industries, including manufacturing and autonomous driving. For example, autonomous driving systems need to anticipate what will happen in a traffic scene consisting of many moving objects. Until recently, this task was typically treated as a problem of computer vision. However, more recent approaches have begun to use GNNs [12]. These GNN-based methods demonstrate that including relational information, such as how limbs are connected, can enable algorithms to develop physical intuition about how a person or animal moves with higher accuracy and less data.

In figure 1.13, we give an example of how a body can be thought of as a "mechanical" graph. The input graphs for these physical reasoning systems have elements that reflect the problem. For instance, when reasoning about a human or animal body, a graph could consist of nodes that represent points on the body where limbs connect. For systems of free bodies, the nodes of a graph could be individual objects such as bouncing balls. The edges of the graph then represent the physical relationship (e.g., gravitational forces, elastic springs, or rigid connections) between the nodes. Given these inputs, GNNs learn to predict future states of a set of objects without explicitly calling on physical/mechanical laws [13]. These methods are a form of *edge prediction*; that is, they predict how the nodes connect over time. Furthermore, these models have to be dynamic to account for the temporal evolution of the system. We consider these problems in detail in chapter 6.

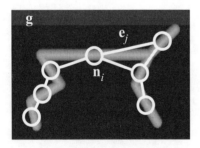

Figure 1.13   A graph representation of a mechanical body, taken from Sanchez-Gonzalez [13]. The body's segments are represented as nodes, and the mechanical forces binding them are edges.

1.4   *When to use a GNN?*

Now that we've explored real-world applications of GNNs, let's identify some underlying characteristics that make problems suitable for graph-based solutions. While the cases of the previous section clearly involved data that was naturally modeled as a graph, it's crucial to recognize that GNNs can also be effectively applied to problems where the graph-like nature may not be immediately obvious.

So, instead of simply stating that GNNs are useful for graph problems, this section will help you recognize patterns and relationships within your data that could benefit from graph-based modeling, even if those relationships aren't immediately apparent. Essentially, there are three types of criteria for identifying GNN problems: implicit relationships and interdependencies; high dimensionality and sparsity; and complex nonlocal interactions.

1.4.1   *Implicit relationships and interdependencies*

Graphs are versatile data structures that can model a wide range of relationships. Even when a problem doesn't initially appear to be graph-like, even if your dataset is tabular, it's beneficial to explore whether implicit relationships or interdependencies might exist that could be represented explicitly. Implicit relationships are connections that aren't immediately documented or obvious within the data but can still play a significant role in understanding the underlying patterns and behaviors.

KEY INDICATORS

To determine if your problem might benefit from modeling implicit relationships with graphs, consider whether there are hidden or indirect connections between entities in your dataset. For example, in customer behavior analysis, customers may appear as independent entities in a tabular dataset containing their purchases, demographics, and other details. However, they could be connected through social media influence, peer recommendations, or shared purchasing patterns, forming an underlying network of interactions.

Another indicator is the presence of entities that share common attributes or activities without a direct or documented relationship. In the case of investors, for example, two or more investors may not have any formal connection but might frequently co-invest in the same companies under similar conditions. Such patterns of co-investment could indicate a shared strategy or influence. In this scenario, a graph representation can be created where nodes represent individual investors, and edges are formed between nodes when two or more investors co-invest in the same company. Additional attributes, such as investment size, timing, or the types of companies invested in can be added to nodes or edges, allowing GNNs to identify patterns, trends, or even potential collaboration opportunities.

Additionally, consider whether the data involves entities that are interconnected through shared references or co-occurrence patterns. Document and text data may not immediately suggest a graph structure, but if documents cite each other or share common topics or authors, they can be represented as nodes in a graph, with edges reflecting these relationships. Similarly, terms within documents can form co-occurrence networks, which are useful for tasks such as keyword extraction, document classification, or topic modeling.

By identifying these key indicators in your data, you can uncover hidden or implicit relationships that can be represented explicitly through graphs. Such representations allow for more advanced analyses using GNNs, which can effectively capture and model these relationships, leading to more accurate predictions and deeper insights into the data.

1.4.2   *High dimensionality and sparsity*

Graph-based models are particularly effective in handling high-dimensional data where many features may be sparse or missing. These models excel in situations where there are underlying structures connecting sparse entities, allowing for more meaningful analysis and improved performance.

KEY INDICATORS

To determine if your problem involves high-dimensional and sparse data suitable for GNNs, consider whether your dataset contains numerous entities with limited direct interactions or relationships. For example, in recommender systems, user-item interaction data may appear tabular, but it's inherently sparse—most users only interact with a small subset of the available items. By representing users and items as nodes and representing their interactions (e.g., purchases or clicks) as edges, GNNs can exploit network effects to make more accurate recommendations. These models can also address the cold-start problem by uncovering both explicit and implicit relationships, leading to better performance in recommending new items to users or engaging new users with existing items.

Another indicator that your problem may be suitable for graph-based models is when the data represents entities that are sparsely connected but share significant characteristics. In drug discovery, for example, molecules are represented as graphs, with atoms as nodes and chemical bonds as edges. This representation captures the inherent sparsity of molecular structures, where most atoms form only a few bonds, and large portions of the molecule may be distant from each other in the graph. Traditional machine learning methods often struggle to predict properties of new molecules due to this sparsity, as they don't account for the full structural context.

Graph-based models, particularly GNNs, overcome these challenges by capturing both local atomic environments and global molecular structures. GNNs learn hierarchical features from fine-grained atomic interactions to broader molecular properties, and their ability to remain invariant to the ordering of atoms ensures consistent predictions. By using the graph structure of molecules, GNNs make accurate predictions from sparse, connected data, thereby accelerating the drug discovery process.

By recognizing these key indicators in your data, you can identify situations where graph-based models can effectively handle high-dimensional and sparse datasets. Representing such data as graphs allows GNNs to capture and use underlying structures, resulting in more accurate predictions and deeper insights across various applications.

1.4.3 Complex, nonlocal interactions

Certain problems require understanding how distant elements in a dataset influence each other. In these cases, GNNs provide a framework to capture these complex interactions, where the predicted value or label of a particular data point depends not just on the features of its immediate neighbors but also on those of other related data points. This capability is especially useful when relationships extend beyond direct connections to involve multiple levels or degrees of separation.

However, some standard GNNs, which rely primarily on local message passing, may struggle to capture long-range dependencies effectively. Advanced architectures or modifications, such as those incorporating global attention, nonlocal aggregation, or hierarchical message-passing, can better address these challenges [14].

KEY INDICATORS

To determine if your problem involves complex, nonlocal interactions suitable for GNNs, consider whether the outcome or behavior of one entity depends on the attributes or actions of entities that aren't directly connected to it but may be indirectly connected through other entities. For example, in supply chain optimization, a delay in one supplier may not only affect its immediate downstream customers but could cascade through multiple levels of the network, influencing distributors and final consumers.

Another indicator is whether the problem involves scenarios where information, influence, or effects propagate through a network over time. In healthcare and epidemiology, for instance, a disease outbreak might spread from a small cluster of patients through their interactions with shared healthcare providers, common environments, or overlapping social networks. Such propagation requires an approach that captures the indirect transmission pathways of information or effects.

To close this section, in determining whether your problem is a good candidate for a GNN, ask yourself these questions:

- Are there implicit relationships or interdependencies in my data that I could model?
- Do the interactions between entities exhibit complex, nonlocal dependencies that go beyond immediate connections?
- Is the data high-dimensional and sparse, with a need to capture underlying relational structures?

If the answer to any of these questions is yes, consider framing your problem as a graph and applying GNNs to unlock new insights and predictive capabilities.

1.5 Understanding how GNNs operate

In this section, we'll explore how GNNs work, starting from the initial collection of raw data to the final deployment of trained models. We'll examine each step, highlighting the processes of data handling, model building, and the unique message-passing technique that sets GNNs apart from traditional deep learning models.

1.5.1 *Mental model for training a GNN*

Our mental model covers the data sourcing, graph representation, preprocessing, and model development workflow. We start with raw data and end up with a trained GNN model and its outputs. Figure 1.14 illustrates and visualizes topics related to these stages, annotated with the chapters in which these topics appear.

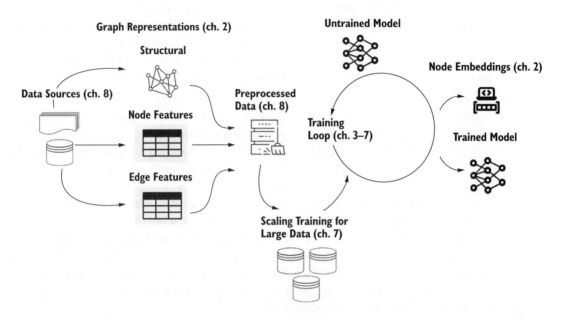

Figure 1.14   Mental model of the GNN project. We start with raw data, which is transformed into a graph data model that can be stored in a graph database or used in a graph processing system. From the graph processing system (and some graph databases), exploratory data analysis and visualization can be done. Finally, for graph machine learning, data is preprocessed into a form that can be submitted for training.

While not all workflows include every step or stage of this process, most will incorporate at least some elements. At different stages of a model development project, different parts of this process will typically be used. For example, when *training* a model, data analysis and visualization may be needed to make design decisions, but when *deploying* a model, it may only be necessary to stream raw data and quickly preprocess it for ingestion into a model. Though this book touches on the earlier stages in this mental model, the bulk of the book is focused on how to train different types of GNNs. When the other topics are discussed, they serve to support this main focus.

The mental model shows the core tasks of applying GNNs to machine learning problems, and we'll be returning to this process repeatedly throughout the rest of the book. Let's examine this diagram from end to end.

The first step in training a GNN is structuring this raw data into a graph format, if it isn't already. This requires deciding which entities in the data to represent as nodes and edges, as well as determining the features to assign to them. Decisions must also be made about data storage—whether to use a graph database, processing system, or other formats.

For machine learning, the data must be preprocessed for training and inference, involving tasks such as sampling, batching, and splitting the data into training, validation, and test sets. Throughout this book, we use PyTorch Geometric (PyG), which offers specialized classes for preprocessing and data splitting while preserving the graph's structure. Preprocessing is covered in most chapters, with more in-depth explanations available in appendix B.

After processing the data, we can then move on to the model training. In this book, we cover several architectures and training types:

- Chapters 2 and 3 discuss convolutional GNNs, where we first use a GCN layer to produce graph embeddings (chapter 2) and then train a full GCN and Graph-SAGE models (chapter 3).
- Chapter 4 explains graph attention networks (GATs), which adds attention to our GNNs.
- Chapter 5 introduces GNNs for unsupervised and generative problems, where we train and use a variational graph autoencoder (VGAE).
- Chapter 6 then explores the advanced concept of spatiotemporal GNNs, based on graphs that evolve over time. We train a neural relational inference (NRI) model, which combines an autoencoder structure with a recurrent neural network.

  Most of the examples provided for the GNNs mentioned so far are illustrated with code examples which use small-scale graphs that can fit into memory on a laptop or desktop computer.

- In chapter 7, we delve into strategies for handling data that exceeds the processing capacity of a single machine.
- In chapter 8, we close with some considerations for graph and GNN projects, such as practical aspects of working with graph data, as well as how to convert nongraph data into a graph format.

1.5.2 Unique mechanisms of a GNN model

Although there are a variety of GNN architectures at this point, they all tackle the same problem of dealing with graph data in a way that is permutation invariant. They do this via encoding and exchanging information across the graph structure during the learning process.

In a conventional neural network, we first need to initialize a set of parameters and functions. These include the number of layers, the size of the layers, the learning rate, the loss function, the batch size, and other hyperparameters. (These are all treated in detail in other books on deep learning, so we assume you're familiar with these terms.) Once we've defined these features, we then train our network by iteratively updating the weights of the network, as shown in figure 1.15.

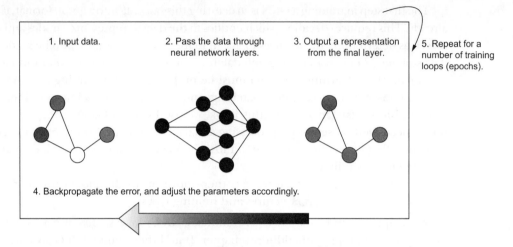

Figure 1.15   Process for training a GNN, which is similar to training most other deep learning models

Explicitly, we perform the following steps:

1 Input our data.
2 Pass the data through neural network layers that transform the data according to the parameters of the layer and an activation rule.
3 Output a representation from the final layer of the network.
4 Backpropagate the error, and adjust the parameters accordingly.
5 Repeat these steps a fixed number of *epochs* (the process by which data is passed forward and backward to train a neural network).

For tabular data, these steps are exactly as listed, as shown in figure 1.16. For graph-based or relational data, these steps are similar except that each epoch relates to one iteration of message passing, which is described in the next subsection.

1.5.3   *Message passing*

Message passing, which is touched on throughout the book, is a central mechanism in GNNs that enables nodes to communicate and share information across a graph [15]. This process allows GNNs to learn rich, informative representations of graph-structured data, which is essential for tasks such as node classification, link prediction, and graph-level prediction. Figure 1.17 illustrates the steps involved in a typical message-passing layer.

The message-passing process begins with the Input (step 1) of the initial graph, where every node and edge have their own features. In the Collect step (step 2), each node gathers information from its immediate neighbors—these pieces of information are referred to as "messages." This step ensures that each node has access to the features of its neighbors, which are crucial for understanding the local graph structure.

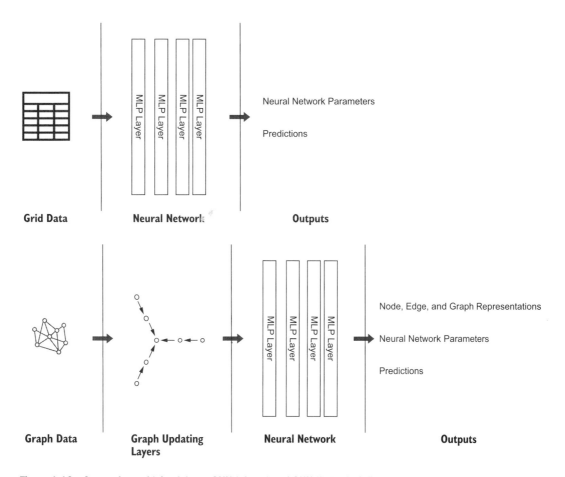

Figure 1.16 Comparison of (simple) non-GNN (above) and GNN (below). GNNs have a layer that distributes data among its vertices.

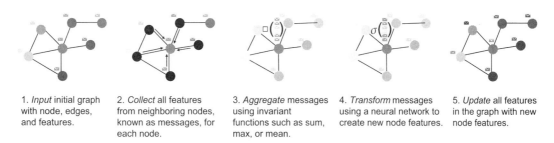

1. *Input* initial graph with node, edges, and features.

2. *Collect* all features from neighboring nodes, known as messages, for each node.

3. *Aggregate* messages using invariant functions such as sum, max, or mean.

4. *Transform* messages using a neural network to create new node features.

5. *Update* all features in the graph with new node features.

Figure 1.17 Elements of our message passing layer. Each message passing layer consists of an aggregation, a transformation, and an update step.

Next, in the Aggregate step (step 3), the collected messages from neighboring nodes are combined using an invariant function, such as sum, mean, or max. This aggregation consolidates the information from a node's neighborhood into a single vector, capturing the most relevant details about its local environment.

In the Transform step (step 4), the aggregated messages are processed by a neural network to produce a new representation for each node. This transformation allows the GNN to learn complex interactions and patterns within the graph by applying nonlinear functions to the aggregated information.

Finally, during the Update step (step 5), the features of each node in the graph are replaced or updated with these new representations. This completes one round of message passing, incorporating information from neighboring nodes to refine each node's features.

Each message-passing layer in a GNN allows nodes to gather information from nodes that are further away, or more "hops" away, in the graph. Repeating these steps over multiple layers enables the GNN to capture more complex dependencies and long-range interactions within the graph.

By using message passing, GNNs efficiently encode the graph structure and data into useful representations for a variety of downstream tasks. Advanced architectures, such as those incorporating global attention or hierarchical message passing, further enhance the model's ability to capture long-range dependencies across the graph, enabling more robust performance on diverse applications.

Summary

- Graph neural networks (GNNs) are specialized tools for handling relational, or relationship-centric, data, particularly in scenarios where traditional neural networks struggle due to the complexity and diversity of graph structures.
- GNNs have found significant applications in areas such as recommendation engines, drug discovery, and mechanical reasoning, showcasing their versatility in handling large and complex relational data for enhanced insights and predictions.
- Specific GNN tasks include node prediction, edge prediction, graph prediction, and graph representation through embedding techniques.
- GNNs are best used when data is represented as a graph, indicating a strong emphasis on relationships and connections between data points. They aren't ideal for individual, standalone data entries where relational information is insignificant.
- When deciding if a GNN solution is a good fit for your problem, consider cases that have characteristics such as implicit relationships, high-dimensionality, sparsity, and complex nonlocal interactions. By understanding these fundamentals, practitioners can evaluate the suitability of GNNs for their specific problems, implement them effectively, and recognize their tradeoffs and limitations in real-world applications.

- Message passing is a core mechanism of GNNs, which enables them to encode and exchange information across a graph's structure, allowing for meaningful node, edge, and graph-level predictions. Each layer of a GNN represents one step of message passing, with various aggregation functions to combine messages effectively, providing insights and representations useful for machine learning tasks.

Graph embeddings

2

This chapter covers

- Exploring graph embeddings and their importance
- Creating node embeddings using non-GNN and GNN methods
- Comparing node embeddings on a semi-supervised problem
- Taking a deeper dive into embedding methods

Graph embeddings are essential tools in graph-based machine learning. They transform the intricate structure of graphs—be it the entire graph, individual nodes, or edges—into a more manageable, lower-dimensional space. We do this to compress a complex dataset into a form that's easier to work with, without losing its inherent patterns and relationships, the information to which we'll apply a graph neural network (GNN) or other machine learning method.

Graphs, as we've learned, encapsulate relationships and interactions within networks, whether they're social networks, biological networks, or any system where entities are interconnected. Embeddings capture these real-life relationships in a compact form, facilitating tasks such as visualization, clustering, or predictive modeling.

There are numerous strategies to derive these embeddings, each with its unique approach and application: from classical graph algorithms that use the network's topology, to linear algebra techniques that decompose matrices representing the graph, and more advanced methods such as GNNs [1]. GNNs stand out because they can integrate the embedding process directly into the learning algorithm itself.

In traditional machine learning workflows, embeddings are generated as a separate step, serving as a dimensionality-reduction technique in tasks such as regression or classification. However, GNNs merge embedding generation with the model's learning process. As the network processes inputs through its layers, the embeddings are refined and updated, making the learning phase and the embedding phase inseparable. This means that GNNs learn the most informative representation of the graph data during training time.

Using graph embeddings can significantly enhance your data science and machine learning projects, especially when dealing with complex networked data. By capturing the essence of the graph in a lower-dimensional space, embeddings make it feasible to apply a variety of other machine learning techniques to graph data, opening up a world of possibilities for analysis and model building.

In this chapter, we begin with an introduction to graph embeddings and a case study on a graph of political book purchases. We start with Node2Vec (N2V) to establish a baseline with a non-GNN approach, guiding you through its practical application. In section 2.2, we shift to GNNs, offering a hands-on introduction to GNN-based embeddings, including setup, preprocessing, and visualization. Section 2.3 provides a comparative analysis of N2V and GNN embeddings, highlighting their applications. The chapter then rounds off with a discussion of the theoretical aspects of these embedding methods, with a special focus on the principles behind N2V and the message-passing mechanism in GNNs. The process we take in this chapter is illustrated in figure 2.1.

NOTE Code from this chapter can be found in notebook form at the GitHub repository (https://mng.bz/qxnE). Colab links and data from this chapter can be accessed in the same location.

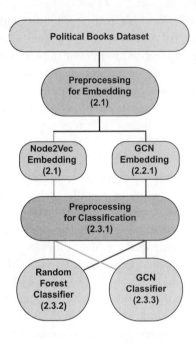

1. Preprocess the
   Political Books dataset
   for embedding.

2. Use N2V and GCN to
   create embeddings from
   the preprocessed data.

3. Prepare the N2V
   embeddings and the GCN
   embeddings for semi-
   supervised classification.

4. Embeddings are used as
   features in a random
   forest classifier (tabular
   features) and a GCN
   classifier (node features).

Figure 2.1   Summary of
process and objectives in
chapter 2

2.1   *Creating embeddings with Node2Vec*

Understanding the relationships within a network is a core task in many fields, from social network analysis to biology and recommendation systems. In this section, we'll explore how to create node embeddings using *Node2Vec (N2V)*, a technique inspired by Word2Vec from natural language processing (NLP) [2]. N2V captures the context of nodes within a graph by simulating random walks, allowing us to understand the neighborhood relationships between nodes in a low-dimensional space. This approach is effective for identifying patterns, clustering similar nodes, and preparing data for machine learning tasks.

To make this process accessible, we'll use the Node2Vec Python library, which is beginner-friendly, although it may be slower on larger graphs. N2V helps create embeddings that capture the structural relationships between nodes, which we can then visualize to uncover insights about the graph's structure. Our workflow involves several steps:

1 *Load data and set N2V parameters.* We start by loading our graph data and initializing N2V with specific parameters to control the random walks, such as walk length and the number of walks per node.

2 *Create embeddings.* N2V generates node embeddings by performing random walks on the graph, effectively summarizing each node's local neighborhood into a vector format.

3 *Transform embeddings.* The resulting embeddings are saved and then transformed into a format suitable for visualization.

4 *Visualize embeddings in two dimensions.* We use UMAP, a dimensionality reduction technique, to project these embeddings into two dimensions, making it easier to visualize and interpret the results.

Our data is the Political Books dataset, which comprises books (nodes) connected by frequent co-purchases on Amazon.com during the 2004 US election period (edges) [3]. Using this dataset provides a compelling example of how N2V can reveal underlying patterns in co-purchasing behavior, potentially reflecting broader ideological groupings among book buyers [4]. Table 2.1 provides key information about the Political Books graph.

Table 2.1   Overview of the Political Books dataset

Books in the political genre co-purchased on Amazon.com	
Number of nodes (books)	105
Left-leaning nodes	41.0%
Right-leaning nodes	46.7%
Neutral nodes	12.4%
Number of edges Edges represent the prevalence of a co-purchase between two books.	441

The Political Books dataset contains the following:

- *Nodes*—Represent books about US politics sold by Amazon.com.
- *Edges*—Indicate frequent co-purchasing by the same buyers, as suggested by Amazon's "customers who bought this book also bought these other books" feature.

In figure 2.2, books are shaded based on their political alignment—darker shade for liberal, lighter shade for conservative, and striped for neutral. The categories were assigned by Mark Newman through a qualitative analysis of book descriptions and reviews posted on Amazon.

This dataset, compiled by Valdis Krebs and available through the GNN in Action repository (https://mng.bz/qxnE) or the Carnegie Mellon University website (https://mng.bz/mG8M), contains 105 books (nodes) and 441 edges (co-purchases). If you want to learn more about the background of this dataset, Krebs has written an article with this information [4].

Using N2V, we aim to explore the structure of this collection of books, uncovering insights based on political leanings and the potential associations between different book categories. By visualizing the embeddings created by N2V, we can gain a better understanding of how books are grouped and which ones might share a common audience, providing valuable insights into consumer behavior during a politically charged period.

Figure 2.2   Graph visualization of the Political Books dataset. Right-leaning books (nodes) are in a lighter shade and are clustered in the top half of the figure, left-leaning are darker shaded circles and clustered in the lower half of the figure, and neutral political stance are dark squares and appear in the middle. When two nodes are connected, it indicates that they have been purchased together frequently on Amazon.com.

From the visualization, note that the data is already clustered in a logical way. This is thanks to the *Kamada-Kawai algorithm* graph algorithm, which exploits the topological data only without the metadata and is useful for visualizing the graph. This graph visualization technique positions nodes in a way that reflects their connections, aiming for an arrangement where closely connected nodes are near each other but less connected nodes are farther apart. It achieves this by treating the nodes like points connected by springs, iteratively adjusting their positions until the "tension" in the springs is minimized. This results in a layout that naturally reveals clusters and relationships within the graph based purely on its structure.

For the Political Books dataset, the Kamada-Kawai algorithm helps us visualize books (nodes) based on how often they are co-purchased on Amazon, without using any external information such as political alignment or book titles. This gives us an initial view of how books are grouped together by buying behavior. In the next steps, we'll use methods such as N2V to create embeddings that capture more detailed patterns and further distinguish different book groups.

2.1.1 Loading data, setting parameters, and creating embeddings

We use the `Node2Vec` and `NetworkX` libraries for our first hands-on encounter with graph embeddings. After installing these packages using pip, we load our dataset's graph data, which is stored in .gml format (Graph Modeling Language, GML), using the `NetworkX` library and generate the embeddings with the `Node2Vec` library.

GML is a simple, human-readable plain text file format used to represent graph structures. It stores information about nodes, edges, and their attributes in a structured way, making it easy to read and write graph data. For instance, a .gml file might contain a list of nodes (e.g., books in our dataset) and edges (connections representing co-purchases) along with additional properties such as labels or weights. This format is widely used for exchanging graph data between different software and tools. By loading the .gml file with `NetworkX`, we can easily manipulate and analyze the graph in Python.

In the `Node2Vec` library's `Node2Vec` function, we can use the following parameters to specify the calculations done and the properties of the output embedding:

- *Size of the embedding* (`dimensions`)—Think of this as how detailed each node's profile is, as in how many different traits you're noting down. The standard detail level is 128 traits, but you can tweak this based on how complex you want each node's profile to be.
- *Length of each walk* (`Walk Length`)—This is about how far each random walk through your graph goes, with 80 steps being the usual journey. If you want to see more of the neighborhood around a node, increase this number.
- *Number of walks per node* (`Num Walks`)—This tells us how many times we'll take a walk starting from each node. Starting with 10 walks gives a good overview, but if you want a fuller picture of a node's surroundings, consider going on more walks.
- *Backtracking control (Return Parameter,* `p`)—This setting helps decide if our walk should circle back to where it's been. Setting it at 1 keeps things balanced, but adjusting it can make your walks more or less exploratory.
- *Exploration Depth (In-Out Parameter,* `q`)—This one's about choosing between taking in the broader neighborhood scene (e.g., a breadth-first search with `q` greater than 1) or diving deep into specific paths (e.g., a depth-first search with `q` less than 1), with 1 being a mix of both.

Adjust these settings based on what you're looking to understand about your nodes and their connections. Want more depth? Tweak the exploration depth. Looking for broader context? Adjust the walk length and the number of walks. In addition, keep in mind that the size of your embeddings should match the level of detail you need. In general, it's a good idea to try different combinations of these parameters to see the effect on the embeddings.

For this exercise, we'll use the first four parameters. Deeper details on these parameters are found in section 2.4.

The code in listing 2.1 begins by loading the graph into a variable called `books_graph`, using the `read_gml` method from the `NetworkX` library. Next, a N2V `model` is initialized with the loaded graph. This model is set up with specific parameters: it will create 64-dimensional embeddings for each node, use walks of 30 steps long, perform 200 walks starting from each node to gather context, and run these operations in parallel across four workers to speed up the process.

The N2V model is then trained with additional parameters defined in the `fit` method. This involves setting a context window size of 10 nodes around each target node to learn the embeddings, considering all nodes at least once (`min_count=1`), and processing four words (nodes, in this context) each time during training.

Once trained, we access the node embeddings using the `model`'s `wv` method (reflecting its NLP heritage, wv stands for word vectors). For our downstream tasks, we map each node to its embedding using a dictionary comprehension.

Listing 2.1   Generating N2V embeddings

```
import NetworkX as nx
from Node2Vec import Node2Vec
books_graph = nx.read_gml('PATH_TO_GML_FILE')
node2vec = Node2Vec(books_graph, dimensions=64,
 walk_length=30, num_walks=200, workers=4)
model = node2vec.fit(window=10, min_count=1,\
batch_words=4)
embeddings = {str(node): model.wv[str(node)]\
 for node in gml_graph.nodes()}
```

Loads the graph data from a GML file into a NetworkX graph object

Initializes the N2V model with specified parameters for the input graph

Trains the N2V model

Extracts and stores the node embeddings generated by the N2V model in a dictionary

2.1.2 Demystifying embeddings

Let's explore what these embeddings are and why they are valuable. An *embedding* is a dense numerical vector that represents the identity of a node, edge, or graph in a way that captures essential information about its structure and relationships. In our context, an embedding created by N2V captures a node's position and neighborhood within the graph using topological information. This means it summarizes how the node is connected to others, effectively capturing its role and importance in the network. Later, when we use GNNs to create embeddings, they will also encapsulate the node's features, providing an even richer representation that includes both structure and attributes. We get deeper into theoretical aspects of embeddings in section 2.4.

These embeddings are powerful because they transform complex, high-dimensional graph data into a fixed-size vector format that can be easily used in various analyses and machine learning tasks. For example, they allow us to perform exploratory data analysis by revealing patterns, clusters, and relationships within the graph. Beyond this, embeddings can be directly used as features in machine learning models, where each dimension of the vector represents a distinct feature. This is particularly useful in applications where understanding the structure and connections between data points, such as in social networks or recommendation systems, can significantly improve model performance.

To illustrate, consider the node representing the book *Losing Bin Laden* in our Political Books dataset. Using the command `model.wv['Losing Bin Laden']`, we retrieve its dense vector embedding. This vector, shown in figure 2.3, captures various aspects of the book's role within the network of co-purchased books, providing a compact, informative representation that can be used for further analysis or as input to other models.

```
node_embedding = model.wv['Losing Bin Laden']
print(node_embedding)
```

```
[-0.28512368 -0.28379866  0.07767913 -0.07288406 -0.24679649 -0.3374484
  0.10274333  0.22401962 -0.39017093 -0.04263842  0.09780863 -0.15985246
 -0.1009391  -0.22627886 -0.06378957 -0.22466789  0.0773036   0.29056177
  0.1982294  -0.20018347  0.3876377   0.29315162  0.02515198  0.09390416
  0.30616233 -0.03660265 -0.27499264  0.01168824  0.40593293  0.12043843
  0.07061908  0.01209513  0.10041909  0.08560859 -0.24474025 -0.16583996
  0.10278559  0.12812535  0.14702478  0.01101081  0.28402498 -0.0639701
 -0.10733705  0.06112047  0.19346236 -0.05111938 -0.22928146 -0.05850201
 -0.04507062  0.02164907 -0.06584382 -0.01047416  0.12176199  0.3322272
  0.2000668   0.3096481  -0.16011229 -0.1627484  -0.06112075  0.45193997
  0.20894942 -0.3192235  -0.12022863 -0.00771468]
```

Figure 2.3   Extracting the embedding for the node associated with the political book *Losing Bin Laden*. The output is a dense vector represented as a Python list.

These embeddings can be used for exploratory data analysis to see the patterns and relationships in a graph. However, their usage extends further. One common application is to use these vectors as features in a machine learning problem that uses tabular data. In that case, each element in our embedding array will become a distinct feature column in the tabular data. This can add a rich representation of each node to complement other attributes in model training. In the next section, we'll look at how to visualize these embeddings to gain deeper insights into the patterns and relationships they represent.

2.1.3   *Transforming and visualizing the embeddings*

Visualization methods such as Uniform Manifold Approximation and Projection (UMAP) are powerful tools for reducing high-dimensional datasets into lower-dimensional space [5]. UMAP is particularly effective for identifying inherent clusters and visualizing complex structures that are difficult to perceive in high-dimensional data. Compared to other methods, such as t-SNE, UMAP excels in preserving both local and global structures, making it ideal for revealing patterns and relationships across different scales in the data.

While N2V generates embeddings by capturing the network structure of our data, UMAP takes these high-dimensional embeddings and maps them onto a lower-dimensional space (typically two or three dimensions). This mapping aims to keep similar nodes close together while also preserving broader structural relationships, providing a more comprehensive visualization of the graph's topology. After obtaining our N2V embeddings and converting them into a numerical array, we initialize the UMAP model with two components to project our data onto a 2D plane. By carefully selecting parameters such as the number of neighbors and minimum distance, UMAP can balance between revealing fine-grained local relationships and maintaining global distances between clusters.

By using UMAP, we gain a more accurate and interpretable visualization of our graph embeddings as shown in the following listing, allowing us to explore and analyze patterns, clusters, and structures more effectively than with traditional methods such as t-SNE.

Listing 2.2   Visualizing the embeddings using UMAP

```
node_embeddings = [embeddings[str(node)] \        Transforms the embeddings
for node in gml_graph.nodes()]                    into a list of vectors for UMAP
node_embeddings_array = np.array(node_embeddings)

umap_model = umap.UMAP(n_neighbors=15, min_dist=0.1, n_components=2, \
random_state=42)
umap_features = umap_model.fit_transform\
(node_embeddings_array)                           Initializes and fits UMAP

plt.scatter(umap_features[:, 0], \                Plots the nodes with
umap_features[:, 1], color=node_colors, alpha=0.7)  UMAP embeddings and
                                                  color by their value
```

The resultant figure 2.4 encapsulates the political book graph's embeddings as distilled by N2V and subsequently visualized through UMAP. The nodes appear in different shades according to their political alignment. The visualization unfolds a discernible structure, with potential clusters that correspond to the various political leanings.

You might wonder why we don't just reduce the dimensions of the N2V embeddings from 64 to 2 and visualize them directly, bypassing UMAP altogether? In listing 2.3, we

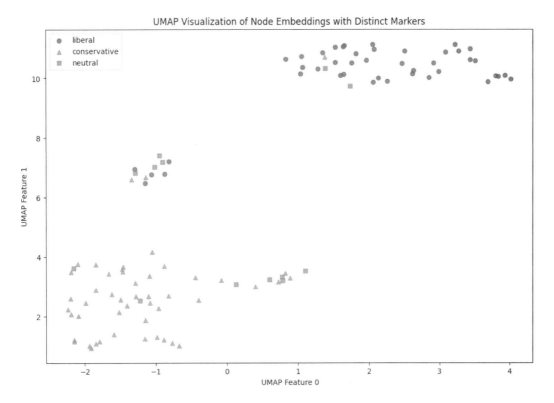

Figure 2.4   Embeddings of the Political Books dataset graph generated by N2V and visualized using UMAP. Shape and shading variations distinguish the three political classes.

show this approach, applying a 2D N2V transformation directly to our `books_graph` object. (For more technical detail and theory of these methods, see section 2.4.)

The `dimensions` parameter is set to 2, aiming for a direct 2D representation suitable for immediate visualization without further dimensionality reduction. The other parameters are kept the same.

Once the model is fitted with the specified window and word batch settings, we extract the 2D embeddings and store them in a dictionary keyed by the string representation of each node. This enables a direct mapping from the node to its embedding vector.

The extracted 2D points are compiled into a NumPy array and plotted. We use the standard `Matplotlib` library to create a scatterplot of these points using the prepared color scheme to represent the political leaning of each node visually.

Listing 2.3   Visualizing 2D N2V embeddings without t-SNE

```
node2vec = Node2Vec(gml_graph, dimensions=2, \
walk_length=30, num_walks=200, workers=4)
```

Initializes N2V with 2D embeddings for visualization

```
model = node2vec.fit(window=10, min_count=1,\
 batch_words=4)
```
Trains N2V model with specified
window and walks settings

```
embeddings_2d = {str(node): model.wv[str(node)] \
for node in gml_graph.nodes()}
```
Maps nodes to their
2D embeddings

```
points = np.array([embeddings_2d[node] \
for node in gml_graph.nodes()])
```
Forms an array of 2D points
for each node's embedding

```
plt.scatter(points[:, 0], points[:, 1], \
color=node_colors, alpha=0.7)
```
Plots the 2D embeddings
with specified node colors

The outcome shows how the books are separated by political leanings, similar to the
UMAP result, but where the books are more bunched together (see figure 2.5). The
two embeddings are then shown in figure 2.6.

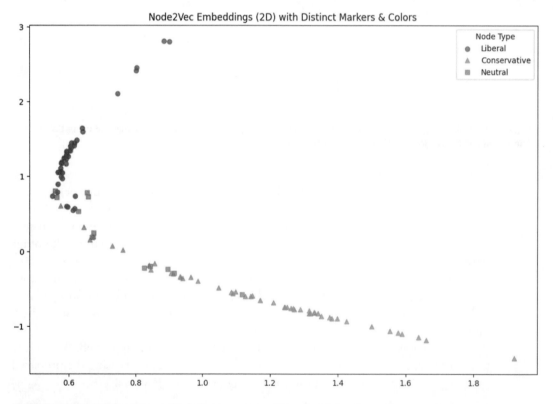

**Figure 2.5   Embeddings of the Political Books dataset graph generated and visualized by N2V for two dimensions.
Shape and shading variations distinguish the three political classes. Here, we see a similar clustering by political
leaning as earlier in figure 2.4 but more bunched together.**

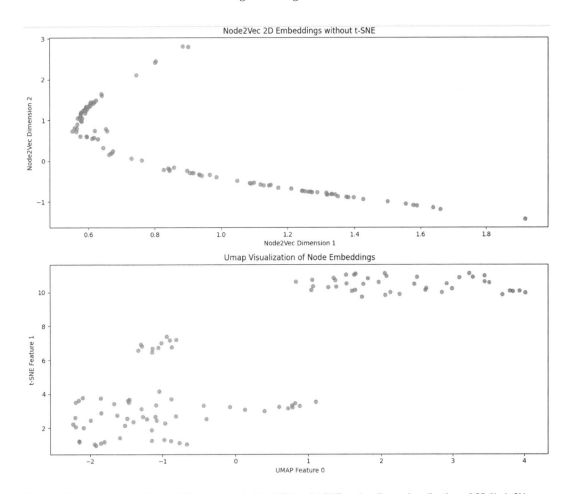

Figure 2.6 **Comparison of embeddings generated by N2V and t-SNE and a direct visualization of 2D Node2Vec**

It's clear that both methods know to separate the books into groups based on political leanings. N2V is less expressive in how it separates the books, bunching them together across the two dimensions. Meanwhile, UMAP is better for spreading out the books in two dimensions. The relevant benefit or information contained within these dimensions depends on the task at hand.

2.1.4 Beyond visualization: Applications and considerations of N2V embeddings

While visualizing N2V embeddings offers intuitive insights into the dataset's structure, their usage extends far beyond graphical representation. N2V is an embedding method designed specifically for graphs; it captures both the local and global structural properties of nodes by simulating random walks through the graph. This process allows

N2V to create dense, numerical vectors that summarize the position and context of each node within the overall network.

These embeddings can then serve as feature-rich inputs for a variety of machine learning tasks, such as classification, recommendation, or clustering. For example, in our Political Books dataset, embeddings could help predict a book's political leaning based on its co-purchase patterns or could recommend books to users with similar political interests. They might even be used to forecast future sales based on the content of a book.

However, it's important to understand the nature of N2V's learning approach, which is *transductive*. Transductive learning is designed to work only with the specific dataset it was trained on and can't generalize to new, unseen nodes without retraining the model. This characteristic makes N2V highly effective for static datasets where all nodes and edges are known up front but less suitable for dynamic settings where new data points or connections frequently appear. Essentially, N2V focuses on extracting detailed patterns and relationships from the existing graph rather than developing a model that can easily adapt to new data.

While this transductive nature has its limitations, it also offers significant advantages. Because N2V uses the full structure of the graph during training, it can capture intricate relationships and dependencies that might be missed by more generalized methods. This makes N2V particularly powerful for tasks where the complete, fixed structure of the data is known and stable. However, to apply N2V effectively, it's crucial to ensure that the graph data is represented in a way that captures all relevant features. In some cases, additional edges or nodes may need to be added to the graph to fully represent the underlying relationships.

For those interested in a deeper understanding of transductive models and how N2V's approach compares to other methods, further details are provided in section 2.4.2. That section will explore the tradeoffs between transductive and inductive learning in greater depth [6, 7], helping you understand when each approach is most appropriate.

While N2V is effective for generating embeddings that capture the structure of a fixed graph, real-world data often demands a more flexible and generalizable approach. This need brings us to our first GNN architecture for creating node embeddings. Unlike N2V, which is a transductive method limited to the specific nodes and edges in the training data, GNNs can learn in an *inductive* manner. This means GNNs are capable of generalizing to new, unseen nodes or edges without requiring retraining on the entire graph.

GNNs achieve this by not only understanding the network's complex structure but also by incorporating node features and relationships into the learning process. This approach allows GNNs to adapt dynamically to changes in the graph, making them well-suited for applications where the data is continually evolving. The shift from N2V to GNNs represents a key transition from focusing on deep analysis within a static dataset to a broader applicability across diverse, evolving networks. This adaptability sets the stage for a wider range of graph-based machine learning applications that require flexibility and scalability. In the next section, we'll explore how GNNs go beyond the capabilities of N2V and other transductive methods, allowing for more versatile and powerful models that can handle the dynamic nature of real-world data.

2.2 Creating embeddings with a GNN

While N2V provides a powerful method for generating embeddings by capturing the local and global structure of a graph, it's fundamentally a transductive approach, meaning it can't easily generalize to unseen nodes or edges without retraining. Although there have been extensions to N2V that enable it to work in inductive settings, GNNs are inherently designed for inductive learning. This means they can learn general patterns from the graph data that allow them to make predictions or to generate embeddings for new nodes or edges without needing to retrain the entire model. This gives GNNs a significant edge in scenarios where flexibility and adaptability are crucial.

GNNs not only incorporate the structural information of the graph, like N2V, but they also use node features to create richer representations. This dual capacity allows GNNs to learn both the complex relationships within the graph and the specific characteristics of individual nodes, enabling them to excel in tasks where both types of information are important.

That said, while GNNs have demonstrated impressive performance across many applications, they don't universally outperform methods such as N2V in all cases. For instance, N2V and other random walk-based methods can sometimes perform better in scenarios where labeled data is scarce or noisy, thanks to their ability to work with just the graph structure without needing additional node features.

2.2.1 Constructing the embeddings

Unlike N2V, GNNs learn graph representations and perform tasks such as node classification or link prediction simultaneously during training. Information from the entire graph is processed through successive GNN layers, each refining the node embeddings without requiring a separate step for their creation.

To demonstrate how a GNN extracts features from graph data, we'll perform a straightforward pass-through using an untrained model to generate preliminary embeddings. Even without the optimization typically involved in training, this approach will show how GNNs use message passing (explored further in section 2.4.4) to update embeddings, capturing both the graph's structure and its node features. When optimization is added, these embeddings become tailored to specific tasks such as node classification or link prediction.

DEFINING OUR GNN ARCHITECTURE

We initiate our process by defining a simple GCN architecture, as shown in listing 2.4. Our `SimpleGNN` class inherits from `torch.nn.Module` and is composed of two `GCN-Conv` layers, which are the building blocks of our GNN. This architecture is shown in figure 2.7, consisting of the first layer, a message passing layer (`self.conv1`), an activation (`torch.relu`), a dropout layer (`torch.dropout`), and a second message passing layer.

Listing 2.4   Our `SimpleGNN` class

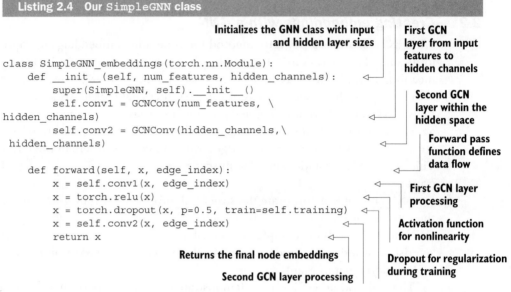

Initializes the **GNN** class with input and hidden layer sizes

First GCN layer from input features to hidden channels

Second GCN layer within the hidden space

Forward pass function defines data flow

First GCN layer processing

Activation function for nonlinearity

Dropout for regularization during training

Returns the final node embeddings

Second GCN layer processing

```
class SimpleGNN_embeddings(torch.nn.Module):
    def __init__(self, num_features, hidden_channels):
        super(SimpleGNN, self).__init__()
        self.conv1 = GCNConv(num_features, \
hidden_channels)
        self.conv2 = GCNConv(hidden_channels,\
 hidden_channels)

    def forward(self, x, edge_index):
        x = self.conv1(x, edge_index)
        x = torch.relu(x)
        x = torch.dropout(x, p=0.5, train=self.training)
        x = self.conv2(x, edge_index)
        return x
```

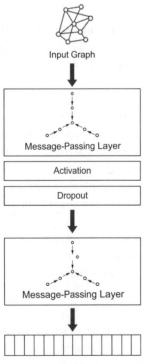

Figure 2.7   Architecture diagram of the `SimpleGNN` model

Let's talk about the architecture aspects specific to GNNs. The activation and dropout are common in many deep learning scenarios. The GNN layers, however, are different from conventional deep learning layers in a fundamental way. The core principle that allows GNNs to learn from graph data is message passing. For each GNN layer, in addition to updating the layer's weights, a "message" is gathered from every node or edge neighborhood and used to update an embedding. Essentially, each node sends messages to its neighbors and simultaneously receives messages from them. For every node, its new embedding is computed by combining its own features with the aggregated messages from its neighbors, through a combination of nonlinear transformations.

In this example, we're going to be using a graph convolutional network (GCN) to act as our message-passing GNN layers. We describe GCNs in much more detail in chapter 3. For now, you just need to know that GCNs act as message-passing layers that are critical in constructing embeddings.

DATA PREPARATION

Next, we prepare our data. We'll start with the same graph from the previous section, `books_gml`, in its `NetworkX` form. We have to convert this `NetworkX` object into a tensor form that is suitable to use with PyTorch operations. Because PyTorch Geometric (PyG) has many functions that convert graph objects, we can do this quite simply with `data = from_NetworkX(gml_graph)`. Method `from_NetworkX` specifically translates the edge lists and node/edge attributes into PyTorch tensors.

For GNNs, generating node embeddings requires initializing node features. In our case, we don't have any predefined node features. When no node features are available or they aren't informative, it's common practice to initialize the node features randomly. A more effective approach is to use *Xavier initialization*, which sets the initial node features with values drawn from a distribution that keeps the variety of activations consistent across layers. This technique ensures that the model starts with a balanced representation, preventing problems such as vanishing or exploding gradients.

By initializing `data.x` with Xavier initialization, we provide the GNN with a starting point that allows it to learn meaningful node embeddings from noninformative features. During training, the network adjusts these initial values to minimize the loss function. When the loss function is aligned with a specific target, such as node prediction, the embeddings learned from the initial random features will become tailored to the task at hand, resulting in more effective representations. We randomize the node features using the following:

```
data.x = torch.randn((data.num_nodes, 64), dtype=torch.float)
'nn.init.xavier_uniform_(data.x) '
```

We could have also used the embeddings from the N2V exercise to use as node features. Recall the `node_embeddings` object from section 2.1.3:

```
node_embeddings = [embeddings[str(node)] for node in gml_graph.nodes()]
```

From this, we can convert the node embedding to a PyTorch tensor object and assign it to the node feature object, `data.x`:

```
node_features = torch.tensor(node_embeddings, dtype=torch.float)
data.x = node_features
```

PASSING THE GRAPH THROUGH THE GNN

With the structure of our GNN model defined and our graph data formatted for PyG, we proceed to the embedding generation step. We initialize our model, `SimpleGNN`, specifying the number of features for each node and the size of the hidden channels within the network.

```
model = SimpleGNN(num_features=data.x.shape[1], hidden_channels=64)
```

Here, we specify 64 hidden channels because we want to compare the resulting embeddings to the ones we produced using the `node2vec` method, which had 64 dimensions. Because the second GNN layer is the last layer, the output will be a 64-element vector.

Once initialized, we switch the model to evaluation mode using `model.eval()`. This mode is used during inference or validation phases when we want to make predictions or assess model performance without modifying the model's parameters. Specifically, `model.eval()` turns off certain behaviors specific to training, such as *dropout*, which randomly deactivates some neurons to prevent overfitting, and *batch normalization*, which normalizes inputs across a mini-batch. By disabling these features, the model provides consistent and deterministic outputs, ensuring that the evaluation accurately reflects its true performance on unseen data.

It's important to disable gradient computations because they're not necessary for the forward pass and embedding generation. So, we employ `torch.no_grad()`, which ensures that the computational graph that records operations for backpropagation isn't constructed, preventing us from accidentally changing performance.

Next, we pass our node-feature matrix (`data.x`) and the edge index (`data.edge_index`) through the model. The result is `gnn_embeddings`, a tensor where each row corresponds to the embedding of a node in our graph—a numerical representation learned by our GNN, ready for downstream tasks such as visualization or classification:

```
model.eval()
with torch.no_grad():
    gnn_embeddings = model(data.x, data.edge_index)
```

After producing these embeddings, we use UMAP to visualize them, as we did in section 2.1.3. Since we've been working with PyTorch tensor data types running on a GPU, we need to convert our embeddings to a NumPy array data type to use analysis methods outside of PyTorch, which are done on a CPU:

```
gnn_embeddings_np = gnn_embeddings.detach().cpu().numpy()
```

With this conversion, we can produce the UMAP calculations and visualization following the process we used in the N2V case. The resulting scatterplot (figure 2.8) is a first glimpse at the clusters within our graph. We add different shadings based on each node's label (left-, right-, or neutral-leaning) to see that similar leaning books are fairly well grouped, given that these embeddings were constructed from topology alone.

Next, let's discuss both how GNN embeddings are used and how they differ from those produced with N2V.

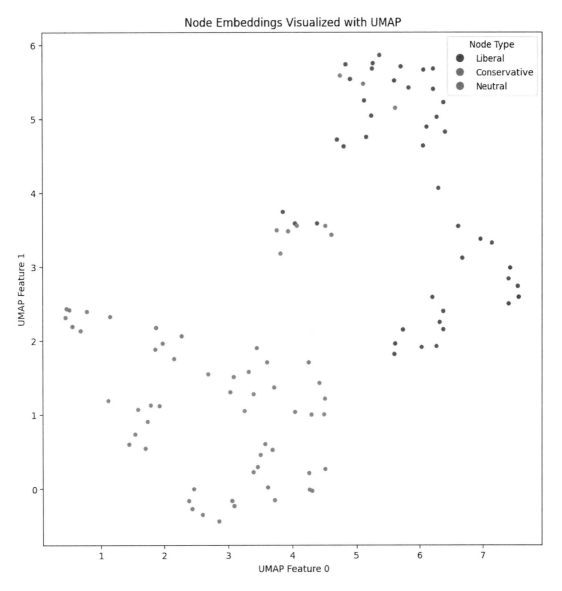

Figure 2.8 Visualization of embeddings generated from passing a graph through a GNN

2.2.2   *GNN vs. N2V embeddings*

Throughout this book, we predominantly use GNNs to generate embeddings because this embedding process is intrinsic to a GNN's architecture. While embeddings play a pivotal role in the methodologies and applications we explore in the rest of the book, their presence is often subtle and not always highlighted. This approach allows us to focus on the broader concepts and applications of GNN-based machine learning without getting slowed down by the technicalities. Nonetheless, it's important to acknowledge that the underlying power and adaptability of embeddings are central to the advanced techniques and insights we get into throughout the text.

GNN-produced node embeddings are particularly powerful because they enable us to tackle a broad range of graph-related tasks by using their inductive nature. Inductive learning allows these embeddings to generalize to new, unseen nodes or even entirely new graphs without needing to retrain the model. In contrast, N2V embeddings are limited to the specific graphs they were trained on and can't easily adapt to new data. Let's reiterate the key ways in which GNN embeddings differ from other embedding methods, such as N2V [1, 3].

ADAPTABILITY TO NEW GRAPHS

One of the critical features of GNN embeddings is their adaptability. Because GNNs learn a function that maps node features to embeddings, this function can be applied to nodes in new graphs without needing to be retrained, provided the nodes have similar feature spaces. This inductive capability is particularly valuable in dynamic environments where the graph may evolve over time or in applications where the model needs to be applied to different but structurally similar graphs. N2V, on the other hand, needs to be reapplied for each new graph or set of nodes.

ENHANCED FEATURE INTEGRATION

GNNs inherently consider node features during the embedding process, allowing for a complex and nuanced representation of each node. This integration of node features, alongside the structural information, offers a more comprehensive view compared to N2V and other methods that focus on a graph's topology. This capability makes GNN embeddings particularly suited for tasks where node features contain significant additional information.

TASK-SPECIFIC OPTIMIZATION

GNN embeddings are trained alongside specific tasks, such as node classification, link prediction, or even graph classification. Through end-to-end training, the GNN model learns to optimize the embeddings for the task at hand, leading to potentially higher performance and efficiency compared to using pre-generated embeddings such as those from N2V.

That said, while GNN embeddings offer clear advantages in terms of adaptability and applicability to new data, N2V embeddings have their strengths, particularly in capturing nuanced patterns within a specific graph's structure. In practice, the choice between GNN and N2V embeddings may depend on the specific requirements of the task, the nature of the graph data, and the constraints of the computational environment.

For tasks where the graph structure is static and well-defined, N2V might provide a simpler and computationally efficient solution. Conversely, for dynamic graphs, large-scale applications, or scenarios requiring the incorporation of node features, GNNs will often be the more robust and versatile choice. Additionally, when the task itself is not well-defined and the work is exploratory, N2V is likely faster and easier to use.

We've now successfully built our first GNN embedding. This is the key first step for all GNN models, and everything from this point will build on it. In the next section, we give an example of some of these next steps and show how to use embeddings to solve a machine learning problem.

2.3   *Using node embeddings*

Semi-supervised learning, which involves a combination of labeled and unlabeled data, provides a valuable opportunity to compare different embedding techniques. In this chapter, we'll explore how GNN and N2V embeddings can be used to predict labels when the majority of the data lacks labels.

Our task involves the Political Books dataset (`books_graph`), where nodes represent political books and edges indicate co-purchase relationships. To make the process clearer, let's review the steps taken so far and outline our next steps, as illustrated in figure 2.9.

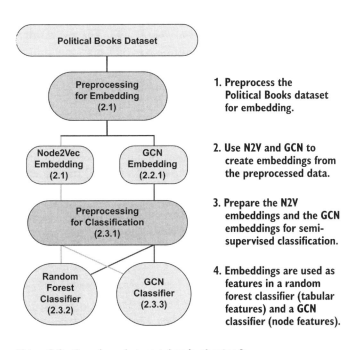

Figure 2.9   **Overview of steps taken in chapter 2**

We began with the `books_graph` dataset in graph format and performed light preprocessing to prepare the data for embedding. For N2V, this involved converting the dataset from a .gml file to a `NetworkX` format. For the GNN-based embeddings, we converted the `NetworkX` graph into a PyTorch tensor and initialized the node features using Xavier initialization to ensure balanced variability across layers.

After preparing the data, we generated embeddings using both N2V and GCNs. Now, in this section, we'll apply these embeddings to a semi-supervised classification problem. This involves further processing to define the classification task, where only 20% of the book labels are retained, simulating a realistic scenario with sparse labeled data.

We'll use the two sets of embeddings (N2V and GCN) with two different classifiers: a random forest classifier (to use the embeddings as tabular features) and a GCN classifier (to use the graph structure and node features). The goal is to predict the political orientation of the books, with the remaining 80% of the labels inferred based on the given embeddings.

2.3.1   *Data preprocessing*

To start, we do a little more preprocessing to our `books_gml` dataset (see listing 2.5). We must format the labels in a suitable way for the learning process. Because all the nodes are labeled, we also have to set up the semi-supervised problem by randomly selecting the nodes from which we hide the labels.

Nodes associated with attribute `'c'` are classified as `'right'`, while those with `'l'` are classified as `'left'`. Nodes that don't fit these criteria, including those with neutral or unspecified attributes, are categorized as `'neutral'`. These classifications are then placed into a NumPy array, `labels`, for optimized computational handling.

Then, an array, `indices`, is created, representing the positional indexes of all nodes within the dataset. A subset of these indices, corresponding to 20% of the total node count, is designated as our labeled data.

To manage the labeled and unlabeled data, Boolean masks, `labelled_mask` and `unlabelled_mask`, are initialized and populated. The `labelled_mask` is set to `True` for indices selected as labeled; these are the ground truth labels for corresponding nodes. Similarly, `unlabelled_mask` is set to `False`. These masks segment the dataset for training and evaluation, ensuring that algorithms are correctly trained and validated on the correct subsets of data.

Listing 2.5   Preprocessing for semi-supervised problem

```
labels = []
for node, data in gml_graph.nodes(data=True):     ⟵  Extracts labels
    if data['value'] == 'c':                           and handles
        labels.append('right')                         neutral values
    elif data['value'] == 'l':
        labels.append('left')
    else:
        labels.append('neutral')
```

```
labels = np.array(labels)
                                          Random seed for
random.seed(52)                           reproducibility

indices = list(range(len(labels)))        ⬅─── Indices of all nodes

labelled_percentage = 0.2                         20% of data to
                                                  keep as labeled
labelled_indices = random.sample(indices, \
int(labelled_percentage * len(labels)))
                                                     Selects a subset of indices
                                                     to remain labeled
labelled_mask = np.zeros(len(labels), dtype=bool)
unlabelled_mask = np.ones(len(labels), dtype=bool)
                                                  Initializes masks for
                                                  labeled and unlabeled data
labelled_mask[labelled_indices] = True
unlabelled_mask[labelled_indices] = False
                                                  Updates masks

labelled_labels = labels[labelled_mask]
unlabelled_labels = labels[unlabelled_mask]       Uses masks to split the dataset

label_mapping = {'left': 0, 'right': 1, 'neutral': 2}
numeric_labels = np.array([label_mapping[label] for label in labels])

                                            Transformed labels to numerical form
```

Now we transform the data for model training, as shown in listing 2.6. For the GNN-derived embeddings, X_train_gnn and y_train_gnn are assigned arrays of embeddings and corresponding numeric labels filtered by a labelled_mask. This mask is a Boolean array indicating which nodes in the graph are part of the labeled subset, ensuring that only data points with known labels are included in the training set.

For N2V embeddings, a similar approach is adopted with an added preprocessing step to align the embeddings with their corresponding labels. The embeddings for each node are aggregated into NumPy array X_n2v in the same order as the nodes appear in the books_graph. This ensures consistency between the embeddings and their labels, a crucial step for supervised learning tasks. Subsequently, X_train_n2v and y_train_n2v are populated with N2V embeddings and labels, again applying the labelled_mask to filter for the labeled data points.

Listing 2.6 Preprocessing: constructing training data

```
X_train_gnn = gnn_embeddings[labelled_mask]
Y_train_gnn = numeric_labels[labelled_mask]       For GNN embeddings

X_n2v = np.array([embeddings[str(node)] \          For N2V embeddings
for node in gml_graph.nodes()])
X_train_n2v = X_n2v[labelled_mask]                 Ensures N2V embeddings are in
y_train_n2v = numeric_labels[labelled_mask]        the same order as labels
```

The extra alignment step for the N2V embeddings isn't necessary for the GNN embeddings because GNN models inherently maintain the order of nodes as they process the entire graph in a structured manner. As a result, the output embeddings from a GNN are naturally ordered in correspondence with the input graph's node order.

In contrast, N2V generates embeddings through independent random walks starting from each node, and the order of the resulting embeddings doesn't necessarily match the order of nodes in the original graph data structure. Therefore, an explicit alignment step is required to ensure that each N2V embedding is correctly associated with its corresponding label, as extracted from the graph. This step is critical for supervised learning tasks where the correct matching of features (embeddings) to labels is essential for model training and evaluation. For this task, we use the attribute `index_to_key`, which contains the identifiers of the nodes in the order they are processed and stored within the model.

2.3.2 *Random forest classification*

With our data prepped, we use GNN and N2V embeddings from sections 2.1 and 2.2 as input features for a `RandomForestClassifier`, as shown in listing 2.7.

Listing 2.7 **Preprocessing: constructing training data**

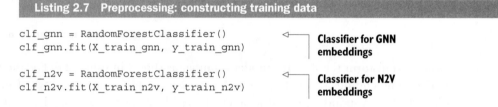

```
clf_gnn = RandomForestClassifier()                    ⊲⎯⎤ Classifier for GNN
clf_gnn.fit(X_train_gnn, y_train_gnn)                    ⎦ embeddings

clf_n2v = RandomForestClassifier()                    ⊲⎯⎤ Classifier for N2V
clf_n2v.fit(X_train_n2v, y_train_n2v)                    ⎦ embeddings
```

This approach allows us to directly compare the embeddings' predictive power, where we compare results in table 2.2.

Table 2.2 Classification performance

Embedding Type	Accuracy	F1 Score
GNN	83.33%	82.01%
N2V	84.52%	80.72%

For this basic classification exercise, we'll evaluate the performance of our models using two fundamental metrics:

- *Accuracy*—This metric measures the proportion of correct predictions made by the model out of all predictions. It provides a straightforward assessment of how often the classifier correctly identifies the political orientation of the books. For instance, an accuracy of 84.52% means that the model correctly predicted the orientation of the books approximately 85 times out of 100.
- *F1 score*—This is a more nuanced metric that balances precision and recall, which is particularly useful in cases where the data is imbalanced—meaning the classes aren't equally represented. It provides a harmonic mean of precision

(the number of true positive predictions divided by the total number of positive predictions) and recall (the number of true positive predictions divided by the total number of actual positives). A higher F1 score indicates a model's robust performance in correctly identifying both the presence and absence of the different classes, minimizing both false positives and false negatives.

The performance metrics reveal that N2V embeddings yield a slightly higher accuracy of 84.52% when used within a `RandomForestClassifier`, compared to 83.33% for GNN embeddings. However, GNN embeddings achieve a marginally better F1 score of 82.01%, compared to 80.72% for N2V embeddings. This nuanced difference underscores potential tradeoffs between the two embedding types: while N2V provides slightly better overall prediction accuracy, GNN embeddings may offer a more balanced performance across both the majority and minority classes.

In general, the inductive nature of GNNs presents a robust framework for learning node representations for graphs of many different sizes. Even on smaller graphs, GNNs can effectively learn the underlying patterns and interactions between nodes, as evidenced by the higher F1 score, indicating a better balance between precision and recall in classification tasks.

In this context, the choice between GNN and N2V embeddings might also hinge on the specific goals of the analysis and the performance metrics of greatest interest. If the priority is achieving the highest possible accuracy and the dataset is unlikely to expand significantly, N2V could be the more suitable option. Conversely, if the task values a balance between precision and recall and there's potential for applying the learned model to similar but new graphs, GNNs offer valuable flexibility and robustness, even for smaller datasets. Having used the N2V and GNN embeddings as inputs to a random forest model, let's next study what happens when we use them as inputs to a full end-to-end GNN model.

2.3.3   *Embeddings in an end-to-end model*

In the previous section, we used GNN and N2V embeddings as static inputs to a traditional machine learning model, namely a random forest classifier. Here, we use an end-to-end GNN model applied to the same problem of label prediction. By *end-to-end*, we mean that the embeddings will be generated while we also predict labels. This means that the embeddings here won't be static because, as the GNN learns, it will update the node embeddings.

To build this model, we'll use the same tools as before—the `books_gml` dataset, and the `SimpleGNN` architecture. We'll change the GNN slightly, by adding a log `softmax` activation at the end, to facilitate the output for a three-label classification problem. We'll also slightly modify the output of our `SimpleGNN` class, allowing us to observe the embeddings as well as the predictive output. Our process includes the following:

- Data prep
- Model/architecture modification

- Establish the training loop
- Study performance
- Study embeddings pre-training and post-training

DATA PREP

Assuming we use the `books_gml` data set, the process to transform it for use within the PyG framework remains the same. We'll train two versions of the data: one with node features initialized randomly, and one with node features using the N2V embeddings.

MODEL MODIFICATION

We use the same `SimpleGNN` class with modifications. First, in this enhanced version of the `SimpleGNN` class, we extend its functionality to provide a predictive output for each node. This is achieved by applying a log `softmax` activation to the embeddings produced by the second GCN layer. The log `softmax` output provides a normalized log probability distribution over the potential classes for each node for the classification task.

Second, we introduce dual outputs. The method returns two values: the raw embeddings from the `conv2` layer, which capture the node representations, and the log `softmax` of these embeddings. For us to observe both the embedding and the predictions, we have the `forward` method return both. In addition to this two-layer model, we added two layers to this architecture to have a four-layer model for comparison, as shown in listing 2.8.

Listing 2.8   Preprocessing: Constructing training data

```python
class SimpleGNN_inference(torch.nn.Module):
    def __init__(self, num_features, hidden_channels):
        super(SimpleGNN, self).__init__()
        self.conv1 = GCNConv(num_features, hidden_channels)
        self.conv2 = GCNConv(hidden_channels, hidden_channels)

    def forward(self, x, edge_index):
        # First Graph Convolutional layer
        x = self.conv1(x, edge_index)
        x = F.relu(x)
        x = F.dropout(x, training=self.training)

        # Second Graph Convolutional layer
        x = self.conv2(x, edge_index)                    ← Predicts classes by passing
        predictions = F.log_softmax(x, dim=1)              the final conv layer through
                                                           a log softmax

        return x, predictions       ← The class returns both the
                                       last embedding and the
                                       prediction.
```

ESTABLISH THE TRAINING LOOP

We program the training loop for the GNN model in a semi-supervised learning context, as shown in listing 2.9. This loop iterates over a specified number of epochs, where an epoch represents a complete pass through the entire training dataset.

Within each epoch, the model's parameters are updated to minimize a loss function, which quantifies the difference between the predicted outputs and the actual labels for the nodes in the training set. For those familiar with programming deep learning training loops, this should be very familiar. For those who could do with a quick reminder, the following describes some of the key steps in initializing and running the training loop:

- *Optimizer initialization*—The optimizer is initialized with a specific learning rate when it's created. For example, here we use the Adam optimizer, with an initial learning rate of 0.01.
- *Zeroing the gradients*—`optimizer.zero_grad()` ensures that the gradients are reset before each update, preventing them from accumulating across epochs.
- *Model forward pass*—The model processes the node features (`data.x`) and the graph structure (`data.edge_index`) to produce output predictions. In semi-supervised settings, not all nodes have labels, so the model's output includes predictions for both labeled and unlabeled nodes.
- *Applying the training mask*—`out_masked = out[data.train_mask]` applies a mask to the model's output to select only the predictions corresponding to labeled nodes. This is crucial in semi-supervised learning, where only a subset of nodes has known labels.
- *Loss computation and backpropagation*—Loss function `loss_fn` compares the selected predictions (`out_masked`) with the true labels of the labeled nodes (`train_labels`). The `loss.backward()` call computes the gradient of the loss function with respect to the model parameters, which is then used to update these parameters via `optimizer.step()`.
- *Logging*—The training loop prints the loss at regular intervals (every 10 epochs in this case) to monitor the training progress.

Listing 2.9 Training loop

```
for epoch in range(3000):                      ◁—┐ Number of epochs
    optimizer.zero_grad()

    _, out = model(data.x, data.edge_index)    ◁—┤ Passes both node features and
                                                    edge_index to the model

    out_masked = out[data.train_mask]          ◁—┐ Applies the training
                                                    mask to select only
    loss = loss_fn(out_masked, train_labels)   ◁—┤ the outputs for the
    loss.backward()                                 labeled nodes
    optimizer.step()

    if epoch % 10 == 0:                        ◁—┐ Computes the loss
        print(f'Epoch {epoch}, Log Loss: {loss.item()}')    using only the labeled
                                                             nodes

                                               Prints the loss
                                               every 10 epochs
```

This process iteratively refines the model's parameters to improve its predictions on the labeled portion of the dataset, with the goal of learning a model that can generalize well to the unlabeled nodes and potentially to new, unseen data.

GNN RESULTS: RANDOMIZED VS. N2V NODE FEATURES

Let's compare the classification task comparing the GNN performance from the randomized node features versus the N2V node features, as shown in table 2.3.

Table 2.3   Classification performance of the GNN model where the input graph uses different node features

Model	GNN Accuracy	GNN F1 Score
Two-layer, randomized features	82.27%	82.14%
Two-layer, N2V features	87.79%	88.10%
Four-layer, randomized features	86.58%	86.90%
Four-layer, N2V features	88.99%	89.29%

The table summarizes the performance of different GNN models based on their accuracy and F1 score. It highlights that GNNs using N2V features consistently outperform those using randomized features across all model configurations. Specifically, the four-layer GNN with N2V features achieves the highest accuracy and F1 score, indicating the effectiveness of incorporating meaningful node representations derived from N2V embeddings. If we had more information about specific features for the node, as we do in chapter 3, the GNN embeddings may further improve accuracy for the GNN model.

RESULTS: GNN VS. RANDOM FOREST

We now compare the performance of the GNN model from this section with the random forest model from the previous section (see table 2.4).

Table 2.4   Comparison of classification performance between the GNN model and the random forest model

Model	Data Input	Accuracy	F1 Score
Random forest	Embedding from GNN	83.33%	82.01%
Random forest	Embedding from N2V	84.52%	80.72%
Two-layer simple GNN	Graph with randomized node features	82.27%	82.14%
Two-layer simple GNN	Graph with n2v embeddings as node features	87.79%	88.10%
Four-layer simple GNN	Graph with randomized node features	86.58%	86.90%
Four-layer simple GNN	Graph with n2v embeddings as node features	88.99%	89.29%

Figure 2.10 visualizes the results from table 2.4. Overall, the GNN models outperformed the random forest models.

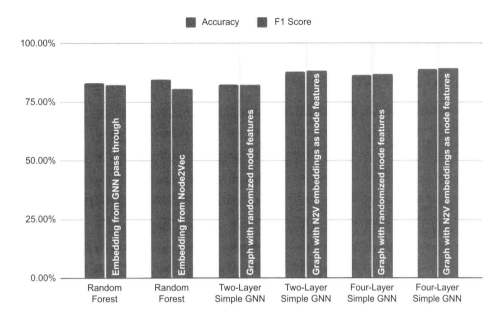

Figure 2.10 **Chart comparing the classification performance of the random forest with the GNN. Only one GNN model is outperformed by the random forest: The two-layer model trained on graph data with randomized node features is outperformed in terms of accuracy.**

When comparing the performance of the GNN models with the random forest models, we can make several observations. Random forest, when trained on embeddings derived from GNN pass-through or N2V embeddings, achieves comparable accuracy to the two-layer simple GNN model. However, when considering the F1 score, both GNN models outperform random forest. Notably, the four-layer simple GNN model, especially when using N2V embeddings as features, exhibits significantly better performance than the random forest model, showcasing higher accuracy and F1 score.

This indicates that while random forest may outperform simpler GNN architectures such as the two-layer model in terms of accuracy, the more complex GNN architectures demonstrate superior performance in terms of F1 score, especially when using sophisticated node embeddings such as N2V. Therefore, the choice between random forest and GNN should consider both accuracy and F1 score, as well as the complexity of the model architecture and the nature of the input features, to achieve optimal performance for the given task and dataset.

It's important to note that this short example didn't extensively fine-tune either the GNN or the random forest models. Further optimization of both types of models could potentially lead to significant improvements in their performance. Fine-tuning hyperparameters, adjusting model architectures, and optimizing training processes could all contribute to enhancing the accuracy and F1 score of both GNNs and random forest classifiers. Therefore, while the results presented here provide starting insights into the performance on a small graph dataset, we suggest you try out the models and experiment with performance.

2.4 Under the Hood

This section gets deeper into the theoretical foundations of graph representations and embeddings, particularly in the context of GNNs. It emphasizes the importance of embeddings in transforming complex graph data into lower-dimensional, manageable forms that retain essential information.

We distinguish between two primary types of learning: transductive and inductive. Transductive methods, such as N2V, optimize embeddings specifically for the training data, making them effective within a known dataset but less adaptable to new data. In contrast, inductive methods, as exemplified by GNNs, enable generalization to new, unseen data by integrating both graph structure and node features during training. This section also examines the mechanisms behind N2V (random walk) and GNNs (message passing).

2.4.1 Representations and embeddings

Understanding graph representations and the role of embeddings is crucial for effectively applying GNNs in machine learning. Representations convert complex graph data into simpler, manageable forms without losing essential information, facilitating analysis and interpretation of the underlying structures within graphs. In the context of GNNs, representations enable the processing of graph data in a way that is compatible with machine learning algorithms, ensuring that the rich and complex structures of graphs are preserved.

Traditional methods such as adjacency matrices and edge lists provide a foundational way to represent graph structures, but they often fall short in capturing richer information, such as node features or subtle topological details. This limitation is where graph embeddings come into play. A graph embedding is a low-dimensional vector representation of a graph, node, or edge that retains essential structural and relational information. Much like reducing a high-resolution image to a compact feature vector, embeddings condense the graph's complexity while preserving its distinguishing characteristics.

Embeddings simplify data handling and open new possibilities for machine learning applications. They enable visualization of complex graphs in two or three dimensions, allowing us to explore their inherent structures and relationships more intuitively. Furthermore, embeddings serve as versatile inputs for various downstream tasks, such as node classification and link prediction, as demonstrated in earlier sections of this chapter. By providing a bridge between raw graph data and machine learning models, embeddings are key to unlocking the full potential of GNNs.

THE SIGNIFICANCE OF NODE SIMILARITY AND CONTEXT

An important use of graph embeddings is to encapsulate the notion of similarity and context within the graph. In a spatial context, proximity (or similarity) often translates to a measurable distance or angle between points.

For graphs, however, these concepts are redefined in terms of connections and paths. The similarity between nodes can be interpreted through their connectivity, that is, how many "hops" or steps it takes to move from one node to another, or the likelihood of traversing from one node to another during random walks on the graph (figure 2.11).

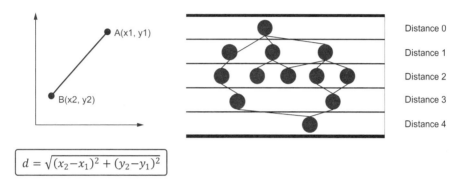

Figure 2.11   Comparison of similarity concepts: using distance on a plane (left) and using steps along a graph (right)

Another way to think about proximity is in terms of probability: Given two nodes (node A and node B), what is the chance that I will encounter node B if I start to hop from node A? In figure 2.12, if the number of hops is 1, the probability is 0, as there is no way to reach node B from node A in one hop. However, if the number of hops is 2,

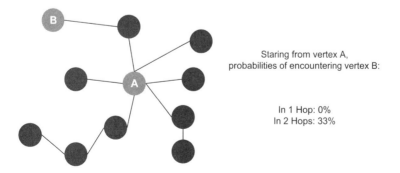

Figure 2.12   Illustrating the notion of proximity computed in terms of probability: given a walk from node A, the probability of encountering node B is a measure of proximity.

then we need to first count to see how many different possible routes there are. Let's also assume that no node can be encountered twice in a traversal and that each direction is equally likely. With these assumptions, there are three unique routes of 2 hops starting from node A. Of those, only one leads to node B. Thus, the probability is one out of three, or 33%. This probabilistic approach to measuring proximity between nodes offers a nuanced understanding of the graph's topology, meaning that graph structures can be encoded within a probability space.

The ideas explained here are relevant as we approach the topic of inductive and transductive methods as applied to graph embeddings. Both of these methodologies use the notion of node proximity, although in distinct ways, to generate embeddings that capture the essence of node relationships and graph structure. Inductive methods excel in generalizing to accommodate new, unseen data, enabling models to adapt and learn beyond their initial training set. Conversely, transductive methods specialize in optimizing embeddings specifically for the training data itself, making them highly effective within their learned context but less flexible when introduced to new data.

2.4.2   *Transductive and inductive methods*

The way an embedding is created determines the scope of its subsequent usage. Here we examine embedding methods that can be broadly classified as transductive and inductive. Transductive embedding methods learn representations for a fixed set of nodes in a single, static graph:

- These methods directly optimize individual embeddings for each node.
- The entire graph structure must be available during training.
- These methods can't naturally generalize to unseen nodes or graphs.
- Adding new nodes requires retraining the entire model.
- Examples include DeepWalk [8], N2V, and matrix factorization approaches.
- Transductive methods allow us to reduce the scope of the prediction problem. For transduction, we're only concerned with the data we're presented with.
- These methods are computationally costly for large amounts of data.

Inductive embedding methods learn a function to generate embeddings, allowing generalization to unseen nodes and even entirely new graphs:

- These methods learn to aggregate and transform node features and local graph structure.
- These methods can generate embeddings for previously unseen nodes without retraining.
- Node attributes or structural features are often used.
- These methods are more flexible and scalable for dynamic or expanding graphs.
- Examples include GraphSAGE, GCNs, and graph attention networks (GATs).

Let's illustrate this with two examples:

- *Example 1: Email spam detection*—An inductive model for email spam detection is trained on a dataset of labeled emails (spam or not spam) and learns to generalize from the training data. Once trained, the model can classify new incoming emails as spam or not spam without needing to retrain.

  Transductive wouldn't be better in this example because models would require retraining with every new batch of emails, making them computationally expensive and impractical for real-time spam detection.

- *Example 2: Semi-supervised learning for community detection in social networks*—A transductive model uses the entire graph to identify communities within a social network. Using a combination of labeled and unlabeled nodes, the model exploits the network in a better way: inductive models wouldn't take full advantage of the specific network structure and node interconnections because they only process part of the data—the training set. This isn't enough information for accurate community detection.

Table 2.5 compares the types of graph representation we've learned so far, consisting of representations generated by both nonembedding methods, and embedding methods.

Table 2.5 Different methods of graph representation

Representation	Description	Examples
Basic data representations	<ul><li>Great for analytical methods that involve network traversal</li><li>Useful for some node classification algorithms</li><li>Information provided: Node and edge neighbors</li></ul>	<ul><li>Adjacency list</li><li>Edge list</li><li>Adjacency matrix</li></ul>
Transductive (shallow) embeddings	<ul><li>Useless for data not trained on</li><li>Difficult to scale</li></ul>	<ul><li>DeepWalk</li><li>N2V</li><li>TransE</li><li>RESCAL</li><li>Graph factorization</li><li>Spectral techniques</li></ul>
Inductive embeddings	<ul><li>Models can be generalized to new and structurally different graphs</li><li>Represents data as vectors in continuous space</li><li>Learns a mapping from data (new and old) to positions within the continuous space</li></ul>	<ul><li>GNNs can be used to inductively generate embeddings</li><li>Transformers</li><li>N2V with feature concatenation</li></ul>

Summary of terms related to transductive embedding methods

Two additional terms related to embedding methods and sometimes used interchangeably with it are *shallow methods* and *encoders*. Here, we'll briefly distinguish these terms.

Transductive methods, explained earlier, are a large class of methods of which graph embedding is one application. So, outside of our present context of representation learning, the attributes of transductive learning remain the same.

In machine learning, *shallow* is often used to refer to the opposite of deep learning models or algorithms. Such models are distinguished from deep learning models in that they don't use multiple processing layers to produce an output from input data. In our context of graph/node embeddings, this term also refers to methods that aren't based on deep learning, but more specifically points to methods that mimic a simple lookup table, rather than a generalized model produced from a supervised learning algorithm.

Any method that reproduces a low dimensional representation of data, an embedding, is often known as an *encoder*. This encoder simply matches a given data point such as a node (or even an entire graph) to its respective embedding in low dimensional space. GNNs can be broadly understood as a class of encoders, similar to Transformers. However, there are specific GNN encoders, such as the graph autoencoder (GAE), which you'll meet in chapter 5.

2.4.3   *N2V: Random walks across graphs*

Random walk approaches construct embeddings by using random walks across the graph. With these, the similarity between two nodes, A and B, is defined as the probability that one will encounter node B on a random graph traversal from node A (as we described in section 2.4.1). These walks are unrestricted, with no restriction preventing a walk from backtracking or encountering the same node multiple times.

For each node, we perform a random walk within its neighborhood. As we perform more and more random walks, we begin to notice similarities in the types of nodes we encounter. A potential mental model is exploring a city or forest. In a distinct neighborhood, for example, as we take the same streets or paths multiple times, we begin to notice that houses have a similar style and trees have a similar species.

The result of a random walk method is a vector of nodes visited for each walk, with different starting nodes. In the upcoming figure 2.13, we show some examples of how we can walk (or search) across a graph.

DeepWalk is one method that creates embeddings by performing several random walks of a fixed size for each node and calculating embeddings from each of these. Here, any path is equally likely to occur, making the walks unbiased and meaning that all nodes connected by an edge are equally likely to be encountered at each step. The output for a DeepWalk on the graph in figure 2.13 might be the vector [u, s1, s3] or the vector [u, s1, s2, s4, s5]. Each of these vectors contains the unique nodes visited in a random walk.

N2V improved on DeepWalk by introducing tunable bias in these random walks. The idea is to be able to trade off learnings from a node's close-by neighborhood and from further away. N2V captures this in two parameters:

- p—Controls the probability that the path walked will return to the previous node.
- q—Controls the probability of whether a depth-first search (DFS, a hopping strategy that emphasizes faraway nodes) or breadth-first search (BFS, a strategy that emphasizes nearby nodes). DFS and BFS are illustrated in figure 2.13, where we demonstrate what happens for four hops.

To mimic the DeepWalk algorithm, both p and q would be set to 0 such that the search is *unbiased*. So, for figure 2.13, the output for N2V could be [u, s1,s2] or [u,s4,s5,s6] depending on whether the walks are BFS or DFS.

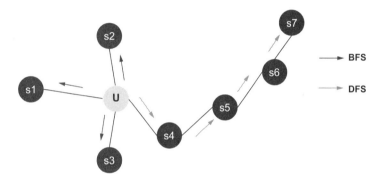

Figure 2.13   Depth-first search (DFS) and breadth first search (BFS) on a graph where embeddings are generated based on random walks using these graph-traversal strategies. DFS (light arrows) prioritizes going deep down one path, while BFS (dark arrows) prioritizes checking all adjacent and nearby paths.

Once we have the vector of nodes, we create embeddings by using a neural network to predict the most likely neighboring node for a given node. Usually, this neural network is shallow, with one hidden layer. After training, the hidden layer becomes that node's embedding.

2.4.4   *Message passing as deep learning*

Deep learning methods in general are composed of building blocks, or layers, that take some tensor-based input and then produce an output that is transformed as it flows through the various layers. At the end, more transformations and aggregations are applied to yield a prediction. However, often the output of the hidden layers is directly exploited for other tasks within the model architecture or are used as inputs to other models. This is what we saw in our classification problem in section 2.3. We constructed a vector of visited nodes, and these nodes were then passed to a deep learning model. The deep learning model learned to predict future nodes based on a starting node. But the actual embeddings were contained within *the hidden layer* of the network.

TIP   For a refresher on deep learning, read *Deep Learning with Python* by François Chollet (Manning, 2021).

We show the classic architecture for a deep feed-forward neural network, specifically a multilayer perceptron (MLP), in figure 2.14. Briefly, the network takes a node vector as input, and the hidden layers are trained to produce an output vector that achieves some task, such as identifying a node class. The input vector may be flattened images, and the output may be a single number reflecting where there is a dog or cat in the image. For the N2V example, the input is a vector of starting nodes, and the output is the corresponding other node vectors that are visited after traversing the graph from the starting node. In the image example, the output is the explicit task function, namely to classify images based on whether they contain a dog or cat. In N2V, the output is implicit in the graph structure. We know the subsequent nodes that are visited, but we're interested in the way the network has encoded the data, that is, how it has built an embedding of the node data. This is contained within the hidden layer, where typically we just take the last layer.

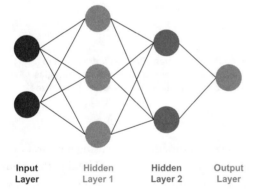

| Input Layer | Hidden Layer 1 | Hidden Layer 2 | Output Layer |

Figure 2.14   Structure of a multilayer perceptron

For GNNs, the input will be the entire graph structure, and the output will be the embeddings. Therefore, the model is explicit in how it constructs the embeddings. However, the output isn't restricted to embeddings. Instead, we can have the output as a classification, such as whether the book has a specific political affiliation in that node in the graph. The embeddings are again implicit in the hidden layers. However, the entire process is wrapped into a single model, so we don't need to extract this data. Instead, we've used the embeddings to achieve our goal, such as node classification.

While the architecture of GNNs is very different from feed-forward neural networks, there are some parallels. In many of the GNNs we learn about, a graph in tensor form is passed into the GNN architecture, and one or more iterations of message passing is applied. The message-passing process is shown in figure 2.15.

1. *Input* initial graph with node, edges, and features.

2. *Collect* all features from neighboring nodes, known as messages, for each node.

3. *Aggregate* messages using invariant functions such as sum, max, or mean.

4. *Transform* messages using a neural network to create new node features.

5. *Update* all features in the graph with new node features.

Figure 2.15 Elements of our message-passing layer. Each message-passing layer consists of an aggregation, a transformation, and an update step.

In chapter 1, we first discussed the idea of message passing. In its simplest form, message passing reflects that we're taking information or data from nodes or edges and sending it somewhere else [1]. The messages are the data, and we're passing the messages across the structure of our graph. Each message can contain information from either sender or receiver, or often both.

We can now explain further why message passing is so important to GNNs. The message passing step updates the information about each node by using the node information and nodes neighborhood information (both in terms of nearby node data and the edge data connecting them). Message passing is how we construct representations about our graph. These are the critical mechanisms that build graph embeddings, which inform other tasks such as node classification. There are two important aspects to consider when constructing these node (or edge) embeddings.

First, we need to think about what is inside a message. In our earlier example, we had a list of books on political topics. This dataset only had information about the books' co-purchasing connections and their political leaning labels. However, if we had additional information such as the book length, author name, or even the synopsis, then those node features could be contained within our messages. However, it's important to remember that it could also be edge data, such as when another book was bought together, that could also be contained in messages. In fact, sometimes messages can contain both node and edge data.

Second, we need to think about how much local information we want to consider when making each embedding. We want to know how much of the neighborhood to sample. We already discussed this when we introduced random walk methods. We need to define how many hops to take when sampling our graph.

Both the data and the number of hops are critical to message passing in GNNs. The features, either node or edge data, are the messages, and the number of hops is the number of times we pass a message. Both of these are controlled by the layers of a GNN. The number of hidden layers is the number of hops that we'll be sending messages. The input to each hidden layer is the data contained in a message. This is almost always the case for GNNs but it's worth noting that it isn't always true. Sometimes, other mechanisms such as attention can determine the depth of message-passing samples from the neighborhood. We'll discuss graph attention networks (GATs) in chapter 4. Until then, understanding that the number of layers in a GNN reflects the number of hops undertaken during message passing is a good intuition to have.

For a feed-forward network, like the one on the left in figure 2.15, information is passed between the nodes of our neural network. In a GNN, this information comprises the messages that we send over our graph. For each message-passing step, the vertex in our neural network collects information from nodes or edges one hop away. So, if we want our node representations to take account of nodes from three hops away from each node, we need three hidden message-passing layers. Three layers may not seem like very many, but the amount of a graph we cover scales exponentially with the number of hops. Intuitively, we can understand this as a type of six degrees of separation principle—that all people are only six degrees of social separation apart from each other. This would mean that you and I could be connected by six short hops across the global combined social network.

Different message-passing schemes lead to different flavors of GNNs. So, for each GNN we study in this book, we'll pay close attention to the math and code implementation for message passing. One important aspect is how we aggregate messages, which we'll discuss in chapter 3 when we discuss GCNs in depth.

After message passing, the resulting tensor is passed through feed-forward layers that result in a prediction. In the left of figure 2.16, which illustrates a GNN model for node prediction, the data flows through message-passing layers, the tensor then passes through an additional MLP and activation function to output a prediction. For example, we could use our GNN to classify whether employees are likely to join a new company or have good recommendations.

However, as with the feed-forward neural network illustrated previously, we can also output just the hidden layers and work directly with that output. For GNNs, this output is the graph, node, or edge embeddings.

One final note on message passing in GNNs is that in each step in the message-passing layer of our GNNs, we'll be passing information from nodes to another node one hop away. Importantly, a neural network then takes the data from the one-hop neighbors and applies a nonlinear transformation. This is the beauty of GNNs; we're applying many small neural networks at the level of individual nodes and/or edges to build embeddings of the graph features. Therefore, when we say that a message-passing

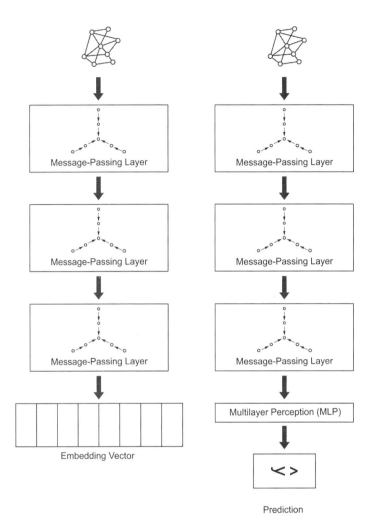

Figure 2.16 **A simple GNN architecture diagram (left). A graph is input on the left, encountering node-information-passing layers. This is followed by MLP layers. After an activation is applied, a prediction is yielded. A GNN architecture (right).**

layer is like the first layer of a neural network, we're really saying that it's the first layer of many individual neural networks that are all learning on local node data or edge-specific data. In practice, the overall code constructing and training is the same as if it were one single transformation, but the intuition that we're applying individual non-linear transformations will become useful as we travel deeper into the workings of complex GNN models.

Summary

- Node and graph embeddings are powerful methods to extract insights from our data, and they can serve as inputs/features in our machine learning models. There are several independent methods for generating such embeddings. GNNs have embedding built into the architecture.
- Graph embeddings, including node and edge embeddings, serve as foundational techniques to transform complex graph data into structured formats suitable for machine learning tasks.
- We explored two main types of graph embeddings: N2V, a transductive method, and GNN-based embeddings, an inductive method, each with distinct characteristics and applications.
- N2V operates on fixed datasets using random walks to establish node contexts and similarities, but it doesn't generalize to unseen data or graphs.
- GNNs, on the other hand, are versatile, inductive frameworks that can generate embeddings for new, unseen data, making them adaptable across different graph structures.
- The comparison of embeddings in machine learning tasks, such as semi-supervised learning, reveals the importance of choosing the right embedding method based on the data size, complexity, and specific problem at hand.
- Despite the effectiveness of random forest classifiers in handling both N2V and GNN embeddings for smaller graphs, GNNs demonstrate a unique ability to use graph topology and node features, particularly in larger and more complex graphs.
- Embeddings can be used as features in traditional machine learning models and in graph data visualization and insight extraction.

Part 2

Graph neural networks

Now that you understand the basics, it's time to roll up your sleeves and dive into the core architectures that make graph neural networks (GNNs) work. This section bridges the theoretical and practical by introducing key GNN architectures and applying them to real-world problems. You'll explore foundational models such as graph convolutional networks (GCNs), GraphSAGE, and graph attention networks (GATs), as well as graph autoencoders (GAEs)—each designed to harness the unique structure of graph data.

These architectures come to life through real-world applications. They have been used for fake review detection, product category prediction, and molecular graph generation for drug discovery. By blending cutting-edge models with highly effective use cases, this part of the book provides both the understanding and practical tools needed to unlock the transformative potential of GNNs in your projects.

3

Graph convolutional networks and GraphSAGE

This chapter covers

- Introducing GraphSAGE and graph convolutional networks
- Applying convolutional graph neural networks to generate product bundles from Amazon
- Key parameters and settings for graph convolutional networks and GraphSAGE
- More theoretical insights, including convolution and message passing

In the first two chapters of this book, we explored fundamental concepts related to graphs and graph representation learning. All of this served to set us up for part 2, where we'll explore distinct types of graph neural network (GNN) architectures, including convolutional GNNs, graph attention networks (GATs), and graph autoencoders (GAEs).

In this chapter, our goal is to understand and apply graph convolutional networks (GCNs) and GraphSAGE [1, 2]. These two architectures are part of a larger class of GNNs that approach deep learning by applying convolutions to graph data.

Convolutional operations are relatively common in deep learning models, particularly for image-based tasks that rely heavily on convolutional neural networks (CNNs). To learn more about CNNs and their application to computer vision, we recommend checking out *Deep Learning with Python* (Manning, 2024) or *Deep Learning with PyTorch* (Manning, 2023).

We provide a short primer on convolutions later in the chapter, but essentially convolutional operations can be understood as performing a spatial or local averaging across entities. For example, in images, CNN layers form representations at incrementally larger pixel subdomains. For GCNs, we'll apply the same idea of a local averaging, but with neighborhoods of nodes.

In this chapter, you'll learn how to apply convolutional GNNs to a node prediction problem, key parameters and settings for GCN and GraphSAGE, ways to optimize performance for convolutional GNNs, and relevant theoretical topics, including graph convolution and message passing. Additionally, we'll explore the Amazon Products dataset. This chapter is structured as follows: first, we jump into the product category prediction problem and create baseline models (section 3.1); then we adjust our models using neighborhood aggregation (section 3.2); next, we optimize our models using general deep learning methods (section 3.3); following that, we explain relevant theory in more detail (section 3.4); and finally, we dig deeper into the Amazon Products dataset used in this chapter and later in the book (section 3.5).

This chapter is designed to immerse you immediately in the application of convolutional GNNs, equipping you with the essential knowledge needed to deploy these models effectively. The initial sections provide you with the minimum toolkit for a functioning understanding of convolutional GNNs in practice.

However, when facing challenging modeling problems, deeper comprehension becomes invaluable. The latter sections of the chapter cover underlying principles of the layers, settings, and parameters introduced earlier. They are crafted to enhance your conceptual grasp, ensuring that your practical skills are complemented by a thorough theoretical understanding. This holistic approach aims to not only enable you to apply GNNs but to innovate and adapt them to the nuanced demands of real-world problems.

> **NOTE**   While *GraphSAGE* refers to a specific individual architecture, it may be confusing that *GCN* also refers to a specific architecture and not the entire class of GNNs based on convolutions. So, in this chapter, we'll use *convolutional GNNs* to refer to this entire class of GNNs, which include GraphSAGE and GCN. We'll use *GCN* to refer to the individual architecture introduced by Thomas Kipf and Max Welling [1].

> **NOTE**   Code from this chapter can be found in notebook form at the GitHub repository (https://mng.bz/wJMW). Colab links and data from this chapter can be accessed in the same locations.

3.1 *Predicting consumer product categories*

Let's start our exploration of convolutional GNNs with a product management problem using the Amazon Products dataset (see table 3.1). Imagine you're a product manager aiming to enhance sales by identifying and promoting emerging trends in product bundles. You have a dataset derived from Amazon's product co-purchasing network, containing a rich set of relationships between products based on customer buying behavior. Your task is to use insights about product categories and co-purchasing patterns to uncover hidden and appealing product bundles that resonate with your customers.

Table 3.1 Overview of the Amazon Products dataset

Amazon co-purchases organized by product category	
Number of nodes (products)	~2,500,000
Node features	100
Node categories	47
Total number of edges	~61,900,000

To tackle this, we introduce GCNs and GraphSAGE—two convolutional GNN architectures. This section will guide you through training these models on the Amazon Products dataset. We'll focus on two tasks: identifying a product's category and finding sets of product bundles by analyzing the similarity between product embeddings produced by the trained models.

> **NOTE** If you want to get deeper into the theory behind GCN and GraphSAGE, see section 3.4. For details about the Amazon Products dataset, see section 3.5.

Following our model training process, in this section, we'll do the following:

- *Preprocess our dataset*—We'll take the Amazon Products dataset and reduce its size to work with systems with minimal resources.
- *Construct our model classes*—We'll focus on two convolutional GNNs: GCN and GraphSAGE. We'll initially create model classes and instantiate them with default parameters.
- *Code our training and validation loops*—We'll train the models with a validation step for each epoch. To compare the two models, we'll train them simultaneously with the same batches.
- *Assess model performance*—We'll take a look at training curves. Then, we'll use traditional classification metrics and observe the ability of the model to predict particular categories.

Our immediate goal is to develop first passes of our trained models. So, at this point, the emphasis isn't on performance optimization but on covering the essential steps to get a baseline model working. Subsequent sections will refine these approaches, enhancing performance and efficiency.

3.1.1   Loading and processing the data

We start by downloading the Amazon Products dataset from the Open Graph Benchmark (OGB) site (https://ogb.stanford.edu/). This dataset is large for a single machine, taking up 1.3 GB. This includes 2.5 million nodes (products) and 61.9 million edges (co-purchases).

To make working with this data manageable for systems with smaller memory capacity and less powerful processors, we'll reduce its size. We simply take the nodes that have the first 10,000 node indices in the original graph and create a subgraph based on those. Depending on your problem, there are other strategies to create subgraphs. In chapter 8, we look at creating subgraphs in more depth.

In creating a subset graph, there is often bookkeeping that must be done to ensure our node subset has a consistent and logical ordering and is connected to the correct labels and features. We must also filter out edges that are connected to nodes from outside the subset. Lastly, we want to make sure we can call back the original indices of the subset in case we want to call back useful information; for example, for the Amazon Products dataset, we can access the SKU (Amazon Standard Identification Number, ASIN) numbers and product categories of each node using their original indices.

So, we relabel the nodes with a consistent ordering. Then, we reassign the respective node features and labels to correspond to the new indices. Even though we choose nodes with the first 10,000 indices, this may not be so in any particular case. Here's how we'll refine and prepare the data for modeling in four steps:

1 *Initialize the subset graph*—We create a new graph object that will store our subset of data. This graph will hold the edges, features, and labels of the nodes that have indices 0–9,999 in our original graph.

2 *Relabel node indices*—To ensure consistency and avoid index mismatches, we relabel the node indices within our subset graph. This relabeling is crucial because operations within GNNs depend heavily on indexing to process node and edge information.

3 *Feature and label assignment*—We assign node features (x) and labels (y) to our new graph object. These features and labels are sliced from the original dataset, corresponding to our specified subset indices.

4 *Edge mask utilization*—The `return_edge_mask` option, used during the subgraph extraction, lets us identify which edges were selected during the subgraph creation. This is useful for tracing back to the original graph's structure or for any structural analysis required later.

By restructuring the data in this manner, we not only make it manageable but also tailor it specifically for efficient processing in subsequent graph-based learning tasks. This setup is foundational as we proceed to construct and evaluate our GNN models in the following sections. The following listing shows the code for implementing that process.

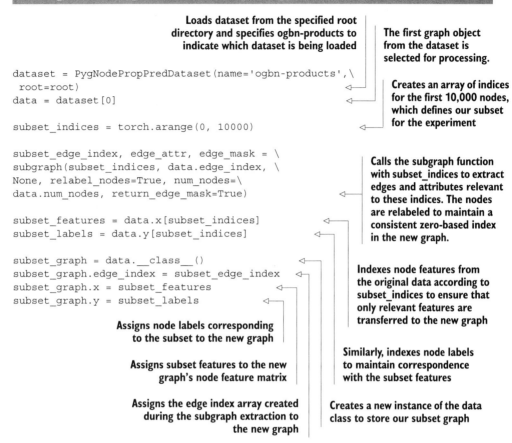

Listing 3.1 Reading in data and creating a subgraph

Loads dataset from the specified root directory and specifies ogbn-products to indicate which dataset is being loaded

The first graph object from the dataset is selected for processing.

```
dataset = PygNodePropPredDataset(name='ogbn-products',\
 root=root)
data = dataset[0]

subset_indices = torch.arange(0, 10000)

subset_edge_index, edge_attr, edge_mask = \
subgraph(subset_indices, data.edge_index, \
None, relabel_nodes=True, num_nodes=\
data.num_nodes, return_edge_mask=True)

subset_features = data.x[subset_indices]
subset_labels = data.y[subset_indices]

subset_graph = data.__class__()
subset_graph.edge_index = subset_edge_index
subset_graph.x = subset_features
subset_graph.y = subset_labels
```

Creates an array of indices for the first 10,000 nodes, which defines our subset for the experiment

Calls the subgraph function with subset_indices to extract edges and attributes relevant to these indices. The nodes are relabeled to maintain a consistent zero-based index in the new graph.

Indexes node features from the original data according to subset_indices to ensure that only relevant features are transferred to the new graph

Similarly, indexes node labels to maintain correspondence with the subset features

Creates a new instance of the data class to store our subset graph

Assigns node labels corresponding to the subset to the new graph

Assigns subset features to the new graph's node feature matrix

Assigns the edge index array created during the subgraph extraction to the new graph

3.1.2 Creating our model classes

After setting up our dataset and preparing a manageable subgraph, we transition to the core of our graph machine learning pipeline: defining the models. In this section, we focus on two popular types of GNNs provided by the PyTorch Geometric (PyG) library: GCN and GraphSAGE.

UNDERSTANDING OUR MODEL ARCHITECTURES

PyG simplifies the construction of GNNs through modular layer objects, each encapsulating a specific type of graph convolution. These layers can be stacked and integrated with other PyTorch modules to build complex architectures tailored to various graph-based tasks.

GCN MODEL

The GCN model uses the `GCNConv` layer, which implements the graph convolution operation as described by Kipf and Welling in their seminal paper [1]. It takes advantage of the spectral properties of graphs to facilitate information flow between nodes, allowing the model to learn representations that embed both local graph structure and node features.

In listing 3.2, the GCN class sets up a two-layer model. Each layer is represented by the GCNConv module, which processes graph data by applying a convolution operation that directly uses the graph's structure.

To summarize its workings, from an input set of node features and the graph structure (edge_index), the network will update node features by aggregating the neighborhood information from each respective node. After the first layer, we apply a rectified linear unit (ReLU) activation function, which adds nonlinearity to the model. The second layer refines these features further.

If we want to look at the node embeddings directly—for instance, to visualize them or to use them in some other analysis—we can just return them right after the second layer. Otherwise, we apply another activation function—in this case, a softmax function—to normalize the outputs for our classification problem.

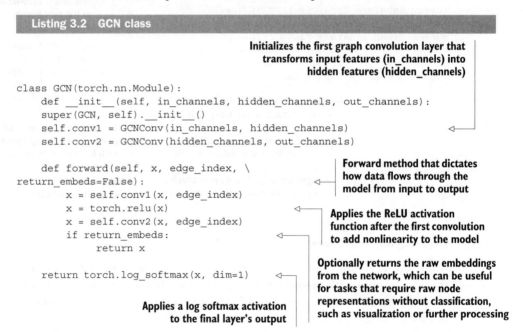

Listing 3.2 GCN class

Initializes the first graph convolution layer that transforms input features (in_channels) into hidden features (hidden_channels)

```
class GCN(torch.nn.Module):
    def __init__(self, in_channels, hidden_channels, out_channels):
        super(GCN, self).__init__()
        self.conv1 = GCNConv(in_channels, hidden_channels)
        self.conv2 = GCNConv(hidden_channels, out_channels)

    def forward(self, x, edge_index, \
return_embeds=False):
        x = self.conv1(x, edge_index)
        x = torch.relu(x)
        x = self.conv2(x, edge_index)
        if return_embeds:
            return x

    return torch.log_softmax(x, dim=1)
```

Forward method that dictates how data flows through the model from input to output

Applies the ReLU activation function after the first convolution to add nonlinearity to the model

Optionally returns the raw embeddings from the network, which can be useful for tasks that require raw node representations without classification, such as visualization or further processing

Applies a log softmax activation to the final layer's output

GRAPHSAGE MODEL

Much like the GCN model, the GraphSAGE model class in our code also sets up a two-layer network, but with the SAGEConv layers. While structurally similar in code, Graph-SAGE is a significant shift from GCN in theory. Unlike GCN's full reliance on the entire graph's adjacency matrix, GraphSAGE is designed to learn from randomly sampled neighborhood data, making it particularly well-suited for large graphs. This sampling approach allows GraphSAGE to scale effectively by focusing on localized regions of the graph.

GraphSAGE uses the `SAGEConv` layer, which supports various aggregation functions—mean, pool, and long short-term memory (LSTM)—offering flexibility in how node features are aggregated. After each `SAGEConv` layer, similar to the GCN model, a nonlinearity is applied. If node embeddings are required directly for tasks such as visualization or further analysis, they can be returned immediately following the second layer. Otherwise, a softmax function is applied to normalize the outputs for classification tasks.

The key difference in PyG's implementation of these models lies in their efficiency and scalability with large datasets. Both models learn node representations, but GraphSAGE provides a significant advantage for practical applications involving very large graphs. Unlike GCN, which can operate on sparse data representations but still processes information from the entire graph structure, GraphSAGE doesn't require the entire adjacency matrix. Instead, it samples local neighborhoods, which allows it to handle vast networks efficiently without overwhelming memory resources by having to load the entire graph representation.

Listing 3.3 GraphSAGE class

Initializes the first graph convolution layer that transforms input features (in_channels) into hidden features (hidden_channels)

```
class GraphSAGE(torch.nn.Module):
    def __init__(self, in_channels, hidden_channels, out_channels):
        super(GraphSAGE, self).__init__()
        self.conv1 = SAGEConv(in_channels, \
        hidden_channels)
        self.conv2 = SAGEConv(hidden_channels, out_channels)

    def forward(self, x, edge_index, \
    return_embeds=False):
        x = self.conv1(x, edge_index)
        x = torch.relu(x)
        x = self.conv2(x, edge_index)
        if return_embeds:
            return x

    return torch.log_softmax(x, dim=1)
```

Forward method that dictates how data flows through the model from input to output

Applies the ReLU activation function after the first convolution to add nonlinearity to the model

Optionally returns the raw embeddings from the network, which can be useful for tasks that require raw node representations without classification, such as visualization or further processing

Applies a log softmax activation to the final layer's output

INTEGRATION AND CUSTOMIZATION

While we use default settings in this introductory example, both models are highly customizable. Parameters such as the number of layers, hidden dimensions, and types of aggregation functions (for GraphSAGE) can be adjusted to optimize performance for specific datasets or tasks. Next, we'll train these models on our subset graph and evaluate their performance to demonstrate their practical applications and effectiveness.

3.1.3 *Model training*

With our data ready and our models set up, let's get into the training process. Training is relatively straightforward, as it follows typical machine learning routines but applied to graph data. We'll be training two models simultaneously—GCN and Graph-SAGE—by feeding them the same data each epoch. This parallel training allows us to directly compare the performance and efficiency of these two model types under identical conditions. Here's a concise breakdown of the training loop:

- *Initialize optimizers*—Set up Adam optimizers with a learning rate of 0.01. This helps us fine-tune the model weights effectively during training.
- *Training and validation loops*—For each epoch, run the training function, which processes the data through the model to compute losses and update weights. Concurrently, validate the model on unseen data to monitor overfitting and adjust training strategies accordingly.
- *Track progress*—Record losses for both training and validation phases to visualize the learning curve and adjust parameters if needed.
- *Conclude with testing*—After training, the models are evaluated on a separate test set to gauge their generalization capabilities.

By maintaining a consistent training regimen for both models, we ensure that any differences in performance can be attributed to the models' architectural differences rather than varied training conditions. The following listing contains the annotated code of our training logic.

Listing 3.4   Training loop

```
gcn_model = GCN(in_channels=dataset.num_features,\
 hidden_channels=64, out_channels=\
dataset.num_classes)                              Initializes models for
                                                  the GCN and GraphSAGE
graphsage_model = GraphSAGE(in_channels=d\
ataset.num_features, hidden_channels=64, \        Initializes models for
out_channels=dataset.num_classes)                 the GCN and GraphSAGE

optimizer_gcn = torch.optim.Adam\                 Sets up optimizers for the
(gcn_model.parameters(), lr=0.01)                 GCN and GraphSAGE models
optimizer_sage = torch.optim.Adam(\               Sets up optimizers for the
graphsage_model.parameters(), lr=0.01)            GCN and GraphSAGE models
criterion = torch.nn.CrossEntropyLoss()           Initializes the cross-entropy loss
                                                  function for the classification task
def train(model, optimizer, data):                Train functions used every epoch
    model.train()
    optimizer.zero_grad()
    out = model(data.x, data.edge_index)
    loss = criterion(out[data.train_mask], data.y[data.train_mask].squeeze())
    loss.backward()
    optimizer.step()
    return loss.item()
```

```
def validate(model, data):                      ⟵┐  Validation functions
    model.eval()                                   │  used every epoch
    with torch.no_grad():
        out = model(data.x, data.edge_index)
        val_loss = criterion(out[data.val_mask],
    data.y[data.val_mask].squeeze())
    return val_loss.item()


train_loss_gcn = []                  ⟵┐  Sets up arrays to capture
val_loss_gcn = []                     │  losses for each model
train_loss_sage = []
val_loss_sage = []

                                                          ┐  Training and
                                                          │  validation loop
for epoch in range(200):                           ⟵─────┘
    loss_gcn = train(gcn_model, optimizer_gcn, subset_graph)
    train_loss_gcn.append(loss_gcn)
    val_loss_gcn.append(validate(gcn_model, subset_graph))

    loss_sage = train(graphsage_model, optimizer_sage, subset_graph)
    train_loss_sage.append(loss_sage)
    val_loss_sage.append(validate(graphsage_model, subset_graph))

    if epoch % 10 == 0:
        print(f'Epoch {epoch}, GCN Loss: \
{loss_gcn:.4f}, GraphSAGE Loss: \
{loss_sage:.4f}, GCN Val Loss: \
{val_loss_gcn[-1]:.4f}, GraphSAGE \
Val Loss: {val_loss_sage[-1]:.4f}')
```

Now that we've set up and trained our models, it's time to see how well they perform. The next section will look at the training and validation loss curves to understand how the models learned over time. It will check out key metrics such as accuracy, precision, recall, and F1 scores to evaluate how well our models can predict product categories based on our graph data. All of this is to understand our models and to figure out where we can improve them in later sections.

3.1.4 Model performance analysis

For the next section, we'll look at the model performance of the GCN and Graph-SAGE models. We'll first examine the training curves and point out that we have to improve the overfitting in a subsequent chapter. Then, we'll look at the F1 and log loss scores, followed by examining accuracy for the product categories.

TRAINING CURVES

During the training process, we saved the losses for each model for every epoch. *Loss* is a measure of how well our model is able to make correct predictions, with lower values being better.

Using Matplotlib, we use this data to plot training loss and validation loss curves, shown in figure 3.1. Such curves track the performance of the model on training and

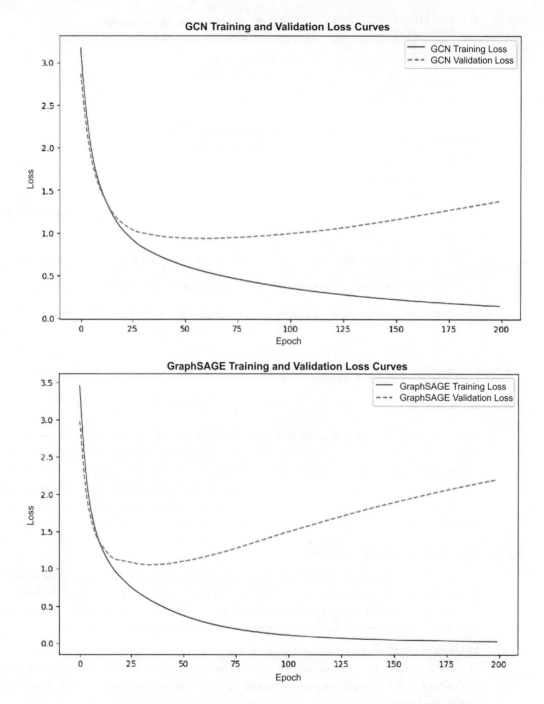

Figure 3.1   Training and validation loss curves for the GCN model (left) and GraphSAGE model (right) trained in this section. The divergence of the validation from the training curve signals over-fitting, where the model learns the training data too well and at the expense of generalizing to new data.

validation datasets over the course of the training process. Ideally, both losses should decline over time. However, in our curves, we see a divergence beginning near epoch 20. The validation loss curves reach a nadir and then begin to climb. Meanwhile, the training loss continues to decline. Our models' performance continues to improve on the training data but degrades on the validation data past some optimal point. This is the classic overfitting problem, which we'll address later in the chapter.

In our training process, we've saved the instance of the model with the best performance, which is the instance with the lowest validation loss. Next, we look at two classification metrics to assess performance: log loss and F1 score.

CLASSIFICATION PERFORMANCE: F1 AND LOG LOSS

Given the overfitting problems shown earlier, we turn to the classification performance of our models to establish a baseline for our improvement efforts. We use our validation sets to establish F1 and log loss scores, shown in table 3.2. (The F1 score is weighted, which measures F1 for each class separately, then averages them, weighing each class by its proportion of the total data.)

The middling scores indicate that the models have much room for improvement. Our F1 scores don't exceed 80%, while the log loss scores are no lower than 1.25.

Table 3.2 Classification performance of our models, by F1 score and log loss

	F1 Score	Log Loss
GCN	0.781	1.25
GraphSAGE	0.733	1.88

In this case, GCN performs better for both metrics. To improve these scores for a multiclass problem, we could look more deeply at the model's capability to predict individual classes and examine its performance for imbalanced classes.

MODEL PERFORMANCE AT A CLASS LEVEL

The Amazon Products dataset comes with two useful files that map each node with its class, and each node with its individual Amazon product number (ASIN). To evaluate the performance of our baseline models by class, we take the node class information and create a table, as shown in figure 3.2, summarizing prediction accuracy for the 25 classes containing the most items.

Along with accuracy, in this table, we examine the biggest mispredictions for each class. From this information, let's make some high-level observations:

- *Performance by category*—Both models show variability in their prediction accuracy across different product categories. The Books category and CDs & Vinyl category have high accuracy rates. This can be due to their relatively high number of samples. It could also indicate that these categories are more distinct or well-defined, making it easier for the model to distinguish them. The first factor, number of samples, is easy to adjust because we're using 10,000 product nodes and can draw millions more from our dataset. You can give it a try by adjusting the size of the subset in the provided code.

To improve less distinctive classes, we need to make a deeper exploration of the node features to determine how distinctive the classes are relative to each other and to brainstorm ways to enhance those features to bring out their novelty.

- *Performance by model*—Looking over all the classes, GraphSAGE generally appears to perform better than GCN in most categories, as seen from the higher percentages of correct predictions. This suggests that GraphSAGE's approach of aggregating features from a node's neighborhood might be more effective for this dataset.
- *Misclassifications*—Common misclassifications tend to occur between categories that might share similar characteristics or be frequently purchased together. For example, the misclassification between Books and Movies & TV or between Electronics and Cell Phones & Accessories suggests that items in these categories may share overlapping features or are often bought by similar customer segments.

Category	N	% of Correct Predictions		Most Frequent Incorrect Prediction	
		GCN	GraphSage	GCN	GraphSage
Books	3077	96.30%	95.52%	CDs & Vinyl	CDs & Vinyl
CDs & Vinyl	887	95.83%	97.18%	Movies & TV	Books
Toys & Games	753	88.84%	87.78%	Books	Books
Sports & Outdoors	658	83.89%	83.43%	Toys & Games	Clothing, Shoes & Jewelry
Health & Personal Care	601	81.53%	83.19%	Beauty	Beauty
Home & Kitchen	577	87%	84.75%	Toys & Games	Sports & Outdoors
Cell Phones & Accessories	568	95.60%	94.37%	Books	Books
Movies & TV	559	89.98%	88.37%	Books	Books
Beauty	531	87.76%	89.83%	Health & Personal Care	Health & Personal Care
Grocery & Gourmet Food	317	92.11%	93.69%	Health & Personal Care	Health & Personal Care
Pet Supplies	243	95.06%	90.95%	Books	Health & Personal Care
Patio, Lawn & Garden	219	87.67%	79%	Sports & Outdoors	Books
Arts, Crafts & Sewing	218	81.65%	81.65%	Toys & Games	Books
Clothing, Shoes & Jewelry	160	68.75%	77.50%	Sports & Outdoors	Sports & Outdoors
Electronics	139	61.87%	68.35%	Books	Books
Video Games	123	86.18%	84.55%	Toys & Games	Books

Figure 3.2   Classification performance (accuracy) by product category, comparing GCN and GraphSAGE

Though we generally don't want misclassifications, observing the classes most likely to be misconstrued for another could inform us about common customer perceptions or confusions between product categories, highlighting potential areas for marketing and product placement strategies.

The next two sections will improve the models' performance from these baseline results by taking advantage of the properties of our GNNs (section 3.2) and by using well-known deep learning methods (section 3.3). To end this section, let's use our models to come up with a product bundle for our product manager.

3.1.5 *Our first product bundle*

In the beginning of this section, we discussed our use case of a product manager who wants to enhance sales by introducing product bundles. Let's use one of our newly trained models to suggest a bundle for a given product. We'll group together the nodes whose embeddings are most similar to a selected node, forming a bundle based on their similarity. Later in the chapter, as we improve the models, we'll come back to the exercise.

> **NOTE** The code won't be reviewed extensively here but can be found in the repository.

NODE ID TO PRODUCT NUMBER

One key file provided in the Amazon Products dataset is a comma-separated values (CSV) file mapping for node index to Amazon product ID (ASIN). In the repository, this is used to create a Python dictionary of node ID (key) to ASIN (value). Using a node's ASIN, we can access information about the product using a URL in this format: www.amazon.com/dp/{ASIN}. (Given the age of the dataset, a few ASINs don't have web pages currently, but the vast majority we tested do at the time of writing.)

To create a product bundle, we work with node embeddings. We choose an individual product node and then find the six most similar products to it. This takes four steps:

1 Produce node embeddings by running our nodes through our trained GNN.
2 Create a similarity matrix using the node embeddings.
3 Sort the top five embeddings by similarity to our chosen product.
4 Convert the node indices of these top embeddings to product IDs.

A seed may be set to ensure reproducibility. Otherwise, your results will differ with every run of your program.

PRODUCE NODE EMBEDDINGS

Like chapter 2, we run our nodes through the model to produce an embedding instead of a prediction. In contrast to chapter 2, we have a trained model for this purpose that has learned from the node features and the co-purchasing relationships of our dataset. To accomplish this, we put our model into evaluation mode (`eval()`), disable gradient computations that support backpropagation (`no_grad()`), and then run a forward pass of the graph data through the model. Earlier, when defining the model class, we enabled an option to return an embedding or a prediction (`return_embeds`):

```
gcn_model.eval()

with torch.no_grad():
    gcn_embeddings = gcn_model(subset_graph.x, \
subset_graph.edge_index, return_embeds=True)
```

CREATE A SIMILARITY MATRIX

A similarity matrix is a set of data, usually in tabular form, that contains the similarities between all pairs of items in a set. In our case, we use cosine similarity, and compare the embeddings of all the nodes in our set. SciKit Learn's `cosine_similarity` function accomplishes this:

```
gcn_similarity_matrix = cosine_similarity(gcn_embeddings.cpu().numpy())
```

LIST THE ITEMS CLOSEST IN SIMILARITY TO A CHOSEN NODE

To identify items most similar to a specific node, we begin by selecting a node—referred to by its index as `product_idx`. Using the cosine similarity matrix, we examine how closely related each node is to our chosen node by sorting the similarities in descending order. The top entries from this sorting (specifically, the first six, where `top_k` is set to 6) represent the nodes most similar to our selected node. Notably, the list includes the selected node itself, So, for practical purposes, we consider the next five nodes to effectively create a bundle of similar items:

```
product_idx = 123
top_k = 6
top_k_similar_indices_gcn = np.argsort(-
gcn_similarity_matrix[product_idx])[:top_k]
```

CONVERT THE NODE INDICES TO PRODUCT IDs

From here, using the index-to-ASIN dictionary will identify the product bundle from the node indices. With this done, let's pick a product node at random and generate a product bundle around it.

PRODUCT BUNDLE DEMO

At random, we pick node #123. Using our index-to-ASIN dictionary, we get ASIN: B00BV1P6GK. This ASIN belongs to the product Funko POP Television: Adventure Time Marceline Vinyl Figure, as shown in figure 3.3. The category of this product is Toys & Games.

Figure 3.3 Our selected product, Funko POP Television: Adventure Time Marceline Vinyl Figure. In this section, a product bundle will be generated for this product.

Marceline, the hundreds-of-years-old Vampire Queen, is one of the main characters in the popular animated TV series *Adventure Time.* Marceline is known for her rock star persona, love of music, and playing her bass guitar, which is often a focal point in her appearances. Her persona is reflected in the figurine, which is smiling and has a relaxed but confident pose.

Adventure Time is an animated series that follows the surreal and epic adventures of a boy named Finn and his magical dog Jake in the mystical Land of Ooo, filled with princesses, vampires, ice kings, and many other bizarre characters.

For a collection based on the *Adventure Time* series, one may expect a variety of vinyl figures representing the show's eclectic cast of characters. Let's see what our system generates.

Using the process outlined earlier, the bundle shown in figure 3.4, was generated. There is one *Adventure Time* vinyl figure included. The rest of the choices seem unrelated at first glance, but maybe this set is a nonintuitive bundle. Let's take a closer look:

- *First ranked similarity: Funko POP Television: Adventure Time Finn with Accessories*—Finn is the central character from *Adventure Time*, a recommendation we expected. This suggests that fans of Marceline might also appreciate or collect merchandise related to other main characters from the same show.
- *Second ranked similarity: Funko My Little Pony: DJ Pon-3 Vinyl Figure*—This item might seem out of context at first glance, but it may indicate a crossover interest in animated series. DJ Pon-3, or Vinyl Scratch, from *My Little Pony* is a musical character like Marceline, appealing to those who enjoy characters associated with music.

Selected Product	Funko POP Television: Adventure Time Marceline Vinyl Figure
1st Ranked Similarity	Adventure Time 5" Finn with Accessories
2nd Ranked Similarity	Funko My Little Pony: DJ Pon-3 Vinyl Figure
3rd Ranked Similarity	My Little Pony: Twilight Sparkle
4th Ranked Similarity	Plastic Gold Coins 288ct With 24 Pirate Themed Tattoos
5th Ranked Similarity	Handheld Brass Telescope with Wooden Box - Pirate Navigation

Figure 3.4 A product bundle centered on the Marceline product. The recommendations are members of the Toy & Games category. The themes of these products connect loosely to the selected product.

- *Third ranked similarity: Funko My Little Pony: Twilight Sparkle Vinyl Figure*—Similar to DJ Pon-3, Twilight Sparkle from *My Little Pony* represents another connection to a popular animated series. This inclusion could appeal to collectors who enjoy fantasy themes and strong female characters.
- *Fourth and fifth ranked similarities: Pirate-themed accessories (Gold Coins, Tattoos, Handheld Brass Telescope with Wooden Box)*—These items are less directly related to "Adventure Time" or "My Little Pony", but they enhance the theme of adventure and exploration, which is a significant element of both series.

All in all, this is not a bad product bundle from our baseline models! Wrapping up this introductory section on model training and evaluation, we've now established a solid foundation for understanding and using GNNs. This understanding is crucial as we progress to section 3.2, where we'll dive deeper into neighborhood aggregation, an effective tool to enhance performance. Then, in section 3.3, we'll draw from general deep learning approaches to further optimize the models' performances.

3.2   Aggregation methods

In this section, we extend the product category analysis from the previous section and take a deeper look into the characteristics of GNNs that influence their performance on tasks such as product categorization. Specifically, we explore aggregation methods, techniques that have a large influence on the performance of convolutional GNNs. Neighborhood aggregation allows nodes to gather and integrate feature information from their local node neighborhoods, capturing contextual relevance within the larger network.

We start with the simple aggregations mean, sum, and max, each applied over all layers of a model. Then, we survey a few more advanced implementations in PyG: unique aggregations applied per layer, list aggregations, aggregation functions, and a layer-wise aggregation known as jumping knowledge networks (JK-Nets). Finally, we provide some guidelines on applying such methods.

3.2.1   Neighborhood aggregation

One way graph data structures are different is that nodes are interconnected through edges, creating a network where nodes can be directly linked or separated by several degrees. This spatial arrangement means that any given node may be in close proximity to certain other nodes, forming what we call its *neighborhood*. The concept of a node's neighborhood is critical as it often holds key insights into the node's characteristics and that of the overall graph.

In convolutional GNNs, node neighborhoods are used through a process known as *neighborhood aggregation*. This technique involves gathering and combining feature information from a node's immediate neighbors to capture both their individual and collective properties. By doing so, a node's representation is enriched with the contextual information provided by its surroundings, which enhances the model's capability to learn more complex and nuanced patterns within the graph.

Neighborhood aggregation operates under the premise that nodes in proximity to each other are likely to influence each other more significantly than those farther away. This is particularly advantageous for tasks where the relationship and interaction between nodes are predictive of their behaviors or properties.

NEIGHBORHOOD AGGREGATION IN PYG

In the PyG layers GCN (`GCNconv`) and GraphSAGE (`SAGEConv`), neighborhood aggregation is implemented in different ways. In GCN, a weighted average aggregation is built into the layer; if you want to tweak it, you must create a customized version of this layer. In this section, we'll mostly focus on GraphSAGE, which allows you to set an aggregation via a parameter. An upcoming section will examine a layer-wise aggregation used in GCN.

In `SAGEConv`, the `aggr` parameter specifies the type of aggregation. The options include, but are not limited to the following:

- *Sum aggregation*—A simple aggregation that sums up all neighbor node features.
- *Mean aggregation*—Computes the mean of the neighbor node features. This is often used for its simplicity and effectiveness in averaging feature information, helping to smooth out anomalies in the data.
- *Max aggregation*—Takes the maximum feature value among all neighbors for each feature dimension. This can help when the most prominent features are more informative than average features, capturing the most significant signals from the neighbors.
- *LSTM aggregation*—A relatively compute- and memory-intensive method that uses an LSTM network to process features of the ordered sequence of neighbor nodes. It considers the sequence of nodes, which can be crucial for tasks where the order of node processing affects the results. As such, special care must be taken to arrange a dataset's nodes and edges for training.

Choosing among these types will depend on the characteristics of a given graph, and the prediction goals. If you don't have a good feel for which method will be more effective for your graph and your use case, trial and error can suffice to choose the aggregation method. In addition, while some of the aggregation options can be applied out of the box, others—such as LSTM aggregation, which relies on a trained LSTM network—require some thought to be put into data preparation.

To see the effect of different aggregations, we add the `aggr` parameter to our model class and then proceed to train as in section 3.1, swapping out the mean, sum, and max aggregations. It should be noted that the mean aggregation is the default for the `SAGEConv` layer, so it's equivalent to our GraphSAGE baseline model. Creating a *GraphSAGE* class with aggregations would look like the following listing.

Listing 3.5 GraphSAGE class with aggregation parameter

```
class GraphSAGE(torch.nn.Module):
    def __init__(self, in_channels, \
```

```
hidden_channels, out_channels, agg_func='mean'):
        super(GraphSAGE, self).__init__()
        self.conv1 = SAGEConv(in_channels, \
hidden_channels, aggr=agg_func)
        self.conv2 = SAGEConv(hidden_channels, \
out_channels, aggr=agg_func)

    def forward(self, x, edge_index):
        x = self.conv1(x, edge_index)
        x = F.relu(x)
        x = self.conv2(x, edge_index)

    return F.log_softmax(x, dim=1)
```

> Sets keyword parameter for aggregation

> First GraphSAGE layer with specified aggregation

> Second GraphSAGE layer with specified aggregation

RESULTS OF USING MEAN, MAX, AND SUM AGGREGATIONS

Table 3.3 compares the models using F1 score and log loss as performance metrics. The table shows that the model using max aggregation is the best under both measures. The results for the model using max aggregation shows the highest F1 score of 0.7449 and the lowest log loss of 2.1039, suggesting that max aggregation is a little more capable at identifying and using the most influential features in the prediction task. The model that uses mean aggregation is equivalent to the model trained in section 3.1. We observe that the max aggregation out-performs the other two. Overall, the performance using different aggregations is very similar to that of our baseline GraphSAGE model.

Table 3.3   Classification performance for GraphSAGE models with different settings for neighborhood aggregation

Aggregation Type	F1 Score	Log Loss
Mean (default)	0.7406	2.1214
Sum	0.7384	2.2496
Max	0.7449	2.1039

What model should be chosen if separate models had the highest F1 score and log loss? For example, what if the max aggregation model scored highest for F1, but the mean aggregation model took the highest for log loss? This will depend on the context of your application, your requirements for prediction, and the consequences of potential errors.

In a healthcare situation, such as predicting patient readmissions within 30 days of discharge, for example, the choice of model can significantly affect patient outcomes and resource allocation. A model with a high F1 score would have a more balanced precision and recall, making it better in situations where missing a readmission could be costly or dangerous. It would be expected to identify more patients at risk, allowing for timely interventions. However, this could also result in higher false positives, leading to unnecessary treatments and increased costs.

A model that exhibits low log loss, on the other hand, offers high confidence in its predictions, prioritizing the accuracy of each prediction over the number of positive cases detected. This model is useful when resource allocation needs to be precise or when treatments have substantial side effects.

Coming back to our product manager who is deciding which products and product bundles to allocate marketing dollars to, having more confident predictions would be desirable in preventing wasted marketing efforts. The lower likelihood of false positives helps in efficiently using resources, but at the risk of missing some revenue-generating bundle configurations due to conservative predictions.

In this section, we used a simple string argument for the `aggr` parameter. PyG, however, has a wide set of tools to incorporate a variety of aggregation methods into your models. We explore these in the next section.

3.2.2 Advanced aggregation tools

This section explores more advanced aggregation tools within PyG. We begin by assigning distinct aggregation methods to different layers within a multilayer architecture. Next, we explore the combination of various aggregation strategies—such as `'mean'`, `'max'`, and `'sum'`—within a single layer. Finally, we revisit GCNs to examine the jumping knowledge (JK) method.

USING MULTIPLE AGGREGATIONS ACROSS LAYERS

In a multilayer GraphSAGE model, you can of course adjust the aggregation function at each layer independently. For example, you might use mean aggregation at the first layer to smooth features but switch to max aggregation at a subsequent layer to highlight the most significant of the resulting neighbor features.

As a first exercise in our exploration, let's apply a couple of permutations of aggregations to two layers and see if these configurations outperform our previous results. We use the code from before, swapping out the `aggr` settings for `conv1` and `conv2`. For one model, we use *mean* for the first layer and *max* at the second. For the other model, we use *sum* for the first layer and *max* at the second. Table 3.4 summarizes the results.

Table 3.4 Classification performance for GraphSAGE models with different settings for neighborhood aggregation

Aggregation Type	F1 Score	Log Loss
Mean (default)	0.7406	2.1214
Sum	0.7384	2.2496
Max	0.7449	2.1039
Layered: Mean → Max	0.7316	2.2041
Layered: Sum → Max	0.7344	2.345

We have middling results at best for our dataset. The model with only max aggregation outperforms the newer models. Let's move on to combining several aggregations for each layer.

LIST AGGREGATIONS AND AGGREGATION FUNCTIONS

In PyG, the concept of using a list for specifying aggregation functions allows you to customize your models with multiple aggregation strategies simultaneously. This feature is significant as it enables the model to use different aspects of graph data, potentially enhancing model performance by capturing various properties of the graph. In a way, you're aggregating your aggregations. For instance, you could combine 'mean', 'max', and 'sum' aggregations in a single layer to capture average, most significant, and summed structural properties of the neighborhood.

This works in PyG by passing a list of aggregation functions, either as strings or as Aggregation module instances, into the MessagePassing class. PyG resolves these strings against a predefined set of aggregation functions or can directly use an aggregation function as the aggr argument. For example, using the keyword 'mean' invokes the MeanAggregation() function.

There are a universe of combinations to try, but let's try two examples to demonstrate, mixing familiar aggregations, 'max', 'sum', and 'mean'; and a set of more exotic aggregations, SoftmaxAggregation and StdAggregation [3]. They can be applied to our conv1 layer as follows (table 3.5 compares these results with previous results):

```
    self.conv1 = SAGEConv(in_channels,\
hidden_channels, aggr=['max', 'sum', 'mean'])

    self.conv1 = SAGEConv(in_channels,\
hidden_channels, aggr=[SoftmaxAggregation(),\
StdAggregation() ])
```

Table 3.5 Classification performance for GraphSAGE models with list aggregations added

Aggregation type	F1 score	Log loss
Mean (default)	0.7406	2.1214
Sum	0.7384	2.2496
Max	0.7449	2.1039
Layered: Mean→Max	0.7316	2.2041
Layered: Sum→Max	0.7344	2.345
List (standard)	0.7484	2.622
List (exotic)	0.745	2.156

Figure 3.5 visualizes the performance comparison from table 3.5. While the F1 scores are very similar, there is a slight performance boost in F1 score from the "standard" list aggregation, though with the drawback of a much higher log loss.

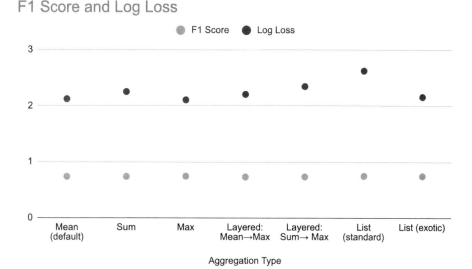

Figure 3.5 **Performance comparison visualized from table 3.5. While the F1 scores are very similar, the standard list aggregation performs slightly better with respect to log loss.**

Given the results of our quick survey of these aggregation methods applied to the GraphSAGE layer, you might conclude that sticking with the default setting is often the best option. However, the potential for performance improvements through tailored aggregation strategies suggests that further exploration could be beneficial.

In the upcoming section 3.2.3, we'll review some considerations in applying these aggregation methods. Before that, we'll come back to the GCN layer to examine the JK aggregation method.

JUMPING KNOWLEDGE NETWORKS

Jumping knowledge (JK) is a novel approach for node representation learning on graphs that addresses limitations of existing models such as GCNs and GraphSAGE [4]. It focuses on overcoming a problem of neighborhood aggregation models in which models are sensitive to the graph's structure, causing inconsistent learning quality across different graph parts.

Jumping knowledge networks (JK-Nets) allow flexible usage of different neighborhood ranges for each node, thereby adapting to local neighborhood properties and task-specific requirements. This adaptation results in improved node representations by enabling the model to selectively use information from various neighborhood depths based on the node and the subgraph's context. JK has been implemented for the GCN layer in PyG, as shown in listing 3.6.

Its main parameter, `mode`, specifies the aggregation scheme used to combine outputs from different layers. The options are listed here:

- `'cat'`—Concatenates the outputs from all layers along the feature dimension. This approach preserves all information from each layer but increases the dimensionality of the output.
- `'max'`—Applies max pooling across the layer outputs. This method takes the maximum value across all layers for each feature, which can help in capturing the most significant features from the graph while being robust against less informative signals.
- `'lstm'`—Uses a bidirectional LSTM to learn attention scores for each layer's output. The outputs are then combined based on these learned attention weights, allowing the model to focus on the most relevant layers dynamically based on the input graph structure.

Listing 3.6   GCN class with `JumpingKnowledge` layer

```
class CustomGCN(torch.nn.Module):
    def __init__(self, in_channels, hidden_channels, out_channels):
        super(CustomGCN, self).__init__()
        self.conv1 = GCNConv(in_channels, hidden_channels)
        self.conv2 = GCNConv(hidden_channels, out_channels)

        self.jk = JumpingKnowledge(mode='cat')        ◁── Initializes JK with
                                                          concatenation mode

    def forward(self, x, edge_index):
        layer_outputs = []               ◁── List to save outputs
                                             from each layer for JK
        x1 = self.conv1(x, edge_index)
        x1 = F.relu(x1)
        layer_outputs.append(x1)         ◁── Appends the layer
                                             outputs list
        x2 = self.conv2(x1, edge_index)
        layer_outputs.append(x2)

                                         │  Applies JK aggregation
        x = self.jk(layer_outputs)    ◁──┤  to the collected layer
                                         │  outputs
        return x
```

In the listing, for the initialization, a `JumpingKnowledge` layer is initialized with the mode set to `'cat'` (concatenate), indicating that the features from each layer will be concatenated to form the final node representations.

In the forward pass, `layer_outputs` is initialized as an empty list to store the outputs from each convolutional layer. This list will be used by the `JumpingKnowledge` layer.

- The first convolutional layer processes the input `x` and the graph structure `edge_index`, and applies a ReLU activation function to introduce nonlinearity.
- The output of the first layer (`x1`) is then added to the `layer_outputs` list.
- After the second convolutional layer, the second output (`x2`) is also added to the `layer_outputs` list.

- Then, the JumpingKnowledge layer takes the list of outputs from all the previous layers and aggregates them according to the specified mode ('cat'). In concatenation mode, the feature vectors from each layer are concatenated along the feature dimension.

Table 3.6 compares the classification performance for GCN models. The baseline GCN model from section 3.1 is compared to a version using the JumpingKnowledge aggregation method. The baseline model has a better F1 score, while the JK model outperforms in log loss.

Table 3.6   Classification performance for GCN models

Model	F1 Score	Log Loss
Baseline GCN	0.781	1.42
JK (GCN)	0.699	1.36

The results show that choosing between the baseline and JK versions involves a tradeoff between higher recall/precision and higher prediction certainty. This tradeoff should be carefully considered based on the specific requirements and goals of the task at hand. Further exploration in section 3.2.3 will review some considerations in applying these aggregation methods effectively.

3.2.3   *Practical considerations in applying aggregation*

Choosing the right aggregation method is a technical decision that should be informed by the specific characteristics and needs of the dataset at hand as well as the use case. For datasets where the local neighborhood structure is crucial, using mean or sum aggregations could potentially blur essential features. In contrast, max aggregation could help highlight critical attributes. For example, in a social network graph where influencer detection is key, max aggregation might be more effective. On the other hand, if what we want to do is represent typical features, max aggregation may overemphasize outliers. In a dataset of financial transactions, where we want to understand typical user behavior, a max aggregation could distort the common behavioral features in favor of one or two large but uncommon transactions.

The task itself can dictate the choice of aggregation method. Tasks that require capturing the most influential features might benefit from max aggregation, while those needing a general representation may find mean aggregation sufficient. In a recommendation system for products, max aggregation could help identify the most important product features that drive purchases. Additionally, the nature of the graph's topology should guide the aggregation method. Densely connected graphs might require different strategies compared to sparsely connected graphs to avoid over-smoothing or under-representation of node features. For instance, a transportation network graph with varying node connectivity might need different aggregations at different layers.

Given the dataset's complexity, empirical testing of different aggregation methods is essential. Experimentation can help identify which methods best capture the relational dynamics and feature distributions of the dataset. This is particularly important for more exotic aggregation methods, where intuition alone may not suffice to determine their effectiveness. The scalability of the chosen aggregation method to handle millions of nodes and edges efficiently is also crucial. It's important to balance computational efficiency with the sophistication of the method, especially for real-time applications such as recommendation systems.

Aggregation methods should be considered alongside other model enhancements such as feature engineering, node embedding techniques, and regularization strategies to address overfitting and improve model generalization. For instance, combining effective aggregation methods with advanced embedding techniques (e.g., Node2Vec) or incorporating dropout for regularization could significantly boost model performance.

While there is no one-size-fits-all aggregation method, a thoughtful combination of techniques, backed by empirical validation, can significantly enhance model performance and applicability. This strategic approach not only aids in accurate product categorization but also in crafting effective recommendation systems that are crucial in e-commerce settings.

This section explored and applied different aggregations to our models. The next section will round out our exploration of convolutional GNNs by applying regularization and adjusting the depth of our models. We'll consolidate our improvements into a final model, from which we'll generate another product bundle based on the Marceline figurine to see if there is improvement.

3.3   *Further optimizations and refinements*

Up to now, the GCN and GraphSAGE layers have been introduced via a product management example. We established a baseline using the default settings in section 3.1. In section 3.2, we examined the use of neighborhood and layer aggregation. In this section, we'll consider other ways we can refine and improve our model. In the first subsections, we'll introduce two other adjustments: the use of dropout and model depth. Dropout is a well-known regularization technique that can reduce overfitting, and model depth is an adjustment that has a unique meaning for GNNs.

In section 3.3.3, we synthesize these insights to develop a model that incorporates multiple improvements and observe the cumulative performance uplift. Finally, in section 3.3.4, we revisit our product bundle problem. We create a new product bundle using the refined model of section 3.3.3 and compare its performance to the bundle created in section 3.1.

3.3.1   *Dropout*

Dropout is a regularization technique used to prevent overfitting in neural networks by randomly dropping units during training. This helps the model generalize better by reducing its dependency on specific neurons.

In PyG, the `dropout` function works similarly to the standard PyTorch dropout, meaning it randomly sets some elements of the input tensor and the hidden-layer activations to 0 during the training process. During each forward pass in training, inputs and activations are set to 0 according to the specified dropout rate. This helps prevent overfitting by ensuring that the model doesn't rely too heavily on any particular input or activation.

The structure of the graph, including its vertices (nodes) and edges, remains unchanged during dropout. The graph's topology is preserved, and only the neural network's activations are affected. This distinction is crucial as it maintains the integrity of the graph while still using dropout to improve model robustness. PyG does have functions that can drop nodes or drop edges during training, but the dropout built into `GCNConv` and `SAGEConv` refers to the traditional deep learning dropout.

In PyG, both the GraphSAGE and GCN layers use `dropout` rate as a parameter, with a default of 0. Figure 3.6 illustrates the performance of GCN models with varying dropout rates (0%, 50%, and 85%). As shown, higher dropout rates can help mitigate overfitting, as indicated by the reduced gap between training and validation losses. For the 85% case, the higher dropout rate could be causing the model to converge more slowly, or it could be a sign of overfitting. More testing is warranted to find out.

Next, let's examine model depth and how it's implemented for convolutional GNNs.

3.3.2   *Model depth*

In GNNs, a *layer* refers to the number of hops or message-passing steps. Each layer allows nodes to aggregate information from their immediate neighbors, effectively increasing the receptive field by one hop per layer. A three-layer model, for example, would interrogate the neighborhood three hops away from each node. The *depth* of a GNN, then, refers to the number of layers in the network, analogous to the depth in traditional deep learning models but with key differences due to graph-structured data.

If a GNN has too few layers, it may not capture sufficient information from the graph, leading to poor representation learning, as each node can only aggregate information from a limited neighborhood. Conversely, increasing the number of layers can lead to *over-smoothing*, where node features become too similar, making it difficult to distinguish between different nodes. With each additional layer, nodes aggregate information from a larger neighborhood, diluting the unique features of individual nodes. Various metrics and methods have been proposed to measure and mitigate this effect.

The performance of GNNs with different depths can vary significantly. Typically, GNNs with 2 or 3 layers perform competitively on many tasks, balancing the need for sufficient neighborhood information without causing over-smoothing. While deeper

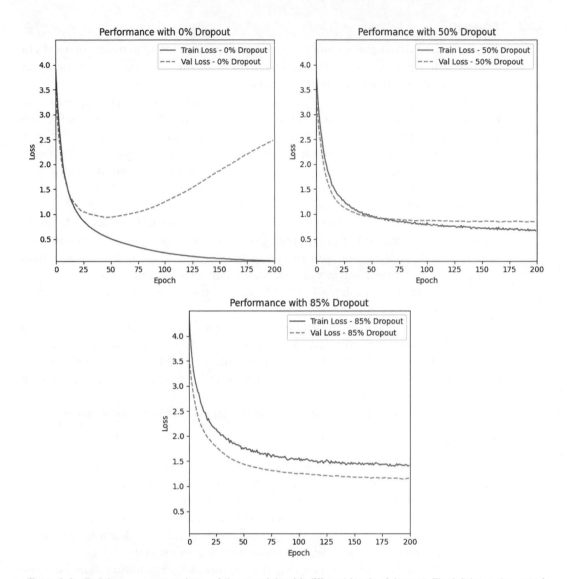

Figure 3.6   Training curve comparisons of three models with different levels of dropout. The left has a dropout of 0%, the middle a dropout of 50%, and the right a dropout of 85%. For our model and dataset, adding dropout indeed ameliorates overfitting. The model with 85% dropout could show signs of either underfitting or slowly converging, requiring more experimentation.

GNNs can theoretically capture more complex patterns, they often suffer from over-smoothing and increased computational complexity. Very deep GNNs, such as those with 50 or more layers, can lead to higher validation loss, indicating over-fitting and/or over-smoothing.

Figure 3.7 compares the performance of GNNs with different depths (e.g., 2 layers, 10 layers, and 50 layers). We see that the 2-layer model achieves a good balance

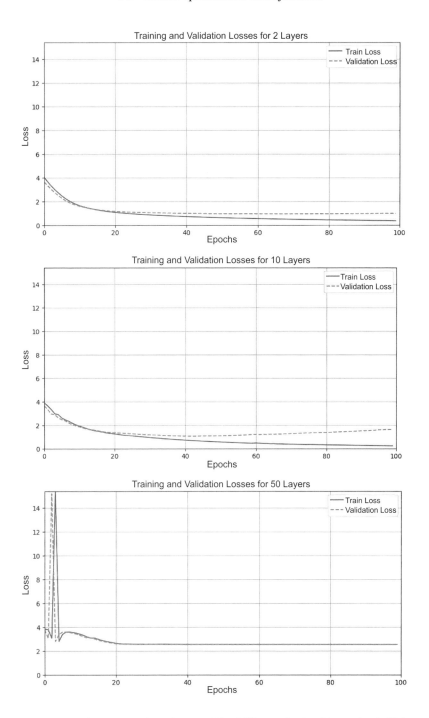

Figure 3.7 Training curves for trained models of different depths: 2 layers (top), 10 layers (middle), 50 layers (bottom). The 2-layer model has the best profile with no signs of overfitting or performance degradation.

between training and validation loss. In the 10-layer GNNs, we see some improvement in training loss but also signs of over-smoothing from the higher validation loss. The 50-layer model shows degraded training and validation loss, which indicates severe over-smoothing or over-fitting.

Balancing the depth of the model is critical to achieving optimal performance in GNNs. Too few layers may result in weak representation learning, while too many layers can lead to over-smoothing, where node features become indistinguishable. In the next section, we apply what we've learned about tuning our model in this chapter, resulting in a refined model that will outperform our baseline.

3.3.3   *Improving the baseline model's performance*

Given all the insights gained in this chapter, let's train models that synthesize these learnings and compare them against the baseline. Some key takeaways from the previous sections that we'll incorporate are listed here:

- *Model depth*—We'll keep it low, at two layers.
- *Neighborhood aggregation*—We'll use max aggregation and experiment with two list aggregations. The same aggregation will be used on both layers.
- *Dropout*—We'll use 50% dropout on both layers.

The following listing shows a GraphSAGE class with adjustable dropout, layer depth, and aggregations.

Listing 3.7   GraphSAGE class

```
class GraphSAGEWithCustomDropout(torch.nn.Module):
    def __init__(self, in_channels, \
hidden_channels, out_channels, num_layers, \
dropout_rate=0.5, aggr='mean'):
        super(GraphSAGEWithCustomDropout, self).__init__()
        self.layers = torch.nn.ModuleList\
([SAGEConv(in_channels, hidden_channels, aggr=aggr)])
        for _ in range(1, num_layers-1):
            self.layers.append(SAGEConv\
(hidden_channels, hidden_channels, aggr=aggr))
        self.layers.append(SAGEConv\
(hidden_channels, out_channels, aggr=aggr))
        self.dropout_rate = dropout_rate

    def forward(self, x, edge_index):
        for layer in self.layers[:-1]:
            x = F.relu(layer(x, edge_index))
            x = F.dropout(x, p=self.dropout_rate, training=self.training)
        x = self.layers[-1](x, edge_index)
        return F.log_softmax(x, dim=1)
```

> The layer is initialized with number of layers, dropout rate, and aggregation type.

> The loop applies the aggregation to each layer.

We trained three models using the preceding class:

```
model_1 = GraphSAGEWithCustomDropout\
(subset_graph.num_features, 64, \
dataset.num_classes, 2, dropout_rate=.5, \
aggr= 'max').to(device)

model_2 = GraphSAGEWithCustomDropout\
(subset_graph.num_features, 64, \
dataset.num_classes, 2, dropout_rate=0.5, \
aggr=['max', 'sum', 'mean']).to(device)

model_3 = GraphSAGEWithCustomDropout\
(subset_graph.num_features, 64, \
dataset.num_classes, 2, dropout_rate=0.50,\
 aggr=[SoftmaxAggregation(), \
StdAggregation() ] ).to(device)
```

Table 3.7 summarizes the performance of different GraphSAGE models with various aggregation methods and a baseline model using the default mean aggregation. The results indicate that all the improved models outperform the baseline in both F1 score and log loss. Notably, Model 2, which uses a combination of `'max'`, `'sum'`, and `'mean'` aggregations, achieved the highest F1 score of 0.8828. Model 3, with a combination of `SoftmaxAggregation()` and `StdAggregation()`, shows the best log loss at 0.5764, suggesting it has the highest prediction certainty among the tested configurations.

Table 3.7   Two-layer GraphSAGE models using 50% dropout and different aggregation types

GraphSAGE Model	Aggregation Type	F1 Score	Log Loss
Model 1	`'max'`	0.8674	0.594
Model 2	`['max', 'sum', 'mean']`	0.8876	0.660
Model 3	`[SoftmaxAggregation(), StdAggregation()]`	0.8829	0.574
Baseline model	Mean (default)	0.7406	2.1214

The confusion matrix in figure 3.8 visualizes the classification performance of Model 1 with max aggregation. The majority of values are along the diagonal, indicating that the model is correctly classifying most instances. However, there are off-diagonal elements, representing misclassifications, for example, instances of class 0 being classified as class 1 or vice versa. The frequency and spread of these misclassifications highlight areas where the model struggles. Additionally, using the bar on the side indicating the count of members per class, the confusion matrix shows how these different classes are distributed. Some classes have higher counts, while others have significantly lower counts, suggesting class imbalance in the dataset.

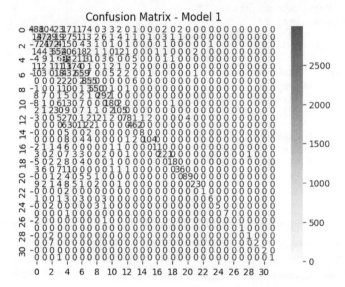

Figure 3.8   Confusion matrix from the two-layer GraphSAGE model with 50% dropout and max aggregation. The strong diagonal pattern indicates good classification performance. The sidebar gives a distribution of the classes, highlighting a class imbalance.

Note that, in all of this, we've been using less than 1% of the dataset's nodes, arbitrarily chosen by index order. Increasing the number of nodes would improve the performance of our models. Additionally, selecting a subgraph in a more meaningful way while keeping the number of nodes the same could also increase performance.

While the current models show significant improvement, several other strategies can be considered to further enhance performance. Increasing the dataset size by using a larger subset can provide more training data, potentially improving model generalization. Refining subgraph selection based on domain knowledge or using graph sampling techniques can ensure that more meaningful data is used for training. Hyperparameter optimization, systematically tuning hyperparameters using tools such as Hyperopt, can help find the optimal settings for the model. Hyperopt allows for efficient searching of the hyperparameter space using algorithms such as Bayesian optimization. Exploring more sophisticated aggregation functions or custom aggregations tailored to the specific characteristics of the dataset can also yield improvements. Additionally, implementing regularization methods such as L2 regularization or gradient clipping can stabilize training and prevent over-fitting. Graph preprocessing techniques, such as normalization, feature engineering, and dimensionality reduction on graph features, can enhance the quality of input data, further boosting model performance. Next, we'll select the model that performs highest on log loss to generate another product bundle.

3.3.4 Revisiting the Marcelina product bundle

The models have markedly improved from our baselines in section 3.1. Let's revisit the product bundling problem and recommend one for our product manager based on our refined GraphSAGE model from the earlier section. Using the process from section 3.1.5 results in the bundle in figure 3.9, which is displayed with the original bundle for comparison.

Selected Product	Funko POP Television: Adventure Time Marceline Figure
1st Ranked Similarity	Adventure Time 5" Finn with Accessories
2nd Ranked Similarity	"The Sword of Shannara" Paperback Book
3rd Ranked Similarity	"Wild Kratts: Wildest Animal Adventures" DVD Set
4th Ranked Similarity	Marvel The Amazing Spider-Man 2 Motorized Spider Force Web Blaster
5th Ranked Similarity	Marvel Super Hero Mashers Spider-Man Figure 6 Inches

Figure 3.9   Product bundles centered on the Marceline product. The upper bundle is from the improved model from section 3.3.3, while the lower bundle is from the baseline model of section 3.1.5. The new recommendations are members of the Toy & Games, Books, and Movies & TV categories.

What do you think of this new bundle? Is it an improvement, that is, more likely to drive purchases than the former bundle? This new bundle incorporates items from Toys & Games, Books, and Movies & TV categories, which is a diverse product selection. The introduction of the *Wild Kratts: Wildest Animal Adventures* DVD alongside the adventure book *The Sword of Shannara* and action figures reflects a pivot toward a more family-oriented and child-friendly product mix.

This new bundle's potential for driving purchases is grounded in the enhanced understanding of customer purchase behaviors and preferences captured by the updated model. The bundle seems well-suited for gifting purposes, catering to both the collectors of pop culture memorabilia (e.g., the Marceline figure and related collectibles) and young fans of fantasy and adventure narratives.

The shift from a more generic collection of toys to a focused, theme-oriented bundle could likely increase its attractiveness as a purchase. The inclusion of both entertainment (*Wild Kratts: Wildest Animal Adventures* DVD) and literary (*The Sword of Shannara*) elements, in addition to the collectible figures, provides a more comprehensive entertainment experience centered around popular themes of adventure and exploration. This could appeal to parents looking for engaging and themed gifts that also offer educational value, such as the animal- and nature-related content of Wild Kratts.

It's crucial to consider the psychological effect of a well-curated bundle. By aligning the products more closely with identified customer interests and cross-selling patterns, the bundle not only caters to existing demand but also encourages additional purchases by enhancing perceived value by how the bundled items complement each other.

Ultimately, the decision on whether this new bundle is an improvement over the original should be validated through customer feedback and sales data. Tracking the sales performance of both bundles (as well as bundles suggested by human product managers) and gathering direct customer insights through surveys or A/B testing would be beneficial to quantitatively assess which bundle performs better in terms of sales and customer satisfaction. This data-driven approach will confirm the theoretical benefits of the advanced modeling techniques used in the new bundle's creation.

With this, we conclude the hands-on product example of this chapter. The next two sections are optional as they dive deeper into the theory of convolutional GNNs and take a closer look at the Amazon Products dataset.

3.4   *Under the hood*

Now that we've created and refined a working convolutional GNN, let's dig deeper into the elements of a GNN to better understand how they work. Such knowledge can help when we want to design new GNNs or troubleshoot a GNN.

In chapter 2, we introduced the idea of using GNN layers to produce a prediction or create embeddings using message passing. Here's that architecture diagram again, reproduced in figure 3.10.

Let's get below the surface of a GNN layer and examine its elements. Then, we'll tie this to the concept of aggregation functions.

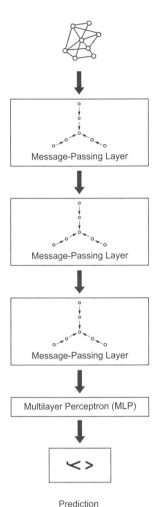

Prediction

Figure 3.10 Node embedding architecture diagram from chapter 2

3.4.1 Convolution methods

Let's first consider one of the most popular architectures for deep learning, the convolutional neural network (CNN). CNNs are typically used for computer vision tasks such as segmentation or classification. A CNN layer can be thought of as having a sequence of operations that are applied to input data:

$$\text{Layer: Filter} \rightarrow \text{Activation function} \rightarrow \text{Pooling}$$

The output of each entire layer is some transformed data that makes some downstream task easier or more successful. These transformation operations include the following:

- *Filter (or kernel operation)*—A process that transforms the input data. The filter is used to highlight some specific features of the input data and consists of learnable weights that are optimized by an objective or loss function.
- *Activation Function*—A nonlinear transformation applied to the filter output.
- *Pooling*—An operation that reduces the size of the filter output for subsequent learning tasks.

CNNs and many GNNs share a common foundation: the concept of convolution. You read about the concept of convolution when we discussed the three operations used in a CNN. Convolution in both CNNs and GNNs is all about learning by establishing *hierarchies of localized patterns* in the data. For CNNs this might be used for image classification, whereas a convolutional GNN, such as a GCN, might use convolution to predict features of nodes. To emphasize this point, CNNs apply convolution to a fixed grid of pixels to identify patterns in the grid. GCN models apply convolution to graphs of nodes to identify patterns in the graph.

I referred to the *concept* of convolution in the previous paragraph because the convolution can be implemented in different ways. Theoretically, convolution relates to the mathematical convolution operator, which we'll be discussing in more detail shortly. For GNNs, convolution can be separated into spatial and spectral methods [1, 5, 6]:

- *Spatial*—Sliding a window (filter) across a graph.
- *Spectral*—Filtering a graph signal using spectral methods.

SPATIAL METHODS

In traditional deep learning, convolutional processes learn data representations by applying a special filter called a *convolutional kernel* to input data. This kernel is smaller in size than the input data and is applied by moving it across the input data. This is shown in figure 3.11, where we apply our convolutional kernel (the matrix in the center) to an image of a lion. The resulting image has been inverted due to our convolutional kernel, which has negative values for all non-center elements. We can see that some of the features have been emphasized, such as the outline of the lion. This highlights the filtering aspect of convolutions.

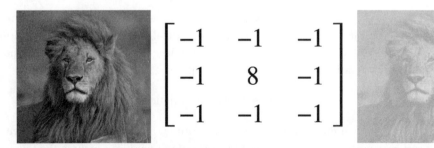

Figure 3.11 A convolution of an input image (left). The kernel (middle) is passed over the image of an animal, resulting in a distinct representation (right) of the input image. In a deep learning process, the parameters of the filter (the numbers in the matrix) are learned parameters.

This use of convolutional networks is particularly common in the computer vision domain. For example, when learning on 2D images, we can apply a simple CNN of a few layers. In each layer, we pass a 2D filter (kernel) over each image. The 3×3 filter works on an image many times its size. We can produce learned representations of the input image by doing this over successive layers.

For graphs, we want to apply this same idea of moving a window across our data, but now we need to make adjustments to account for the relational and non-Euclidian topology of our data. For images, we're dealing with rigid 2D grids; for graphs, we're dealing with data that has no fixed shape or order. Without a predefined ordering of the nodes in a graph, we use the concept of a *neighborhood*, consisting of a starting node, and all of its one-hop neighbors (i.e., all nodes within one hop from the central node). Then, our sliding window moves across a graph by moving across its node neighborhoods.

In figure 3.12, we see an illustration comparing convolution applied to grid data and applied to graph data. In the grid case, pixel values are filtered around the nine pixels immediately surrounding the central pixel (marked with a gray dot). However, for a graph, node attributes are filtered based on all nodes that can be connected by one edge. Once we have the nodes that we'll be considering, we then need to perform some operation on the nodes. This is known as the *aggregation operation*; for example, all the node weights in a neighborhood might be averaged or summed, or we might take the max value. What is important for graphs is that this operation is *permutation invariant*. The order of the nodes shouldn't matter.

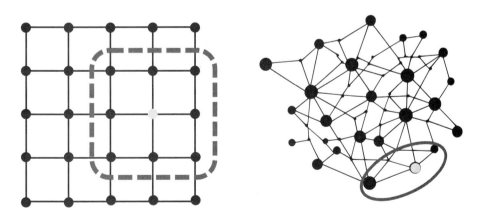

Figure 3.12   A comparison of convolution over grid data (left; e.g., a 2D image) and over a graph (right).

SPECTRAL METHODS

To introduce the second method of convolution, let's examine the concept of a graph signal [6]. In the field of information processing, *signals* are sequences that can be examined in either time or frequency domains. When studying a signal in the time domain, we consider its dynamics, namely how it changes over time. From the frequency domain, we consider how much of the signal lies within each frequency band.

We can also study the signal of a graph in an analogous way. To do this, we define a graph signal as a vector of node features. Thus, for a given graph, its set of node weights can be used to construct its signal. As a visual example, in figure 3.13, we have a graph with values associated with each node, where the height of each respective bar represents some node feature.

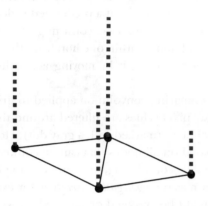

Figure 3.13   A random positive graph signal on the vertices of the graph. The height of each vertical bar represents the signal value at the node where the bar originates.

To operate on this graph signal, we represent the graph signal as a matrix, where each row is a set of features associated with a particular node. We can then apply operations from signal processing on the graph matrix. One critical operation is that of the Fourier transform. The Fourier transform can express a graph signal, its set of node features, into a frequency representation. Conversely, an inverse Fourier transform will revert the frequency representation into a graph signal.

ABOVE AND BEYOND: LIMITATIONS OF TRADITIONAL DEEP LEARNING METHODS TO GRAPHS

Why can't we apply CNNs directly to a graph structure? The reason is because graph representations have an ambiguity that image representations don't. CNNs, and traditional deep learning tools in general, can't resolve this ambiguity. A neural network that can deal with this ambiguity is said to be *permutation equivariant* or *permutation invariant*.

Let's illustrate the ambiguity of a graph versus an image by considering the image of the lion shown earlier. A simple representation of this set of pixels is as a 2D matrix (with dimensions for height and width). This representation will be unique: if we swap out two rows of the image, or two columns, we don't have an equivalent image. Similarly, if we swap out two columns or rows of the matrix representation of the image (as shown in figure 3.14), we don't have an equivalent matrix.

This isn't the case with a graph. Graphs can be represented by adjacency matrices (described in chapter1 and appendix A), such that each row and column element stands for the relation between two nodes. If an element is nonzero, it means that the row node and column node are linked. Given such a matrix, we can repeat our

Figure 3.14 **The image of a lion is unique (left). If we swap out two columns (right), we end up with a distinct photo with respect to the original.**

previous experiment and swap out two rows as we did with the image. Unlike the case of the image, we end up with a matrix that represents the graph we started with. We can do any number of permutations or rows and columns and end up with a matrix that represents the same graph.

Returning to the convolution operation, to successfully apply a convolutional filter or a CNN to the graph's matrix representation, such an operation or layer would have to yield the same result no matter the ordering of the adjacency matrix (because every ordering describes the same thing). CNNs fail in this respect.

Finding convolutional filters that can be applied to graphs has been solved in a variety of ways. In this chapter, we examined two ways this has been done: spatial and spectral methods. (For a deeper discussion and derivation of convolutional filters applied to graphs, see [7].)

3.4.2 *Message passing*

Both spatial and spectral approaches describe how we can combine data on our graph. Spatial methods look at the graph structure and combine data across spatial neighborhoods. Spectral methods look at the graph signal and use methods from signal processing, such as the Fourier transform to combine data across the graph. Implicit to both these methods is the idea of message passing.

In chapter 3, we introduced message passing as a way to extract more information from our graphs. Let's go step-by-step and consider what message passing does. First, the messages from each node or edge are collected from neighboring nodes. Second, we transform these messages to encode the data as feature vectors. Finally, we update the node or edge data to include these messages. The result is that each node or edge ends up containing individual data as well as data from the rest of the graph. The amount of data that becomes encoded in these nodes is reflected by the number of hops or message-passing steps. This is the same as the number of layers in a GNN. In figure 3.15, we show a mental model for message passing.

The output of each message-passing layer is a set of embeddings or features. In the aggregation step, we gather the messages from the graph neighborhoods. In the transfor-

1. *Input* initial graph with node, edges, and features.

2. *Collect* all features from neighboring nodes, known as messages, for each node.

3. *Aggregate* messages using invariant functions such as sum, max, or mean.

4. *Transform* messages using a neural network to create new node features.

5. *Update* all features in the graph with new node features.

Figure 3.15   Elements of our message-passing layer. Each message-passing layer consists of an aggregation, a transformation, and an update step.

mation step, we apply a neural network to the aggregated messages. Finally, in the update step, we alter the features of the nodes or edges to include the message passing data.

In this way, a GNN layer is similar to a CNN layer. It can be interpreted as a sequence of operations that are applied to input data:

$$\text{Layer: Aggregate} \rightarrow \text{Transform} \rightarrow \text{Update}$$

As we explore different GNNs in this book, we'll return to this set of operations, as most types of GNNs can be seen as modifications of these elements. For example, in this chapter, you're learning about GCNs as a specific type of aggregation. In the next chapter, you'll learn about GATs, which combine both transformation and aggregation steps by learning how to aggregate messages using an attention mechanism.

To build this message-passing step, let's work through the preceding process, adding more detail. The first two steps can be understood as a type of filter, similar to the first step of a conventional neural network. First, we aggregate node or edge data using our *aggregation operator*. For example, we might sum the features, average the features, or choose the maximum values. The most important thing is that the order of the nodes shouldn't matter for the final representation. The reason that the order shouldn't matter is that we want our models to be permutation equivariant, which means that subtraction or division wouldn't be suitable.

Once we've aggregated information from all node or collected all the messages, we then transform them into *embeddings* by passing the new messages through a neural network and an activation function. Once we have these transformed embeddings, we apply an activation function and then combine them with the node or edge data and the previous embeddings.

The activation function is a nonlinear transformation that is applied to the transformed and aggregated messages. We need the function to be nonlinear; otherwise, the model would be linear, regardless of how many layers it has, similar to a linear (or logistic, in our case) regression model. These are standard activation functions used in artificial neural networks, such as the ReLU, which is the maximum value between zero and the input value. The pooling step then reduces the overall size of the filter output for any graph-level learning tasks. For node prediction, this can be omitted, which we'll do here.

We can combine the previous description into a single expression for the message-passing operation. First, let's assume that we're working with node embeddings as we'll do in this chapter. We want to transform the data for node n into a node embedding. We can do so using the following formula:

$$\text{Transform}(u) = \sigma(W a * \text{Aggregate}(u)) \qquad \textbf{(3.1)}$$

Here, u represents the nodes. The learnable weights are given by W_a, which will be tuned based on the loss function, and σ is the activation function. To build the embeddings, we need to take all the node data and combine it into a single vector. This is where the aggregation function comes in. For GCNs, the aggregation operator is summation. Therefore,

$$\text{Aggregate Function}(u) = \sum_{V \in N(u)} h_v \qquad \textbf{(3.2)}$$

where, for node u, h_v is data from node v in the neighborhood of node u, $N(u)$. Combining both equations, we can construct a general formula for constructing node embeddings:

$$\text{Transform}(u) = \sigma \left(W a * \sum_{V \in N(u)} h_v \right) \qquad \textbf{(3.3)}$$

For the preceding formula, we see that a node and its neighborhood play a central part. Indeed, this is one of the main reasons that GNNs have proven to be so successful. We also see that we need to make a choice on both our activation function and our aggregation function. Finally, these are updated to include the previous data at each node:

$$\text{Update}(u) = h'_n = \text{Concat}(h_n, \text{Transform}(u)) \qquad \textbf{(3.4)}$$

Here, we're concatenating the messages together. It's also possible to use other methods to update the message information, and the choice depends on the architecture used.

This update equation is the essence of message passing. For each layer, we're *updating* all the node data using the *transformed* data that contains all *aggregated* messages. If we have only one layer, we perform this operation only once, we're aggregating the information from the neighbors one hop away from our starting node. If we run these operations for multiple iterations, we aggregate nodes within two hops of our central node into the node feature data. Thus, the number of GNN layers is directly tied to the size of the neighborhoods we're interrogating with our model.

These are the fundamentals for what operations are being performed during a message-passing step. The variations of things such as aggregation or activation functions highlight key differences in the architecture of a GNN.

3.4.3   *GCN aggregation function*

The key distinction between GCN and GraphSAGE is that they perform different aggregation operations. GCN is a spectral-based GNN, whereas GraphSAGE is a spatial method. To better understand the difference between the two, let's look at implementing them both.

First, we need to understand how to apply convolution to graphs. Mathematically, the convolutional operation can be expressed as the combination of two functions that produces a third function as

$$\text{Convolution} = g(x) = f(x) \odot h(x) \tag{3.5}$$

where $f(x)$ and $h(x)$ are functions, and the operator represents element-wise multiplication. In the context of CNNs, the image and the kernel matrices are the functions in equation 3.6:

$$\text{Convolution} = \text{image}() \odot \text{filter}() \tag{3.6}$$

This mathematical operation is interpreted as the kernel sliding over the image, as in the sliding window method. We can convert the preceding description to matrices or tensors describing our data. To apply the convolution of equation 3.7 to graphs, we use the following ingredients:

- Matrix representations of the graph:
    - Vector $\mathbf{x}$ as the graph signal
    - Adjacency matrix $\mathbf{A}$
    - Laplacian matrix $\mathbf{L}$
    - A matrix of eigenvectors of the Laplacian $\mathbf{U}$
- A parameterized matrix for the weights, $\mathbf{H}$
- Fourier transform based on the matrix operations: $\mathbf{U}^{\mathrm{T}}\mathbf{x}$

This leads to the expression for spectral convolution over a graph:

$$\text{Graph Convolution} = \mathbf{x} *_{\mathrm{G}} \mathbf{H} = \mathbf{U}(\mathbf{U}^{\mathrm{T}}\mathbf{x} \circ \mathbf{U}^{\mathrm{T}}\mathbf{H}) \tag{3.7}$$

Because this operation isn't a simple element-wise multiplication, we're using the symbol $*_{\mathrm{G}}$ to express this operation. Several convolutional-based GNNs build on equation 3.8; next, we'll examine the GCN version.

GCNs introduced changes to the convolution equation (3.8) to simplify operations and to reduce computational cost. These changes include using a filter based on a polynomial rather than a set of matrices and limiting the number of hops to one. This reduces the computational complexity from quadratic to linear, which is significant. However, the key thing to note is that GCNs updated the aggregation function that we described earlier. This will still use a summation but includes a normalization term.

Previously, the aggregation operator was summation. This can lead to problems in graphs where the degree of nodes can have high variance. If a graph contains nodes whose degrees are high, those nodes will dominate. To solve this, one method is to replace summation with averaging. The aggregation function is then expressed as

$$m_{N(u)} = \sum_{v \in N(u)} \frac{h_u}{\sqrt{|N(u)|\,|N(v)|}} \tag{3.8}$$

Therefore, for GCN message passing, we have

$$\text{GCN Updated Node Embeddings} = h_u^{(k)} = \sigma\left(W^{(k)} \sum_{v \in N(u)} \frac{h_u}{\sqrt{|N(u)|\,|N(v)|}}\right) \tag{3.9}$$

where

- h is the updated node embedding.
- sigma, σ, is a nonlinearity (i.e., activation function) applied to every element.
- W is a trained weight matrix.
- $|N|$ denotes the count of the elements in the set of graph nodes

The summed factor,

$$\sum_{v \in N(u)} \frac{h_u}{\sqrt{|N(u)|\,|N(v)|}} \tag{3.10}$$

is a special normalization called *symmetric normalization*. Additionally, GCNs include self-loops such that node embeddings include both neighborhood data and data from the starting node. So, to implement a GCN, the following operations must occur:

- Graph nodes adjusted to contain self-loops
- Matrix multiplication of the trained weight matrix and the node embeddings
- Normalization operations summing the terms of the symmetric normalization

In figure 3.16, we explain each of the terms used in a message-passing step in detail.

So far this has all been theoretical. Let's next look at how we implement this in PyG.

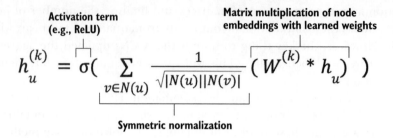

Figure 3.16   Mapping of key computational operations in the GCN embedding formula

3.4.4   GCN in PyTorch Geometric

In the PyG documentation, you can find source code that implements the GCN layer, as well as a simplified implementation of the GCN layer. In the following, we'll point out how the source code implements the preceding key operations.

In table 3.8, we break down key steps in the computation of the GCN embeddings and tie them to functions in the source code. These operations are implemented using a class and a function:

- Function `gcn_norm` performs normalization and add self-loops to the graph.
- Class `GCNConv` instantiates the GNN layer and performs matrix operations.

Table 3.8   Mapping key computational operations in the GCN embedding formula

Operation	Function/Method
Add self-loops to nodes	`gcn_norm()`, annotated in listing 3.8
Multiply weights and embeddings $W^{(k)}h_u$	`GCNConv.__init__`; `GCNConv.forward`
Symmetric normalization	`gcn_norm()`, annotated in listing 3.8

In listing 3.8, we show the code in detail for the `gcn_norm` function and class and use annotation to highlight the key operations. This normalization function is a key aspect for the GCN architecture. The `gcn_norm` arguments are as follows:

- `edge_index`—The node representations are in a tensor or sparse tensor form.
- `edge_weight`—An array of one-dimensional edge weights is optional.
- `num_nodes`—This is a dimension of the input graph.
- `improved`—This introduces an alternative method to add self-loops from the Graph U-Nets paper [8].
- `Add_self_loops`—Adding self-loops is the default, but it's optional.

Listing 3.8   The `gcn_norm` function

> Performs symmetric normalization of the input
> graph and adds a self-loop to the input graph

```
def gcn_norm(edge_index, edge_weight=None, num_nodes=None, improved=False,
            add_self_loops=True, dtype=None):                              ◁┐

    fill_value = 2. if improved else 1.              ◁─┤ The fill_value parameter is used in the
                                                        alternative self-loop operation.

    if isinstance(edge_index, SparseTensor):                                    ◁─┐
        adj_t = edge_index                                          If the graph input is a
        if not adj_t.has_value():                                   sparse tensor, the first
            adj_t = adj_t.fill_value(1., dtype=dtype)               block of code in the if-
        if add_self_loops:                                          statement will apply.
            adj_t = fill_diag(adj_t, fill_value)                   Otherwise, the second
        deg = sparsesum(adj_t, dim=1)                                   will apply.
        deg_inv_sqrt = deg.pow_(-0.5)
        deg_inv_sqrt.masked_fill_(deg_inv_sqrt == float('inf'), 0.)
        adj_t = mul(adj_t, deg_inv_sqrt.view(-1, 1))
        adj_t = mul(adj_t, deg_inv_sqrt.view(1, -1))
        return adj_t

    else:                                                                        ◁─
        num_nodes = maybe_num_nodes(edge_index, num_nodes)

        if edge_weight is None:
            edge_weight = torch.ones((edge_index.size(1), ), dtype=dtype,
                                    device=edge_index.device)

        if add_self_loops:
            edge_index, tmp_edge_weight = add_remaining_self_loops(
                edge_index, edge_weight, fill_value, num_nodes)
            assert tmp_edge_weight is not None
            edge_weight = tmp_edge_weight

        row, col = edge_index[0], edge_index[1]
        deg = scatter_add(edge_weight, col, dim=0, dim_size=num_nodes)
        deg_inv_sqrt = deg.pow_(-0.5)
        deg_inv_sqrt.masked_fill_(deg_inv_sqrt == float('inf'), 0)
        return edge_index, deg_inv_sqrt[row] * edge_weight * deg_inv_sqrt[col]
```

In practice, we can simplify the implementation of the normalization considerably by using some functions from PyTorch and PyG. In listing 3.9, we show a shortened version of normalizing the adjacency matrix. First, we compute the in-degree for each node and then calculate the inverse square root. We then use this to create a new edge weighting and apply the degree-based inverse square root to this weighting. Finally, we create a sparse tensor that represents the adjacency matrix and assign this to our data.

Listing 3.9   Normalizing using PyTorch and PyG

```
    edge_index = data.edge_index
    num_nodes = edge_index.max().item() + 1    ◁—— Assumes node indices start from 0

    deg = torch.zeros(num_nodes, \
    dtype=torch.float).to(edge_index.device)
    deg.scatter_add_(0, edge_index[1],              Computes in-degree
                torch.ones(edge_index.size(1))\     for each node
.to(edge_index.device))

    deg_inv_sqrt = deg.pow(-0.5)                    Computes the degree-based
    deg_inv_sqrt[deg_inv_sqrt == float('inf')] = 0  inverse square

    edge_weight = torch.ones(edge_index.size(1))\       Creates a new
    .to(edge_index.devic)                         ◁——  edge_weight tensor
    edge_weight = deg_inv_sqrt[edge_index[0]]*edge_weight*\
    deg_inv_sqrt[edge_index[1]]                          ◁——  Applies
                                                               deg_inv_sqrt to
    num_nodes = edge_index.max().item() + 1       ◁——         edge weights

    adj_t = torch.sparse_coo_tensor(indices=edge_index,\    Assumes
    values=edge_weight, size=(num_nodes, num_nodes))        node indices
    data.adj_t = adj_t.coalesce()                           start from 0
```

Creates a sparse tensor
and assigns to data

In the following listing, we have excerpts of the `GCNConv` class, which calls on the `gcn_norm` function as well as the matrix operations.

Listing 3.10   The `GCNConv` class

```
class GCNConv(MessagePassing):

    def __init__(self, in_channels: int, out_channels: int,
improved: bool = False, cached: bool = False,
        add_self_loops: bool = True, normalize: bool = True,
        bias: bool = True, **kwargs):

        self.lin = Linear(in_channels, out_channels, bias=False,
                        weight_initializer='glorot')
    def forward(self, x: Tensor, edge_index: Adj,
                edge_weight: OptTensor = None) -> Tensor:

if self.normalize:                                          ◁——
    if isinstance(edge_index, Tensor):
        cache = self._cached_edge_index
            if cache is None:
                edge_index, edge_weight = gcn_norm(
                edge_index, edge_weight, x.size(self.node_dim),
                self.improved, self.add_self_loops)
                if self.cached:
                    self._cached_edge_index = (edge_index, edge_weight)
```

The forward propagation function performs symmetric normalization given one of two options: that the input graph is a tensor or a sparse tensor. The source code for a tensor input is included here.

```
        else:
            edge_index, edge_weight = cache[0], cache[1]

    x = self.lin(x)                          ⊲────┐  **Linear transformation of**
                                                  │  **the node feature matrix**
    out = self.propagate(edge_index, x=x,\
edge_weight=edge_weight, size=None)          ⊲────┐  **Message**
                                                  │  **propagation**
    if self.bias is not None:                ⊲──┐
        out += self.bias                        │  **There is an optional additive**
                                                │  **bias to the output.**
    return out
```

3.4.5 *Spectral vs. spatial convolution*

In the previous section, we talked about interpreting convolution in two ways: (1) via a thought experiment of sliding a window filter across part of a graph consisting of a local neighborhood of linked nodes, and (2) by processing graph signal data through a filter. We also discussed how these two interpretations highlight two branches of convolutional GNNs: the spatial method and the spectral method. Sliding window and other spatial methods rely on a graph's geometrical structure to perform convolution. Spectral methods instead use graph signal filters.

There is no clear demarcation between the spectral and spatial methods, and often one type can be interpreted as the other. For example, one contribution of GCN is the demonstration that its spectral derivation could be interpreted in a spatial way. However, at the time of writing, spatial methods are preferred because they have fewer restrictions and, in general, offer less computational complexity. We've highlighted additional aspects of both spectral and spatial methods in table 3.9.

Table 3.9 A comparison of spectral and spatial convolutional methods

Spectral	Spatial
Operation: performing a convolution using a graph's eigenvalues	Operation: aggregation of node features in node neighborhoods
▪ Must be undirected ▪ Operation dependent on node features ▪ Generally less computationally efficient	▪ Not required to be undirected ▪ Operation not dependent on node features ▪ Generally more computationally efficient

3.4.6 *GraphSAGE aggregation function*

GraphSAGE improved on the computational cost of GCNs by limiting the number of neighboring nodes used in the aggregation operation. Instead, GraphSAGE aggregates from a randomly selected sample of the neighborhood. The aggregation operator is more flexible (e.g., it can be a summation or an average), but the messages that are considered are now only a subset of all messages. Mathematically, we can write this as

$$h_{(k)} = \sigma \left(W_{(k)} \cdot \text{Aggregate} \left(h_{(k-1)}, \left\{ h_{(k-1)}, \forall u \in S \right\} \right) \right) \tag{3.11}$$

where $\forall u \in S$ denotes that the neighborhood is picked from a random sample, S, of the total neighborhood. From the GraphSAGE paper [2], we have the general embedding updating process, which the paper introduces as Algorithm 1, reproduced here in figure 3.17.

1. **Input:**

- A graph G with nodes V and edges E
- Features x_v for each node v in V
- A maximum depth K (the number of layers or iterations)
- Weight matrices W^k for each layer k
- A nonlinear activation function σ (e.g., ReLU)
- Functions $AGGREGATE_k$ for combining node features from neighbors

2. **Output:**

- A vector representation z_v for each node v in the graph

Steps:

1. **Initialize Node Features:**

- Start by setting the initial hidden state h_v^0 of each node v to its input features x_v.

2. **Iterative Layer Updates:**

- For each layer k from 1 to K:
  - For each node v in the graph:
    - **Aggregate Neighbor Features:** Collect the hidden states h_u^{k-1} from all neighboring nodes u of v using the aggregation function $AGGREGATE_k$.
    - **Update Node Features:** Combine the aggregated features with the current node's features h_v^{k-1} using

$$h_v^k \leftarrow \sigma \left(W^k \cdot \text{CONCAT}(h_v^{k-1}, h_{\mathcal{N}(v)}^k) \right)$$

    - Normalize the updated feature vector h_v^k for stability.

3. **Final Output:**

- The final node representation z_v is the hidden state h_v^K after the last iteration.

Figure 3.17   Algorithm 1, the GraphSAGE embedding generation algorithm from the GraphSAGE paper [2]

The basics of this algorithm can be described as follows:

1 For every layer/iteration *and* for every node:
   a Aggregate the embeddings of the neighbors.
   b Concatenate neighbor embeddings with the central node.
   c Matrix multiply that concatenation with the Weights matrix.
   d Multiply that result with an activation function.
   e Apply a normalization.
2 Update node features, z, with node embeddings, h.

Let's take a closer look at what this means for the message-passing step. We've defined message passing for GraphSAGE as follows:

GraphSage Updated

$$\text{Node Embeddings} = h_{(k)} = \sigma \left(W_{(k)} \cdot \text{Aggregate} \left(h_{(k-1)}, \{ h_{(k-1)}, \forall u \in S \} \right) \right) \quad \textbf{(3.12)}$$

If we choose the mean as the aggregation function, this becomes

$$h_{(k)}v \leftarrow \sigma\left(W \cdot \text{MEAN}\right)\left\{h_{(k-1)}, v\right\} \cup \left\{h_{(k-1)}, u, \forall u \in N(v)\right\} \tag{3.13}$$

For implementation, we can further reduce this to

$$\mathbf{x}'_i = \mathbf{W}_i \mathbf{x}_i + \mathbf{W}_i \cdot \text{mean}_{j \in N(i)}\,\mathbf{x}_j \tag{3.14}$$

where x'_i denotes the generated central node embeddings, and x_i and x_j are the input features of the central and neighboring nodes, respectively. The weight matrices are applied to both central nodes and neighboring nodes, as shown in figure 3.18, but only the neighboring nodes have an aggregation operator (in this case, the mean).

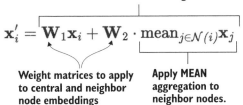

Concatenate central node to neighbor nodes.

$$\mathbf{x}'_i = \mathbf{W}_1 \mathbf{x}_i + \mathbf{W}_2 \cdot \text{mean}_{j \in \mathcal{N}(i)} \mathbf{x}_j$$

Weight matrices to apply to central and neighbor node embeddings

Apply MEAN aggregation to neighbor nodes.

Figure 3.18   Mapping key computational operations in the GraphSAGE embedding formula

We've now seen all the main features of the GraphSAGE algorithm. Let's next look at how we implement this in PyG.

3.4.7 *GraphSAGE in PyTorch Geometric*

In table 3.10, we break down the key operations and where they occur in PyG's GraphSAGE class. The key operations are aggregation of the neighbor embeddings, concatenation of a node's neighbors' embeddings with that node's embeddings, multiplication of weights with the concatenation, and application of an activation function.

Table 3.10   Mapping key computational operations in the GCN embedding formula

Operation	Function/Method
Aggregate the embeddings of the neighbors (sum, mean, or other).	`SAGEConv.message_and_aggregate`
Concatenate neighbor embeddings with that of the central node.	`SAGEConv.forward`
Matrix multiply that concatenation with the Weights matrix.	`SAGEConv.message_and_aggregate`

Table 3.10   Mapping key computational operations in the GCN embedding formula *(continued)*

Operation	Function/Method
Apply an activation function.	If the `project` parameter is set to `True`, done in `SAGEConv.forward`
Apply a normalization.	`SAGEConv.forward`

For GraphSAGE, PyG also has source code to implement this layer in the `SAGEConv` class, excerpts of which are shown in the following listing.

Listing 3.11   The GraphSAGE class

```
class SAGEConv(MessagePassing):
    ...
    def forward(self, x, edge_index, size):

        if isinstance(x, Tensor):
            x: OptPairTensor = (x, x)

        if self.project and hasattr(self, 'lin'):
            x = (self.lin(x[0]).relu(), x[1])

        out = self.propagate(edge_index, x=x, size=size)
        out = self.lin_l(out)
        x_r = x[1]

        if self.root_weight and x_r is not None:
            out += self.lin_r(x_r)

        if self.normalize:
            out = F.normalize(out, p=2., dim=-1)
        return out

    def message(self, x_j):
        return x_j

    def message_and_aggregate(self, adj_t, x):
        adj_t = adj_t.set_value(None, layout=None)
        return matmul(adj_t, x[0], reduce=self.aggr)
    ...
```

If the project parameter is set to True, this applies a linear transformation with an activation function (ReLU, in this case) to the neighbor nodes.

Propagates messages and applies a linear transformation

Assigns the root node to a variable

If the root_weight parameter is set to True and a root node exists, this will add (concatenate) the transformed root node features to the output.

If the normalize parameter is set to True, L2 normalization will be applied to the output features.

Matrix multiplication with an aggregation. Setting the aggr parameter establishes the aggregation scheme (e.g., mean, max, lstm; default is add). adj_t is the sparse matrix representation of the input; using such a representation speeds up calculations.

3.5   *Amazon Products dataset*

In both this chapter and chapter 5, we use the Amazon Products dataset [9]. This dataset explores product relationships, particularly co-purchases, which are products purchased in the same transaction. This co-purchase data is a great dataset for benchmarking methods for predicting both nodes and edges. We give a bit more information about the dataset in this section.

To illustrate the concept of co-purchases, in figure 3.19, we show six example co-purchase images for an online customer. For each product, we include a picture, a plain text product label, and a bold text category label.

Figure 3.19 **Examples of co-purchases on Amazon.com. Each product is represented by a picture, a plain text product title, and a bold text product category. We see that some co-purchases feature products that are obvious complements of one another, while other groupings are less so.**

Some of these co-purchase groups seem to fit together well, such as the book purchases or the clothing purchases. Other co-purchases are less explainable, such as an Apple iPod being purchased with instant meals, or beans being purchased with a wireless speaker. In those less obvious groupings, there may be some latent product relationship, or maybe it's just mere coincidence. Examining the data at scale can provide clues.

To show how the co-purchasing graph would appear at a small scale, figure 3.20 takes one of the images from the previous figure and represents the products as nodes, with the edges between them representing each co-purchase. For one customer and one purchase, this is a small graph, with only four nodes and six edges. But for the same customer over time, for a larger set of customers with the same tastes in food, or even all the customers, it's easy to imagine how this graph can scale with more products and product connections branching from these few products.

The construction of this dataset is a long journey in itself, which is very much of interest to graph construction and the decisions that have to be made to get a meaningful and useful dataset. Put simply, this dataset was derived from purchasing log data from Amazon, which directly showed co-purchases, and from text data from product reviews, which was used to indirectly show product relationships. (For the in-depth story, see [8]).

To explore the product relationships, we can use the Amazon Products co-purchasing graph, a dataset of products that have been bought together in the same transaction (defined as a co-purchase). In this dataset, products are represented by nodes with

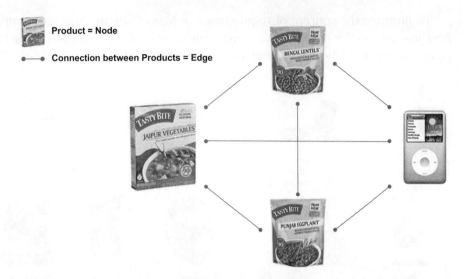

Figure 3.20   A graph representation of one of the co-purchases from figure 3.19. Each product's picture is a node, and the co-purchases are the edges (shown as lines) between the products. For the four products shown here, this graph is only the co-purchasing graph of one customer. If we show the corresponding graph for all customers of Amazon, the number of products and edges could feature tens of thousands of product nodes and millions of co-purchasing edges.

both the type of product that was bought, which are the category labels, and some feature information. The feature information takes the product description and first applies a natural language processing (NLP) method, the bag-of-words algorithm, to convert the strings into numerical values. Then, to convert this into the same fixed length, the creators of the dataset used principal component analysis (PCA) to convert this into a vector of length 100.

Meanwhile, co-purchases are represented by edges, which refers to two products that were bought together. In total, the dataset, `ogbn-products`, consists of 2.5 million nodes (products) and 61.9 million edges (co-purchases). The dataset is provided through the Open Graph Benchmark (OGB) dataset, mentioned at the beginning of the chapter, with a usage license from Amazon. Each node has 100 features. There are 47 categories that are used as targets in a classification task. We note that the edges here are undirected and unweighted.

In figure 3.21, we see that the categories with the highest counts of nodes are Books (668,950 nodes), CDs & Vinyl (172,199 nodes), and Toys & Games (158,771 nodes). The lowest are Furniture and Decor (9 nodes), Digital Music (6 nodes), and an unknown category (#508510) with 1 node.

We also observe that many categories have very low proportions in the dataset. The mean count of nodes per label/category is 52,107; the median count is 3,653. This highlights that there is a strong class imbalance in our dataset. This can pose a challenge for typical tabular results.

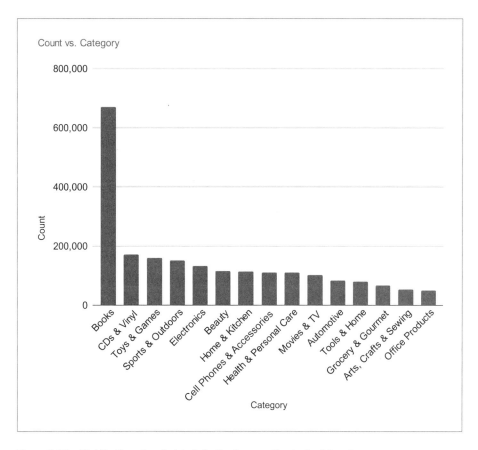

Figure 3.21 **Distribution of node labels in the Amazon Products dataset**

In this chapter, we explored the fundamentals of graph convolutional networks (GCNs) and GraphSAGE, two powerful architectures for learning on graph-structured data. We applied these models to a practical product categorization problem using the Amazon Products dataset, demonstrating how to implement, train, and refine GNNs. We also delved into the theoretical underpinnings of these models, examining concepts like neighborhood aggregation, message passing, and the distinctions between spectral and spatial convolution methods. By combining hands-on implementation with theoretical insights, this chapter has provided a comprehensive foundation for understanding and applying convolutional GNNs to real-world graph learning tasks. In the next chapter, we study a special convolutional GNN that uses the attention mechanism, the Graph Attention Network (GAT).

Summary

- GCNs and GraphSAGE are GNNs that use convolution, done by spatial and spectral methods, respectively.
- These GNNs can be used in supervised and semi-supervised learning problems. We applied them to the semi-supervised problem of predicting product categories.
- The Amazon Products dataset, `ogbn-products`, consists of a set of products (nodes) linked by being purchased in the same transaction (co-purchases). Each product node has a set of features, including its product-category. This dataset is a popular benchmark for graph classification problems. We can also study how it was constructed to get insights on graph creation methodology.
- Selecting subgraphs based on domain knowledge or using graph sampling techniques ensures more meaningful data is used for training. This can improve the performance of the models by focusing on relevant parts of the graph.
- Different aggregation methods, such as mean, max, and sum, have varied effects on model performance. Experimenting with multiple aggregation strategies can help capture various properties of the graph data, potentially enhancing model performance.
- Exploring more sophisticated aggregation functions or custom aggregations tailored to the specific characteristics of the dataset can yield performance improvements. Examples include `SoftmaxAggregation` and `StdAggregation`.
- Depth in GNNs is analogous to the number of hops or message-passing steps. While deeper models can theoretically capture more complex patterns, they often suffer from over-smoothing, where node features become too similar, making it difficult to distinguish between different nodes.
- Empirical testing of different aggregation methods and model configurations is essential. Experimentation helps determine which methods best capture the relational dynamics and feature distributions of the dataset.

Graph attention networks

In this chapter, we extend our discussion of convolutional graph neural network (convolutional GNN) architectures by looking at a special variant of such models, the graph attention network (GAT). While these GNNs use convolution as introduced in the previous chapter, they extend this idea with an *attention mechanism* to highlight important nodes in the learning process [1, 2]. In contrast to the conventional convolutional GNN, which weights all nodes equally, the attention mechanism allows the GAT to learn what aspects in its training to put extra emphasis on.

As with convolution, *attention* is a widely used mechanism in deep learning outside of GNNs. Architectures that rely on attention (particularly *transformers*) have seen such success in addressing natural language problems that they now dominate the field. It remains to be seen if attention will have a similar effect in the graph world.

GATs shine when dealing with domains where some nodes have more importance than the graph structure suggests. Sometimes in a graph, there can be a single high-degree node that has an outsized importance on the rest of the graph, and the vanilla message passing (covered in the previous chapter) will likely capture its significance thanks to the node's many neighbors. However, sometimes a node can have a large effect despite having a similar degree to other nodes. Some examples include social networks, where some members of a network have more influence on generating or spreading information and news; fraud detection, where a small set of actors and transactions drive deception; and anomaly detection, where a small subset of people, behaviors, or events will fall outside the norm [3–5]. GATs are especially well suited to these types of problems.

In this chapter, we'll apply GATs to the domain of fraud detection. In our problem, we detect fake customer reviews from the Yelp website. For this, we use a network of user reviews derived from a dataset that contains Yelp reviews for hotels and restaurants in the Chicago area [6, 7].

After an introduction to the problem and the dataset, we first train a baseline model without the graph structure before applying two versions of the GAT model to the problem. At the end, we discuss class imbalance and some ways to address this.

Code snippets will be used to explain the process, but the majority of code and annotation can be found in the repository. As with previous chapters, we provide a deeper dive into the theory in section 4.5 at the end of the chapter.

> **NOTE** Code from this chapter can be found in notebook form at the GitHub repository (https://mng.bz/JYoP). Colab links and data from this chapter can be accessed in the same location.

4.1 *Detecting spam and fraudulent reviews*

On consumer-oriented websites and e-commerce platforms such as Yelp, Amazon, and Google Business Reviews, it's common for user-generated reviews and ratings to accompany the presentation and description of a product or a service. In the United States, more than 90% of adults trust and rely on these reviews and ratings when making a purchase decision [3]. At the same time, many of these reviews are fake. Capital One estimated that 30% of online reviews weren't real in 2024 [5]. In this chapter, we're going to be training our model to detect fake reviews.

Spam or fraudulent review detection has been a well-trodden area in machine learning and natural language processing (NLP). As such, several datasets from primary consumer sites and platforms are available. In this chapter, we're going to use review data from Yelp.com, a platform of user reviews and ratings that focuses on consumer services. On Yelp.com, users can look up local businesses in their proximity and browse basic information about the business and written feedback from users. Yelp uses internally developed tools and models to filter reviews based on their trustworthiness. The process we'll use to approach the problem is shown in figure 4.1.

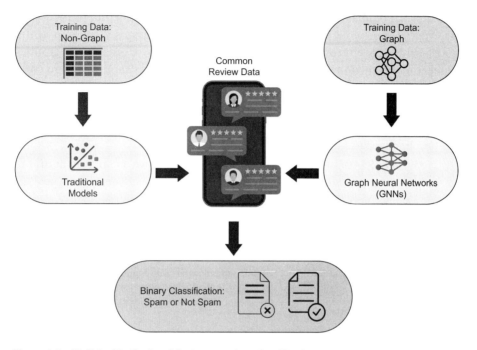

Figure 4.1   We'll tackle the fraudulent user review classification problem using both non-graph and graph data.

First, we'll establish baselines using non-GNN models and tabular data: logistic regression, XGBoost, and scikit-learn's multilayer perceptron (MLP). Then, we'll apply graph convolutional network (GCN) and GAT to the problem, introducing graph structural data.

This fraudulent review problem can be tackled as a node classification problem. We'll use GAT to perform node classification of the Yelp reviews, sifting the fraudulent from the legitimate reviews. This classification is binary: "spam" or "not spam."

We expect that the graph structural data and attention mechanism will give an edge to the attention-based GNN models. We'll follow this process in this chapter:

- Load and preprocess the dataset
- Define baseline models and results
- Implement the GAT solution and compare it to baseline results

4.2   *Exploring the review spam dataset*

Derived from a broader Yelp review dataset, our data focuses on reviews from Chicago's hotels and restaurants. It has also been preprocessed so that the data has a graph structure. This means we're going to be using a specialized version of the Yelp Multirelational dataset, characterized by its graph structure and its focus on consumer reviews from many Chicago-based hotels and restaurants. The Yelp Multirelational dataset is derived from the Yelp Review dataset and processed into a graph. This dataset contains the following (final version of the dataset is summarized in table 4.1):

- *45,954 nodes*—Each node represents an individual review, with 14.5% of them flagged as likely fraudulent and created by a bot to skew the reviews.
- *Preprocessed node features*—Our nodes come with 32 features that have been normalized to facilitate machine learning algorithms.
- *3,892,933 edges*—Edges connect reviews that have a common author or review a common business. While the original dataset had multiple types of relational edges, we use one with homogenous edges for easier analysis.
- *No user or business IDs*—Distinguishing IDs have been removed.

Table 4.1 Overview of the Yelp Multirelational dataset

Yelp Review dataset for the city of Chicago processed into a graph, with node features based on review text and user data	
Number of nodes (reviews)	45,954
Filtered (fraudulent) nodes	14.5%
Node features	32
Total number of edges (edges are assumed to be homogenous in our analysis)	3,846,979
Reviews with a common writer	49,315
Reviews of a common business and written in the same month	73,616
Reviews of a common business that share the same rating	3,402,743

Next, table 4.2 shows examples of text reviews from this dataset, ordered by the star rating system.

Table 4.2 Sampling of reviews from the YelpChi dataset for one restaurant, in descending order by rating (5 being the highest)

Rating (1–5)	Date	Review*
5	7/7/08	Perfection. Snack has become my favorite late lunch/early dinner spot. Make sure to try the butter beans!!!
4	7/1/13	Ordered lunch for 15 from Snack last Friday. On time, nothing missing and the food was great. I have added it to the regular company lunch list, as everyone enjoyed their meal.

Table 4.2 Sampling of reviews from the YelpChi dataset for one restaurant, in descending order by rating (5 being the highest) *(continued)*

Rating (1–5)	Date	Review*
3	12/8/14	The food at snack is a selection of popular Greek dishes. The appetizer tray is good as is the Greek salad. We were underwhelmed with the main courses. There are 4-5 tables here so it's sometimes hard to get seated.
2	9/10/13	Been meaning to try this place for a while-highly recommended by a friend. Had the tuna sandwich . . . good but got TERRIBLY SICK afterword. Also, sage tea was nice.
1	8/12/12	Lackluster service, soggy lukewarm spinach pie and two-day-old cucumber salad. Go to Local instead!

*Spelling, grammar, and punctuation are uncorrected in these reviews.

4.2.1 Explaining the node features

Highlights of this dataset are its node features. These were extracted from available metadata such as ratings, timestamps, and review text. They are divided into the following:

- Characteristics of the text review
- Characteristics of the reviewer
- Characteristics of the reviewed business

These features are then further divided into behavioral and textual features:

- Behavioral features highlight patterns of behavior and actions of the reviewers.
- Textual features are based on the text found in the reviews.

The process for calculating these features was developed by Rayana and Akoglu [7] and Dou [9]. Taking the original formulas from Rayana and Akoglu, Dou preprocessed and normalized the feature data that we use in this example. A summary of the features is shown in figure 4.2. (For more details on definitions and how they were calculated, refer to the original paper [8].) These node features are summarized here:

- Reviewer and business features:

  Behavioral:

  – *Max. number of reviews written in a day (MNR)*—High value suggests spam.
  – *Ratio of positive reviews (4-2 star) (PR)*—High value suggests spam.
  – *Ratio of negative reviews (1-2 star) (NR)*—High value suggests spam.
  – *Avg. rating deviation (avgRD)*—High value suggests spam.
  – *Weighted rating deviation (WRD)*—High value suggests spam.
  – *Burstiness (BST)*—Specifically, the time frame between the user's first and last review. High value suggests spam.
  – *Entropy of rating distribution (ERD)*—Low value suggests spam.
  – *Entropy of temporal gaps Δt's (ETG)*—Low value is spam indicative.

Text-based:

- *Avg. review length in words (RL)*—Low value suggests spam.
- *Avg./Max. content similarity measured with cosine similarity using a bag-of-bigrams approach (ACS, MCS)*—High value suggests spam.

■ Review features:

Behavioral:

- *Rank order among all the reviews of a product*—Low value suggests spam.
- *Absolute rating deviation from product's average rating (RD)*—High value is suspicious.
- *Extremity of rating (EXT)*—High values (4-5 stars) are considered spammy.
- *Thresholded rating deviation of review (DEV)*—High deviation is suspicious.
- *Early time frame (ETF)*—Reviews that appear too early are suspicious.
- *Singleton Reviewer Detection (ISR)*—If the review is a user's sole review, it's marked as suspicious.

Text-based:

- *Percentage of ALL-capital words (PCW)*—High values are suspicious.
- *Percentage of capital letters (PC)*—High values are suspicious.
- *Review length in words*—Low values are suspicious.
- *Ratio of 1st person pronouns like "I", "my" (PP1)*—Low values are suspicious.
- *Ratio of exclamation sentences (RES)*—High values are suspicious.
- *Ratio of subjective words*—Detected by *sentiWordNet (SW)*—High values are suspicious.
- *Ratio of objective words*—Detected by *sentiWordNet (OW)*—Low values are suspicious.
- *Frequency of review*—Approximated using *locality-sensitive hashing (F)*—High values are suspicious.
- *Description length based on unigrams and bigrams (DLu, DLb)*—Low values are suspicious.

Figure 4.2 gives a summary of the set of features.

This diverse mix of features requires varying degrees of intuition to interpret. These features not only help in understanding the behavior of reviewers but also in deducing the context and essence of the reviews. It's clear that certain features, such as Singleton Reviewer Detection or Review Length in Words can provide immediate insights, while others, such as Entropy of Temporal Gaps Δt's, require a more considered understanding. Let's next examine the distributions of these features present in the data.

Reviewer and Business Features		
	Feature Name	**Suspicious Indicator**
	User and Product Features	
Behavioral	Max. number of reviews written in a day (**MNR**)	High value suggests spam.
	Ratio of positive reviews (4-5 star) (**PR**)	High value suggests spam.
	Ratio of negative reviews (1-2 star) (**NR**)	High value suggests spam.
	Avg. rating deviation (**avgRD**)	High value suggests spam.
	Weighted rating deviation (**WRD**)	High value suggests spam.
	Burstiness (**BST**)	High value suggests spam.
	Entropy of rating distribution (**ERD**)	Low value suggests spam.
	Entropy of temporal gaps Δt's (**ETG**)	Low value is spam indicative.
Text	Avg. review length in words (**RL**)	Low value suggests spam.
	Avg./Max. content similarity (**ACS, MCS**)	High value suggests spam.
	Review Features	
Behavioral	Rank order among all the reviews of a product	Long value suggests spam.
	Absolute rating deviation from product's average rating (**RD**)	High value is suspicious.
	Extremity of rating (**EXT**)	High values (4-5 stars) are considered spammy.
	Tresholded rating deviation of review (**DEV**)	High deviation is suspicious.
	Early time frame (**ETF**)	Reviews that appear too early are suspicious.
	Singleton review detection (**ISR**)	If a user's sole review, it's marked as suspicious.
Text	Percentage of ALL-capital words (**PCW**)	High values are suspicious.
	Percentage of capital letters (**PC**)	High values are suspicious.
	Review length in words	Low values are suspicious.
	Ratio of first-person pronouns like "I", "my" (**PP1**)	Low values are suspicious
	Ratio of exclamation sentences (**RES**)	High values are suspicious.
	Ratio of subjective words (**SW**)	High values are suspicious.
	Ratio of objective words (**OW**)	Low values are suspicious.
	Frequency of review (**F**)	High values are suspicious.
	Description length based on unigrams and bigrams (**DLu, DLb**)	Low values are suspicious.

Figure 4.2 Summary definitions of node features used in the example. A label of high means that a high value of the data indicates a tendency toward spamminess. Likewise, a label of low means that a low value of the data indicates a tendency toward spamminess. (For more details on the derivation of these features, refer to [7].)

4.2.2 Exploratory data analysis

In this section, we download and explore the dataset with a focus on node features. Node features will serve as the main tabular features in our non-graph baseline models.

The dataset can be downloaded from Yingtong Dou's GitHub repository (https://mng.bz/Pdyg), compressed in a zip file. The unzipped file will be in MATLAB format. Using the `loadmat` function from the `scipy` library and a utility function from Dou's repository, we can produce the objects we need to start (see listing 4.1):

- A `features` object containing the node features
- A `labels` object containing the node labels
- An adjacency list object

Listing 4.1   Load data

```
prefix = 'PATH_TO_MATLAB_FILE/'

data_file = loadmat(prefix +  'YelpChi.mat')

labels = data_file['label'].flatten()
features = data_file['features'].todense().A

yelp_homo = data_file['homo']
sparse_to_adjlist(yelp_homo, prefix +\
 'yelp_homo_adjlists.pickle')
```

`loadmat` is a scipy function that loads MATLAB files.

Retrieves the node labels and features, respectively

Retrieves and pickles an adjacency list. "Homo" means that this adjacency list will be based on a homogenous set of edges; that is, we get rid of the multirelational nature of the edges.

Once the adjacency list is extracted and pickled, it can then be called in the future using

```
with open(prefix + 'yelp_homo_adjlists.pickle', 'rb') as file:
    homogenous = pickle.load(file)
```

With the data loaded, we can now perform some exploratory data analysis (EDA) to analyze the graph structure and node features.

4.2.3   *Exploring the graph structure*

To better understand fraud within our dataset, we explore the underlying graph structure. By analyzing the connected components and various graph metrics, we can get an overview of the network's topology. This understanding will reveal the data's inherent characteristics and make sure there are no potential blockers to effective GNN training. We present a detailed analysis of the connected components, density, clustering coefficients, and other key metrics.

To perform this structural EDA, we use our adjacency list to examine the structural nature of our graph using the `NetworkX` library. In the following snippet of code, we load the adjacency list object, convert it into a `NetworkX` graph object, and then interrogate this graph object for three basic properties. The longer code can be found in the repository:

```
with open(prefix + 'yelp_homo_adjlists.pickle', 'rb') as file:
homogenous = pickle.load(file)
g = nx.Graph(homogenous)
print(f'Number of nodes: {g.number_of_nodes()}')
print(f'Number of edges: {g.number_of_edges()}')
print(f'Average node degree: {len(g.edges) / len(g.nodes):.2f}')
```

From the EDA, we obtain the properties listed in table 4.3.

Table 4.3   Graph properties

Property	Value/details
Number of nodes	45,954
Number of edges	3,892,933
Average node degree	84.71
Density	~0.00
Connectivity	The graph isn't connected.
Average clustering coefficient	0.77
Number of connected components	26
Degree distribution (first 10 nodes)	[4, 4, 4, 3, 4, 5, 5, 6, 5, 19]

Let's dig into these properties. The graph is relatively large with 45,954 nodes and 3,892,933 edges. This means the graph has a considerable level of complexity and will likely contain intricate relationships. The average node degree is 84.71, suggesting that, on average, nodes in the graph are connected to around 85 other nodes. This indicates that the nodes in the graph are reasonably well connected, and there's a possibility of rich information flow between them. The graph's density is close to 0.00, which indicates it's quite sparse. In other words, the number of actual connections (edges) is much lower than the number of possible connections. The density of a graph is its number of edges divided by its total possible edges.

The graph isn't fully connected and consists of 26 separate connected components. The presence of multiple connected components may require special consideration in modeling, especially if different components represent distinct data clusters or phenomena. The average clustering coefficient of 0.77 is relatively high. This metric gives an idea of the graph's "cliquishness." A high value means that nodes tend to cluster together, forming tightly knit groups. This could be indicative of local communities or clusters within the data, which can be crucial in understanding patterns or anomalies, especially in fraud detection.

Given that we have 26 distinct components, it's important to examine them to plan for model training. We want to know whether the components are roughly the same size, are a mix of sizes, or have one or two components dominating. Do the properties of these separate graphs differ significantly? We run a similar analysis on the 26 components and summarize the properties in table 4.4, with the components displayed in descending order in terms of the number of nodes. The first column contains the identifier of the component. From this table, we observe that one large component dominates the dataset.

Table 4.4   Properties of the 26 graph components, sorted in descending order by number of nodes

Component ID	Number of nodes	Number of edges	Average node degree	Density	Average clustering coeff
3	45,900	38,92810	169.62	0	0.77
4	13	60	9.23	0.77	0.77
2	6	14	4.67	0.93	0.58
1, 22	3	6	4	2	1
5–9, 14, 17, 24, 26	2	3	3	3	0
7–21, 23, 25	1	1	2	0	0

In the bottom three rows, several components have identical properties and are put in the same row to save space.

We see here that component 3 is the dominant component, followed by 25 components that are tiny in comparison. These tiny components probably won't have a strong influence over our model, so we'll focus on component 3. Let's contrast this component with the overall graph, found in table 4.5. Most of the properties are very similar or the same, with the exception of the average node degree, for which component 3 is twice as large.

Table 4.5   Comparing the largest component of the graph, component 3, to the overall graph

Attribute	Component No. 3	Overall Graph	Insight/Contrast
Number of nodes	45,900	45,954	Component 3 contains almost all nodes from the entire graph.
Number of edges	3,892,810	3,892,933	Component 3 contributes almost all edges of the entire graph.
Average node degree	169.62	84.71	Nodes in component 3 are more densely connected than in the overall graph.
Density	0.00	0.00	Both the component and the entire graph are sparse; this property is mainly driven by component 3.
Average clustering coefficient	0.77	0.77	Component 3 matches the overall graph in terms of clustering, indicating its dominance in defining the graph's structure.

For our GNN modeling purposes, what should we take away from this structural analysis? Primarily, the overwhelming dominance of component 3 in both nodes and edges underscores its significance in our dataset; almost the entirety of the graph's structure is encapsulated within this single component. This suggests that the patterns, relationships, and anomalies within component 3 will heavily influence the model's training and outcomes. The higher average node degree in component 3, compared to the overall graph, indicates a richer interconnectedness, emphasizing the importance of capturing these dense connections effectively. Furthermore, the identical density and clustering coefficient values between component 3 and the entire graph highlight that this component is highly representative of the dataset's overall structural properties. We have two options:

1 Assume that the other components will have a minor effect on the model and train without making any adjustments.

2 Model only component 3 itself, completely leaving the data of the smaller components out of the training and test data.

We looked at the structural properties of the graph data to get a glimpse into the characteristics of the graph and got some valuable insights to guide GNN model design and training for understanding potential fraud patterns. Next, we deep dive into the node features.

4.2.4 Exploring the node features

Having explored the structural nature of our graph, we turn to the node features. In the code at the beginning of this section, we pulled out the node features from the data file:

```
features = data_file['features'].todense().A
```

> **NOTE** As discussed previously, these feature definitions were handcrafted by Rayana and others [7, 8]. Guided by the feature generation process, Dou et al. [8] did the nontrivial work of further processing the Yelp review dataset to create a set of normalized node features.

With some additional work, shown in the code repository, we also add some tags and descriptions to the features before we create a chart distribution for each feature (example plots are shown in figures 4.3 to 4.5). Each set of plots corresponds to features describing the review text, the reviewer, and the business. We want to use these plots to check that the node features can be useful in distinguishing fraud. Figure 4.3 shows the distributions of two of the features derived from the characteristics of the reviews.

Figure 4.4 shows the distributions of two of the features derived from the characteristics of the reviewers.

Finally, figure 4.5 shows two of the distributions of the features derived from the characteristics of the restaurant or hotel being reviewed.

By examining the histograms for the 32 node features, we can make several observations. First, there's a pronounced skewness in many of the features. Specifically, features such as Rank, RD, and EXT lean toward a right-skewed distribution. This indicates that the majority of data points fall on the histogram's left side, but a few higher-value points stretch the histogram toward the right. Conversely, features such as MNR_user, PR_user, and NR_user, among others, display a left-skewed distribution. In these cases,

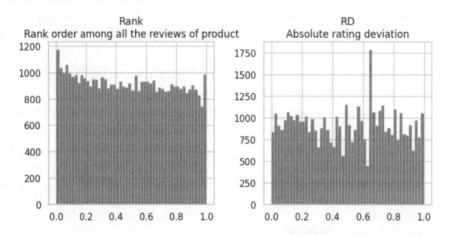

Figure 4.3   Distribution plots of 2 of the 15 normalized node features based on the review (see section 4.2.1 for feature definitions)

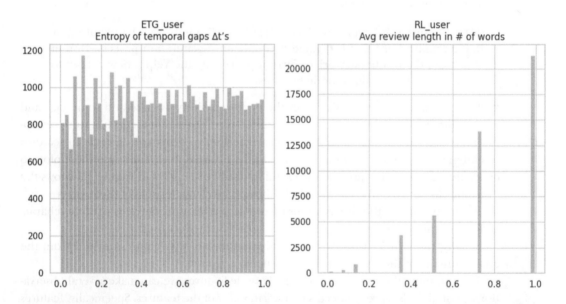

Figure 4.4   Distribution plots of two of the nine normalized node features based on the reviewer (see section 4.2.1 for feature definitions)

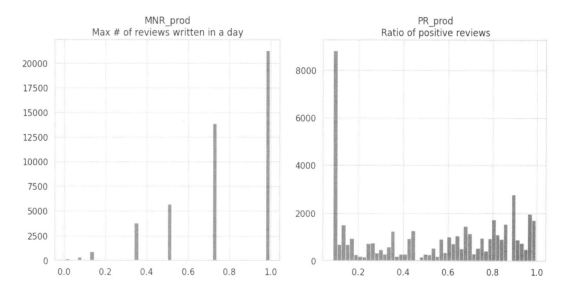

Figure 4.5   Distribution plots of two of the eight normalized node features based on the business being reviewed (see section 4.2.1 for feature definitions)

most of the data points concentrate on the histogram's right side, with a few lower-value points stretching the histogram to the left.

Some features also exhibit a bimodal distribution, meaning that there are two distinct peaks or groups within the data. This suggests that segmenting the data and creating separate models for each group could be a useful strategy.

Lastly, the long tails in several histograms suggest there are some outliers. Given that certain models, such as linear regression, are highly sensitive to extreme values, addressing these outliers could be crucial in refining and improving our model. This could mean opting for outlier-resistant models, developing strategies to mitigate their effect, or even removing them altogether.

Given those general insights, let's examine one of the feature plots more closely. PP1 is the ratio of first-person pronouns (i.e., I, me, us, our, etc.) to second person pronouns (you, your, etc.) in the review. This feature was developed due to an observation that spam reviews typically contain more second person pronouns. From the distribution plot for PP1, we observe that the distribution is skewed left, with a tail that peaks at low values. Thus, if a low ratio is an indicator of a spammy review, this feature would be good at distinguishing spam reviews.

To conclude our exploration of the node features, this data exhibits diverse characteristics, with many opportunities for model training. Further preprocessing, which could involve outlier handling, skewed feature transformation, data segmentation, and feature scaling, may be crucial in optimizing the model's predictive performance.

Our exploration of the review spam dataset revealed some patterns, anomalies, and insights. From the intricate structural characteristics of the dataset, represented largely by dominant component 3, to the node features that provide promising indications for distinguishing between genuine and fraudulent reviews, we've laid the groundwork for our model training.

In section 4.3, we'll embark on training our baseline models. These initial models serve as a foundation, helping us gauge the effectiveness of basic model performance. Through these models, we'll harness the potential of the data's graph structure and node features to separate fraud and spam from genuine reviews.

4.3   Training baseline models

Given our dataset, we'll begin the training phase by first developing three baseline models: logistic regression, XGBoost, and an MLP. Note that for these models, the data will have a tabular format, with the node features serving as our columnar features. There will be one row or observation for every node of our graph dataset. Next, we'll develop an additional GNN baseline by training a GCN to evaluate the effect of introducing graph structured data to our problem.

We now split our tabular data into test and train sets, and apply the three baseline models. First, the test/train splitting:

```
from sklearn.model_selection import train_test_split
split = 0.2
xtrain, xtest, ytrain, ytest = train_test_split\
(features, labels, test_size = \
split, stratify=labels, random_state = 99)
```
⊲ Splits data into test and train sets with an 80/20 split

```
print(f'Required shape is {int(len(features)*(1-split))}')
print(f'xtrain shape = {xtrain.shape}, \
xtest shape = {xtest.shape}')
print(f'Correct split = {int(len(features)*(1-split))\
 == xtrain.shape[0]}')
```
⊲ Double-checks the object shapes

We can use this split data for each of the three models. For this training, we're only using the node features and labels. There is no use of the graph data structure or geometry. For the baseline models and for the GNNs, we'll mainly rely on Receiver Operating Characteristic (ROC) and Area Under the Curve (AUC) to gauge performance and to compare the performance of our GAT models.

4.3.1   Non-GNN baselines

We start by using a logistic regression model with the scikit-learn implementation and the default hyperparameters:

```
from sklearn.linear_model import LogisticRegression
from sklearn.metrics import accuracy_score
from sklearn.metrics import roc_auc_score, f1_score

clf = LogisticRegression(random_state=0)\
.fit(xtrain, ytrain)
```
⊲ Logistic regression model instantiation and training

```
ypred = clf.predict_proba(xtest)[:,1]
acc = roc_auc_score(ytest,ypred)                ◁────  Accuracy score

print(f"Model accuracy (logression) = {100*acc:.2f}%")
```

This model yields an AUC of 76.12%. For the ROC performance, we'll also use a function from scikit-learn. We'll also recycle the true positive rate (`tpr`) and false positive rate (`fpr`) to compare with our other baseline models:

```
from sklearn.metrics import roc_curve
fpr, tpr, _ = roc_curve(ytest,ypred)            ◁┐  ROC curve calculation,
                                                 │  yielding false positive
plt.figure(1)                                    │  rate (fpr) and true
plt.plot([0, 1], [0, 1])                         │  positive rate (tpr)
plt.plot(fpr, tpr)
plt.xlabel('False positive rate')
plt.ylabel('True positive rate')
plt.show()
```

In figure 4.6, we see the ROC curve. We find that the curve is relatively balanced between false positives and false negatives but that the overall specificity is quite poor, given how near it is to the diagonal.

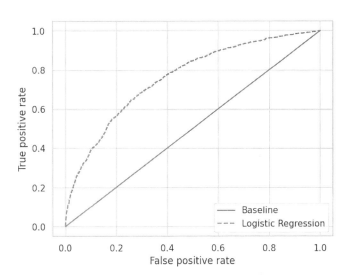

Figure 4.6 ROC curve for logistic regression baseline model (orange line) and chance line (blue diagonal line). An AUC of 76% indicates a model that can be improved.

XGBOOST

The XGBoost baseline follows the logistic regression, as shown in listing 4.2. We use a barebones model with the same training and test sets. For comparison, we differentiate the names of the generated predictions (named `pred2`), the true positive rate (`tpr2`), and the false positive rate (`fpr2`).

Listing 4.2   XGBoost baseline and plot

```
import xgboost as xgb
xgb_classifier = xgb.XGBClassifier()

xgb_classifier.fit(xtrain,ytrain)
ypred2 = xgb_classifier.predict_proba(xtest)[:,1]
acc = roc_auc_score(ytest,ypred2)

print(f"Model accuracy (XGBoost) = {100*acc:.2f}%")

fpr2, tpr2, _ = roc_curve(ytest,ypred2)

plt.figure(1)
plt.plot([0, 1], [0, 1])
plt.plot(fpr, tpr)
plt.plot(fpr2, tpr2)
plt.xlabel('False positive rate')
plt.ylabel('True positive rate')
plt.show()
```

For comparison, we name the XGBoost predictions "ypred2".

For comparison, we distinguish the tpr and fpr of XGBoost and plot them alongside the logistic regression result.

Figure 4.7 shows the ROC curves for XGBoost and logistic regression. It's clear that XGBoost has superior performance for this metric.

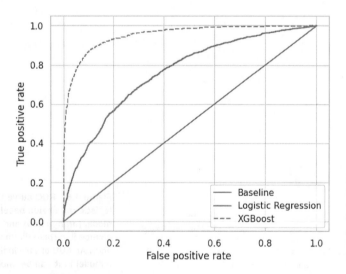

Figure 4.7   ROC curve for the XGBoost (dotted line), shown with the logistic regression curve (solid line). We see that the XGBoost curve shows a better performance than the logistic regression. The diagonal line is the chance line.

XGBoost fares better than logistic regression with this data, yielding an AUC of 94%, and with a superior ROC curve. This highlights that even a simple model can be suitable for some problems, and it's always a good idea to check performance.

MULTILAYER PERCEPTRON

For the MLP baseline, we use PyTorch to build a simple, three-layer model, as shown in listing 4.3. As with PyTorch, we establish the model using a class, defining the layers and the forward pass. In the MLP, we use binary cross-entropy (BCE) as the loss function, which is commonly used in binary classification problems.

Listing 4.3 MLP baseline and plot

```python
import torch
import torch.nn as nn
import torch.nn.functional as F

class MLP(nn.Module):
    def __init__(self, in_channels, out_channels, hidden_channels=[128,256]):
        super(MLP, self).__init__()
        self.lin1 = nn.Linear(in_channels,hidden_channels[0])
        self.lin2 = nn.Linear(hidden_channels[0],hidden_channels[1])
        self.lin3 = nn.Linear(hidden_channels[1],out_channels)

    def forward(self, x):
        x = self.lin1(x)
        x = F.relu(x)
        x = self.lin2(x)
        x = F.relu(x)
        x = self.lin3(x)
        x = torch.sigmoid(x)

        return x

model = MLP(in_channels = features.shape[1],\
 out_channels = 1)

epochs = 100
lr = 0.001
wd = 5e-4
n_classes = 2
n_samples = len(ytrain)

w= ytrain.sum()/(n_samples - ytrain.sum())

optimizer = torch.optim.Adam(model.parameters()\
,lr=lr,weight_decay=wd)
criterion = torch.nn.BCELoss()

xtrain = torch.tensor(xtrain).float()
ytrain = torch.tensor(ytrain)

losses = []

for epoch in range(epochs):
    model.train()
    optimizer.zero_grad()
    output = model(xtrain)
```

- Imports needed packages for this section
- Defines the MLP architecture using a class
- Instantiates the defined model
- Sets key hyperparameters
- Added to the account for class imbalance
- Defines the optimizer and the training criterion
- Uses BCE loss as the loss function
- Converts training data to torch data types: torch tensors
- The training loop. In this example, we've specified 100 epochs.

```
loss = criterion(output, ytrain.reshape(-1,1).float())
loss.backward()
losses.append(loss.item())

ypred3 = model(torch.tensor(xtest,dtype=torch.float32))

acc = roc_auc_score(ytest,ypred3.detach().numpy())
print(f'Epoch {epoch} | Loss {loss.item():6.2f}\
| Accuracy = {100*acc:6.3f}% | # True\ Labels = \
{ypred3.detach().numpy().round().sum()}', end='\r')

optimizer.step()
```

```
fpr, tpr, _ = roc_curve(ytest,ypred)
fpr3, tpr3, _ = roc_curve(ytest,ypred3.detach().numpy())
```

Differentiates the tpr and fpr for comparison

```
plt.figure(1)
plt.plot([0, 1], [0, 1])
plt.plot(fpr, tpr)
plt.plot(fpr2, tpr2)
plt.plot(fpr3, tpr3)
plt.xlabel('False positive rate')
plt.ylabel('True positive rate')
plt.show()
```

Plots all three ROC curves together

Figure 4.8 shows the ROC results for logistic regression, XGBoost, and an MLP.

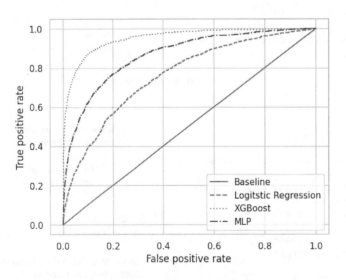

Figure 4.8   ROC curves for all three baseline models. The curves for logistic regression and MLP overlap. The XGBoost model shows the best performance for this metric. The diagonal line is the chance line.

The MLP run for 100 epochs yields an accuracy of 85.9% in the middle of our baselines. Its ROC curve is only slightly better than the logistic regression models. These results are summarized in table 4.6.

Table 4.6   Log loss and ROC AUC for the three baseline models

Model	Log Loss	ROC AUC
logistic regression	0.357	75.90%
XGBoost	0.178	94.17%
Multilayer perceptron	0.295	85.93%

To summarize this section, we've run three baseline models to use as benchmarks against our GNN models. These baselines used no structural graph data, only a set of tabular features derived from the node features. We didn't attempt to optimize these models, and XGBoost ended up performing the best with an accuracy of 89.25%. Next, we'll train one more baseline using GCN and then apply the GATs.

4.3.2 GCN baseline

In this section, we'll apply GNNs to our problem, starting with the GCN from chapter 3 before moving on to a GAT model. We anticipate that our GNN models will outperform other baselines thanks to the graph structural data, and the models with an attention mechanism will be best. For the GNN models, we need to make some changes to our pipeline. A lot of this has to do with the data preprocessing and data loading.

DATA PREPROCESSING

One critical first step is to prepare the data for use by our GNNs. This follows some of what has already been covered in chapters 2 and 3. The code for this is provided in listing 4.4, where we take the following steps:

- *Establish the train/test split.* We use the same `test_train_split` function from before, slightly tweaked to produce indices, and we only keep the resulting indices.
- *Transform our dataset into PyG tensors.* For this, we start with the homogenous adjacency list generated in an earlier section. Using NetworkX, we convert this to a NetworkX `graph` object. From there, we use the PyG `from_networkx` function to convert this to a PyG `data` object.
- *Apply the train/test split to the converted data objects.* For this, we use the indices from the first step.

We want to show a variety of ways to arrange the training data for ingestion. So, for the GCN, we'll run the entire dataset through the model, while in the GAT example, we'll batch the training data.

Listing 4.4   Converting the datatypes of our training data

```
from torch_geometric.transforms import NormalizeFeatures

split = 0.2
indices = np.arange(len(features))
```
**Establishes the train/test split.
We'll only use the index variables.**

```
xtrain, xtest, ytrain, ytest, idxtrain, idxtest\
 = train_test_split(features labels,indices, \
stratify=labels, test_size = split, \
random_state = 99)
```
Establishes the train/test split. We'll only use the index variables.

```
g = nx.Graph(homogenous)
print(f'Number of nodes: {g.number_of_nodes()}')
print(f'Number of edges: {g.number_of_edges()}')
print(f'Average node degree: {len(g.edges) / len(g.nodes):.2f}')
data = from_networkx(g)
data.x = torch.tensor(features).float()
data.y = torch.tensor(labels)
data.num_node_features = data.x.shape[-1]
data.num_classes = 1 #binary classification
```
Takes the adjacency list and transforms it into PyG data objects

```
A = set(range(len(labels)))
data.train_mask = torch.tensor([x in idxtrain for x in A])
data.test_mask = torch.tensor([x in idxtest for x in A])
```
Establishes the train/test split in the data objects

With the preprocessing done, we're ready to apply the GCN and GAT solutions. We detailed the GCN architecture in chapter 3. In listing 4.5, we establish a two-layer GCN, trained over 1,000 epochs. We choose two layers due to the insight from chapter 3 that, in general, a low model depth improves performance and prevents oversmoothing.

Listing 4.5 GCN definition and training

```
class GCN(torch.nn.Module):
    def __init__(self, hidden_layers = 64):
        super().__init__()
        torch.manual_seed(2022)
        self.conv1 = GCNConv(data.num_node_features, hidden_layers)
        self.conv2 = GCNConv(hidden_layers, 1)

    def forward(self, data):
        x, edge_index = data.x, data.edge_index

        x = self.conv1(x, edge_index)
        x = F.relu(x)
        x = F.dropout(x, training=self.training)
        x = self.conv2(x, edge_index)

        return torch.sigmoid(x)

device = torch.device("cuda"\
 if torch.cuda.is_available() \
else "cpu")
print(device)
model = GCN()
model.to(device)
data.to(device)
```
Defines a two-layer GCN architecture

Instantiates the model and puts the model and data on the GPU

```
lr = 0.01
epochs = 1000

optimizer = torch.optim.Adam(model.parameters(), lr=lr, weight_decay=5e-4)
criterion = torch.nn.BCELoss()

losses = []
for e in range(epochs):                ◁—— Training loop
    model.train()
    optimizer.zero_grad()
    out = model(data)                           ◁—┐

    loss = criterion(out[data.train_mask], \         For each epoch, we feed the
    data.y[data.train_mask].\                        entire data object through the
    reshape(-1,1).float())                           model and then use the training
    loss.backward()                         ◁—┘      mask to calculate the loss.
    losses.append(loss.item())

    optimizer.step()

    ypred = model(data).clone().cpu()
    pred = data.y[data.test_mask].clone().cpu().detach().numpy()
    true = ypred[data.test_mask].detach().numpy()
    acc = roc_auc_score(pred,true)

    print(f'Epoch {e} | Loss {loss:6.2f} \           Calculates false positive
    | Accuracy = {100*acc:6.3f}% \                   rate (fpr) and true
    | # True Labels =\ {ypred.round().sum()}')       positive rate (tpr)
fpr, tpr, _ = roc_curve(pred,true)          ◁—┘
```

APPLYING THE SOLUTIONS

One item of note is the use of the masks in our training. While we establish loss using the nodes in the training mask, for forward propagation, we must pass the entire graph through the model. Why is this so? Unlike traditional machine learning models that work on independent data points (e.g., rows in a tabular dataset), GNNs operate on graph-structured data where the relationships between nodes are critical. When training a GCN, each node's embedding is updated based on its neighbors' information. Because this message-passing process involves aggregating information from a node's local neighborhood, the model needs access to the entire graph structure so that it can compute these aggregations correctly and accurately perform this process.

So, during training, even though we're only interested in the prediction for certain nodes (those in the training set), passing the entire graph through the model ensures that all necessary context is considered. If only part of the graph were passed through the model, the network would lack the complete information needed to propagate messages correctly and update node representations effectively.

A training session of 100 epochs for the GCN yields an accuracy of 94.37%. By introducing the graph data, we see incremental improvement against the XGBoost model. Table 4.7 compares the model performance levels.

Table 4.7 AUC for the four baseline models

Model	AUC
Logistic regression	75.90%
XGBoost	94.17%
Multilayer perceptron	85.93%
GCN	94.37%

To summarize, we've seen that including graph structural information using a GNN model slightly improves performance compared to a purely feature-based or tabular model. It's clear that the XGBoost model has shown impressive results even without the use of graph structures. However, the GCN model's marginally better performance underlines the potential of GNNs in using relational information embedded in graph data.

In the next phase of our study, our attention will turn to graph attention networks (GATs). GATs have an attention mechanism that is especially tailored to learning how to weigh the significance of neighbors during a message-passing step. This can potentially offer even better model performance. In the next section, we'll delve into the details of training GAT models and comparing their outcomes with the baselines we've established. Let's proceed with GAT model training.

4.4 *Training GAT models*

To train our GAT models, we'll apply two PyG implementations (GAT and GATv2) [2]. In this section, we'll dive straight into training the models without discussing what attention means for machine learning models and why it's helpful. However, for a short overview on attention and why attention might be all you need, see section 4.5.

We'll be training two different GAT models. These both follow the same fundamental idea—that we're replacing the aggregation operator in our GCN with an attention mechanism to learn what messages (node features) the model should pay the most attention to. The first—GATConv—is a simple extension to the GCN in chapter 3 with the attention mechanism. The second is a slight variation to this model known as GATv2Conv. This model is the same as GATConv except that it addresses a limitation in the original implementation, namely that the attention mechanism is *static* over individual GNN layers. Instead, for GATv2Conv, the attention mechanism is dynamic across layers.

To reiterate this, the original GAT model only computes the attention weights once per training loop by using individual node and neighborhood features, and these weights are static across all layers. In GATv2, the attention weights are calculated on the node features as they are transformed through the layers. This allows GATv2 to be more expressive, learning to emphasize the influence of node neighborhoods throughout the trained model.

Both models introduce a significant computational overhead due to the introduction of the attention mechanism. To address this, we introduce mini-batching to our training loop.

4.4.1   Neighborhood loader and GAT models

From an implementation point of view, one key difference between the previously studied convolutional models and our GAT models is the much larger memory requirements of GAT models [9]. The reason for this is that GAT requires a calculation of attention scores for every attention head and for every edge. This in turn requires the PyTorch `autograd` method to hold tensors in memory that can scale up considerably, depending on the number of edges, heads, and (twice) the number of node features.

To get around this problem, we can divide our graph into batches and load these batches into the training loop. This is in contrast to what we did with our GCN model where we trained on one single batch (the entire graph). PyG's `NeighborLoader` (in its `dataloader` module) allows such mini-batch training, where we provide implementation code for this in listing 4.6. (PyG function `NeighborLoader` is based on the "Inductive Representation Learning on Large Graphs" paper [10].) The key input parameters for `NeighborLoader` are

- `num_neighbors`—How many neighbor nodes will be sampled, multiplied by the number of iterations (i.e., GNN layers). In our example, we specify 1,000 nodes over two iterations.
- `batch_size`—The number of nodes selected for each batch. In our example, we set the batch size to be `128`.

Listing 4.6   Setting up `NeighborLoader` for GAT

```
from torch_geometric.loader import NeighborLoader

batch_size = 128
loader = NeighborLoader(
    data,
    num_neighbors=[1000]*2,        # Samples 1,000 neighbors for each node in two iterations
    batch_size=batch_size,
    input_nodes=data.train_mask)   # Uses a batch size for sampling training nodes

sampled_data = next(iter(loader))
print(f'Checking that batch size is \
{batch_size}: {batch_size == \
sampled_data.batch_size}')
print(f'Percentage fraud in batch: \
{100*sampled_data.y.sum()/\
len(sampled_data.y):.4f}%')
sampled_data
```

In creating our GAT model, there are two key changes to make relative to our GCN class. First, because we're training in batches, we want to apply a batch-norm layer.

Batch normalization is a technique used to normalize the inputs of each layer in a neural network to have a mean of 0 and a standard deviation of 1. This helps stabilize and accelerate the training process by reducing internal covariate shift, allowing the use of higher learning rates, and improving the overall performance of the model.

Second, we note that our GAT layers have an additional input parameter—heads—which is the number of multihead attentions. In our example, our first GATConv layer has two heads, as specified in listing 4.7.

The second GATConv layer, which is the output layer, has one head. In this GAT model, because we want the final layer to have a single representation for each node for our task, we use one head. Multiple heads would result in a confusing output with multiple node representations.

Listing 4.7   GAT-based architecture

GAT layers have a heads parameter, which determines the number of attention mechanisms in each layer. In this implementation, the first layer (conv1) uses multiple heads for richer feature extraction, while the final output layer (conv2) uses a single head to aggregate the learned information into a # single output for each node.

```python
class GAT(torch.nn.Module):
    def __init__(self, hidden_layers=32, heads=1, dropout_p=0.0):
        super().__init__()
        torch.manual_seed(2022)
        self.conv1 = GATConv(data.num_node_features,\
 hidden_layers, heads, dropout=dropout_p)
        self.bn1 = nn.BatchNorm1d(hidden_layers*heads)
        self.conv2 = GATConv(hidden_layers * heads, \
1, dropout=dropout_p)

    def forward(self, data, dropout_p=0.0):
        x, edge_index = data.x, data.edge_index
        x = self.conv1(x, edge_index)
        x = self.bn1(x)
        x = F.relu(x)
        x = F.dropout(x, training=self.training)
        x = self.conv2(x, edge_index)

        return torch.sigmoid(x)
```

Because mini-batch training is being performed, a batch-norm layer is added.

Our training routine for GAT is similar to the single-batch GCN, which we provide in the following listing, except that we now need a nested loop for each batch.

Listing 4.8   Training loop for GAT

```python
lr = 0.01
epochs = 1000

model = GAT(hidden_layers = 64,heads=2)
model.to(device)
```

```
optimizer = torch.optim.Adam(model.parameters(), lr=lr,weight_decay=5e-4)
criterion = torch.nn.BCELoss()

losses = []
for e in range(epochs):                                    ┌── Nested loop for mini-
    epoch_loss = 0.                                        │   batch training. Each
    for i, sampled_data in enumerate(loader):    ◄─────────┤   iteration here is a batch
        sampled_data.to(device)                           │   of nodes loaded by
        model.train()                                     │   NeighborLoader.
        optimizer.zero_grad()
        out = model(sampled_data)
        loss = criterion(out[sampled_data.train_mask],\
sampled_data.y[sampled_data.train_mask].\
reshape(-1,1).float())
loss.backward()
epoch_loss += loss.item()

        optimizer.step()

        ypred = model(sampled_data).clone().cpu()
        pred = sampled_data.y[sampled_data.test_mask]\
.clone().cpu().detach().numpy()
        true = ypred[sampled_data.test_mask].detach().numpy()
        acc = roc_auc_score(pred,true)
    losses.append(epoch_loss/batch_size)

    print(f'Epoch {e} | Loss {epoch_loss:6.2f}\
    | Accuracy = {100*acc:6.3f}% |
    # True Labels = {ypred.round().sum()}')
```

The steps outlined previously are the same for GATv2Conv, which can be found in our repository. Training GATConv and GATv2Conv yields accuracies of 95.65% and 95.10%, respectively. As shown in table 4.8, our GAT models outperform the baseline models and GCN. Figure 4.9 shows the ROC results of the GCN and GAT models. Figure 4.10 shows the ROC results of the GCN, GAT, and GATv2 models.

Table 4.8 ROC AUC of the models

Model	ROC AUC (%)
Logistic regression	75.90
XGBoost	94.17
Multilayer perceptron	85.93
GCN	94.37
GAT	95.65
GATv2	95.10

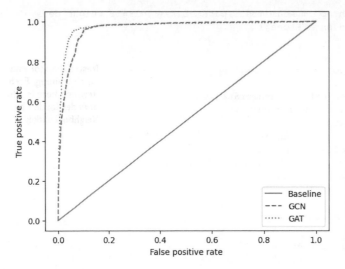

Figure 4.9   ROC curves for GCN and GATConv. The GATConv model shows the best performance for this metric because it has a higher AUC and because its false positive rate is markedly lower. The diagonal line is the chance line.

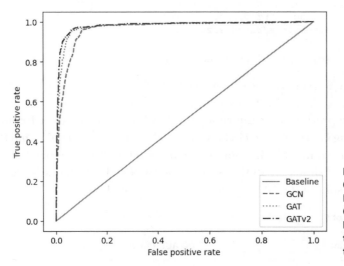

Figure 4.10   ROC curves for GCN, GATConv, and GATv2. Both GAT models outperform GCN. GATv2 has the same higher false positive profile than GAT but has a similar true positive rate.

When observing the ROC curves, we see that both GAT models outperform the GCN. We also see that both have better false positive rates. This is crucial for fraud/spam detection as false positives can lead to genuine transactions/users being incorrectly flagged, causing inconvenience and loss of trust. For GATv2, we notice that for true positive rates, its performance is the same as for GCN and GAT. This indicates that while it's conservative in not mislabeling genuine transactions as fraudulent, it might miss some actual frauds. These insights can lead to paths to refine the models or to decision-making about which to use. Despite the favorable AUC curves and scores, we must address one final problem that affects the usability of our GAT models: class imbalance.

4.4.2   *Addressing class imbalance in model performance*

Class imbalance is a critical challenge in GNN problems, where the minority class, often representing rare but important instances (e.g., fraudulent activities), is significantly underrepresented compared to the majority class. In our dataset, only 14.5% of the nodes are labeled as fraudulent, making it challenging for the model to effectively learn from this sparse data. While high AUC scores may suggest good overall performance, they can be misleading, masking poor performance on the minority class that is crucial for a balanced evaluation. A deeper analysis reveals a critical oversight: class imbalance significantly undermines our precision and F1 scores.

In response to this challenge, several methods have been developed specifically for GNNs to address class imbalance. Traditional techniques such as the Synthetic Minority Over-sampling Technique (SMOTE) have been adapted to create graph-specific methods such as GraphSMOTE, which generates synthetic nodes and edges to balance the class distribution without disrupting the graph structure. Other approaches include resampling techniques (both over-sampling and under-sampling), cost-sensitive learning, architectural modifications, and attention mechanisms that focus on minority class features [11, 12].

While these methods help improve model performance, they come with unique challenges, such as preserving the graph's topology, maintaining node dependencies, and ensuring scalability. Recent advancements, such as Graph-of-Graph Neural Networks (G2GNN), have been developed to handle these problems more effectively. By understanding and applying these strategies, we can enhance the robustness and fairness of GNN models in real-world applications where class imbalance is a common problem. Taking the GATv2 model from the previous section as the illustration, we compare its F1, recall, and precision with that of XGBoost in table 4.9. XGBoost has superior performance, while GATv2 struggles to handle the imbalanced data.

Table 4.9   Comparing F1, recall, and precision between the GATv2 and XGBoost models trained in this chapter

Metric	GATv2	XGBoost
F1 score	0.254	0.734
Precision	0.145	0.855
Recall	1	0.643

The GATv2 model's performance reflects a common challenge faced in scenarios with significant class imbalances. With the minority class constituting only 14.5% of the data, the model emphasizes maximizing recall, achieving a perfect recall score of 1.000. This suggests that the model correctly identifies every instance of the minority class, avoiding any missed detections of potentially crucial cases. However, this comes at a significant cost to precision, which is notably low at 0.145. This indicates that while the GAT is effective in detecting all true positives, it also misclassifies many negative cases as positive, leading to a high number of false positives. As a result, the F1 score, which reflects both precision and recall, is low at 0.254, highlighting the inefficiency of the model in balancing detection with accuracy.

To alleviate this, we implemented two strategies aimed at mitigating class imbalance: SMOTE illustrated in figure 4.11 and a custom reshuffling approach shown in figure 4.12.

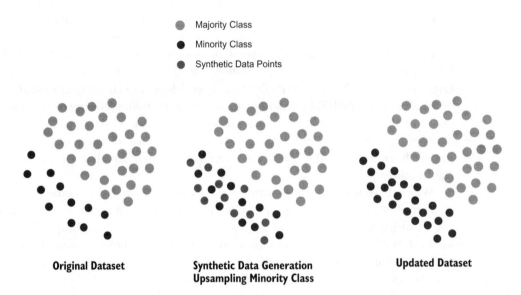

Figure 4.11   An illustration of SMOTE, which seeks to provide a more balanced dataset by upsampling the minority class. On the left, we begin with the original dataset. In the middle, SMOTE creates synthetic data in the minority class. On the right, with the synthetic data added to the minority class, the dataset is more balanced.

SMOTE was used to generate synthetic nodes, reflecting the average degree characteristics of the original dataset, and to artificially enhance the representation of minority classes. The reshuffling method took a different approach by avoiding the generation of synthetic data. Instead, it ensures a balanced class representation in each training batch by redistributing the majority class data across the batches. This is achieved using the `BalancedNodeSampler` class, which guarantees that each batch has an equal number of nodes from both the majority and minority classes. For each batch, the sampler randomly selects a balanced set of nodes, extracts the corresponding subgraph, and re-indexes the nodes to maintain consistency. A typical batch redistribution from this process is illustrated in figure 4.12. This class is shown in listing 4.9.

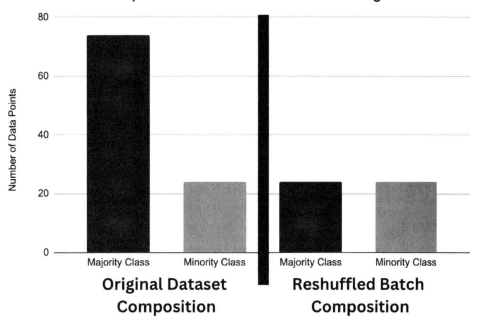

Figure 4.12   Illustration of the reshuffling method using an example of 100 data points, with 76 in the majority class and 24 in the minority class. When creating batches for training, each batch is made to contain equal portions of the majority and minority classes.

Listing 4.9   `BalancedNodeSampler` class

```
class BalancedNodeSampler(BaseSampler):
    def __init__(self, data, num_samples=None):
        super().__init__()
        self.data = data
        self.num_samples = num_samples

    def sample_from_nodes(self, index, **kwargs):
        majority_indices = torch.\
where(self.data.y == 0)[0]
        minority_indices = torch.\
where(self.data.y == 1)[0]

        if self.num_samples is None:
            batch_size = min(len(majority_indices),\
 len(minority_indices))
        else:
            batch_size = self.num_samples // 2

        majority_sample = majority_indices[torch.randperm\
(len(majority_indices))[:batch_size]]
        minority_sample = minority_indices[torch.randint\
(len(minority_indices), (batch_size,))]
```

Optional: defines fixed sampling size per class

Indices for the majority class

Indices for the minority class

Determines balanced batch size

Randomly selects nodes for both classes

```
        batch_indices = torch.cat\
((majority_sample, minority_sample))
```
Combines samples from both classes into a single batch

```
        mask = torch.zeros(self.data.num_nodes, dtype=torch.bool)
        mask[batch_indices] = True
        row, col = self.data.edge_index
        mask_edges = mask[row] & mask[col]
        sub_row = row[mask_edges]
        sub_col = col[mask_edges]
```
Creates a mask for sampled nodes

Filters edges between sampled nodes

```
        new_index = torch.full((self.data.num_nodes,), -1, dtype=torch.long)
        new_index[batch_indices] = \
torch.arange(batch_indices.size(0))
        sub_row = new_index[sub_row]
        sub_col = new_index[sub_col]
```
Re-indexes sampled nodes

```
        return SamplerOutput(
            node=batch_indices,
            row=sub_row,
            col=sub_col,
            edge=None,
            num_sampled_nodes=[len(batch_indices)],
            metadata=(batch_indices, None)
        )
```

In this case, SMOTE didn't yield performance improvement. Therefore, we'll focus on the results of applying the reshuffling method. The metrics in table 4.10 demonstrate that our interventions have not only improved the fairness of the models but also enhanced their robustness by better capturing the minority class without sacrificing overall accuracy. While the reshuffling method's AUC doesn't exceed XGBoost (94.17%), it handles the class imbalance well with superior F1, precision, and recall.

Table 4.10   Comparing F1, precision, recall, and AUC of the GATv2 model trained with a class reshuffling method

Metric	Value
Mean validation F1 score	0.809
Mean validation precision	0.878
Mean validation recall	0.781
Mean validation AUC	0.914

4.4.3   *Deciding between GAT and XGBoost*

The choice between using XGBoost and GATs should be informed by specific use-case requirements and constraints. XGBoost offers efficiency and speed, which are advantageous for projects with limited computational resources or when quick model training is required. However, GATs provide the added benefit of deeply integrating node relational data, which is essential for projects where internode relationships are pivotal to understanding complex data patterns.

GATs are particularly valuable for their ability to be integrated into broader deep learning frameworks, offering enhanced node embeddings that encapsulate rich contextual information, thus making them suitable for complex relational datasets.

Our exploration into methods for addressing class imbalance has significantly informed our understanding of model performance in real-world scenarios. These insights are crucial for the effective development of robust and effective models, especially in fields where precision and recall are critically balanced. In the next, optional section, we go deeper into the concepts underlying GATs.

4.5 Under the hood

In this section, we discuss some of the additional details about attention and GATs. This is provided for those who want to know what's going on under the hood, but you can safely skip this section if you're more interested in learning how to apply the models. We dive into the equations from the GAT paper [8] and explain attention from a more intuitive perspective.

4.5.1 Explaining attention and GAT models

In this section, we provide a foundational overview of attention mechanisms. Attention, self-attention, and multihead attention are explained conceptually. Then, GATs are positioned as an extension of convolutional GNNs.

CONCEPT 1: THE VARIOUS ATTENTION MECHANISM TYPES

Attention is one of the most important concepts introduced into deep learning in the past decade. It's the basis for the, now famous, transformer model that powers many of the breakthroughs in generative models such as large language models (LLMs). Attention is the mechanism by which a model can learn what aspects in its training to put extra emphasis on [13, 14]. What are the various types of attention in a model?

ATTENTION

Imagine you're reading a novel where the storyline isn't linear but rather jumps around, connecting various characters, events, or even parallel storylines. While reading a chapter about a specific character, you remember and consider other parts of the book where this character has appeared or been mentioned. Your understanding of this character at any given moment is influenced by these different parts of the book.

In deep learning and GNNs, attention serves a similar purpose. When processing a sentence in an NLP problem, attention means the model can learn the importance of neighboring words. For a GNN considering a specific node in a graph, the model uses attention to weigh the importance of neighboring nodes. This helps the model decide which neighboring nodes are most relevant when trying to understand the current node, similar to how you remember relevant parts of the book to better understand a character.

SELF-ATTENTION

Imagine reading a sentence in the novel that refers to multiple characters and events, some of which are related in complex ways. To understand this sentence fully, you have to recall how each character and event relate to each other, all within the scope of that sentence. You might find yourself focusing more on certain characters or events that are crucial to understanding the context of the sentence you're currently reading.

For a GNN using self-attention, each node in a graph not only considers its immediate neighbors but also takes into account its own features and position in the graph. By doing this, each node receives a new representation influenced by a weighted context of itself and other nodes, which helps in tasks that require understanding the relationships between nodes in a complex graph.

MULTIHEAD ATTENTION

Suppose you're a member of a book club that is reading the novel, and each member of your club is asked to focus on different aspects of the novel—one on character development, another on plot twists, and yet another on thematic elements. When you all come together to discuss, you get a multifaceted understanding of the book.

Similarly, in GNNs, multihead attention allows the model to have multiple "heads," or attention mechanisms, focusing on various aspects or features of the neighboring nodes. These different heads can learn different patterns or relationships within the graph, and their outputs are usually aggregated to form a more complete understanding of each node's role within the larger graph.

CONCEPT 2: GATS AS VARIANTS OF CONVOLUTIONAL GNNS

GATs extend convolutional GNNs by incorporating attention mechanisms. In traditional convolutional GNNs such as GCNs, the contributions from all neighbors during the message-passing step are equally weighted when aggregated. GATs, however, add in attention scores to the aggregation function to weigh these contributions. This is still permutation invariant (by design) but more descriptive than the summation operation in GCNs.

PyG IMPLEMENTATIONS

PyG offers two versions of GAT layers. The two are distinguished by the types of attention used and the calculation of attention scores:

- GATConv—Based on Veličković's paper [1], this layer uses self-attention to calculate attention scores across the entire graph. It can also be configured to use multihead attention, thereby employing multiple "heads" to focus on various aspects of the input nodes.
- GATv2Conv—This layer improves upon GATConv by introducing *dynamic attention*. Here, self-attention scores are recalculated in a node-specific context across

layers, making the model more expressive in how it learns to weigh node representations constructed during the message-passing step within each layer of a GNN. As with `GATConv`, it supports multihead attention to capture various features or aspects more effectively.

TRADEOFFS VS. OTHER CONVOLUTIONAL GNNS

As implemented in PyG, GAT layers have advantages due to the use of attention. There are performance tradeoffs to consider, however. Key factors to consider are:

- *Performance*—GATs generally have higher performance than standard convolutional GNNs as they can focus on the most relevant features.
- *Training time*—Increased performance comes at the cost of more time required to train the models due to the added complexity of computing the attention mechanisms.
- *Scalability*—The computational cost also affects the scalability, making GATs less suitable for very large or dense graphs.

4.5.2 Over-smoothing

You've learned how to change the aggregation operation used in the message-passing step to include more complicated methods, such as attention mechanisms. However, there is always a risk of performance degradation when applying multiple rounds of message passing. This effect, known as *over-smoothing*, occurs because, after multiple rounds of message passing [15], the updated features can converge to similar values. An example of this is shown in figure 4.13.

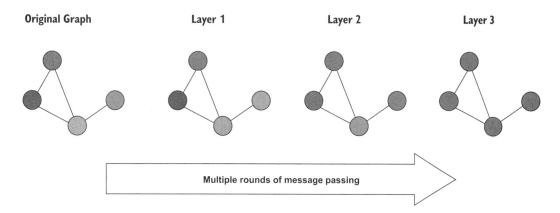

Figure 4.13 Example of over-smoothing based on changing node features

As we know, message passing occurs at each layer of a GNN. In fact, a GNN that has many layers is more at risk of over-smoothing than one that has fewer layers. This is one of the reasons why GNNs are typically more shallow than traditional deep learning models.

Another cause of over-smoothing happens when a problem has a significant long-range (in terms of number of hops) task that needs solving. For example, a node could be influenced by a far-off node. This is also known as having a large "problem radius." Whenever we have a graph where nodes can have a very large effect on other nodes despite being multiple hops away, then the problem radius should be considered large. For example, social media networks might have a large problem radius if certain individuals such as celebrities can influence other individuals despite being distantly connected. Usually, this occurs when a graph is sufficiently large to have distantly connected nodes.

In general, if you think a problem may be at risk of over-smoothing, be careful with how many layers you introduce to the GNN, that is, how deep you make it. However, note that certain architectures appear less at risk of over-smoothing than others. For example, GraphSAGE samples a fixed number of neighbors and aggregates their information. This sampling can mitigate over-smoothing. On the other hand, GCNs are more at risk because they don't have this sampling process, and while the attention mechanism partially lowers the risk, GATs can also suffer from over-smoothing because the aggregation is still local.

4.5.3   *Overview of key GAT equations*

In this section, we'll briefly cover the key equations given in the GAT paper by Veličković et al. [1] and tie them to the concepts we've covered about GATs. GATs use attention mechanisms to learn which neighboring nodes are more important when updating a node's features. They do this by computing attention scores (equations 1–3), which are then used to weigh and combine the features of neighboring nodes (equations 4–6). The use of multihead attention enhances the model's expressiveness and robustness, allowing it to learn from multiple perspectives simultaneously. This approach can be computationally expensive, but it generally improves the performance of GNNs on various tasks such as node classification and link prediction.

ATTENTION COEFFICIENTS CALCULATION (EQUATIONS 4.1–4.3)

The first step in using GATs is to compute the attention scores or coefficients for each pair of connected nodes. These coefficients indicate how much "attention" or importance a node should give to its neighbor. Raw attention scores [1] are calculated as

$$e_{ij} = a(\mathbf{W}\mathbf{h}_i, \mathbf{W}\mathbf{h}_j) \qquad\qquad (4.1)$$

Here, e_{ij} represents the raw attention score from node iii to its neighbor j:

- $\mathbf{h}_i$ and $\mathbf{h}_j$ are the feature vectors (representations) of nodes i and j.
- $\mathbf{W}$ is a learnable weight matrix that linearly transforms the features of each node to a higher dimensional space.
- α is an attention mechanism (usually a neural network) that computes the importance score for each node pair.

The idea is to assess how much information node i should consider from node j. Normalized attention coefficients [1] are calculated as

$$\alpha_{ij} = \text{softmax}_j(e_{ij} = \frac{\exp(e_{ij})}{\sum_{k \in \mathcal{N}_i} \exp(e_{ik})}$$ (4.2)

Once we have raw scores e_{ij}, we normalize them using a softmax function:

- α_{ij} represents the normalized attention coefficient that quantifies the importance of node j's features to node i.
- The softmax ensures that all attention coefficients for a given node iii sum up to 1, making them comparable across different nodes.

Following is a detailed computation of attention coefficients [1]:

$$\alpha_{ij} = \frac{\exp(\text{LeakyReLU}(\mathbf{a}^T[\mathbf{Wh}_i \| \mathbf{Wh}_j]))}{\sum_{k \in \mathcal{N}_i} \exp(\text{LeakyReLU}(\mathbf{a}^T[\mathbf{Wh}_i \| \mathbf{Wh}_k]))}$$ (4.3)

Here, the attention mechanism α is implemented using a single-layer feed-forward neural network with parameters $\mathbf{a}$. The term $\mathbf{a}^T[\mathbf{Wh}_i \| \mathbf{Wh}_j]$ involves concatenating the transformed feature vectors of nodes i and j, and then applying a linear transformation followed by a nonlinear activation (leaky rectified linear unit [leaky ReLU]).

NODE REPRESENTATION UPDATE (EQUATIONS 4.4–4.6)

After computing the attention coefficients, the next step is to use them to aggregate information from the neighbors and update the node representations with attention [1]:

$$\mathbf{h}' = \sigma\left(\sum_{j \in \mathcal{N}_i} \alpha_{ij}\mathbf{Wh}_j\right)$$ (4.4)

This equation computes the new representation $\mathbf{h}_i'$ for node i:

- The term $\sum_{j \in \mathcal{N}_i} \alpha_{ij}\mathbf{Wh}_j$ represents a weighted sum of the neighboring node features, where each feature vector is weighted by its corresponding attention coefficient α_{ij}.
- σ is a nonlinear activation function (like ReLU or sigmoid) that introduces nonlinearity into the model, helping it learn complex patterns.

The multihead attention mechanism [1] is calculated as

$$\mathbf{h}' = \|_{k=1}^{K} \sigma\left(\sum_{j \in \mathcal{N}_i} \alpha_{ij}^k \mathbf{W}^k \mathbf{h}_j\right)$$ (4.5)

To stabilize the learning process, GATs use multihead attention, as discussed earlier:

- Here, K attention heads independently compute different sets of attention coefficients and corresponding weighted sums.
- The results from all heads are concatenated to form a richer, more expressive node representation.

The following shows averaging for multihead attention in the final layer [1]:

$$\mathbf{h}' = \sigma\left(\frac{1}{K}\sum_{k=1}^{K}\sum_{j\in N_i}\alpha_{ij}^k\mathbf{W}^k\mathbf{h}_j\right) \qquad (4.6)$$

In the final prediction layer of the network, instead of concatenating the outputs from different heads, we take their average. This reduces the dimensionality of the final output and simplifies the model's prediction process.

Summary

- A graph attention network (GAT) is a specialized type of graph neural network (GNN) that incorporates attention mechanisms to focus on the most relevant nodes during the learning process.
- GATs excel in domains where certain nodes have disproportionate importance, such as social networks, fraud detection, and anomaly detection.
- The chapter uses a dataset derived from Yelp reviews, focusing on detecting fake reviews for hotels and restaurants in Chicago. Reviews are represented as nodes, with edges representing shared characteristics (e.g., common authors or businesses).
- GATs were applied to this dataset to classify nodes (reviews) as fraudulent or legitimate. The GAT models showed improvements over baseline models such as logistic regression, XGBoost, and graph convolutional networks (GCNs).
- GATs are memory-intensive due to their need to compute attention scores for all edges. To handle this, mini-batching with the `NeighborLoader` class in PyTorch Geometric (PyG) was used.
- The GAT layers in PyG, such as `GATConv` and `GATv2Conv`, apply different types of attention to graph learning problems.
- Strategies such as SMOTE and class reshuffling can be employed to address class imbalance. For our case, class reshuffling significantly improved model performance.

Graph autoencoders 5

This chapter covers

- Distinguishing between discriminative and generative models
- Applying autoencoders and variational autoencoders to graphs
- Building graph autoencoders with PyTorch Geometric
- Over-squashing and graph neural networks
- Link prediction and graph generation

So far, we've covered how classical deep learning architectures can be extended to work on graph-structured data. In chapter 3, we considered convolutional graph neural networks (GNNs), which apply the convolutional operator to identify patterns within the data. In chapter 4, we explored the attention mechanism and how this can be used to improve performance for graph-learning tasks such as node classification.

Both convolutional GNNs and attention GNNs are examples of *discriminative models*, as they learn to discriminate between different instances of data, such as whether a photo is of a cat or a dog. In this chapter, we introduce the topic of *generative models* and explore them through two of the most common architectures, autoencoders and variational autoencoders (VAEs). Generative models aim to learn the entire dataspace rather than separating boundaries *within* the dataspace, as do discriminative models. For example, a generative model learns how to generate images of cats and dogs (learning to reproduce aspects of a cat or dog, rather than learning just the features that separates two or more classes, such as the pointed ears of a cat or the long ears of a spaniel).

As we'll discover, discriminative models learn to separate boundaries in dataspace, whereas generative models learn to model the dataspace itself. By approximating the dataspace, we can sample from a generative model to create new examples of our training data. In the preceding example, we can use our generative model to make new images of a cat or dog, or even some hybrid version that has features of both. This is a very powerful tool and important knowledge for both beginner and established data scientists. In recent years, deep generative models, generative models that use artificial neural networks, have shown amazing ability in many language and vision tasks. For example, the family of DALL-E models are able to generate new images from text prompts while models such as OpenAI's GPT models have dramatically changed the capabilities of chatbots.

In this chapter, you'll learn how to extend generative architectures to act on graph-structured data, leading to graph autoencoders (GAEs) and variational graph autoencoders (VGAEs). These models are distinct from previous chapters, which focused on discriminative models. As we'll see, generative models model the entire dataspace and can be combined with discriminative models for downstream machine learning tasks.

To demonstrate the power of generative approaches to learning tasks, we return to the Amazon Product Co-Purchaser Network introduced in chapter 3. However, in chapter 3, you learned how to predict what category an item might belong to given its position in the network. In this chapter, we'll show how to predict where an item should be placed in the network, given its description. This is known as *edge* (or link) *prediction* and comes up frequently, for example, when designing recommendation systems. We'll put our understanding of GAEs to work here to perform edge prediction, building a model that can predict when nodes in a graph are connected. We'll also discuss the problems of over-squashing, a specific consideration for GNNs, and how we can apply a GNN to generate potential chemical graphs.

By the end of this chapter, you should know the basics of when and where to use generative models of graphs (rather than discriminative ones) and how to implement them when we need to.

> **NOTE** Code from this chapter can be found in notebook form at the GitHub repository (https://mng.bz/4aGQ). Colab links and data from this chapter can be accessed in the same location.

5.1 Generative models: Learning how to generate

A classic example of deep learning is, given a set of labeled images, how to train models to *learn* what label to give to new and unseen images. If we consider the example of a set of images of boats and airplanes, we want our model to distinguish between these different images. If we then pass the model a new image, we want our model to correctly identify this as, for example, a boat. Discriminative models learn to discriminate between classes based on their specific target labels. Both convolutional architectures (discussed in chapter 3) and attention-based architectures (covered in chapter 4) are typically used to create discriminative models. However, as we'll see, they can also be incorporated into generative models. To understand this, we first have to understand the difference between discriminative and generative modeling approaches.

5.1.1 Generative and discriminative models

As described in previous chapters, the original dataset that we use to train a model is referred to as our *training data*, and the labels that we seek to predict are our *training targets*. The unseen data is our *test data*, and we want to learn the *target labels* (from training) to classify the test data. Another way to describe this is using conditional probability. We want our models to return the probability of some target, Y, given an instance of data, X. We can write this as $P(Y|X)$, where the vertical bar means that Y is "conditioned" on X.

As we've said, discriminative models learn to discriminate *between* classes. This is equivalent to learning the separating boundaries of the data in the dataspace. In contrast, generative models learn to model the dataspace itself. They capture the entire distribution of data in the dataspace, and, when presented with a new example, they tell us how likely the new example is. Using the language of probability, we say that they model the *joint probability* between data and targets, $P(X,Y)$. A typical example of a generative model might be a model that is used to predict the next word in a sentence (e.g., the autocomplete feature in many modern mobile phones). The generative model assigns a probability to each possible next word and returns those words that have the highest probability. Discriminative models can tell you how likely a word has some specific sentiment, while a generative model will suggest a word to use.

Returning to our image example, a generative model approximates the overall distribution of images. This can be seen in figure 5.1, where the generative model has learned where the points are positioned in the dataspace (rather than how they are separated). This means that generative models must learn more complicated correlations in the data than their discriminative counterparts. For example, a generative model learns that "airplanes have wings" and "boats appear near water." On the other hand, discriminative models just have to learn the difference between "boat" and "not boat." They can do this by looking for telltale signs such as a mast, keel, or boom in the image. They can then largely ignore the rest of the image. As a result, generative models can be more computationally expensive to train and can require larger network architectures. (In section 5.5, we'll describe over-squashing, which is a particular problem for large GNNs.)

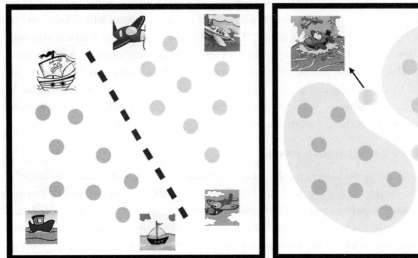
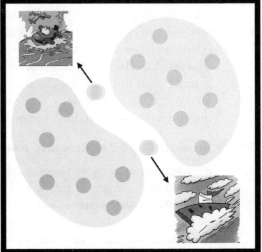

Figure 5.1   Comparison of generative and discriminative tasks. On the left, the discriminative model learns to separate different images of boats and airplanes. On the right, the generative model attempts to learn the entire dataspace, which allows for new synthetic examples to be created such as a boat in the sky or an airplane on water.

5.1.2   Synthetic data

Given that discriminative models are computationally cheaper to train and more robust to outliers than generative models, you might wonder why we want to use a generative model at all. Generative models, however, are efficient tools when labeling data is relatively expensive but generating datasets is easy to do. For example, generative models are increasingly being used in drug discovery where they generate new candidate drugs that might match certain properties, such as the ability to reduce the effects of some disease. In a sense, generative models attempt to learn how to create synthetic data, which allows us to create new data instances. For example, none of the people shown in figure 5.2 exist and were instead created by sampling from the dataspace, approximated using a generative model.

Synthetic examples created by generative models can be used to augment a dataset, which is expensive to collect. Rather than taking lots of pictures of faces under every condition, we can use generative models to create new data examples (e.g., a person wearing a hat, glasses, and a mask) to increase our dataset to contain tricky edge cases. These synthetic examples can then be used to further improve our other models (e.g., one that identifies when someone is wearing a mask). However, when

Figure 5.2   Figure showing synthetic faces (Source: [1])

introducing synthetic data, we must also be careful about introducing other biases or noise into our dataset.

In addition, discriminative models are often used downstream of generative models. This is because generative models are typically trained in a "self-supervised" way, without relying on data labels. They learn to compress (or *encode*) complex high-dimensional data to lower dimensions. These low-dimensional representations can be used to better tease out underlying patterns within our data. This is known as *dimension reduction* and can be helpful in clustering data or in classification tasks. Later, we'll see how generative models can separate graphs into different classes without ever seeing their labels. In cases where annotating each data point is expensive, generative models can be huge cost savers. Let's get on to meeting our first generative GNN model.

5.2   Graph autoencoders for link prediction

One of the fundamental and popular models for deep generative models is the autoencoder. The reason the autoencoder framework is so widely used is because it's incredibly adaptive. Just as the attention mechanisms in chapter 3 can be used to improve on many different models, autoencoders can be combined with many different models, including different types of GNNs. Once the autoencoder structure is understood, the encoder and decoder can be replaced with any type of neural network, including different GNNs such as the graph convolutional network (GCN) and GraphSAGE architectures from chapter 2.

However, we need to take care when applying autoencoders to graph-based data. When reconstructing our data, we also have to reconstruct our adjacency matrix. In this section, we'll look at implementing a GAE using the Amazon Products dataset from chapter 3 [2]. We'll build a GAE for the task of link prediction, which is a common problem when working with graphs. This allows us to reconstruct the adjacency matrix and is especially useful when we're dealing with a dataset that has missing data. We'll follow this process:

1. Define the model:
   a. Create both an encoder and decoder.
   b. Use the encoder to create a latent space to sample from.
2. Define the training and testing loop by including a loss suitable for constructing a generative model.
3. Prepare the data as a graph, with edge lists and node features.
4. Train the model, passing the edge data to compute the loss.
5. Test the model using the test dataset.

5.2.1   *Review of the Amazon Products dataset from chapter 3*

In chapter 3, we learned about the Amazon Products dataset with co-purchaser information. This dataset contains information about a range of different items that were purchased, details about who purchased them and how, and categories for the items, which were the labels in chapter 3. We've already learned about how we can turn this tabular dataset into a graph structure and, by doing so, make our learning algorithms more efficient and more powerful. We've also already used some dimension reduction without realizing it. Principal component analysis (PCA) was applied to the Amazon Products dataset to create the features. Each product description was converted into numerical values using the bag-of-words algorithm, and PCA is then applied to reduce the (now numerical) description to 100 features.

In this chapter, we're going to revisit the Amazon Products dataset but with a different aim in mind. We're going to use our dataset to learn link predictions. Essentially, this means learning the *relations between* nodes in our graph. This has many use cases, such as predicting what movies or TV shows users would like to watch next, suggesting new connections on social media platforms, or even predicting customers who are more likely to default on credit. Here, we're going to use it to predict which products in the Amazon Electronics dataset should be connected together, as we show in figure 5.3. For further details about link prediction, check out section 5.5 at the end of this chapter.

As with all data science projects, it's worth first taking a look at the dataset and understanding what the problem is. We start by loading the data, the same way as we did in chapter 3, which we show in listing 5.1. The data is preprocessed and labeled so it can be loaded using NumPy. Further details on the dataset can be found in [2].

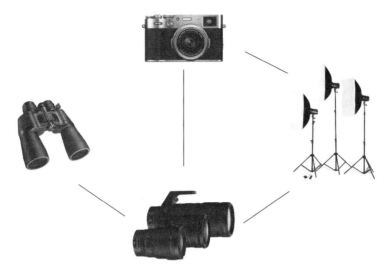

Figure 5.3 The Amazon Electronics dataset, where different products such as cameras and lenses are connected based on whether they have been bought together in the past

Listing 5.1 Loading the data

```
import numpy as np

filename = 'data/new_AMZN_electronics.npz'

data = np.load(filename)

loader = dict(data)
print(loader)
```

The preceding output prints the following:

```
{'adj_data': array([[0., 0., 0., ..., 0., 0., 0.],
       [0., 0., 0., ..., 0., 0., 0.],
       [0., 0., 0., ..., 0., 0., 0.],
       ...,
       [0., 0., 0., ..., 0., 0., 0.],
       [0., 0., 0., ..., 0., 0., 0.]], \
 dtype=float32), 'attr_data': \
array([[0., 0., 0., ..., 0., 1., 0.],
       [0., 0., 0., ..., 0., 0., 0.],
       ...,
       [0., 1., 0., ..., 0., 0., 0.],
       [1., 1., 0., ..., 0., 0., 0.],
       [0., 0., 0., ..., 0., 0., 1.]], \
 dtype=float32), 'labels': \
array([6, 4, 3, ..., 1, 2, 3]), \
```

```
'class_names': array(['Film Photography',\
'Digital Cameras', 'Binoculars & Scopes',
        'Lenses', 'Tripods & Monopods', 'Video Surveillance',
        'Lighting & Studio', 'Flashes'], dtype='<U19')}
```

With the data loaded, we can next look at some basic statistics and details of the data. We're interested in edge or link prediction, so it's worth understanding how many different edges exist. We might also want to know how many components there are and the average degree to understand how connected our graph is. We show the code to calculate this in the following listing.

Listing 5.2   Exploratory data analysis

```
adj_matrix = torch.tensor(loader['adj_data'])
if not adj_matrix.is_sparse:
    adj_matrix = adj_matrix.to_sparse()

feature_matrix = torch.tensor(loader['attr_data'])
labels = loader['labels']

class_names = loader.get('class_names')
metadata = loader.get('metadata')

num_nodes = adj_matrix.size(0)
num_edges = adj_matrix.coalesce().values().size(0)    ⟵    This is only possible
density = num_edges / (num_nodes \                           because the adjacency
* (num_nodes - 1) / 2) if num_nodes \                        matrix is undirected.
> 1 else 0                              ⟵    Ratio of actual edges
                                             to possible edges
```

We also plot the distribution of the degree to see how connections vary, as shown in the following listing and in figure 5.4.

Listing 5.3   Plotting the graph

```
degrees = adj_matrix.coalesce().indices().numpy()[0]    ⟵    Gets row indices
degree_count = np.bincount(degrees, minlength=num_nodes)      for each nonzero
                                                              value
plt.figure(figsize=(10, 5))
plt.hist(degree_count, bins=25, alpha=0.75, color='blue')
plt.xlabel('Degree')
plt.ylabel('Frequency')
plt.grid(True)
plt.show()
```

We find that there are 7,650 nodes, more than 143,000 edges, and an overall density of 0.0049. Therefore, our graph is medium size (~10,000 nodes) but very sparse (density much less than 0.05). We see that the majority of nodes have a low degree (less than 10), but that there is a second peak of edges with a higher degree (around 30) and a longer tail. In total, we see very few nodes with a high degree, which we would expect given the low density of the graph.

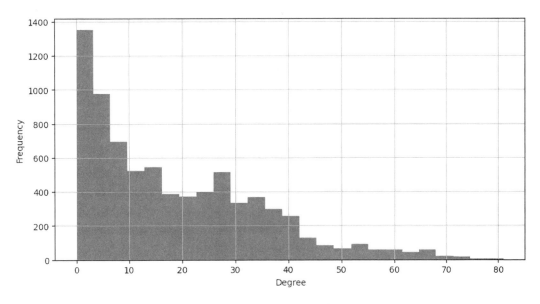

Figure 5.4   Degree distribution for the Amazon Electronics co-purchaser graph

5.2.2   Defining a graph autoencoder

Next, we'll use a generative model, the autoencoder, to estimate and predict links in the Amazon Electronics dataset. In doing so, we're in good company, as link prediction was the problem that GAEs were applied to when first published by Kipf and Welling in 2012 [3]. In their seminal paper, they introduced the GAE and its variational extension, which we'll be discussing shortly, and then applied these models to three classic benchmarks in graph deep learning, the Cora dataset, CiteSeer, and PubMed. Today, most graph deep learning libraries make it very easy to create and begin training GAEs, as these have become one of the most popular graph-based deep generative models. We'll look at the steps required to build one in more detail in this section.

The GAE model is similar to a typical autoencoder. The only difference is that each individual layer of our network is a GNN, such as a GCN or GraphSAGE network. In figure 5.5, we show a schematic for a GAE's architecture. Broadly, we'll be taking our edge data and compressing it into a low-dimensional representation using an encoder network.

The first thing we need to define for our GAE is the encoder, which will take our data and transform it into a latent representation. The code snippet for implementing the encoder is given in listing 5.4. We first import our libraries and then build a GNN where each layer is progressively smaller.

1. Edge data is compressed into a latent representation using the encoder.

2. The latent representation is reconstructed into its original format using the decoder.

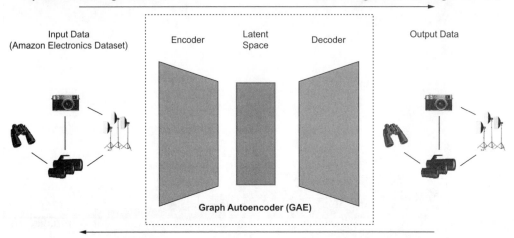

4. The trained model can then be used for edge prediction on unseen test data.

3. The error between reconstructed and original edge data is passed back through the network, and weights are updated.

Figure 5.5   Schematic for the GAE showing the key elements of the model, such as the encoder, latent space, and decoder

Listing 5.4   Graph encoder

```
from torch_geometric.nn import GCNConv          Loads GCNConv
                                                models from PyG

class GCNEncoder(torch.nn.Module):
    def __init__(self, input_size, layers, latent_dim):    Defines the encoder layer
        super().__init__()                                 and initializes it with a
                                                           predefined size
        self.conv0 = GCNConv(input_size, layers[0])
        self.conv1 = GCNConv(layers[0], layers[1])    Defines each of the
        self.conv2 = GCNConv(layers[1], latent_dim)   encoder layer networks

    def forward(self, x, edge_index):
        x = self.conv0(x, edge_index).relu()     Forward pass for the
        x = self.conv1(x, edge_index).relu()     encoder with edge data
        return self.conv2(x, edge_index)
```

Note that we also have to make sure that our forward pass can return the edge data from our graph because we'll be using our autoencoder to reconstruct the graph from the latent space. To put this another way, the autoencoder will be learning how to reconstruct the adjacency matrix from a low-dimensional representation of our feature space. This means it's also learning to predict edges from new data. To do this, we need to make the autoencoder structure learn to reconstruct edges, specifically by changing the decoder. Here, we'll use the inner product to predict edges from the latent space. This is shown in listing 5.5. (To understand why we use the inner product, see the technical details in section 5.5.)

Listing 5.5   Graph decoder

```
class InnerProductDecoder(torch.nn.Module):
    def __init__(self):                          Defines the
        super().__init__()                        decoder layer

def forward(self, z, edge_index):        ◁─┐    States the shape and size of the
        value = (z[edge_index[0]] * \              decoder (which, again, is the
z[edge_index[1]]).sum(dim=1)             ◁─       reverse of the encoder)
        return torch.sigmoid(value)
                                                  Forward pass for the decoder
```

Now we're ready to combine both encoder and decoder together in the GAE class, which contains both submodels (see listing 5.6). Note that we don't initialize the decoder with any input or output sizes now as this is just applying the inner product to the output of our encoder with the edge data.

Listing 5.6   Graph autoencoder

```
class GraphAutoEncoder(torch.nn.Module):
    def __init__(self, input_size, layers, latent_dims):
        super().__init__()
        self.encoder = GCNEncoder(input_size, \     Defines the encoder
layers, latent_dims)                          ◁─    for the GAE
        self.decoder = InnerProductDecoder()  ◁─┐   Defines the
                                                    decoder
    def forward(self, x):
        z = self.encoder(x)
        return self.decoder(z)
```

In PyTorch Geometric (PyG), the GAE model can be made even easier by just importing the GAE class, which automatically builds both decoder and autoencoder once passed to the encoder. We'll use this functionality when we build a VGAE later in the chapter.

5.2.3   *Training a graph autoencoder to perform link prediction*

Having built our GAE, we can proceed to use this to perform edge prediction for the sub models Amazon Products dataset. The overall framework will follow a typical deep learning problem format, where we first load the data, prepare the data, and split this data into train, test, and validation datasets; define our training parameters; and then train and test our model. These steps are shown in figure 5.6.

We begin by loading the dataset and preparing it for our learning algorithms, which we've already done in listing 5.1. For us to use the PyG models for GAE and VGAE, we need to construct an edge index from the adjacency matrix, which is easily

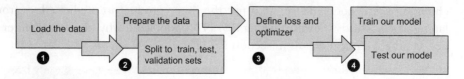

Figure 5.6 Overall steps for training our model for link prediction

done using one of PyG's utility functions, `to_edge_index`, as we describe in the following listing.

Listing 5.7 Construct Edge Index

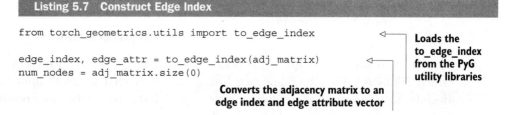

```
from torch_geometrics.utils import to_edge_index          ◁—  Loads the
                                                               to_edge_index
edge_index, edge_attr = to_edge_index(adj_matrix)         ◁—  from the PyG
num_nodes = adj_matrix.size(0)                                 utility libraries
```

Converts the adjacency matrix to an
edge index and edge attribute vector

We then load the PyG libraries and convert our data into a PyG data object. We can also apply transformations to our dataset, where the features and adjacency matrix are loaded as in chapter 3. First, we normalize our features and then split our dataset into training, testing, and validation sets based on the edges or links of the graph, as shown in listing 5.8. This is a vital step when carrying out link prediction to ensure we correctly split our data. In the code, we've used 5% of the data for validation and 10% for test data, noting that our graph is undirected. Here, we don't add any negative training samples.

Listing 5.8 Convert to a PyG object

```
data = Data(x=feature_matrix,
            edge_index=edge_index,          Converts our data to
            edge_attr=edge_attr,            a PyG data object
            y=labels)

device = torch.device('cuda' if torch.cuda.is_available() else 'cpu')

transform = T.Compose([\
    T.NormalizeFeatures(),\
    T.ToDevice(device),                     Transforms our data
    T.RandomLinkSplit(num_val=0.05,\        and splits the links
    num_test=0.1, is_undirected=True,       into train, test, and
    add_negative_train_samples=False)])     validation sets
train_data, val_data, test_data = transform(data)
```

With everything in place, we can now apply GAE to the Amazon Products dataset. First, we define our model, as well as our optimizer and our loss. We apply the binary cross-entropy loss to the predicted values from the decoder and compare against our true edge index to see whether our model has reconstructed the adjacency matrix correctly, as shown in the following listing.

Listing 5.9   Define the model

```
input_size, latent_dims = feature_matrix.shape[1], 16
layers = [512, 256]
model = GraphAutoEncoder(input_size, layers, latent_dims)
model = model.to(device)

optimizer = torch.optim.Adam(model.parameters(), lr=0.01)
criterion = torch.nn.BCEWithLogitsLoss()
```

Specifies the shape of our encoder

Defines a GAE with the correct shape

Our loss now is binary cross-entropy.

It's important to use a binary cross-entropy loss because we want to calculate the probabilities that each edge is a true edge, where true edges correspond to the ones that aren't being hidden and don't need to be predicted (i.e., the positive samples). The encoder learns to compress the edge data but doesn't change the number of edges, whereas the decoder learns to predict edges. In a sense, we're combining both the discriminative and generative steps here. Therefore, the binary cross-entropy gives us a probability where there is likely to be an edge between these nodes. It's binary, as either an edge should exist (label 1) or shouldn't (label 0). We can compare all of those edges that have a binary cross-entropy probability greater than 0.5 to the actual true edges in each epoch of our training loop, as shown in the following listing.

Listing 5.10   Training function

```
def train(model, criterion, optimizer):

    model.train()

    optimizer.zero_grad()
    z = model.encoder(train_data.x,\
    train_data.edge_index)

    neg_edge_index = negative_sampling(\
    edge_index=train_data.edge_index,\
    num_nodes=train_data.num_nodes,
    num_neg_samples=train_data.\
    edge_label_index.size(1), method='sparse')

    edge_label_index = torch.cat(
    [train_data.edge_label_index, neg_edge_index],
    dim=-1,)

    out = model.decoder(z, edge_label_index).view(-1)

    edge_label = torch.cat([
    train_data.edge_label,
    train_data.edge_label.new_zeros\
    (neg_edge_index.size(1))
    ], dim=0)
```

Encodes graph into latent representation

Performs a new round of negative sampling

Combines new negative samples with the edge label index

Generates edge predictions

Combines edge labels with 0s for negative samples

```
loss = criterion(out, edge_label)
loss.backward()
optimizer.step()

return loss
```

Computes loss and
backpropagates

Here, we first encoded our graph into a latent representation. We then perform a round of negative sampling, with new samples drawn for each epoch. Negative sampling takes a random subset of nonexistent labels rather than existing positive ones during training to account for the class imbalance between real labels and nonexistent ones. Once we have these new negative samples, we concatenate them with our original edge labels index and pass these to our decoder to get a reconstructed graph. Finally, we concatenate our true edge labels with the 0 labels for our negative edges and compute the loss between our predicted edges and our true edges. Note that we're not doing batch learning here; instead, we're choosing to train on all data during each epoch.

Our test function, shown in listing 5.11, is much simpler than our training function as it doesn't have to perform any negative sampling. Instead, we just use the true and predicted edges and return a Receiver Operating Characteristic (ROC)/Area Under the Curve (AUC) score to measure the accuracy of our model. Recall that the ROC/AUC curves will range between 0 and 1, and a perfect model, whose predictions are 100% correct, will have an AUC of 1.

Listing 5.11 Test function

```
from sklearn.metrics import roc_auc_score

@torch.no_grad()
def test(data):
    model.eval()
    z = model.encode(data.x, data.edge_index)          ◁── Encodes the graph into a
    out = model.decode(z, \                                 latent representation
    data.edge_label_index).view(-1).sigmoid()          ◁── Decodes the graph
    loss = roc_auc_score(data.edge_label.cpu().numpy(),     using the full edge
                          out.cpu().numpy())                label index
    return loss                                         ◁── Calculates the overall
                                                            ROC/AUC score
```

At each time step, we'll calculate the overall success of a model using all our edge data from our validation data. After training is complete, we then use the test data to calculate the final test accuracy, as shown in the following listing.

Listing 5.12 Training loop

```
best_val_auc = final_test_auc = 0
for epoch in range(1, 201):
    loss = train(model, criterion, optimizer)          ◁── Performs a
    val_auc = test(val_data)                                training step
    if val_auc > best_val_auc:                          ◁── Tests our updated model
                                                            on validation data
```

```
           best_val_auc = val_auc
test_auc = test(test_data)
```
←─┤ **Tests our final
    model on test data**

We find that after 200 epochs, we achieve an accuracy of more than 83%. Even better, when we then use our test set to see how well our model is able to predict edges, we get an accuracy of 86%. We can interpret our model performance as being able to suggest a meaningful item to the purchaser 86% of the time, assuming that all future data is the same as our current dataset. This is a great result and demonstrates how useful GNNs are for recommender systems. We can also use our model to better understand how the dataset is structured or apply additional classification and feature engineering tasks by exploring our newly constructed latent space. Next, we're going to learn about one of the most common extensions to the graph autoencoder model—the VGAE.

5.3   *Variational graph autoencoders*

Autoencoders map data onto discrete points in the latent space. To sample outside of the training dataset and generate new synthetic data, we can interpolate between these discrete points. This is exactly the process that we described in figure 5.1, where we generated unseen combinations of data such as a flying boat. However, autoencoders are deterministic, where each input maps to a specific point in the latent space. This can lead to sharp discontinuities when sampling, which can affect performance for data generation resulting in synthetic data that doesn't reproduce the original dataset as well. To improve our generative process, we need to ensure that our latent space is well-structured, or *regular*. In figure 5.7, for example, we show how to use the Kullback-Liebler divergence (KL divergence) to restructure the latent space to improve reconstruction.

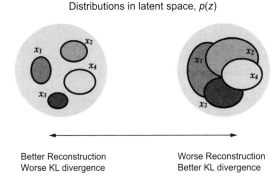

Distributions in latent space, *p(z)*

Better Reconstruction
Worse KL divergence

Worse Reconstruction
Better KL divergence

Figure 5.7   Regular spaces are continuous and compact, but data regions may become less separated. Alternatively, high reconstruction loss typically means data is well separated, but the latent space might be less covered leading to worse generative samples. Here, KL Divergence refers to the Kullback-Liebler divergence.

The KL divergence is a measure of how one probability distribution differs from another. It calculates how much "extra information" is needed to encode values from one distribution (the original data distribution) into another (the latent space). On the left, the data groups (x_i) don't overlap much, which means the KL divergence is higher. On the right, there is more overlap (similarity) between the different data groups, meaning the KL divergence is lower. When building a more regular latent space that has a high KL divergence, we can get very good reconstruction but poor interpolation, while we get the opposite for low KL divergence. More details on this are provided in section 5.5.

Regular means that the space fulfills two properties: continuity and compactness. *Continuity* means that nearby points in the latent space are decoded into approximately similar things, while *compactness* means that any point in the latent space should lead to a meaningful decoded representation. These terms, approximately similar and meaningful, have precise definitions, which you can read more about in *Learn Generative AI with PyTorch* (Manning, 2024; https://mng.bz/AQBg). However, for this chapter, all you need to know is that these properties make it easier to sample from the latent space, resulting in cleaner generated samples and potentially higher model accuracy.

When we regularize a latent space, we use variational methods that model the entire dataspace in terms of probability distributions (or densities). As we'll see, the main benefit of using variational methods is that the latent space is well structured. However, variational methods don't necessarily guarantee higher performance, so it's often important to test both the autoencoder and the variational counterpart when using these types of models. This can be done by either looking at the reconstruction score (e.g., mean squared error) on the test dataset, applying some dimension reduction method to the latent encodings (e.g., t-SNE or Uniform Manifold Approximation and Projection [UMAP]), or using task-specific measures (e.g., the Inception Score for images or ROUGE/METEOR for text generation). Specifically for graphs, measures such as the maximum mean discrepancy (MMD), graph statistics, or graph kernel methods can all be used to compare against different synthetically generated graph copies.

In the next few sections, we'll go into more detail on what it means to model a dataspace as a probability density and how we can transform our graph autoencoder into a VGAE with just a few lines. These depend on some key probabilistic machine learning concepts such as the KL divergence and the reparameterization trick, which we give an overview of in section 5.5. For more of a deep dive into these concepts, we recommend *Probabilistic Deep Learning* (Manning, 2020). Let's build a VGAE architecture and apply it to the same Amazon Products dataset as before.

5.3.1 Building a variational graph autoencoder

The VGAE architecture is similar to the GAE model. The main difference is that the output of a *variational* graph encoder is generated by sampling from a probability density. We can characterize density in terms of its mean and variance. Therefore, the output of the encoder will now be the mean and variance for each dimension of our previous space. The decoder then takes this sampled latent representation and decodes it to appear like the input data. This can be seen in figure 5.8, where the high-level model is that we now extend our previous autoencoder to output mean and variance rather than point estimates from the latent space. This allows our model to make probabilistic samples from the latent space.

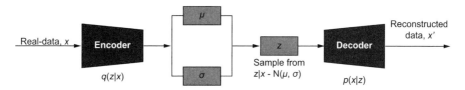

Figure 5.8 Structure of a general VAE, where we now sample from a probability density in the latent space rather than a point estimate as with typical autoencoders. VGAEs extend the VAE architecture to apply to graph-structured data.

We have to adapt our architecture and also change our loss to include an additional term for regularizing the latent space. Listing 5.13 provides a code snippet for the VGAE. The similarities between listing 5.4 and the `VariationalGCNEncoder` layer in listing 5.13 include that we've doubled the dimensionality of our latent space and now return the mean and the log variance from our encoder at the end of our forward pass.

Listing 5.13 `VariationalGCNEncoder`

```
class VariationalGCNEncoder(torch.nn.Module):
  def __init__(self, input_size, layers, latent_dims):
    super().__init__()
    self.layer0 = GCNConv(input_size, layers[0])
    self.layer1 = GCNConv(layers[0], layers[1])
    self.mu = GCNConv(layers[1], latent_dims)
    self.logvar = GCNConv(layers[1], latent_dims)

  def forward(self, x, edge_index):
    x = self.layer0(x, edge_index).relu()
    x = self.layer1(x, edge_index).relu()
    mu = self.mu(x, edge_index)
    logvar = self.logvar(x, edge_index)
    return mu, logvar
```

Adds in mean and log variance variables to sample from

Forward pass returns mean and log variance variables

When we discussed the GAE, we learned that the decoder uses the inner product to return the adjacency matrix, or edge list. Previously we explicitly implemented the inner dot product. However, in PyG, this functionality is built in. To build a VGAE structure, we can call the VGAE function, shown in the following listing.

Listing 5.14 Variational graph autoencoder (VGAE)

```
from torch_geometric.nn import VGAE
model = VGAE(VariationalGCNEncoder(input_size,\
  layers, latent_dims))
```

Uses the VGAE function from the PyG library to build the autoencoder

This functionality makes it much simpler to build a VGAE, where the VGAE function in PyG takes care of the reparameterization trick. Now that we have our VGAE model, the next thing we need to do is amend the training and testing functions to include the KL divergence loss. The training function is shown in the following listing.

> **Listing 5.15 Training function**

```
def train(model, criterion, optimizer):          As we are using the PyG VGAE function,
    model.train()                                 we need to use the encode and
    optimizer.zero_grad()                         decode methods.
    z = model.encode(train_data.x, train_data.edge_index)          ◁───┐

    neg_edge_index = negative_sampling(
    edge_index=train_data.edge_index, num_nodes=train_data.num_nodes,
    num_neg_samples=train_data.edge_label_index.size(1), method='sparse')

    edge_label_index = torch.cat(
    [train_data.edge_label_index, neg_edge_index],
    dim=-1,)
    out = model.decode(z, edge_label_index).view(-1)          ◁───┘

    edge_label = torch.cat([
    train_data.edge_label,
    train_data.edge_label.new_zeros(neg_edge_index.size(1))
    ], dim=0)

    loss = criterion(out, edge_label)              Adds in the regularizing
+ (1 / train_data.num_nodes) * model.kl_loss()     term of the loss given by
                                                   the KL divergence
    loss.backward()
    optimizer.step()

    return loss
```

This is the same training loop that we used in listing 5.12 to train our GAE model. The only differences are that we include an additional term to our loss that minimizes the KL divergence and we change the `encoder` and `decoder` method calls to `encode` and `decode` (which we also need to update in our test function). Otherwise, the training remains unchanged. Note that thanks to the added PyG functionality, these changes are considerably less involved than when we made the changes in PyTorch earlier. However, going through each of those extra steps gives us more intuition about the underlying architecture for a GAE.

We can now apply our VGAE to the Amazon Products dataset and use this to perform edge prediction, which yields an overall test accuracy of 88%. This is slightly higher than our accuracy for GAE. It's important to note that VGAEs won't necessarily give higher accuracy. As a result, you should always try a GAE as well as a VGAE and run careful model validation when using this architecture.

5.3.2 *When to use a variational graph autoencoder*

Given that the accuracy for the VGAE was similar to the GAE, it's important to realize the limitations of both methods. In general, GAEs and VGAEs are great models to use when you want to build a generative model or where you want to use one aspect of your data to learn another aspect. For example, we might want to make a graph-based model for pose prediction. We can use both GAE and VGAE architectures to predict future poses based on video footage. (We'll see a similar example in later chapters.) When we do so, we're using the GAE/VGAE to learn a graph of the body, conditioned on what the future positions of each body part will be. However, if we're specifically interested in generating new data, such as new chemical graphs for drug discovery, VGAEs are often better as the latent space is more structured.

In general, GAEs are great for specific reconstruction tasks such as link prediction or node classification, while VGAEs are better for where the tasks require a larger or more diverse range of synthetic samples, such as where you want to generate entirely new subgraphs or small graphs. VGAEs are also often better suited for when the underlying dataset is noisy, compared to GAEs which are faster and more suitable for graph data with clear structure. Finally, note that VGAEs are less prone to overfitting due to their variational approach, and they may generalize better as a result. As always, your choice of architecture depends on the problem at hand.

In this chapter, we've learned about two examples of generative models, the GAE and VGAE models, and how to implement these models to work with graph-structured data. To better understand how to use this model class, we applied our models to an edge prediction task. However, this is only one step in applying a generative model.

In many instances where we require a generative model, we use successive layers of autoencoders to further reduce the dimensionality of our system and increase our reconstruction power. In the context of drug discovery and chemical science, GAEs allow us to reconstruct the adjacency matrix (as we did here) as well as reconstruct types of molecules and even the number of molecules. GAEs are used frequently in many sciences and industries. Now you have the tools to try them out too.

In the next section, we'll demonstrate how to use the VGAE to generate new graphs with specific qualities, such as novel molecules that have a high property indicating usefulness as a potential drug candidate.

5.4 *Generating graphs using GNNs*

So far, we've considered how to use a generative model of our graph to estimate edges between nodes. However, sometimes we're also interested in generating not just a node or an edge but the entire graph. This can be particularly important when trying to understand or predict graph-level data. In this example, we'll do exactly that by using our GAE and VGAEs to generate new potential molecules to synthesize, which have certain properties.

One of the fields that GNNs have had the largest effect on has been drug discovery, especially for the identification of new molecules or potential drugs. In 2020, a new antibiotic was proposed that was discovered using a GNN, and, in 2021, a new method for identifying carcinogens in food was published that also made use of GNNs. Since then, there have been many other papers that use GNNs as tools to accelerate the drug discovery pipeline.

5.4.1　*Molecular graphs*

We're going to be considering small molecules that have previously been screened for drugs, as described in the ZINC dataset of around 250,000 individual molecules. Each molecule in this dataset has additional data including the following:

- *Simplified Molecular Input Line Entry System (SMILES)*—A description of the molecular structure or the molecular *graph* in ASCII format.
- *Important properties*—Synthetic accessibility score (SAS), water-octanol partition coefficient ($logP$), and, most importantly, a measure of the quantitative estimate of druglikeness (QED), which highlights how likely this molecule could be as a potential drug.

To make this dataset usable by our GNN models, we need to convert this into a suitable graph structure. Here, we're going to be using PyG for defining our model and running our deep learning routines. Therefore, we first download the data and then convert the dataset into graph objects using NetworkX. We download our dataset in listing 5.16, which generates the following output:

```
       smiles       logP       qed       SAS
0      CC(C)(C)c1ccc2occ(CC(=O)Nc3ccccc3F)c2c1
       5.05060        0.702012      2.084095
1      C[C@@H]1CC(Nc2cncc(-c3nncn3C)c2)C[C@@H](C)C1
       3.11370        0.928975      3.432004
2      N#Cc1ccc(-c2ccc(O[C@@H](C(=O)N3CCCC3)c3ccccc3)...
       4.96778        0.599682      2.470633
3      CCOC(=O)[C@@H]1CCCN(C(=O)c2nc
       (-c3ccc(C)cc3)n3c...
       4.00022        0.690944      2.822753
4      N#CC1=C(SCC(=O)Nc2cccc(Cl)c2)N=C([O-])
       [C@H](C#...     3.60956       0.789027      4.035182
```

Listing 5.16　Create a molecular graph dataset

```python
import requests
import pandas as pd

def download_file(url, filename):
    response = requests.get(url)
    response.raise_for_status()
    with open(filename, 'wb') as f:
        f.write(response.content)
```

```
url = "https://raw.githubusercontent.com/
aspuru-guzikgroup/chemical_vae/master/models/
zinc_properties/250k_rndm_zinc_drugs_clean_3.csv"
filename = "250k_rndm_zinc_drugs_clean_3.csv"

download_file(url, filename)

df = pd.read_csv(filename)
df["smiles"] = df["smiles"].apply(lambda s: s.replace("\n", ""))
```

In listing 5.17, we define a function to convert the SMILES into small graphs, which we then use to create a PyG dataset. We also add some additional information to each object in our dataset, such as the number of heavy atoms that we can use for further data exploration. Here, we use the recursive SMILES depth-first search (DFS) toolkit (RDKit) package (www.rdkit.org/docs/index.html), which is a great open source tool for cheminformatics.

Listing 5.17 Create the molecular graph dataset

```
from torch_geometric.data import Data
import torch
from rdkit import Chem


def smiles_to_graph(smiles, qed):
  mol = Chem.MolFromSmiles(smiles)
    if not mol:
        return None

    edges = []
    edge_features = []
    for bond in mol.GetBonds():
        edges.append([bond.GetBeginAtomIdx(), bond.GetEndAtomIdx()])
        bond_type = bond.GetBondTypeAsDouble()
        bond_feature = [1 if i == bond_type\
        else 0 for i in range(4)]
        edge_features.append(bond_feature)

    edge_index = torch.tensor(edges, dtype=torch.long).t().contiguous()
    edge_attr = torch.tensor(edge_features, dtype=torch.float)
    x = torch.tensor([atom.GetAtomicNum()\
 for atom in mol.GetAtoms()], \
 dtype=torch.float).view(-1, 1)

    num_heavy_atoms = mol.GetNumHeavyAtoms()

    return Data(x=x, edge_index=edge_index,\
 edge_attr=edge_attr, \
qed=torch.tensor([qed], \
dtype=torch.float), \
num_heavy_atoms=num_heavy_atoms)
```

A random sample from our dataset is shown in figure 5.9, which highlights how varied our molecular graphs are and their small size, where each one has less than 100 nodes and edges.

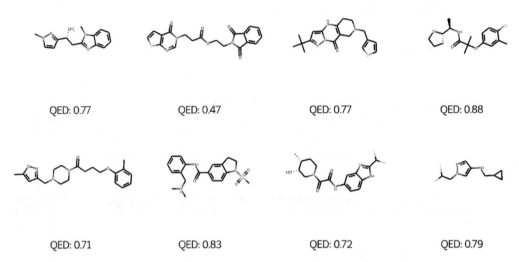

QED: 0.77   QED: 0.47   QED: 0.77   QED: 0.88

QED: 0.71   QED: 0.83   QED: 0.72   QED: 0.79

Figure 5.9   Example molecular graphs with quantitative estimate of druglikeness (QED)

5.4.2   *Identifying new drug candidates*

In figure 5.10, we start to see how QED can vary with different molecular structures. One of the main obstacles to drug discovery is the number of different potential combinations of molecules and how to know which ones to synthesize and then test for drug efficacy. This is far before the stage of introducing the drug to human, animal (in vivo), or sometimes even cellular (in vitro) trials. Even evaluating things such as a molecule's solubility can be a challenge if we use the molecular graph alone. Here, we're going to be focusing on predicting the molecules' QED, to see which ones are most likely to have potential use as a drug. To give an example of how the QED can vary, see figure 5.10, which has four molecules with high (~0.95) and low (~0.12) QED. We can see some qualitative differences between these molecules, such as the increased number of strong bonds for those with low QED. However, estimating the QED directly from the graph is a challenge. To help us with this task, we'll use a GNN to both generate and evaluate new potential drugs.

Our work will be based on two important papers that demonstrated how generative models can be effective tools for identifying new molecules (Gómez-Bombarelli et al. [4] and De Cao et al. [5]). Specifically, Gómez-Bombarelli et al. showed that by constructing a smooth representation of the dataspace, which is the latent space we described earlier in this chapter, it's possible to optimize to find new candidates with specific properties of interest. This work borrows heavily from an equivalent

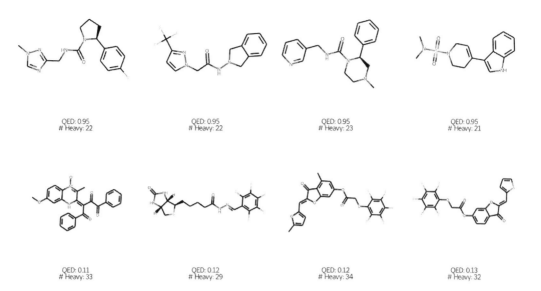

Figure 5.10   Molecules with high QED (top) and low QED (bottom)

implementation in the Keras library, outlined in a posting by Victor Basu [6]. Figure 5.11 reproduces the basic idea from [5].

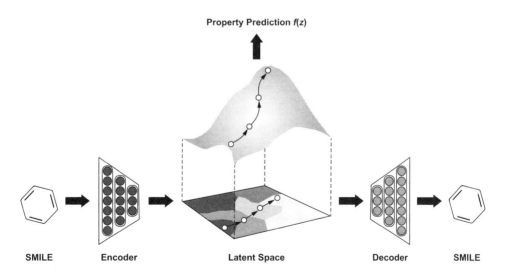

Figure 5.11   Example of how a graph autoencoder that is trained to re-create small graphs can also be used to make property predictions. The property prediction is applied in the latent space and creates a learned gradient of a specific graph property—in our case, the QED value.

In figure 5.11, we can see that the underlying model structure is an autoencoder, just like the ones we've been discussing in this chapter. Here, we pass the SMILES of the molecule as input to the encoder, and this is then used to construct the latent space of different molecular representations. This is shown as regions with different colors representing different groups of molecules. Then, the decoder is designed to faithfully translate the latent space back into the original molecule. This is similar to the autoencoder structure that we showed earlier in figure 5.5.

Alongside the latent space, we now also have an additional function, which is going to predict the property of the molecule. In figure 5.11, the property we'll predict is also the property we're optimizing for. Therefore, by learning how to encode both the molecule and the property, which in our case is QED, into the latent space, we can optimize drug discovery to generate new candidate molecules with a high QED.

In our example, we'll use the VGAE. This model includes two losses: a reconstruction loss that measures the difference between the original input data passed to the encoder and the output from the decoder, as well as a measure of the structure of the latent space, where we use the KL divergence.

Along with these two loss functions, we'll add one more function: a property prediction loss. The property prediction loss estimates the MSE between predicted and actual properties after running the latent representation through a property prediction model, as shown in the middle of figure 5.11.

To train our GNN, we adapt the training loop provided earlier in listing 5.15 to include these individual losses. This is shown in listing 5.18. Here, we have the reconstruction loss as the binary cross-entropy (BCE) for the adjacency matrix, while the property prediction loss considers only QED and can be based on the MSE.

Listing 5.18 Loss for molecule graph generation

```
        def calculate_loss(self, pred_adj, \
    true_adj, qed_pred, qed_true, mu, logvar):
            adj_loss = F.binary_cross_entropy\
    (pred_adj, true_adj)                                 ⟵——— Reconstruction loss

            qed_loss = F.mse_loss\
    (qed_pred.view(-1), qed_true.view(-1))               ⟵——— Property prediction loss

            kl_loss = -0.5 * torch.mean\
    (torch.sum(1 + logvar - mu.pow(2)\
     - logvar.exp(), dim=1))                             ⟵——— KL divergence loss

            return adj_loss + qed_loss + kl_loss
```

5.4.3   *VGAEs for generating graphs*

Now that we have both our training data and loss, we can start to think about the model. Overall, this model will be similar to the ones discussed earlier in the chapter, both GAE and VGAE. However, we need to make some subtle changes to our model to ensure that it's well applied to the problem at hand:

- Use a heterogenous GCN to account for different edge types.
- Train the decoder to generate the entire graph.
- Introduce a property prediction layer.

Let's look at each of these in turn.

HETEROGENEOUS GCN

The small graphs that we're generating will have different edge types that connect the nodes of our graphs. Specifically, we can have a different number of bonds between the atoms such as a single bond, double bond, triple bond, or even *aromatic bonds*, which relate to molecules that are formed into a ring. Graphs with more than one edge type are known as heterogeneous graphs, so we'll need to make our GNN applicable to heterogeneous graphs.

So far, all the graphs we've been considering have been homogenous (only one edge type). In listing 5.19, we show how the GCN, which we discussed in chapter 3, can be adapted to heterogeneous graphs. Here, we explicitly map out some of the different features for heterogeneous graphs. However, it's important to note that many GNN packages already support models for heterogeneous graphs out of the box. For example, PyG has a specific class of models known as `HeteroConv`.

Listing 5.19 shows the code to create a heterogenous GCN. This builds off the message-passing class in PyG, which is fundamental to all GNN models. We also use the PyTorch `Parameter` class to create a new subset of parameters that are specific to the different edge types (relations). Finally, we also specify here that the aggregation operation in the message-passing framework is based on summation (`'add'`). If you're interested, feel free to try other aggregation operations.

Listing 5.19 Heterogenous GCN

```
from torch.nn import Parameter
from torch_geometric.nn import MessagePassing

  class HeterogeneousGraphConv(MessagePassing):
def __init__(self, in_channels, out_channels, num_relations, bias=True):
        super(HeterogeneousGraphConv, self).\
__init__(aggr='add')                          ◁─┐  "Add"
        self.in_channels = in_channels             │  aggregation
        self.out_channels = out_channels
        self.num_relations = num_relations

        self.weight = Parameter(torch.\
Tensor(num_relations, in_channels, \               ┌─  Parameter
out_channels))                             ◁──┘    │  for weights
        if bias:
            self.bias = Parameter(torch.Tensor(out_channels))
        else:
            self.register_parameter('bias', None)

        self.reset_parameters()
```

```
        def reset_parameters(self):
            torch.nn.init.xavier_uniform_(self.weight)
            if self.bias is not None:
                torch.nn.init.zeros_(self.bias)

        def forward(self, x, edge_index, edge_type):

        return self.propagate\
(edge_index, size=(x.size(0),
x.size(0)), x=x, edge_type=edge_type)

        def message(self, x_j, edge_type, index, size):

            W = self.weight[edge_type]
            x_j = torch.matmul(x_j.unsqueeze(1), W).squeeze(1)

            return x_j

        def update(self, aggr_out):
            if self.bias is not None:
                aggr_out += self.bias
            return aggr_out
```

edge_type is used to select the weights.

x_j has shape [E, in_channels], and edge_type has shape [E].

Select the corresponding weights.

With the preceding GNN, we can then compose our encoder as a combination of these individual GNN layers. This is shown in listing 5.20, where we follow the same logic as when we defined our edge encoder (refer to listing 5.13), except that we now switch out our GCN layers for the heterogeneous GCN layers. As we have different edge types, we must now also specify the number of different types (relations) as well as passing the specific edge type into the forward function for our graph encoder. Again, we return both log variance and mean to ensure that the latent space is constructed using distributions rather than point samples.

Listing 5.20   Small graph encoder

```
class VariationalGCEncoder(torch.nn.Module):
    def __init__(self, input_size, layers, latent_dims, num_relations):
        super().__init__()
        self.layer0 = HeterogeneousGraphConv(input_size,
layers[0], num_relations)
        self.layer1 = HeterogeneousGraphConv(layers[0],
layers[1], num_relations)
        self.layer2 = HeterogeneousGraphConv(layers[1],
latent_dims, num_relations)

    def forward(self, x, edge_index, edge_type):
        x = F.relu(self.layer0\
(x, edge_index, edge_type))
        x = F.relu(self.layer1\
(x, edge_index, edge_type))
        mu = self.mu(x, edge_index)
        logvar = self.logvar(x, edge_index)
        return mu, logvar
```

Heterogeneous GCNs

Forward pass GCNs

GRAPH DECODERS

In our previous examples, we used GAEs to generate and predict edges between nodes in a single graph. However, we're now interested in using our autoencoder to generate entire graphs. Therefore, we no longer just consider the inner product decoder to account for the presence of an edge in the graph but instead decode both the adjacency matrix and feature matrix for each small molecular graph. This is shown in listing 5.21.

Listing 5.21 Small graph decoder

```python
class GraphDecoder(nn.Module):
    def __init__(self, latent_dim, adjacency_shape, feature_shape):
    super(GraphDecoder, self).__init__()

    self.dense1 = nn.Linear(latent_dim, 128)
    self.relu1 = nn.ReLU()
    self.dropout1 = nn.Dropout(0.1)

    self.dense2 = nn.Linear(128, 256)
    self.relu2 = nn.ReLU()
    self.dropout2 = nn.Dropout(0.1)

    self.dense3 = nn.Linear(256, 512)
    self.relu3 = nn.ReLU()
    self.dropout3 = nn.Dropout(0.1)

    self.adjacency_output = nn.Linear(512,\
torch.prod(torch.tensor(adjacency_shape)).item())
    self.feature_output = nn.Linear(512,\
torch.prod(torch.tensor(feature_shape)).item())

    def forward(self, z):
        x = self.dropout1(self.relu1(self.dense1(z)))
        x = self.dropout2(self.relu2(self.dense2(x)))        ◁── Generates the
        x = self.dropout3(self.relu3(self.dense3(x)))             adjacency
                                                                  matrix
        adj = self.adjacency_output(x)
        adj = adj.view(-1, *self.adjacency_shape)
        adj = (adj + adj.transpose(-1, -2)) / 2      ◁── Symmetrizes the
        adj = F.softmax(adj, dim=-1)                 ◁──    adjacency matrix

        features = self.feature_output(x)            ◁── Applies softmax
        features = features.view(-1, *self.feature_shape)
        features = F.softmax(features, dim=-1)        ◁── Generates features

        return adj, features                              Applies softmax
```

The majority of this code is typical for decoder style networks. We begin with a small network that matches the dimension for the latent space created using the encoder. We then progressively increase the size of the graph through subsequent layers of the network. Here, we can use simple linear networks, where we include network dropout for performance. At the final layer, we reshape the decoder output into the adjacency and feature matrices. We also ensure that the adjacency matrix is symmetric before applying softmax. We symmetrize the adjacency matrix by adding it to its transpose and dividing by 2. This ensures that node i is connected to j and that j is also connected to i. We then apply softmax to normalize the adjacency matrix, ensuring all outgoing edges from each node sum to 1. There are other choices we could make here such as using the maximum value, applying a threshold, or using the sigmoid function instead of softmax. In general, averaging + softmax is a good approach.

PROPERTY PREDICTION LAYER

All that's left is to combine both encoder and decoder networks into a final model that can be used for molecular graph generation, as shown in listing 5.22. Overall, this follows the same steps as in listing 5.14 earlier, where we define both our encoder and decoder as well as use the reparameterization trick. The only difference is that we also include a simple linear network to predict the property of the graphs, in this case, the QED. This is applied on the latent representation (z), after being reparameterized.

Listing 5.22   VGAE for molecular graph generation

```python
import torch
import torch.nn as nn
import torch.nn.functional as F
from torch_geometric.nn import MessagePassing

class VGAEWithPropertyPrediction(nn.Module):
    def __init__(self, encoder, decoder, latent_dim):
        super(VGAEWithPropertyPrediction, self).__init__()
        self.encoder = encoder
        self.decoder = decoder
        self.property_prediction_layer = nn.Linear(latent_dim, 1)

    def reparameterize(self, mu, logvar):
        std = torch.exp(logvar / 2)
        eps = torch.randn_like(std)
        return eps.mul(std).add_(mu)

    def forward(self, data):
        mu, logvar = self.encoder(data.x, \
data.edge_index, data.edge_attr)
        z = self.reparameterize(mu, logvar)
        adj_recon, x_recon = self.decoder(z)
        qed_pred = self.property_prediction_layer(z)
        return adj_recon, x_recon, qed_pred, mu, logvar, z
```

The output for the model is then both the mean and log variance, which are passed to the KL divergence; the reconstructed adjacency matrix and feature matrix, passed to the reconstruction loss; and the predicted QED values, which are used in the prediction loss. Using these, we can then compute the loss for our network and backpropagate the loss through the network weights to refine the generated graphs to have specifically high QED values. Next, we show how to achieve just that in our training and test loops.

5.4.4   Generating molecules using a GNN

In the previous section, we discussed all the individual parts needed to use a GNN to generate molecules. We'll now bring the different elements together and demonstrate how to use a GNN to create novel graphs that are optimized for a specific property. In figure 5.12, we show the steps to generate molecules with a GNN that have a high QED. These steps include creating suitable graphs to represent small molecules, passing these through our autoencoder, predicting specific molecular features such as QED, and then repeating those steps until we're able to recreate new novel molecular graphs with specific features.

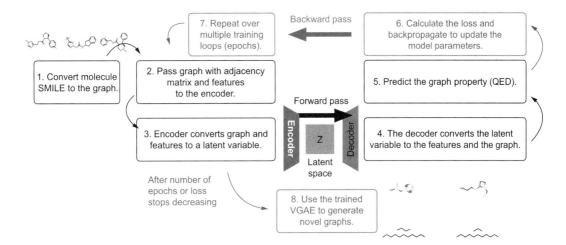

Figure 5.12   Steps to generate molecules with a GNN

The key element that remains is to combine our loss functions with our adapted VGAE model. This is shown in listing 5.23, which defines our training loop. This is similar to previous training loops that you've seen in earlier chapters and examples. The main idea is that our model is used to predict some property of the graph. However, here we're predicting the entire graph, as defined in the predicted adjacency matrix (`pred_adj`) and the predicted feature matrix (`pred_feat`).

The output from our model and the real data are passed to our method for calculating the loss, which contains the reconstruction loss, KL divergence loss, and property prediction loss. Finally, we compute the gradient penalty, which acts as a further regularizer for our model (and defined in more detail in section 5.5). With both loss and gradient calculated, we backpropagate through our model, step our optimizer forwards, and return the loss.

Listing 5.23   Training function for molecule graph generation

```python
def train(model, optimizer, data, test=False):
    model.train()
    optimizer.zero_grad()

    pred_adj, pred_feat, pred_qed, mu, logvar, _ = model(data)

    real_adj = create_adjacency_matrix\
(data.edge_index, data.edge_attr, \
num_nodes=NUM_ATOMS)
    real_x = data.x
    real_qed = data.qed


    loss = calculate_loss\
(pred_adj[0], real_adj, pred_qed, \
real_qed, mu, logvar)                    ←——  Compute losses

    total_loss = loss

    if not test:
        total_loss.backward()
    optimizer.step()
    return total_loss.item()
```

During training time, we find that the model loss decreases, demonstrating that the model is effectively learning how to reproduce novel molecules. We show some of these molecules in figure 5.13.

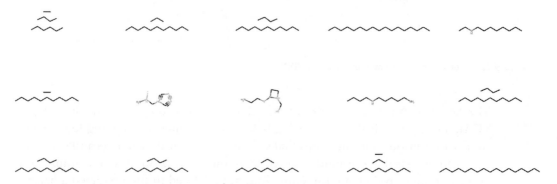

Figure 5.13   Small molecule graphs generated using a GNN

To better understand the distribution of the predicted QED property in our latent space, we apply our encoder to a new subset of data and look at the first two axes of the data as represented in the latent space, as shown in figure 5.14. Here, we can see that the latent space has been constructed to cluster molecules with higher QED together. Therefore, by sampling from regions around this area, we can identify new molecules to test. Future work will be needed to verify our results, but as a first step toward the discovery of new molecules, we've demonstrated that a GNN model may well be used to propose new and potentially valuable drug candidates.

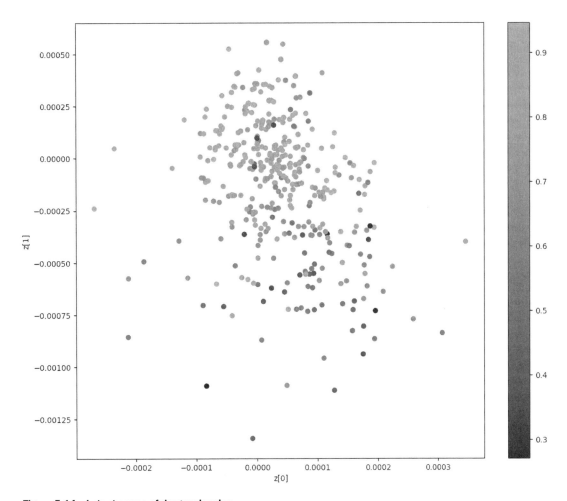

Figure 5.14 **Latent space of drug molecules**

In this chapter, we've focused on generative tasks rather than classical discriminative models. We've shown generative models, such as GAEs and VGAEs, can be used for edge prediction, learning to identify connections between nodes where information is potentially not available. We then went on to show that generative GNNs can be used to discover not just unknown parts of a graph, such as a node or edge, but also entirely new and complicated graphs, when we applied our GNNs to generate new small molecules with a high QED. These results highlight that GNNs are vital tools for those working in chemistry, life sciences, and many other disciplines that deal with many individual graphs.

Moreover, we've learned that GNNs are extremely useful for both discriminative and generative tasks. Here, we consider the topic of small molecule graphs, but GNNs have also been applied to knowledge graphs and small social clusters. In the next chapter, we'll look at how we can learn to generate graphs that are consistent over time by combining generative GNNs with temporal encodings. In that spirit, we take a further step forward and learn how GNNs can be taught how to walk.

5.5   *Under the hood*

Deep generative models use artificial neural networks to model the dataspace. One of the classic examples of a deep generative model is the autoencoder. Autoencoders contain two key components, the encoder and the decoder, both represented by neural networks. They learn how to take data and encode (compress) it into a low dimensional representation as well as decode (uncompress) it again. Figure 5.15 shows a basic autoencoder taking an image as input and compressing it (step 1). This results in the low dimensional representation, or latent space (step 2). The autoencoder then reconstructs the image (step 3), and the process is repeated until the reconstruction error between input image (x) and output image (x*) is as small as possible. The autoencoder is the basic idea behind GAEs and VGAEs.

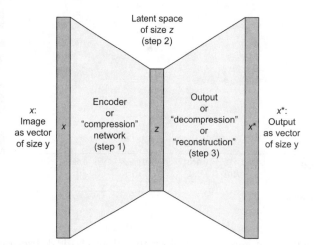

Figure 5.15   Structure of an autoencoder [9]

5.5.1   *Understanding link prediction tasks*

Link prediction is a common problem in graph-based learning, especially in situations where we have incomplete knowledge of our data. This might be because the graph changes over time, for example, where we expect new customers to use an e-commerce service, and we want a model that can give the best suggested products to buy at that time. Alternatively, it may be costly to acquire this knowledge, for example, if we want our model to predict which combinations of drugs lead to specific disease outcomes. Finally, our data may contain incorrect or purposefully hidden details, such as fake accounts on a social media platform. Link prediction allows us to infer relations *between* nodes in our graph. Essentially, this means creating a model that predicts when and how nodes are connected, as shown in figure 5.16.

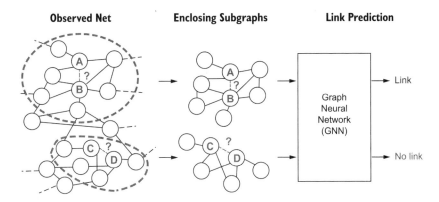

Figure 5.16   Schematic explaining how link prediction is performed in practice. Subsections of the input graph (subgraphs) are passed to the GNN with different links missing, and the model learns to predict when to recreate a link.

For link prediction, a model will take pairs of nodes as input and predict whether these nodes are connected (whether they should be *linked*). To train a model, we'll also need ground-truth targets. We generate these by hiding a subset of links within the graph. These hidden links become the missing data that we'll learn to infer, which are known as *negative samples*. However, we also need a way to encode the information about pairs of nodes. Both of these parts can be solved simultaneously using GAEs, as autoencoders both encode information about the edge as well as predict whether an edge exists.

5.5.2   *The inner product decoder*

Inner product decoders are used for graphs because we want to reconstruct the adjacency matrix from the latent representation of our feature data. The GAE learns how to rebuild a graph (to infer the edges) given a latent representation of the nodes. The inner product in high dimensional space calculates the distance between two positions. We use the inner product, rescaled by the sigmoid function, to gain a probability for an edge between nodes. Essentially, we use the distance between points in the latent space as a probability that a node will be connected when decoded. This allows us to build a decoder that takes samples from our latent space and returns probabilities of whether an edge exists, namely, to perform edge prediction, as shown in figure 5.17.

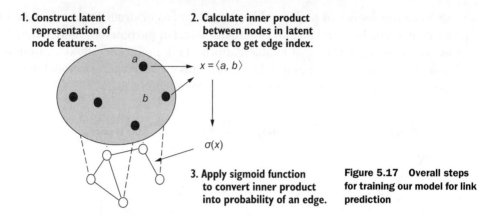

1. **Construct latent representation of node features.**

2. **Calculate inner product between nodes in latent space to get edge index.**

$x = \langle a, b \rangle$

$\sigma(x)$

3. **Apply sigmoid function to convert inner product into probability of an edge.**

Figure 5.17   Overall steps for training our model for link prediction

The inner product decoder works by taking the latent representation of our data and applying the inner product of this data using the passed edge index of our data. We then apply the sigmoid function to this value, which returns a matrix where each value represents the probability that there is an edge between the two nodes.

REGULARIZING THE LATENT SPACE

Put plainly, the KL divergence tells us how much worse we would be doing if we used the wrong probability density when estimating a probability of something. Suppose we have two coins and want to guess how well one coin (which we know is fair) matches the other coin (which we don't know is fair). We're trying to use the coin with the known probability to predict the probability for the coin with unknown probability. If it's a good predictor (the unknown coin actually is fair), then the KL divergence will be zero. The probability densities of both coins are the same; however, if we find that the coin is a bad predictor, then the KL divergence will be large. This is because the two probability densities will be far from each other. In figure 5.18, we can see this explicitly. We're trying to model the unknown probability density Q(z) using the conditional probability density P(Z|X). As the densities overlap, the KL divergence here will be low.

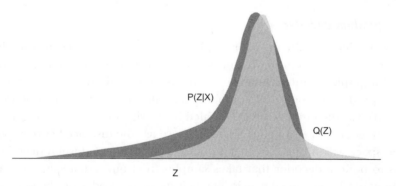

P(Z|X)

Q(Z)

z

Figure 5.18   KL divergence calculates the degree to which two probability densities are distinct. High KL divergence means that they are well separated, whereas low KL divergence means they are not.

Practically, we convert an autoencoder to a VGAE by introducing the KL divergence in the loss. Our intention here is to both minimize the discrepancy between our encoder and decoder as in the autoencoder loss, as well as minimize the difference between the probability distribution given by our encoder and the "true" distribution that was used to generate our data. This is done by adding the KL divergence to the loss. For many standard VGAE, this is given by

$$\text{KL}(p\|q) = -0.5 \left(1 + \text{logvar} - \mu^2 - \sum(\exp(\text{logvar})\right), \tag{5.1}$$

where $(p\|q)$ denotes the divergence of probability p with respect to probability q. The term μ is the mean value of the latent features, and log(var) is the logarithm of the variance. We use this in the loss function whenever we build a VGAE, ensuring that the forward pass returns both the mean and variance to our decoder.

OVER-SQUASHING

We've discussed how GNNs can be used to find out information about a node by propagating node and edge representations through message passing. These are used to make embeddings of individual nodes or edges, which help guide the model to perform some specific tasks. In this chapter, we discussed how to construct a model that constructs latent representations by propagating all of the embeddings created by the message-passing layers into a latent space. Both perform dimension reduction and representation learning of graph-specific data.

However, GNNs have a specific limitation in how much information they can use to make representations. GNNs suffer from something known as *over-squashing*, which refers to how information that is spread many hops across the graph (i.e., message passing) causes a considerable drop in performance. This is because the neighborhood that each node receives information from, also known as its receptive field, grows exponentially with the number of layers of the GNN. As more information is aggregated through message passing across these layers, the important signals from distant nodes become diluted compared to the information coming from nearer nodes. This causes the node representations to become similar or more homogenous, and eventually to converge to the same representations, also known as over-smoothing, which we discussed in chapter 4.

Empirical evidence has shown that this can start to occur with as few as three or four layers [7], as you can see in figure 5.19. This highlights one of the key differences between GNNs and other deep learning architectures: we rarely want to make a very deep model with many layers stacked on top of each other. For models with many layers, other methods are often also introduced to ensure long-range information is included such as skip connections or attention mechanisms.

In the previous example in this chapter, we spoke about using GNNs for drug discovery. Here, we considered an example where the graphs were relatively small. However, when graphs become larger, there is an increasing risk that long-range interactions become important. This is particularly true in chemistry and biology, where nodes at

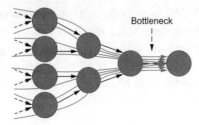

Bottleneck

Bottleneck of GNNs

Figure 5.19   Visualization of over-squashing (Source: Alon and Yahav [7])

extreme ends of a graph can have an outsized influence on the overall properties of the graph. In the context of chemistry, these might be two atoms that are either ends of a large molecule and which decide the overall properties of the molecule such as its toxicity. The range of interactions or information flow that we need to consider to effectively model a problem is known as the *problem radius*. When designing a GNN, we need to make sure that the number of layers is at least as large as the problem radius.

In general, there are several methods for addressing over-squashing for GNNs:

- Ensure that not too many layers are stacked together.
- Add in new "fake" edges between nodes that are very far/many hops apart or introduce a single node that is attached to all other nodes so that the problem radius is reduced to 2.
- Use sampling, such as GraphSAGE, which samples from the neighborhood or introduces skip connections, which similarly skip some local neighbors. For sampling methods, it's important to balance the loss of local information with the gain of more long-range information.

All of these methods are highly problem specific, and you should think carefully about the type of interactions between nodes in your graph when deciding whether long-range interactions are important. For example, in the next chapter, we consider motion prediction where the head has likely little influence on the foot compared to the knee. Alternatively, molecular graphs as described in this chapter will likely have large influences from more distant nodes. Therefore, the most important part in resolving problems such as over-squashing is making sure you have a solid understanding of both your problem and data.

Summary

- Discriminative models learn to separate data classes, while generative models learn to model the entire dataspace.
- Generative models are often used to perform dimension reduction. Principal component analysis (PCA) is a form of linear dimension reduction.
- Autoencoders contain two key components, the encoder and the decoder, both represented by neural networks. They learn how to take data and encode (compress) it into a low dimensional representation as well as decode (uncompress)

it again. For autoencoders, the low dimensional representation is known as the latent space.

- VAEs extend autoencoders to have a regularizing term in the loss. This regularizing term is typically the Kullback-Liebler (KL) divergence, which measures the difference between two distributions—the learned latent distribution and a prior distribution. The latent space of VAEs is more structured and continuous, where each point represents a probability density rather than a fixed-point encoding.
- Autoencoders and variational autoencoders (VAEs) can also be applied to graphs. These are, respectively, graph autoencoders (GAE) and variational graph autoencoders (VGAE). They are similar to typical autoencoders and VAEs, but the decoder element is typically the dot product applied to the edge list.
- GAEs and VGAEs are useful for edge prediction tasks. They can help us predict where there might be hidden edges in our graph.

Part 3

Advanced topics

The evolution of graph neural networks (GNNs) has unlocked a wealth of new possibilities, and this part of the book delves into some of the most exciting and complex frontiers. We begin by examining spatiotemporal GNNs, which model dynamic graphs that evolve over time, along with applications such as pose estimation in motion analysis. Next, we tackle the challenge of scaling GNNs to massive datasets, exploring strategies to efficiently process industrial-scale graphs while maintaining high performance. Finally, we focus on the practical considerations for building and deploying GNN projects, including how to create graph data models from nongraph data, perform ETL (extract, transform, load) and preprocessing from raw data sources, and construct datasets and data loaders with PyTorch Geometric (PyG). Each chapter in this part provides actionable insights and tools to master these advanced topics, empowering you to unlock the full potential of GNNs in your work.

Dynamic graphs: Spatiotemporal GNNs

This chapter covers

- Introducing memory into your deep learning models
- Understanding the different ways to model temporal relations using graph neural networks
- Implementing dynamic graph neural networks
- Evaluating your temporal graph neural network models

So far, all of our models and data have been single snapshots in time. In practice, the world is dynamic and in constant flux. Objects can move physically, following a trajectory in front of our eyes, and we're able to predict their future positions based on these observed trajectories. Traffic flow, weather patterns, and the spread of diseases across networks of people are all examples where more information can be gained when modeled with spatiotemporal graphs instead of static graphs.

Models that we build today might quickly lose performance and accuracy as we deploy them in the real world. These are problems intrinsic to any deep learning (and machine learning) model, known as *out-of-distribution (OOD) generalization*, that is, how well models generalize to entirely unseen data.

In this chapter, we consider how to make models that are suitable for dynamic events. While this doesn't mean they can deal with OOD data, our dynamic models will be able to make predictions about unseen events in the future using the recent past.

To build our dynamic graph-based learning model, we'll consider the problem of pose estimation. *Pose estimation* relates to those classes of problems that predict how bodies (human, animal, or robotic) move over time. In this chapter, we'll consider a body walking and build several models that learn how to predict the next step from a series of video frames. To do this, we'll first explain the problem in more detail and how to understand this as a relational problem before jumping in to see how graph-based learning approaches this problem. As with the rest of our book, further technical details are left to section 6.5 at the end of the chapter.

We'll use much of the material that we've already covered in the book. If you've skipped ahead to this chapter, make sure you have a good understanding of the concepts described in the "Building on what you've learned" sidebar.

NOTE   Code from this chapter can be found in notebook form at the GitHub repository (https://mng.bz/4a8D).

Building on what you've learned

To introduce temporal updates into our GNN, we can build on some of the concepts that we've learned in previous chapters. As a quick refresher, we've summarized some of the main important features from each chapter:

- *Message passing*—In chapter 2, you learned that the main method used by GNNs to learn from relational data is by combining message passing with artificial neural networks. Each layer of a GNN can be understood as one step of message passing.

- *Graph convolutional networks (GCNs)*—In chapter 3, you saw that message passing itself can be understood as the relational form of the convolution operator (as in convolutional neural networks [CNNs]), and this is the central idea behind GCNs. Messages can also be averaged across neighborhoods by only sampling a subset of nearest neighbors. This is used for GraphSAGE and can considerably reduce the total compute needed.

- *Attention*—In chapter 4, we showed how the aggregation function for message passing doesn't need to be restricted to only summing, averaging, or max operations (though the operation must be permutation invariant). Attention allows for a weighting to be learned during training to give more flexible message-passing aggregation functions. Using a graph attention network (GAT) is the basic form of adding attention to message passing.

- *Generative models*—While discriminative models seek to learn separations between data classes, generative models attempt to learn the underlying data-generating process. The autoencoder is one of the most popular frameworks for designing generative models, where data is passed through a neural network bottleneck to create a low-dimensional representation of the data, also called the latent space. These are commonly implemented as graph autoencoders (GAEs) or variational graph autoencoders (VGAEs) for graphs, as we discussed in chapter 5.

6.1 Temporal models: Relations through time

Almost every data problem will, in some way, also be a dynamic problem. In many cases, we can ignore changes in time and build models that are suitable for snapshots of the data that we've collected. For example, image segmentation methods rarely consider video footage to train models.

In chapter 3, we used a GCN to predict suitable products to recommend to customers using data on a customer-purchaser network. We used a toy dataset that had been collected over a period of several years. However, in reality, we'll often have constant streams of data and want to make up-to-date predictions that account for both customer and cultural habit changes. Similarly, when we applied a GAT to a fraud-detection problem, the data we used was a single snapshot of financial records that was collected over a period of several years. However, we didn't account for how financial behaviors changed over time in our model. Again, we would likely want to use this information to predict where an individual's spending behavior abruptly changes to help us detect fraudulent activity.

These are just a few of the many different dynamic problems that we're faced with every day (see figure 6.1). GNNs are unique in that they can model both dynamic and relational changes. This is very important as many of the networks that operate around us are also moving in time. Take, for example, a social network. Our friendships change, mature, and sadly (or fortunately!) weaken over time. We might become stronger friends with work colleagues or friends of friends and see friends from our hometown less frequently. Making predictions for social networks need to account for this.

As another example, we often make predictions about which way to go and when we might arrive based on our knowledge of the roads, traffic patterns, and how much of a rush we're in. A dynamic GNN can also be used to help make use of this data, by treating the road network as a graph and making temporal predictions on how this network will change. Finally, we can consider predicting how two or more objects move together, that is, by estimating their future trajectories. While this might seem less useful than making friends or getting to work on time, predicting trajectories of interacting bodies, such as molecules, cells, objects, or even stars, is vital to many sciences as well as for robotic planning. Again, dynamic GNNs can help us both predict these trajectories and infer new equations or rules that explain them.

These examples are just the tip of the iceberg for applications where we need to model temporal changes. In fact, we're sure that you can think of many others. Given the importance of knowing how to combine relational learning with temporal learning, we'll cover three different methods for building dynamic models, two of which use GNNs: a recurrent neural network (RNN) model, a GAT model, and a neural relational inference (NRI) model. We'll build machine learning models that

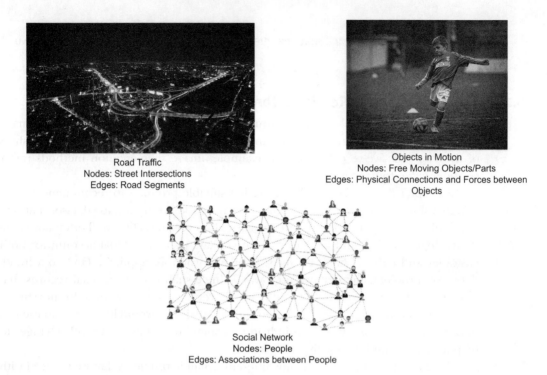

Road Traffic
Nodes: Street Intersections
Edges: Road Segments

Objects in Motion
Nodes: Free Moving Objects/Parts
Edges: Physical Connections and Forces between
Objects

Social Network
Nodes: People
Edges: Associations between People

Figure 6.1   Examples of different dynamic problems

"learn to walk" by estimating how a human pose changes over time. These models
are often deployed in, for example, medical consultations, remote home security
services, and filmmaking. The models are also a great toy problem for us to learn to
walk before we can run. In that spirit, let's first learn more about the data and build
our first benchmark model.

6.2   *Problem definition: Pose estimation*

In this chapter, we'll solve a "dynamic relational" problem with one set of data: preprocessed segmentation of a body walking. This is a useful dataset to explore these
techniques, as a moving body is a textbook example of an interacting system: our foot
moves because our knee moves because a leg moves, and our arms and torso will all
move too. This means that there is a temporal component to our problem.

In a nutshell, our pose estimation problem is about path prediction. More pre-
cisely, we want to know where, for example, a foot will move having followed the rest
of the body for some number of previous timesteps. This type of object tracking is
something that we do every day, for example, when we play sports, catch something
that's falling, or watch a television show. We learn this skill as a child and often take it
for granted. However, as you'll see, teaching a machine to perform this object tracking was a significant challenge up until the emergence of spatiotemporal GNNs.

The skills that we'll use for path prediction are important for many other tasks. Predicting events in the future is useful when we want to predict the next purchase of a customer or understand how weather patterns will change based on geospatial data.

We'll be using the Carnegie Mellon University (CMU) Motion Capture Database (http://mocap.cs.cmu.edu/), which contains many examples of different dynamic poses, including walking, running, jumping, and performing sports moves, as well as multiple people interacting [1]. Throughout this chapter, we'll use the same dataset of subject #35 walking. At each timestep, the subject has 41 sensors that each follow a single joint, ranging from the toes up to the neck. An example of the data from this database is shown in figure 6.2. These sensors track the movement of part of the body across snapshots of their motion. In this chapter, we won't follow the entire motion and consider only a small subset of the motion. We'll use the first 49 frames for our training and validation datasets and 99 frames for our test set. In total, there are 31 different examples of this subject walking. We'll discuss more about the structure of our data in the next section.

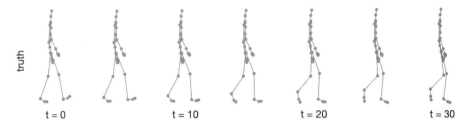

Figure 6.2 Snapshots in time (t = time in seconds) of a human subject walking. The dots represent sensors placed on key joints on the human's body. These snapshots are across 30 seconds. To represent these figures as a graph, the sensor placements (joints) can be represented as nodes, and the body's connections between the joints are the edges.

6.2.1 Setting up the problem

Our aim is to predict the dynamics for all the individual joints. Clearly, we can construct this as a graph because all the joints are connected through edges, as shown previously in figure 6.2. Therefore, it makes sense to use GNNs to solve this problem. However, we'll first compare another approach, which doesn't account for the graph data, to benchmark our GNN models.

DOWNLOADING THE DATA

We've included the steps to download and preprocess the data in our code repository. The data is contained within a zip file where each of the different trials is saved as an advanced systems format (.asf) file. These .asf files are basically just text files that contain the label for each sensor and their xyz coordinates at each timestep. In the following listing, we show a snippet of the text.

Listing 6.1 Example of the sensor data text files

```
1
root 4.40047 17.8934 -21.0986 -0.943965 -8.37963 -7.42612
lowerback 11.505 1.60479 4.40928
upperback 0.47251 2.84449 2.26157
thorax -5.8636 1.30424 -0.569129
lowerneck -15.9456 -3.55911 -2.36067
upperneck 19.9076 -4.57025 1.03589
```

Here, the first number is the frame number, and `root` is specific to the sensors and can be ignored. `lowerback`, `upperback`, `thorax`, `lowerneck`, and `upperneck` denote the positions of the sensors. In total, there are 31 sensors mapping the movement of a man walking. To convert this sensor data into trajectories, we need to calculate the change in position for each sensor. This becomes quite a complicated task, as we need to account for both translational movements and angular rotations for the various sensors between each frame. Here, we'll use the same data files as in the NRI paper [2]. We can use these to map out the trajectories of each individual sensor in x, y, and z, or look at how the sensors are moving in two dimensions to get intuition about how the entire body is moving. Examples of this are shown in figure 6.3, where we focus on the movement of a foot sensor in x, y, and z, as well as the overall movement of the body over time (with the sensor shown as solid black stars).

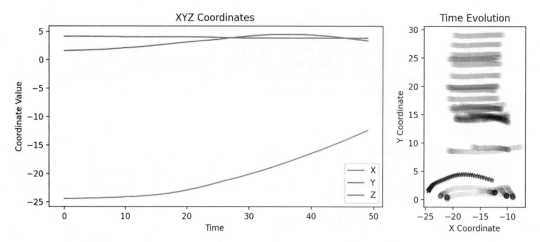

Figure 6.3 Preconstructed spatial trajectories of sensors

Along with the spatial data, we can also calculate the velocity data. This data is provided as separate files for each of the movie frames. An example of the change in velocity data is shown in figure 6.4. As you can see, the velocity data varies around a smaller range. Both spatial and velocity data will be used as the features in our machine learning problem. Here, we now have six features across 50 frames for each of our 31 sensors and across 33 different trials. We can understand this as a multivariate time series problem. We're trying to predict the future evolution of a six-dimensional (three spatial and three velocity) object (each sensor). Our first approach will treat these as independent, looking to predict future positions and velocity based on past sensor data. We'll then switch to treating this as a graph, where we can couple all sensors together.

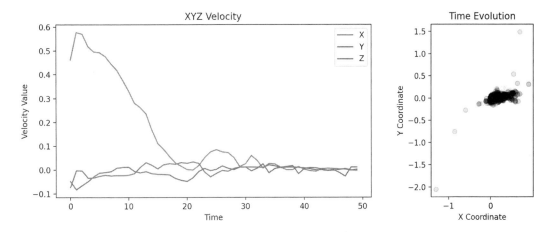

Figure 6.4 **Preconstructed velocity data of sensors**

Currently, this is a relational problem, but we're only considering the node data and not the edge data. Where there is node data and no edge data, we have to be careful not to make too many assumptions. For example, if we chose to connect nodes based on their distance from one another, then we might end up with a very strange-looking skeleton, as shown in figure 6.5. Luckily, we have the edge data as well, which has been built using the CMU dataset and is included in the data provided. This serves as a cautionary tale that GNNs are only as powerful as the graphs they're trained on and that we must take care to ensure that the graph structure is correct. However, if edge data is entirely lacking, then we can attempt to infer the edge data from the node data itself. While we won't be doing this here, note that the NRI model we'll be using has this capability.

We now have all of our data loaded. In total, we have three datasets (training, validation, testing) that each contain 31 individual sensor positions. Each of these sensors contain six features (spatial coordinates) and are connected by an adjacency matrix that is constant in time. The sensor graph is undirected, and the edges are unweighted. The training and validation sets contain 49 frames, and the test sets contain 99 frames.

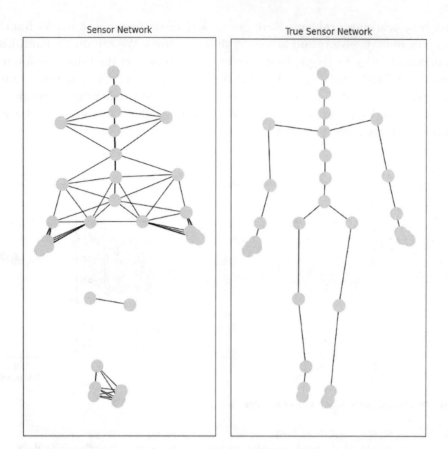

Figure 6.5   Sensor networks showing the error of wrongly inferring graph structures. The nodes are human skeletal connections. The left figure shows a network with edges inferred from node proximity (closest nodes connected to one another). This figure does not reflect a real human skeleton. The true set of edges is shown in the right figure.

6.2.2   Building models with memory

Now that our problem is defined and our data is loaded, let's consider how we might approach the problem of predicting the joint dynamics. First, we need to think about what the underlying aim is. At its core, we'll be involved in sequence prediction, just like autocomplete on a phone or search tool. These types of problems are often approached using networks, such as transformers, for which we use an attention mechanism as in chapter 4. However, before attention-based networks, many deep learning practitioners instead approached sequence prediction tasks by introducing memory into their models [3]. This makes intuitive sense: if we want to predict the future, we need to remember the past.

Let's build a simple model that predicts the next location for all the individual sensors using past events. Essentially, this means we'll build a model that predicts the position of nodes without edge data. An example of what we'll be attempting is shown in figure 6.6. Here, we'll start by preprocessing and preparing our data to be passed to a model that can predict how the data evolves over time. This allows us to predict the changes in the pose given a few input frames.

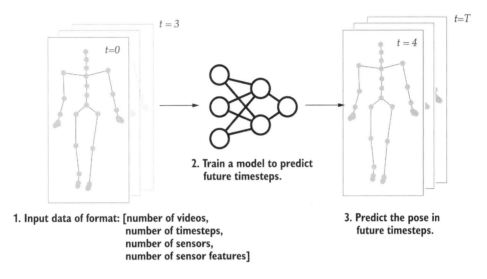

Figure 6.6   Predicting future positions using only sensor data

To introduce memory to our neural networks, we'll start by considering a recurrent neural network (RNN). Similar to convolutional and attention neural networks, RNNs are a broad class of architectures that are fundamental tools for researchers and practitioners alike. For more information about RNNs, see, for example *Machine Learning with TensorFlow* (Manning, 2020, https://mng.bz/VVOW). RNNs can be considered as multiple individual networks that link together. These repeating subnetworks allow for past information to be "remembered" and the effect from past data to affect future predictions. After initializing, each subnetwork takes in input data as well as the output of the last subnetwork, and these are used to make new predictions. In other words, each subnetwork takes input and information from the recent past to build inferences about the data. However, a vanilla RNN will only ever remember the preceding step. They have *very* short-term memory. To improve the effect of the past on the future, we need something stronger.

Long short-term memory (LSTM) networks are another extremely popular neural network architecture for modeling and predicting temporal or sequential information. These networks are special cases of RNN that similarly link multiple subnetworks together. The difference is that LSTMs introduce more complex dependencies in the subnetwork structure. LSTMs are particularly useful for sequential data as they resolve the problem of vanishing gradients that is observed for RNNs. Put simply, *vanishing gradients* refers to where the gradient that we use to train our neural network using gradient descent approaches zero. This is especially likely to happen when we train an RNN that has many layers. (We won't go into the reasons for this here, but if you're interested, read *Deep Learning with Python* (Manning, 2024, https://mng.bz/xKag) for more information.

Gated recurrent unit networks (GRUs) also resolve the problem of vanishing gradients by allowing new information to be added to the memory store about the recent past. This is achieved through a gating structure, where gates within the model architecture help to control the flow of information. These gates also add a new design element to how we can build and adapt our neural networks. We won't consider LSTM here as it's outside the scope of the book, but again we recommend that you check out *Deep Learning with Python* (Manning, 2024, https://mng.bz/xKag) for more information.

CONSTRUCTING A RECURRENT NEURAL NETWORK

Let's now look at how to use an RNN to predict the trajectories of the body sensors over time, which will act as one of our baselines for future performance gains. We won't go into the details of RNNs and GRU architectures but additional information is provided at the end of the chapter in section 6.5.

The idea for this model is that our RNN will predict the future positions for sensors without taking into account relational data. When we start to introduce our graph models, we'll see how this can be improved.

We'll use the same standard training loop for deep learning, as shown in figure 6.7. Once we define our model and define a training and test loop, we use these to train and then test the model. As always, we'll keep the training and testing data completely separate and include a validation set of data to make sure our model isn't overfitting during training.

Figure 6.7   Standard process for training a deep learning model that we'll follow throughout this chapter

The training loop used here is fairly standard, so we'll describe it first. In the training loop definition shown in listing 6.2, we follow the same convention as in previous chapters, looping through model prediction and loss updates over a fixed number of epochs. Here, our loss will be contained in our criterion function, which we define as a simple mean standard error (MSE) loss. We will use a learning rate scheduler, which will reduce the learning rate parameter after our validation loss starts to plateau. We initialize the best loss as infinity and lower the learning rate after the validation loss is less than our best loss for N steps.

Listing 6.2 Training loop

```
num_epochs = 200
train_losses = []
valid_losses = []

pbar = tqdm(range(num_epochs))

for epoch in pbar:

    train_loss = 0.0
    valid_loss = 0.0

    modelRNN.train()
    for i, (inputs, labels) in enumerate(trainloader):
        inputs = inputs.to(device)
        labels = labels.to(device)

    optimizer.zero_grad()

    outputs = modelRNN(inputs)
    loss = criterion(outputs, labels)
    loss.backward()
    optimizer.step()

    train_loss += loss.item() * inputs.size(0)

    modelRNN.eval()
    with torch.no_grad():
        for i, (inputs, labels) in enumerate(validloader):
            inputs = inputs.to(device)
            labels = labels.to(device)

            outputs = modelRNN(inputs)
            loss = criterion(outputs, labels)
            valid_loss += loss.item() * inputs.size(0)

    if valid_loss < best_loss:
        best_loss = valid_loss
        counter = 0
    else:
        counter += 1

    scheduler.step(best_loss)

    if counter == early_stop:
    print(f"\n\nEarly stopping \
initiated, no change \
after {early_stop} steps")
        break

    train_loss = train_loss/len(trainloader.dataset)
    valid_loss = valid_loss/len(validloader.dataset)

    train_losses.append(train_loss)
    valid_losses.append(valid_loss)
```

Initializes loss and accuracy variables

Begins the training loop

Zeros the parameter gradients

Forward + backward + optimize

Updates training loss, multiplying by the number of samples in the current mini-batch

Begins the validation loop

Checks for early stopping

Steps the scheduler

Calculates and stores losses

Both layers are trained (using our training loop in listing 6.3) for a specific task. For both the RNN and the GRU, the format for the data will be the individual trials or videos, the frame timestamp, the number of sensors, and the features of the sensors. By providing the data broken up into individual snapshots of time, the model is able to use the temporal aspects to learn from. Here, we use the RNN to predict the future position for each individual sensor, given the 40 previous frames. For all of our calculations, we'll normalize the data based on the node features (position and velocity) using min-max scaling.

After we finish our training loop, we test our network. As always, we don't want to update the parameters of our network, so we make sure that there is no backpropagated gradient (by selecting `torch.no_grad()`). Note that we choose a sequence length of 40 so that our testing loop is able to see the first 40 frames and then attempt to infer the final 10 frames.

Listing 6.3 Testing loop

```
model.eval()
predictions = []           Sets the model to
test_losses = []           evaluation mode
seq_len = 40

with torch.no_grad():
    for i, (inputs, targets) in enumerate(testloader):
        inputs = inputs.to(device)
        targets = targets.to(device)

        preds = []
        for _ in range(seq_len):
            output = model(inputs)
            preds.append(output)
                                             Updates inputs
            inputs = torch.cat([inputs[:, 1:]\   for the next
, output.unsqueeze(1)], dim=1) \                 prediction

        preds = torch.cat(preds, dim=1)          Computes the
        loss = criterion(preds, targets)         loss for this
        test_losses.append(loss.item())          sequence

        predictions.append(preds.detach().cpu().numpy())   Converts predictions
                                                            to a NumPy array for
    predictions = np.concatenate(predictions, axis=0)      easier manipulation
    test_loss = np.mean(test_losses)                       Computes the
                                                            average test loss
```

Once our models are defined, we can next use the training loop given in listing 6.3 to train our model. At this point, you might be wondering how we'll amend the training loop to correctly account for the temporal element when backpropagating. The good news is that this is handled automatically by PyTorch. We find that the RNN model is able to predict the future positions with 70% accuracy for the validation data and 60% accuracy for the test data.

We also tried a GRU model to predict the future steps taken and found this model is able to get an accuracy of 75% using the validation data. This is quite low but not as low as it might be given the simplicity of the model and the little amount of information that we've passed it. However, when we test the model performance on our test data, we can see that performance falls to 65%. A few example outputs from our model are shown in figure 6.8. Clearly, the model quickly degrades, and the estimated pose position starts to vary widely. For better accuracy, we'll need to use some of the relational inductive biases in the pose data.

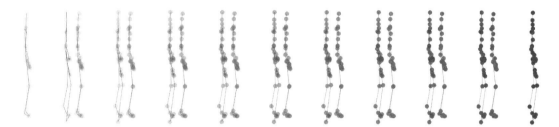

Figure 6.8 **Predicting future movements using an RNN. Here, figures on the left represent the true data, and those on the right represent the predicted data.**

6.3 *Dynamic graph neural networks*

To predict the future evolution of the graph, we need to restructure our data to account for temporal data. Specifically, dynamic GNNs connect different sequential snapshots of the graph's evolution and learn to predict future evolutions [4–6]. One method for doing so is to combine them into a single graph. This temporal graph now contains both per-timestep data and the temporal connections encoded as nodes with temporal edges. We'll first approach the task of pose estimation by taking a naive approach to modeling graph evolution. We'll look at how we can combine our temporal data into one large graph and then predict the future evolution by masking the nodes of interest. We'll use the same GAT network that you saw in chapter 3. Then, in section 6.4, we'll show another method for solving the pose estimation problem by instead encoding each snapshot of the graph and predicting the evolution using a combination of variational autoencoders (VAEs) and RNNs, which is the NRI method [2].

6.3.1 *Graph attention network for dynamic graphs*

We'll look at how to convert our pose estimation problem into a graph-based problem. To do this, we need to construct an adjacency matrix that accounts for temporal information. First, we need to load our data in as a PyTorch Geometric (PyG) data object. We'll use the same location and velocity data that we used to train our RNN. The difference here is that we'll construct a single graph that contains all the data. The code snippet in listing 6.4 shows how we initialize our dataset. We pass the paths for where the location and velocity data are as well as where the edge data is located.

We also pass whether we need to transform our data and the mask and window size that we'll predict over.

Listing 6.4   Loading the data as a graph

```
class PoseDataset(Dataset):
    def __init__(self, loc_path,
                 vel_path,
                 edge_path,
                 mask_path,
                 mask_size,
                 transform=True):

        self.locations = np.load(loc_path)          # Loads the data
        self.velocities = np.load(vel_path)         # from .npy files
        self.edges = np.load(edge_path)

        self.transform=transform                     # Determines the
        self.mask_size = mask_size                   # mask size
        self.window_size = self.locations\
.shape[1] - self.mask_size                           # Determines the
                                                     # window size
```

For all our dataset objects, we need a `get` method inside the class to describe how to retrieve this data, which is shown in listing 6.5. This method combines the location and velocity data into node features. We also provide an option to transform the data using a `normalize_array` function.

Listing 6.5   Set up node features using location and velocity data

```
def __getitem__(self, idx):                          # Concatenates location and
    nodes = np.concatenate((self.locations[idx],     # velocity data for each node
self.velocities[idx]), axis=2)
    nodes = nodes.reshape(-1, nodes.shape[-1])       # Determines
                                                     # the mask size

    if self.transform:                               # Applies normalization
        nodes, node_min, node_max\                   # if transform is True
= normalize_array(nodes)

    total_timesteps = self.window_size + self.mask_size   # Repeats the
    edge_index = np.repeat(self.\                         # edges for the total
edges[None, :], total_timesteps, axis=0)                  # number of timesteps
                                                          # (past + future)

    N_dims = self.locations.shape[2]
    shift = np.arange(total_\                         # Applies the shift to
timesteps)[:, None, None]*N_dims                      # the edge indices
    edge_index += shift
    edge_index = edge_index.reshape(2, -1)           # Flattens the edge indices
                                                     # into two dimensions

    x = torch.tensor(nodes, dtype=torch.float)       # Converts everything
    edge_index = torch.tensor\                       # to PyTorch tensors
(edge_index, dtype=torch.long)
```

```
        mask_indices = np.arange(
            self.window_size * self.\
locations.shape[2],
            total_timesteps * \
self.locations.shape[2]
            )
        mask_indices = torch.tensor(mask_indices, dtype=torch.long)

        if self.transform:
            trnsfm_data = [node_min, node_max]
            return Data(x=x,
                edge_index=edge_index,
                mask_indices=mask_indices,
                trnsfm=trnsfm_data
                )
        return Data(x=x, edge_index=\
edge_index, mask_indices=mask_indices)
```

Calculates the indices
of the masked nodes

We next want to combine all nodes across the different timesteps into one large graph containing all individual frames. This gives an adjacency matrix that covers all different timesteps. (For further details on the idea of temporal adjacency matrices, see section 6.5 at the end of this chapter.) To do this for our pose estimation data, we first construct the adjacency matrix for each timestep, as shown in listing 6.6 and included in listing 6.5.

As shown in figure 6.9, the process begins by representing the graph data across multiple timesteps, where each timestep is treated as a distinct layer (Step 1). All nodes have node feature data (not shown in the figure). For our application, the node feature data consists of location and velocity information.

Nodes within a timestep are connected to each other using intra-timestep edges, that is, connections between nodes on the same timestep layer (Step 2). These edges ensure that each graph at a specific timestep is internally consistent. The nodes are not yet connected across timesteps.

To incorporate temporal relationships, inter-timestep edges (i.e., connections between nodes on different timestep layers) are added to connect corresponding nodes across adjacent timesteps (Step 3). These edges allow information to flow between nodes in different timesteps, enabling temporal modeling of the graph data.

In preparation for predicting future values, the nodes in the last timestep are masked to represent unknown data (Step 4). These masked nodes are treated as the target of the prediction task. Their values are unknown, but they can be inferred by leveraging the features and relationships of the unmasked nodes in earlier timesteps.

The inference process (Step 5) involves using the known features of unmasked nodes from previous timesteps (t = 0 and t = 1) to predict the features of the masked nodes in t = 2. Dotted arrows illustrate how information flows from unmasked nodes to masked nodes, showing the dependency of the predictions on earlier graph data. This transforms the task into a node prediction problem, where the goal is to estimate the features of the masked nodes based on the relationships and features of the unmasked nodes.

Step 1: Sequence of Graphs over Time

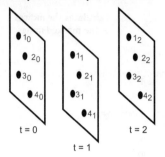

Step 2: Add Intra-Graph Edges (Dark Lines)

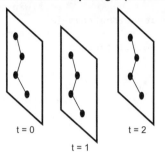

Step 3: Add Inter-Graph Edges (Dotted Lines)

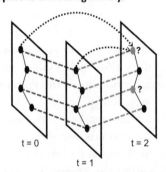

Step 4: Mask Unknown Future Nodes (Gray Nodes)

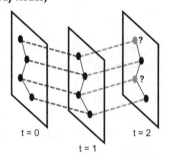

Step 5: Inference from unmasked to masked nodes using node features (location and velocity). This is illustrated for nodes in the first position but applies to all nodes generally.

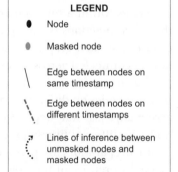

LEGEND
● Node
● Masked node
\ Edge between nodes on same timestamp
\ Edge between nodes on different timestamps
↗ Lines of inference between unmasked nodes and masked nodes

Figure 6.9   Illustration of the spatiotemporal graph construction and inference process. Step 1 shows the sequence of graphs across timesteps with nodes representing entities at each timestep. Step 2 highlights intra-timestep edges (solid lines) connecting nodes within the same graph layer. Step 3 introduces inter-timestep edges (dotted lines) that encode temporal dependencies by linking corresponding nodes across adjacent timesteps. In Step 4, nodes at the final timestep are masked (gray) to represent unknown values for prediction. Step 5 demonstrates the inference process (dashed arrows), where information from unmasked nodes in earlier timesteps is used to estimate the features of masked nodes. The legend clarifies the types of nodes and edges used in the graph representation.

Listing 6.6 Constructing the adjacency matrix

```
    total_timesteps = self.\
window_size + self.mask_size
    edge_index = np.repeat(self.edges[None, :],\
 total_timesteps, axis=0)

    shift = np.arange(total_timesteps)[:, None, \
None] * num_nodes_per_timestep
    edge_index += shift
    edge_index = edge_index.reshape(2, -1)
```

→ **Repeats the edges for the total number of timesteps (past + future)**

→ **Creates a shift for each timestep**

→ **Applies the shift to the edge indices**

Flattens the edge indices into two dimensions

Now that we have the adjacency matrix, the next step is to build a model that can predict future timesteps. Here, we'll use a GAT model, introduced in chapter 4 [7]. We choose this GNN because it can be more expressive than other GNNs, and we want something that is able to account for the different temporal and spatial information. The model architecture is provided in listing 6.7.

This model follows the basic structure outlined in chapter 4. We define the number of layers and heads for our model as well as the relevant input size, which depends on the number of features that we're predicting. Each of our GAT layers has a hidden size and we include dropout and batch normalization to improve performance. We then loop through the number of layers in our model, ensuring that the dimensions are correct to match our target output. We also define our forward function, which predicts the node features for the masked nodes. By unwrapping each timestep into a larger graph, we start to introduce temporal effects as additional network structures that our model can learn.

Listing 6.7 Defining the GAT model

```
class GAT(torch.nn.Module):
    def __init__(self, n_feat,
                 hidden_size=32,
                 num_layers=3,
                 num_heads=1,
                 dropout=0.2,
                 mask_size=10):
        super(GAT, self).__init__()

        self.num_layers = num_layers
        self.heads = num_heads
        self.n_feat = n_feat
        self.hidden_size = hidden_size
        self.gat_layers = torch.nn.ModuleList()
        self.batch_norms = torch.nn.ModuleList()
        self.dropout = nn.Dropout(dropout)
        self.mask_size = mask_size
```

```
            gat_layer = GATv2Conv(self.n_feat,\
    self.hidden_size, heads=num_heads)              First GAT
            self.gat_layers.append(gat_layer)       layer
            middle_size = self.hidden_size*num_heads
            batch_layer = nn.BatchNorm1d\
(num_features=middle_size)                          BatchNorm layer for
            self.batch_norms.append(batch_layer)    the first GAT layer

            for _ in range(num_layers-2):
                gat_layer = GATv2Conv(input_size,\  Intermediate
    self.hidden_size, heads=num_heads)              GAT layers
                self.gat_layers.append(gat_layer)
                batch_layer = nn.BatchNorm1d(num_features\
=middle_size)
                                                    BatchNorm layers
                self.batch_norms.append(batch_layer) for intermediate
                                                    GAT layers
            gat_layer = GATv2Conv(middle_size, self.n_feat)
            self.gat_layers.append(gat_layer)
                                                    Last GAT
                                                    layer
        def forward(self, data):
            x, edge_index = data.x, data.edge_index
            for i in range(self.num_layers):
                x = self.gat_layers[i](x, edge_index)
                if i < self.num_layers - 1:         Don't apply batch
                    x = self.batch_norms[i](x)      normalization and
                    x = torch.relu(x)               dropout to the output
                    x = self.dropout(x)             of the last GAT layer.

            n_nodes = edge_index.max().item() + 1   Only outputs
            x = x.view(-1, n_nodes, self.n_feat)    the last frame
            return x[-self.mask_size:].view(-1, self.n_feat)
```

With both model and dataset defined, let's start training our model and see how it performs. Recall that the RNN and GRU achieved 60% and 65% in test accuracy, respectively. In listing 6.8, we show the training loop for our GAT model. This training loop follows the same structure as that used in previous chapters. We use the MSE as our loss functions and set the learning rate to 0.0005. We calculate the node features of the masked nodes using our GAT and then compare these to the true data, which is stored in `data`. We first train our model and then compare the model predictions using our validation set. Note that because of the multiple graph sequences we're now predicting, this training loop takes more time than previous models. On a V100 GPU through Google Colab, this took under an hour to train.

Listing 6.8 GAT training loop

```
lr = 0.001
criterion = torch.nn.MSELoss()                              Initializes loss and
optimizer = torch.optim.Adam(model.parameters(), lr=lr)     optimizer with
                                                            learning rate
for epoch in tqdm(range(epochs), ncols=300):
    model.train()
    train_loss = 0.0
```

```
for data in train_dataset:
    optimizer.zero_grad()
    out = model(data)

loss = criterion(out, \
data.y.reshape(out.shape[0], -1))
    loss.backward()
    optimizer.step()
    train_loss += loss.item()

model.eval()
val_loss = 0.0
with torch.no_grad():
    for val_data in val_dataset:
        val_out = model(val_data)
            val_loss += criterion(out, \
data.y.reshape(out.shape[0],\
 -1)).item()

    val_loss /= len(val_dataset)
    train_loss /= len(train_dataset)
```

Generates the model's predictions for the input

Computes the loss between the outputs and the targets

Validation loop

Generates the model's predictions for the input

Computes the loss between the outputs and the targets

Finally, we test our trained model using the test set and code shown in the following listing.

Listing 6.9 GAT test loop

```
test_loss = 0
for test_data in test_dataset:
    test_out = model(test_data)
    test_loss += criterion(out,\
data.y.reshape(out.shape[0], -1)).item()
```

Generates the model's predictions for the input

Computes the loss between the outputs and the targets

We find that this naive approach is unable to predict the poses. Our overall test accuracy is 55%, and the predicted graphs look very different from our expectation of the pose's appearance. This is due to the large amount of data that we're now holding in a single graph. We're compressing both node features and temporal data into one graph, and we're not emphasizing the temporal property when defining our model. There are ways to improve this, such as by using temporal encodings to extract the edge data that is unused, as in the temporal GAT (TGAT) model. TGAT treats edges as dynamic rather than static, such that each edge also encodes a timestamp.

However, without this time data, our model has become too expressive such that the overall structure of the pose has diverged significantly from the original structure, as shown with the predicted poses in figure 6.10. Next, we'll investigate how to combine the best of both approaches into a GNN that uses RNN-based predictions by learning on each graph snapshot.

Figure 6.10   Output from the GAT model

6.4   *Neural relational inference*

Our RNN focused entirely on the temporal data but ignored the underlying relational data. This resulted in a model that was able to move in the right direction on average but didn't really alter the individual sensor positions very well. On the other hand, our GAT model ignored temporal data by encoding all individual temporal graphs into a single graph and attempting node prediction on the unknown future graphs. The model caused the sensors to move dramatically, and our resulting graphs looked very unlike how we would expect a human to move.

Neural relational inference (NRI), as mentioned earlier, is a slightly different approach that uses a more complex encoding framework to combine the best of both RNN and GNNs [2]. The architecture for this model is shown in figure 6.11. Specifically, NRI uses an autoencoder structure to embed the information at each timestep. Therefore, the embedding architecture is applied to the entire graph in a similar way to GAE, which we discussed in chapter 5. This encoded graph data is then updated using an RNN. One key point is that NRI evolves the latent representation of the embeddings.

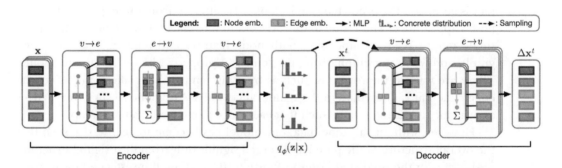

Figure 6.11   Schematic for NRI (Source: Kipf et al. [2]). The model consists of an encoder and decoder layer and several message-passing steps. However, here the messages are passed in the encoder from node to edge, back from edge to node, and then back from node to edge again. For the decoder, messages are passed from node to edge and then from edge to node. The final step takes the latent representation and is used to predict the next step in the temporal evolution of the body.

Let's explore how this model applies to our problem of pose estimation so that we can best understand the different components in the model. We'll use the same format of masking some data during training and then using the test day to identify these masked nodes. Recall that this is equivalent to inferring the future frames in our video. However, we now need to change both the model architecture and the loss. We need to change the model architecture to account for the new autoencoder structure, and we need to adjust the loss to include minimizing the reconstruction loss as well as the Kullbeck-Liebler divergence (KL divergence). For more information on the NRI model and relevant changes, see section 6.5 at the end of the chapter.

The code for the base class of an NRI model is provided in listing 6.10. As is clear in the code, we need to define an encoder and decoder when calling this class. Along with the encoder and decoder, there are some other model-specific details we need to be aware of. First, we need to define the number of variables. This relates to the number nodes in our graph rather than the number of features for each node. In our case, this will be 31, corresponding to each of the different sensors tracking a joint position. We also need to define the different types of edges between the nodes. This will be either 1 or 0, representing whether an edge exists.

We'll assume that the way the nodes, or sensors, connect doesn't change, that is, that the graph structure is static. Note that this model also allows for dynamic graphs where the connectivity changes over time, for example, when different players move around a basketball court. The total number of players is fixed but the number of players that can be passed to changes. In fact, this model was also used to predict how different players would pass using footage from the NBA.

Finally, this model needs some hyperparameters to be set, including the Gumbel temperature and the prior variance. *Gumbel temperature* controls the tradeoff between exploration and exploitation when performing discrete sampling. Here, we need to use a discrete probability distribution to predict the edge type. We discuss this in more detail in section 6.5. *Prior variance* reflects how uncertain we are on the connectivity of the graph before we start. We need to set this because the model assumes we *don't* know the connectivity. In fact, the model learns the connectivity that best helps it to improve its predictions. This is exactly what we're setting when we call the `_initialize_log_prior` function. We're telling the model what our best guess is for a likely connectivity pattern. For example, if we were to apply this model to a sports team, we might use a Gaussian distribution with a high mean for edges between players that frequently pass to each other or even to players on the same team.

To demonstrate our model, we're instead going to assume a uniform prior, which means that all edges are as likely as all others, or in everyday terms "we don't know." The prior variance sets our uncertainty bound for each of the edges. In the following listing, we set it to be 5×10^{-5} for numerical stability, but given that our prior is uniform, it shouldn't have much effect.

Listing 6.10 Base class for the NRI model

```
class BaseNRI(nn.Module):
    def __init__(self, num_vars, encoder, decoder,
            num_edge_types=2,
            gumbel_temp=0.5,
            prior_variance=5e-5):
        super(BaseNRI, self).__init__()
        self.num_vars = num_vars
        self.encoder = encoder
        self.decoder = decoder
        self.num_edge_types = num_edge_types
        self.gumbel_temp = gumbel_temp
        self.prior_variance = prior_variance

        self.log_prior = self._initialize_log_prior()

    def _initialize_log_prior(self):
        prior = torch.zeros(self.num_edge_types)
        prior.fill_(1.0 / self.num_edge_types)
        log_prior = torch.log(prior)\
.unsqueeze(0).unsqueeze(0)
        return log_prior.cuda(non_blocking=True)
```

- Number of variables in the mode
- Encoder neural network
- Decoder neural network
- Gumbel temperature for sampling categorical variables
- Prior variance
- Fills the prior tensor with uniform probabilities
- Takes the log and adds two singleton dimensions

As we discovered in chapter 5, VAEs have a two-component loss—the reconstruction error and the error in representing the distributional properties of the data—captured by the KL-divergence. The total loss function is given in listing 6.11.

Our encoder is passed edge embeddings and then outputs log probabilities of an edge type. The Gumbel-Softmax function converts these discrete logits into a differentiable continuous distribution. The decoder takes this distribution and the edge representations and then converts these back into node data. At this point, we're ready to use the standard loss machinery for VAEs, so we calculate the reconstruction loss as MSE and the KL divergence. For further insight into VAE losses and how the KL divergence is calculated, revisit chapter 5.

Listing 6.11 Loss for the NRI model

```
def calculate_loss(self, inputs,
    is_train=False,
    teacher_forcing=True,
    return_edges=False,
    return_logits=False):

    encoder_results = self.encoder(inputs)
    logits = encoder_results['logits']
    hard_sample = not is_train
    edges = F.gumbel_softmax\
            (logits.view(-1, self.num_edge_types),
            tau=self.gumbel_temp,
            hard=hard_sample).view\
                (logits.shape)
```

- Calculates Gumbel-Softmax using PyTorch's functional API, imported as F in code

```
        output = self.decoder(inputs[:, :-1], edges)

        if len(inputs.shape) == 3: \
target = inputs[:, 1:]
        else:
            Target = inputs[:, 1:, :, :]

        loss_nll = F.mse_loss(\
output, target) / (2 * \
self.prior_variance)
```
⟵ **Negative log likelihood (NLL)
for Gaussian distribution**

```
        probs = F.softmax(logits, dim=-1)
        log_probs = torch.log(probs + 1e-16)
        loss_kl = (probs * \
(log_probs - torch.log(\
torch.tensor(1.0 /
        self.num_edge_types))))).\
sum(-1).mean()
```
⟵ **Adds a small constant
to avoid taking the
logarithm of zero**

⟵ **KL divergence with a uniform
categorical distribution**

```
        loss = loss_nll + loss_kl

        return loss, loss_nll, loss_kl, logits, output
```

Finally, we need our model to be able to predict the future trajectories of the sensors. The code for predicting the future state of the graph is given in listing 6.12. This is a relatively simple function once we have our encoder and decoder trained. We pass the encoder the current graph, and this returns a latent representation of whether an edge exists. We then convert these probabilities into a suitable distribution using Gumbel-Softmax and pass this to our decoder. The output from the decoder is our predictions. We can either get the predictions directly or get both predictions and whether an edge exists.

Listing 6.12   Predicting the future

```
def predict_future(self, inputs, prediction_steps,
    return_edges=False,
    return_everything=False):
    encoder_dict = self.encoder(inputs)
    logits = encoder_dict['logits']
    edges = nn.functional.gumbel_softmax(
        logits.view(-1, \
        self.num_edge_types),
        tau=self.gumbel_temp,\
        hard=True).view(logits.shape\
        )
    tmp_predictions, decoder_state =\
        self.decoder(
        inputs[:, :-1],
        edges,
        return_state=True
    )
```
**Runs the encoder to get
logits for edge types**

**Applies Gumbel-
Softmax to the
edges**

**Runs the decoder to get
the initial predictions
and decoder state**

```
        predictions = self.decoder(
            inputs[:, -1].unsqueeze(1),
            edges,
            prediction_steps=prediction_steps,
            teacher_forcing=False,
            state=decoder_state
            )
    if return_everything:
        predictions = torch.cat([\
            tmp_predictions,\
            Predictions\
            ], dim=1)

    return (predictions, edges)\
        if return_edges else predictions
```

Uses the last input and decoder state to predict future steps

Concatenates initial and future predictions if needed

Returns predictions and edges if specified

This is the basis of the NRI model. We have an encoder that converts our initial node data into edge probabilities. The edge probabilities get passed to our decoder, and the decoder predicts future trajectories conditional on the most likely graph representation. Our encoder will be a simple multilayer perceptron (MLP) that works on graph data. Our decoder needs to be able to make future predictions, so we'll use an RNN to do this, specifically the same GRU model we discussed in section 6.2.2. Let's next meet our encoder and decoder networks so we can apply our model to the data and see how it performs.

6.4.1 Encoding pose data

Now that we know the different parts of our NRI model, let's define our encoder. This encoder will act as the bottleneck to make our problem simpler. After encoding, we'll be left with a low-dimensional representation of the edge data, so we don't need to worry about temporal data at this stage. However, by providing our temporal data together, we're transferring temporal structure into our latent space. Specifically, the encoder takes the temporal patterns and relationships from the input data and preserves this in the compressed, low-dimensional representations. This makes it easier to decode from, making our pose prediction problem easier to solve.

There are several subsets to implementing the encoder. First, we pass the input data, which comprises the different sensors at different frames, across different experiments. The encoder then takes this data, *x*, and performs a message-passing step to transform edge data into node data and then back into edge data. The edge data is then converted to node data again before being encoded in the latent space. This is equivalent to three message-passing steps, from edges to nodes, edges to edges, and edges to nodes again. The repeated transformations are useful for information aggregation through repeated message passing and capturing high-order interactions in the graph. By repeatedly transforming between nodes and edges, the model becomes aware of both local and global structure information.

Throughout this book, we've explored how to use message passing to convert node or edge features into complex representations of nodes or edges. These are at the core of all GNN methods. The NRI model is slightly different from the methods that we've explored before because messages are passed between nodes and edges, rather than node to node or edge to edge. To make explicit what these steps are doing, we'll depart from PyG and code our model in plain PyTorch instead.

In listing 6.13, we show the base class for our encoder, which requires several key features. First, note that we haven't described the actual neural network that will be used to encode the data. We'll introduce this shortly. Instead, we have two message-passing functions, `edge2node` and `node2edge`, as well as an encoding function, `one_hot_recv`.

Listing 6.13   Encoder base class

```
class BaseEncoder(nn.Module):
    def __init__(self, num_vars):
        super(BaseEncoder, self).__init__()
        self.num_vars = num_vars
        edges = torch.ones(num_vars)\
 - torch.eye(num_vars)                          ◁──┐ Creates a matrix
                                                       representing edges
                                                       between variables
        self.send_edges, self.\
recv_edges = torch.where(edges)                  ◁──  Finds the indices
                                                       where edges exist

        one_hot_recv = torch.nn.functional.one_hot(
            self.recv_edges,                           Creates a one-hot
            num_classes=num_vars                       representation for
                                                       receiving edges
            )

        self.edge2node_mat = \
nn.Parameter(one_hot_recv.\                       ◁──  Creates a parameter
float().T, requires_grad=False)                        tensor for edge-to-node
                                                       transformation

    def node2edge(self, node_embeddings):
        send_embed = \
node_embeddings[:, self.send_edges]              ◁──┐ Extracts sender and
        recv_embed = \                                 receiver embeddings
node_embeddings[:, self.recv_edges]              ◁──┘
        return torch.\
cat([send_embed, recv_embed], dim=2)             ◁──  Concatenates sender and
                                                       receiver embeddings

    def edge2node(self, edge_embeddings):
        incoming = torch.\
matmul(self.edge2node_mat, edge_embeddings)      ◁──┐ Multiplies edge
        return incoming / (self.num_vars - 1)    ◁──┘ embeddings with
                                                       edge-to-node matrix
                                                 Normalizes the incoming
                                                 embeddings
```

The first step in our encoder class is to build an adjacency matrix. Here, we assume that the graph is fully connected, such that all nodes are connected to all other nodes but not to themselves. The `node2edge` function takes node embedding data and identifies the direction that these messages have been sent. Figure 6.12 shows an example of how we're building the adjacency matrix.

$$\begin{bmatrix} 1 & 1 & 1 \\ 1 & 1 & 1 \\ 1 & 1 & 1 \end{bmatrix} - \begin{bmatrix} 1 & 0 & 0 \\ 0 & 1 & 0 \\ 0 & 0 & 1 \end{bmatrix} = \begin{bmatrix} 0 & 1 & 1 \\ 1 & 0 & 1 \\ 1 & 1 & 0 \end{bmatrix}$$

Figure 6.12 **Example of creating an adjacency matrix for a fully connected graph with three nodes. The matrix on the left represents a fully connected graph, the matrix in the middle represents the identity matrix, and the matrix on the right shows the final adjacency matrix after subtracting the identity matrix. This results in a graph where each node is connected to every other node with no self-loops.**

The next function call then determines which nodes are sending or receiving data by returning two vectors that contain rows and columns for connected nodes. Recall that in an adjacency matrix, the rows represent receiving nodes and the columns represent sending nodes. The output is then

```
send_edges = tensor([0, 0, 1, 1, 2, 2])
recv_edges = tensor([1, 2, 0, 2, 0, 1])
```

We can interpret this as saying that the node at row 0 sends data to nodes at columns 1 and 2, and so on. This allows us to extract edges between nodes. Once we construct our node embeddings, we then use the sending and receiving data to convert our node data to edges. This is the principle of the `node2edge` function.

The next function we need is how to build `edge2node` based on our `edge_embeddings`. We first construct an `edge2node` matrix. Here, we're using a one-hot encoding method that converts our receiving edges into a one-hot encoded representation. Specifically, we create a matrix where each row denotes whether that category (receiving node) exists. For our simple three-node case, the one-hot encoding method for the receiving edges is shown in figure 6.13.

We then transpose this to switch rows and columns, so that the dimension will be (number of nodes, number of edges), and we convert it into a PyTorch parameter so that we can differentiate over it. Once we have our `edge2node` matrix, we multiple this by our edge embeddings. Our edge embeddings will be of shape (number of edges, embedding size) so that multiplying the `edge2node` matrix by the edge embeddings gives us an object of shape (number of nodes, embedding size). These are our new node embeddings! Finally, we normalize this matrix by the number of possible nodes for numerical stability.

This section is key to understanding the message-passing step in the model. (For further information on message passing, revisit chapter 2 and 3.) As discussed there, once we have a principled way to pass messages between nodes, edges, or some combination of both, we then apply neural networks to these embeddings to get nonlinear representations. To do so, we need to define our embedding architecture. The code for the complete encoder is given in listing 6.14.

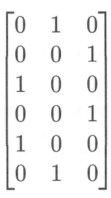 

Figure 6.13 The one-hot encoding matrix representing incoming edges for each node in a fully connected graph with three nodes is shown on the left. Each row corresponds to an edge, and each column corresponds to a node. A 1 in position (i, j) indicates that edge i is directed toward node j. This matrix is used to transform edge embeddings to node embeddings in the `edge2node` function of the encoder base class, enabling the model to aggregate information from incoming edges for each node. In this graph structure, nodes 0, 1, and 2 each send messages to the other two nodes, resulting in a total of six directed edges. The diagram of the three-node graph is shown on the right.

The `RefMLPEncoder` is shown in listing 6.14. This encoder uses four MLPs for message processing, each featuring exponential linear unit (ELU) activation and batch normalization (defined in `RefNRIMLP`, shown in the chapter's code repository).

NOTE   The exponential linear unit (ELU) is an activation function that is useful in smoothing outputs across multiple layers and preventing vanishing gradients. In contrast to ReLUs, ELUs have a smoother gradient built in for negative inputs and allows for negative outputs.

The final part of the network (`self.fc_out`) is a sequence of linear layers with ELU activations between them, ending with a linear layer that outputs the desired embeddings or predictions. The final layer of this sequence is a fully connected layer.

Listing 6.14   NRI MLP encoder

```
class RefMLPEncoder(BaseEncoder):
    def __init__(self,
            num_vars=31,
            input_size=6,
            input_time_steps=50,
            encoder_mlp_hidden=256,
            encoder_hidden=256,
            num_edge_types=2,
            encoder_dropout=0.):
        super(RefMLPEncoder, self).__init__(num_vars)
```

```
        inp_size = input_size * input_time_steps
        hidden_size = encoder_hidden
        num_layers = 3
        self.input_time_steps = input_time_steps

        self.mlp1 = RefNRIMLP\
(inp_size, hidden_size, \
hidden_size, encoder_dropout)
        self.mlp2 = RefNRIMLP\
(hidden_size*2, hidden_size,\
 hidden_size, encoder_dropout)
        self.mlp3 = RefNRIMLP\
(hidden_size, hidden_size,\
 hidden_size, encoder_dropout)
        mlp4_inp_size = hidden_size * 2
        self.mlp4 = RefNRIMLP\
(mlp4_inp_size, hidden_size,\
 hidden_size, encoder_dropout)

        layers = [nn.Linear\
(hidden_size, encoder_mlp_hidden), \
nn.ELU(inplace=True)]
        layers += [nn.Linear\
(encoder_mlp_hidden, \
encoder_mlp_hidden),\
   nn.ELU(inplace=True)] \
   * (num_layers - 2)
        layers.append(nn.\
Linear(encoder_mlp_hidden, \
num_edge_types))
        self.fc_out = nn.Sequential(*layers)
        self.init_weights()
```

Defines MLP layers. RefNRIMLP is a 2-layer fully connected ELU net with batch norm.

Defines the final fully connected layer

Here, we define architectural details related to the encoder. As discussed earlier, there are 31 sensors that we represent using the `num_vars` variable. The number of features is 6, which is the `input_size` for our network. The number of timesteps for our training and validation set is still 50, and our encoder network size will be 256. The number of `edge_types` is 2, and we assume no dropout of the weights. We then initialize our networks, which are typical MLPs, described in our shared repository. The networks include a batch normalization layer and two fully connected layers. Once the network is defined, we also pre-initialize the weights, as shown in listing 6.15. Here, we loop through all the different layers and then initialize the weights using the Xavier initialization approach. This ensures that the gradients in the layers are all approximately of similar scale, which reduces the risk of our loss rapidly diverging—known as blow-up. This is an important step when combining multiple networks with different architectures as we do here. We also set the initial bias to 0.1, which further helps with the stability of training.

Listing 6.15   Weight initialization

```
def init_weights(self):
    for m in self.modules():
        if isinstance(m, nn.Linear):
            nn.init.xavier_normal_(m.weight.data)
            m.bias.data.fill_(0.1)
```

Only applies to linear layers

Initializes weights using Xavier normal initialization

Sets bias to 0.1

Finally, we need to define our forward pass method, as shown in listing 6.16. This is where our message-passing step occurs.

Listing 6.16   Encoder forward pass

```
def forward(self, inputs, state=None, return_state=False):
    if inputs.size(1) > self.input_time_steps:
        inputs = inputs[:, -self.input_time_steps:]
    elif inputs.size(1) < self.input_time_steps:
        begin_inp = inputs[:, 0:1].expand(
        -1,
        self.input_time_steps-inputs.size(1),
        -1, -1
        )
        inputs = torch.cat([begin_inp, inputs], dim=1)

    x = inputs.transpose(1, 2).contiguous()
    x = x.view(inputs.size(0), inputs.size(2), -1)

    x = self.mlp1(x)
    x = self.node2edge(x)
    x = self.mlp2(x)

    x = self.edge2node(x)
    x = self.mlp3(x)

    x = self.node2edge(x)
    x = self.mlp4(x)

    result = self.fc_out(x)
    result_dict = {
        'logits': result,
        'state': inputs,
        }
    return result_dict
```

New shape:
[num_sims, num_atoms, num_timesteps*num_dims]

Passes through first MLP layer (two-layer ELU network per node)

Converts node embeddings to edge embeddings

Passes through the second MLP layer

Converts edge embeddings back to node embeddings

Converts node embeddings to edge embeddings again

Final fully connected layer to get the logits

Our encoder lets our model transform different sets of frames of our sensor graphs into latent representation of edge probabilities. Next, let's explore how to construct a decoder that transforms the latent edge probabilities into trajectory using the recent sensor data.

6.4.2 *Decoding pose data using a GRU*

To transform the latent representations into future frames, we need to account for the temporal evolution of the trajectories. To do so, we train a decoder network. Here, we'll follow the original structure of the NRI paper [2] and use a GRU as our RNN.

We introduced the concept of a GRU in section 6.2.2 earlier. As a quick reminder, gated recurrent units (GRUs) are a type of RNN that uses a gated process to allow RNNs to capture long-term behaviors in the data. They are composed of two types of gates—reset gates and update gates.

For the NRI model, we'll apply GRUs to our edges, rather than across the entire graph. The update gates will be used to determine how much of the node's hidden state should be updated, given the receiving data, and the reset gate decides how much should be erased or "forgotten." To put it another way, we'll use a GRU to predict what the future state of a node should be based on the edge type probabilities from our encoder network.

Let's look at how we construct this step-by-step. The initialization code for our decoder is given in listing 6.17. First, we note some of the variables passed to this network. We again define the number of variables or nodes in our graphs, 31, and the number of input features, 6. We assume there is no dropout of the weights and the hidden size for each layer is 64. Again, we need to make clear that our decoder should be predicting two different types of edges. We'll also skip the first edge type when making predictions as this denotes that there is no edge.

Once we have the input parameters defined, we can introduce the network architecture. The first layer is a simple linear network that needs to have twice the input dimension to account for the mean and variance provided by our encoder, and we define this network for each of the edge types. We then define a second layer to further increase the expressivity of our network. The output from these two linear layers is passed to our RNN, which is a GRU. Here, we have to use a custom GRU to account for both node data and edge data. The output from the GRU is passed to three more neural network layers to provide the future predictions. Finally, we need to define our edge2node matrix and sending and receiving nodes, as we did with our encoder.

Listing 6.17   RNN decoder

```
class GraphRNNDecoder(nn.Module):
    def __init__(self,
        num_vars=31,
        input_size=6,
        decoder_dropout=0.,
        decoder_hidden=64,
        num_edge_types=2,
        skip_first=True):
        super(GraphRNNDecoder, self).__init__()
        self.num_vars = num_vars
        self.msg_out_shape = decoder_hidden
        self.skip_first_edge_type = skip_first
        self.dropout_prob = decoder_dropout
```

```
        self.edge_types = num_edge_types

        self.msg_fc1 = nn.ModuleList\
([nn.Linear(2 * decoder_hidden,\
 decoder_hidden) for _ in \
range(self.edge_types)])
        self.msg_fc2 = nn.ModuleList\
([nn.Linear(decoder_hidden, decoder_hidden)\
 for _ in range(self.edge_types)])

        self.custom_gru = CustomGRU\
(input_size, decoder_hidden)

        self.out_fc1 = nn.Linear\
(decoder_hidden, decoder_hidden)
        self.out_fc2 = nn.Linear(decoder_hidden, decoder_hidden)
        self.out_fc3 = nn.Linear(decoder_hidden, input_size)

        self.num_vars = num_vars
        edges = np.ones(num_vars) - np.eye(num_vars)
        self.send_edges = np.where(edges)[0]
        self.recv_edges = np.where(edges)[1]
        self.edge2node_mat = \
            torch.FloatTensor\
            (encode_onehot(self.recv_edges))
        self.edge2node_mat = self.edge2node_mat.cuda(non_blocking=True)
```

Edge-related layers ← (annotation for `self.msg_fc1` / `self.msg_fc2` blocks)

GRU layers ← (annotation for `self.custom_gru` block)

Fully connected layers ← (annotation for `self.out_fc1` block)

In listing 6.18, we provide the architecture for our GRU. The first overall architecture for this network is the same structure as a typical GRU. We define three hidden layers which represent the reset gates defined by `hidden_r` and `input_r`, the update gates defined by `hidden_i` and `input_i`, and the activation networks defined by `hidden_h` and `input_h`. The forward network, however, needs to account for the aggregated messages from the message-passing output of our encoder. This is shown in the forward pass. We'll pass the edge probabilities in `agg_msgs`, along with the input node data, and these combine to return future predictions. This can be seen in the `predict_future` code in our base NRI class:

```
predictions = self.decoder(inputs[:, -1].unsqueeze(1), edges,
prediction_steps=prediction_steps, teacher_forcing=False,
state=decoder_state)
```

Our decoder gets passed the last time frame of our graphs. The edge data that is output from our encoder is also passed to the decoder.

Listing 6.18   Custom GRU network

```
class CustomGRU(nn.Module):
    def __init__(self,input_size, n_hid,num_vars=31):
        super(CustomGRU, self).__init__()
        self.num_vars = num_vars
        self.hidden_r = nn.Linear
```

```
(n_hid, n_hid, bias=False)
        self.hidden_i = nn.Linear\
(n_hid, n_hid, bias=False)
        self.hidden_h = nn.Linear\
(n_hid, n_hid, bias=False)
```

Defines hidden layer
transformations for
reset, input, and
new gates

```
        self.input_r = nn.Linear\
(input_size, n_hid, bias=True)
        self.input_i = nn.Linear(\
input_size, n_hid, bias=True)
        self.input_n = nn.Linear\
(input_size, n_hid, bias=True)
```

Defines input layer
transformations for
reset, input, and
new gates

```
    def forward(self, inputs, agg_msgs, hidden):
        inp_r = self.input_r(inputs)\
.view(inputs.size(0), self.num_vars, -1)
        inp_i = self.input_i(inputs)\
.view(inputs.size(0), self.num_vars, -1)
        inp_n = self.input_n(inputs)\
.view(inputs.size(0), self.num_vars, -1)
```

Computes reset
gate activations

```
        r = torch.sigmoid(inp_r + \
self.hidden_r(agg_msgs))
        i = torch.sigmoid(inp_i + \
self.hidden_i(agg_msgs))
        n = torch.tanh(inp_n + \
r*self.hidden_h(agg_msgs))
        hidden = (1 - i)*n + i*hidden
```

Computes input
gate activations

Computes new
gate activations

Updates hidden
state

```
    return hidden
```

The output from the decoder network is then the future prediction timesteps. To better understand this, let's look at the forward pass method for our decoder, given in listing 6.19. Our forward pass is given the inputs and sampled edges to build a prediction. There are also four additional arguments that help control the behavior. First, we define a `teacher_forcing` variable. Teaching forcing is a typical method used when training sequential models, such as RNNs. If this is true, we use the ground truth (the real graph) to predict the next time frame. When this is false, we use the output from the model's previous timestep. This makes sure that the model isn't led astray by incorrect predictions during training. Next, we include a `return_state` variable, which allows us to access the hidden representations given by the decoder network. We use this when we predict the future graph evolution, as shown here:

```
tmp_predictions, decoder_state = \
    self.decoder(inputs[:, :-1], edges,
    return_state=True)
predictions = self.decoder\
    (inputs[:, -1].unsqueeze(1), edges,
    prediction_steps=prediction_steps, \
    teacher_forcing=False, state=decoder_state)
```

Let's now discuss the prediction process. First, we predict a temporary prediction set. Then, we use the hidden representations to predict as many steps in the future as is needed. This is particularly useful when we want to predict more than one timestep, as we show in the testing phase of this model. This is controlled by the `prediction_steps` variable, which tells us how many times to loop through our RNN, that is, how many timesteps in the future we want to predict. Finally, we have a `state` variable, which is used to control the information being passed to our decoder. When it's left empty, we initialize a tensor of zeros so that there is no information being passed. Otherwise, we'll use information from previous timesteps.

Listing 6.19   Decoder forward pass

```
def forward(self, inputs, sampled_edges,
    teacher_forcing=False,
    return_state=False,
    prediction_steps=-1,
    state=None):

    batch_size, time_steps, num_vars, num_feats = inputs.size()
    pred_steps = prediction_steps if \
        prediction_steps > 0 else time_steps        ⊲─┤ Determines the number
                                                       of prediction steps

    if len(sampled_edges.shape) == 3:               ┐  Expands the
        sampled_edges = sampled_edges.unsqueeze(1)  │  sampled_edges
        sampled_edges = sampled_edges.expand\       │  tensor if needed
            (batch_size, pred_steps, -1, -1)        ┘

    if state is None:
        hidden = torch.zeros(batch_size,
            Num_vars,                               Initializes the hidden
            Self.msg_out_shape,                     state if not provided
            device=inputs.device)
    else:
        hidden = state                              ⊲─┤ Determines the number
        teacher_forcing_steps = time_steps             of steps to apply
                                                       teacher forcing to

    pred_all = []
    for step in range(pred_steps):                  ┐  Decides the input for
    if step == 0 or (teacher_forcing \              │  this step based on
        and step < teacher_forcing_steps):          │  teacher forcing
        ins = inputs[:, step, :]                     ┘
    else:
        ins = pred_all[-1]

    pred, hidden = self.single_step_forward(        │  Performs a single
        ins,                                        │  forward step using the
        sampled_edges[:, step, :],                  │  ins calculated from
        hidden                                      │  inputs or pred_all (see
        )                                           │  the previous comment)
        pred_all.append(pred)
```

```
preds = torch.stack(pred_all, dim=1)

return (preds, hidden) if return_state else preds
```
◁— Returns predictions and the hidden state

To predict timesteps into the future, we make an additional forward pass that is based on a single timestep, as defined in listing 6.20. This is where our network performs additional message-passing steps. We take our receiver nodes and sending nodes, which are defined from the edge probabilities from our encoder. We ignore the first edges, as these are unconnected nodes, and the network then loops through the different networks for the different edge types to get all edge-dependent messages from the network. This is the critical step that makes our predictions dependent on the graph data. Our GRU then takes the messages from the connected node to inform its predictions of the trajectories. At this step, we're learning to predict how the body is walking from what we've learned about how the body is connected. The output is both the predicted trajectories of the sensors on the body as well as the network data for why it made these predictions, encoded in the hidden weights. This completes the NRI model for estimating poses.

Listing 6.20   Decoder single step forward

```
def single_step_forward(self, inputs, rel_type, hidden):
    receivers = hidden[:, self.recv_edges, :]
    senders = hidden[:, self.send_edges, :]

    pre_msg = torch.cat([receivers, senders], dim=-1)

    all_msgs = torch.zeros(
        pre_msg.size(0),
        pre_msg.size(1),
        self.msg_out_shape,
        device=inputs.device
        )

    start_idx = 1 if self.skip_first_edge_type else 0
    norm = float(len(self.msg_fc2) - start_idx)

    for i in range(start_idx, len(self.msg_fc2)):
        msg = torch.tanh(self.msg_fc1[i](pre_msg))
        msg = F.dropout(msg, p=self.dropout_prob)
        msg = torch.tanh(self.msg_fc2[i](msg))
        msg = msg * rel_type[:, :, i:i+1]
        all_msgs += msg / norm

    agg_msgs = all_msgs.transpose(-2, -1)
    agg_msgs = agg_msgs.matmul(self.edge2node_mat)
    agg_msgs = agg_msgs.transpose\
        (-2, -1) / (self.num_vars - 1)

    hidden = self.custom_gru(inputs, agg_msgs, hidden)
```

Node-to-edge step

Message of size: [batch, num_edges, 2*msg_out]

Runs a separate MLP for every edge type

Sums all the messages per node

GRU-style gated aggregation

```
pred = F.dropout(F.relu\
  (self.out_fc1(hidden)), \
  p=self.dropout_prob)
pred = F.dropout(F.relu\
(self.out_fc2(pred)), \
p=self.dropout_prob)
pred = self.out_fc3(pred)

pred = inputs + pred
return pred, hidden
```

**Builds
output MLP**

6.4.3 Training the NRI model

Now that we've defined the different parts of our model, let's train the model and see how it performs. To train our model, we'll take the following steps:

1 Train an encoder that converts sensor data into a representation of edge probabilities, indicating whether a sensor is connected to another or not.
2 Train a decoder to predict future trajectories, conditional on the probability of there being an edge connecting the different sensors.
3 Run the decoder to predict the future trajectories using a GRU, which is passed the edge probabilities.
4 Reduce the loss based on the reconstructed poses. This loss has two components: the reconstruction loss and the KL divergence.
5 Repeat steps 1 through 4 until training converges.

This is also shown in figure 6.14, and the training loop is given in listing 6.21.

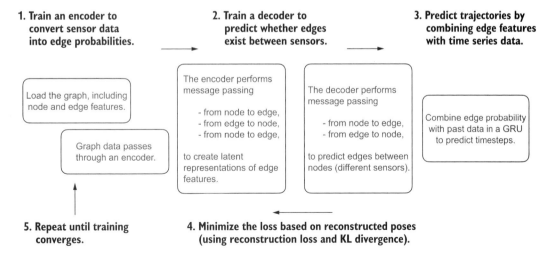

Figure 6.14 Pipeline for the NRI model

Listing 6.21   NRI training loop

```
pbar = tqdm(range(start_epoch, num_epochs + 1), desc='Epochs')
for epoch in pbar:
    model.train()                                    <──── Training loop
    model.train_percent = epoch / num_epochs
    total_training_loss = 0
    for batch in train_data_loader:
        inputs = batch['inputs'].cuda(non_blocking=True)
        loss, _, _, _, _ = model.\
            calculate_loss(inputs,
            is_train=True,
            return_logits=True)
        loss.backward()                    <──── Update the weights.
        optimizer.step()
        optimizer.zero_grad()              <┐  Zero gradients for
        total_training_loss += loss.item()  │  the validation pass

    if training_scheduler is not None:
        training_scheduler.step()

    total_nll, total_kl = 0, 0
    for batch in val_data_loader:
        inputs = batch['inputs'].cuda(non_blocking=True)
        , loss_nll, loss_kl, _, _ = model.calculate_loss(inputs,
        is_train=False,
        teacher_forcing=True,
        return_logits=True)
        total_kl += loss_kl.sum().item()
        total_nll += loss_nll.sum().item()

        total_kl /= len(val_data)
        total_nll /= len(val_data)
        total_loss = total_kl + total_nll
        tuning_loss = total_nll

    if tuning_loss < best_val_result:
        best_val_epoch, best_val_result = epoch, tuning_loss
```

We'll train for 50 epochs with a learning rate of 0.0005, a learning rate scheduler that reduces the learning rate by a factor of 0.5 after 500 forward passes, and a batch size of 8. Most of the training is based on the `calculate_loss` method call, which we defined earlier in listing 6.14. We find that our model loss falls along with the validation loss, reaching a validation loss of 1.21 based on the negative log likelihood (nll). This looks good but let's see how it performs on the test data, where it needs to predict multiple steps into the future. To do so, we need to define a new function, given in the following listing.

Listing 6.22   Evaluating future predictions

```
def eval_forward_prediction(model,
    dataset,
    burn_in,
```

```
forward_steps,
gpu=True, batch_size=8,
return_total_errors=False):

dataset.return_edges = False

data_loader = DataLoader\
  (dataset, batch_size=\
  batch_size, pin_memory=gpu)
model.eval()
total_se = 0
batch_count = 0
all_errors = []

for batch_ind, batch in enumerate(data_loader):
  inputs = batch['inputs']
  with torch.no_grad():
    model_inputs = inputs[:, :burn_in]
    gt_predictions = inputs[:, burn_in:burn_in+forward_steps]
    model_inputs = model_inputs.cuda(non_blocking=True)
    model_preds = model.predict_future(
        model_inputs,
        forward_pred_steps
        ).cpu()
    batch_count += 1
    if return_total_errors:
        all_errors.append(
          F.mse_loss(
            model_preds,
            gt_predictions,
            reduction='none'
          ).view(
            model_preds.size(0),
            model_preds.size(1), -1
          ).mean(dim=-1)
        )
    else:
        total_se += F.mse_loss(
          model_preds,
          gt_predictions,
          reduction='none'
        ).view(
          model_preds.size(0),
          model_preds.size(1),
          -1
        ).mean(dim=-1).sum(dim=0)

 if return_total_errors:
      return torch.cat(all_errors, dim=0)
    else:
          return total_se / len(dataset)
```

This function loads our test data and then calculates the MSE for our predictions given different time horizons. When we test our model, we find that it's able to predict the next timestep with an MSE of 0.00008. Even better, it predicts 40 timesteps into the future with an accuracy of 94%. This is significantly better than our LSTM and GAT models, which achieved 65% and 55%, respectively. The reduction in accuracy over future timesteps is shown in figure 6.15, and the example output is given in figure 6.16.

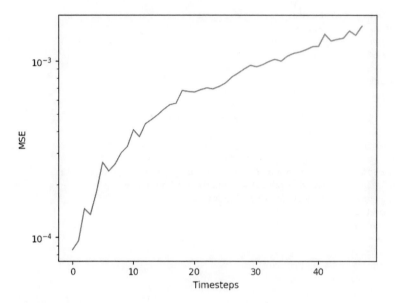

Figure 6.15   Reduction in accuracy as we predict into the future

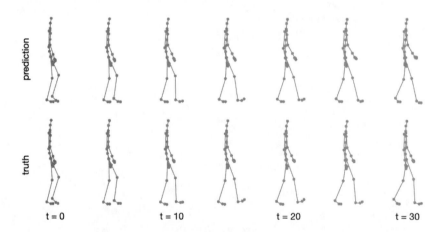

Figure 6.16   Example output from the NRI model

We've covered all the core components for the NRI model, with the full working code provided in the GitHub repository (https://mng.bz/4a8D). The accuracy is impressive and highlights the power of combining generative and graph-based methods with temporal models. This is shown in figure 6.15, where we see good agreement with the predicted pose and the resulting estimated pose.

Furthermore, this method is robust at not just predicting graphs but also learning the underlying structure even when all the graph data isn't available. In this problem, we knew what interaction network to expect. However, there are many instances where we don't know the interaction network. One example is particles that are moving in a confined space. When they are within some interaction radius, then they will influence each other, but not when they are farther away. This is true of organisms from cells to sports players. In fact, the majority of the world involves interacting agents with secret interaction networks. NRI models provide a tool to not only predict the behavior and movement of these agents but also learn about their interaction patterns with other agents. Indeed, the original NRI paper demonstrated this using video tracking data of basketball games and showed that the model can learn typical patterns between ball, ball handler, screener, and defensive matchups for the different players. (For more information, refer to Kipf et al. [2].)

6.5 Under the hood

In this chapter, we showed how to tackle temporal or dynamic problems. Here, we go into more detail for some of the key model components that we used.

6.5.1 Recurrent neural networks

In figure 6.16, we showed a schematic for RNN models. The main difference for RNN models compared to all the other models that we've seen is that the model can cope with sequential data. This means that each timestep has a hidden layer, and output from this hidden layer is combined with new input at subsequent timesteps. In figure 6.17, this is shown in two ways. First, on the left side, we show the temporal updates as a single self-loop denoted by W_{hh}. To get a better understanding of what this self-loop is doing, we've "unfolded" the model in time so that we can explicitly see how our model updates. Here, we change our input, output, and hidden layers (x, y, h) to be temporal variables (x_t, y_t, h_t). At our initial step, t, we update our current hidden layer with input data from x_t and the weights from our previous hidden layer h_{t-1} and then use this to output y_t. The weights from h_t are then passed to h_{t+1} along with the new input at x_{t+1} to infer y_{t+1}.

One of the key features for this model is that when we backpropagate to update our weights, we need to backpropagate through time (BPTT). This is a specific feature for all RNNs. However, most modern deep learning packages make this very straightforward to do and hide all the difficult computational details for the practitioner.

Let's see how to implement an RNN using PyTorch. This is as straightforward as defining a neural network class and then introducing specific RNN layers within the network. For example, in listing 6.23, we show the code for defining a network with a single RNN layer. This is a very basic definition of an RNN, given there is only one hidden layer. However, it's useful to see this example to get some solid intuition on how a model can be trained. For each timestep, our input is passed both to the hidden layer

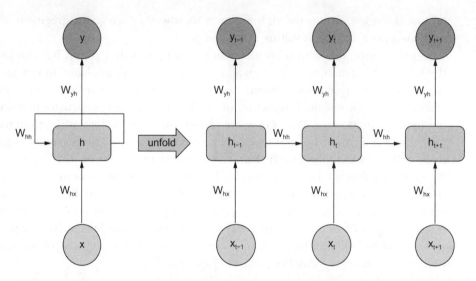

Figure 6.17   Structure for an RNN. Temporal updates as a single self-loop denoted by Whh (left). An unfolded model in time showing the model updates (right). Here, we change our input, output, and hidden layers (x, y, h) to be temporal variables (x_t, y_t, h_t). At our initial step, t, we update our current hidden layer with input data from x_t and the weights from our previous hidden layer h_{t-1} and then use this to output y_t. The weights from ht are then passed to h_{t+1} along with the new input at x_{t+1} to infer y_{t+1}.

and the output. When we perform a forward pass, the output goes back to output and the hidden layer. Finally, we need to initialize our hidden layer with something, so we're using a fully connected layer.

Listing 6.23   Defining an RNN

```
class PoseEstimationRNN(nn.Module):
    def __init__(self, input_size, hidden_size, output_size, num_layers):
        super(PoseEstimationRNN, self).__init__()

        self.hidden_size = hidden_size
        self.num_layers = num_layers

        self.rnn = nn.RNN\                              ◁——  RNN layer
(input_size, hidden_size, \
num_layers, batch_first=True)
        self.fc = nn.Linear(hidden_size, output_size)   ◁——  Fully connected
                                                              layer

    def forward(self, x):
        h0 = torch.zeros(self.num_layers,\              ◁——  Sets the initial hidden
          x.size(0), self.hidden_size)                       and cell states
        H0 = h0.to(x.device)

        out, _ = self.rnn(x, h0)                        ◁——  Forward propagates
        out = self.fc(out[:, -10:, :])                       the RNN
        return out
```
◁—— Passes the output of the last timestep to the fully connected layer

In practice, we often want to use more complicated RNNs. This includes extensions to RNNs such as LSTM networks or GRU networks. We can even stack RNNs, LSTMs, and GRUs together using our deep learning library of choice. A GRU is similar to an RNN in that it's useful for sequences of data. They were specifically designed to resolve one of the key drawbacks of RNNs, the vanishing gradient problem. It uses two gates, which determine both how much past information to keep (the update gates) and how much to forget or throw away (the reset gates). We show an example design for a GRU in figure 6.18. Here, z_t denotes the update gates, and r_t denotes the reset gates. The $\sim h_t$ term is known as the candidate activation and reflects a candidate for the new state of the representations, while the h_t term is the actual hidden state.

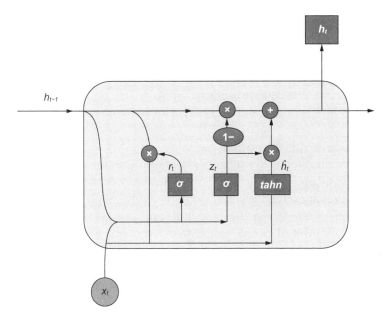

Figure 6.18   Design of the GRU layer, where r_t represents the reset gate, z_t is the update gate, $\sim h_t$ is the candidate function, and h_t is the final actual hidden state

In listing 6.24, we show how to build a model with GRU layers. Here, the majority of the implementation is handled by PyTorch, where the layer is imported from the standard PyTorch library. The rest of the model definition is a typical neural network.

Listing 6.24   GRU

```
class PoseEstimationGRU(nn.Module):
    def __init__(self, input_size, hidden_size, output_size, num_layers):
        super(PoseEstimationGRU, self).__init__()
        self.hidden_size = hidden_size
        self.num_layers = num_layers
```

```
        self.gru = nn.GRU\
(input_size, hidden_size, \
num_layers, batch_first=True)
              self.fc = nn.Linear(hidden_size, output_size)

     def forward(self, x):

          h0 = torch.zeros\
(self.num_layers, \
x.size(0), self.hidden_size)
              h0 = h0.to(x.device)
              out, _ = self.gru(x, h0)
              out = self.fc(out[:, -10:, :])
              return out
```

GRU layer

Fully connected layer

Sets the initial hidden state

Forward propagates the GRU

Passes the output of the last timestep to the fully connected layer

6.5.2   *Temporal adjacency matrices*

When considering temporal graphs, we might start with two nodes connected by one edge, then at each subsequent timestep, another few nodes and/or edges are added. This results in several distinct graphs, each with a differently sized adjacency matrix.

This might present a difficulty when designing our GNN. First, we have different sized graphs at each timestep. This means we won't be able to use node embeddings because the number of nodes will keep changing across input data. One method is to use graph embeddings at each timestep to store the entire graph as a low-dimensional representation. This method is at the heart of many temporal approaches, where graph embeddings are evolved in time rather than the actual graph. We can even use more complex transformations on our graph, such as using an autoencoder model as in our NRI model.

Alternatively, we can transform all the individual graphs at each timestep into one single larger graph by creating a temporal adjacency matrix. This involves wrapping each timestep into a single graph that spans both per-timestep data as well as dynamic temporal data. Temporal adjacency matrices can be useful if a graph is small and we're only interested in a few timesteps in the future. However, they can often become very large and difficult to work with. On the other hand, using temporal embedding methods can often involve multiple complicated subcomponents and become difficult to train. Unfortunately, there is no one-size-fits-all temporal graph, and the best approach is almost always problem specific.

6.5.3   *Combining autoencoders with RNNs*

In this section, to build intuition around the NRI model, we'll summarize its components and illustrate its application in predicting graph structures and node trajectories. To start, in figure 6.19, we repeat the schematic for the NRI model.

In this model, there are two key components. First, we train an encoder to encode the graphs from each frame into the latent space. Explicitly, we use the encoder to

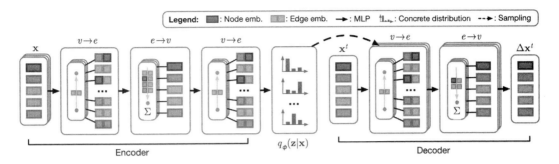

Figure 6.19   Schematic for NRI (Source: Kipf et al. [2]). The model consists of an encoder and decoder layer and several message-passing steps. However, here the messages are passed in the encoder from node to edge, back from edge to node, and then back from node to edge again. For the decoder, messages are passed from node to edge and then from edge to node. The final step takes the latent representation and is used to predict the next step in the temporal evolution of the body.

predict the probability distribution, $q_\varphi(z|x)$ over the latent interactions (z), given the initial graphs (x). Once we've trained the encoder, we then use the decoder to convert samples from this probability distribution into trajectories using the latent encoding as well as previous timesteps. In practice, we use the encoder-decoder structure to infer the trajectories of nodes with different interaction types (or edges).

In this chapter, we've only considered two edge types: where there is or isn't a physical connection between sensors. However, this method can be scaled to consider many different connections, all changing with time. Additionally, the decoder model needs an RNN to effectively capture the temporal data in our graph. To build some intuition around the NRI model, let's repeat the process once more.

1   *Input*—Node data.

2   *Encoding*—

    a   The encoder receives the node data.

    b   The encoder converts the node data into edge data.

    c   The encoder represents the edge data in a latent space.

3   *Latent space*—The latent space represents probabilities of different edge types. Here, we have two edge types (connected and not connected), though multiple edge types are possible for more complex relationships. We always need to include at least two types as otherwise the model would assume all the nodes are connected or, worse, none of them are.

4   *Decoding*—

    a   The decoder takes the edge type probabilities from the latent space.

    b   The decoder learns to reconstruct the future graph state based on these probabilities.

5   *Prediction*—The model predicts future trajectories by learning to predict graph connectivity.

Note that this model gives us graph and trajectory predictions simultaneously! While this might not be helpful for our problem, for cases where we don't know the underlying graph structure such as social media networks or sports teams, this can provide ways to discover new interaction patterns in a system.

6.5.4 *Gumbel-Softmax*

In the NRI model, there is an additional step before calculating both of these losses, which is calculating the probability of an edge using Gumbel-Softmax. The key reason we need to introduce Gumbel-Softmax is that our autoencoder is learning to predict the adjacency matrix representing our edges, that is, the network connectivity, rather than the nodes and their features. Therefore, the end predictions for the autoencoder have to be discrete. However, we're also inferring a probability. Gumbel-Softmax is a popular approach whenever probability data needs to be made discrete.

Here, we have two discrete types of edges, that is, whether something is or isn't connected. This means that our data is *categorical*—each edge is either in category 0 (isn't connected) or category 1 (connected). Gumbel-Softmax is used to draw and score samples from a categorical distribution. In practice, Gumbel-Softmax will approximate the output from our encoder, which comes in the form of log probabilities or *logits*, as a Gumbel distribution, which is an extreme value distribution. This approximates the continuous distribution of our data as a discrete one (edge types) and allows us to then apply a loss function to the distribution.

The temperature of a Gumbel distribution, one of our hyperparameters, reflects the "sharpness" of the distribution, similar to how variance controls the sharpness of a Gaussian distribution. In this chapter, we used a temperature of 0.5, which is about medium sharpness. We also specify Hard as a hyperparameter, which denotes whether one or more categories exist. As discussed, we want it to have two categories when training to represent whether an edge exists. This allows us to approximate the distribution as a continuous one, and then we can backpropagate this through our network as a loss. However, when testing, we can set Hard to True, which means that there is only one category. This makes the distribution fully discrete, meaning we can't optimize using the loss, as discrete variables are nondifferentiable by definition. This is a useful control to make sure that our test loop doesn't propagate any gradients.

Summary

- While some systems can use single snapshots of data to make predictions, others need to consider changes in time to avoid errors or vulnerabilities.

- Spatiotemporal GNNs consider previous timesteps to model how graphs evolve over time.

- Spatiotemporal GNNs can solve pose-estimation problems where we predict the next position of the body given some data on how the body position was in the recent past. In this case, nodes represent sensors placed on body joints, and edges represent the body connections between joints.

- Adjacency matrices can be adapted to consider temporal information by concatenating different adjacency matrices along the diagonal.

- Memory can be introduced into models, including GNNs, such as by using a recurrent neural network (RNN) or a gated recurrent unit network (GRU).

- The neural relational inference (NRI) model combines recurrent networks such as a GRU with autoencoder GNNs. These models can infer temporal patterns, even where adjacency information is unknown.

7
Learning and inference at scale

This chapter covers

- Strategies for handling data overload in small systems
- Recognizing graph neural network problems that require scaled resources
- Seven robust techniques for mitigating problems arising from large data
- Scaling graph neural networks and tackling scalability challenges with PyTorch Geometric

For most of our journey through graph neural networks (GNNs), we've explained key architectures and methods, but we've limited examples to problems of relatively small scale. Our reason for doing so was to allow you to access example code and data readily.

However, real-world problems in deep learning are not often so neatly packaged. One of the major challenges in real-world scenarios is training GNN models when the dataset is large enough to fit in memory or overwhelm the processor [1].

As we explore the challenges of scalability, it's crucial to have a clear mental model of the GNN training process. Figure 7.1 revisits our familiar visualization of this process. At its core, the training of a GNN revolves around acquiring data from a source, processing this data to extract relevant node and edge features, and then using these features to train a model. As the data grows in size, each of these steps can become increasingly resource-intensive, making necessary the scalable strategies we'll explore in this chapter.

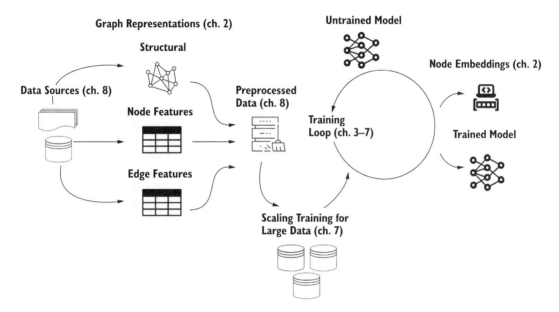

Figure 7.1 Mental model for the GNN training process. We will focus on scaling our system for large data in this chapter.

In deep learning development projects, accounting for large or scaled-up data in training and in deployment can make the difference between a successful and a failed venture. The machine learning engineer working on tight deadlines with demanding stakeholders doesn't have the luxury of spending weeks on long training routines or rectifying errors triggered by processor overloads. Heading off scale problems by planning ahead can prevent such time sinks.

In this chapter, you'll learn how to handle problems that arise when data is too large for a small system. To characterize a scale problem, we focus on three metrics: memory usage during processing or training, the time it takes to train an epoch, and the time it takes for a problem to converge. We explain these metrics and point to how to calculate them in the Python or PyTorch Geometric (PyG) environment.

In this chapter, the emphasis is on scaling from modest beginnings, optimizing from a single machine. While the primary focus of this book isn't on data engineering or architecting large-scale solutions, some of the concepts discussed here might be pertinent in those contexts. To solve scale problems, seven methods are explained that can be used in tandem or by themselves:

- Choosing and configuring the processor (section 7.4)
- Using sparse versus dense representation of your dataset (section 7.5)
- Choosing the GNN algorithm (section 7.6)
- Training in batches based on sampling from your data (section 7.7)
- Using parallel or distributed computing (section 7.8)
- Using remote backends (section 7.9)
- Coarsening your graph (section 7.10)

To illustrate how to make decisions regarding these methods in practice, examples or mini-cases are provided. The fictional company GeoGrid Inc. (hereafter, GeoGrid) is followed through various cases as the company deals with relevant problems related to large data.

In addition, the Amazon Products dataset you encountered in chapter 3, where a graph convolutional network (GCN) and GraphSAGE were used to perform node classification, is used to demonstrate the various methods. For relevant methods, example code can be found in the GitHub repository for this book.

This chapter diverges from previous ones. Whereas earlier chapters honed in on one or two examples to illustrate a range of concepts, the unique nature of scale problems means that various methods will be explored, each accompanied by brief examples. Consequently, this chapter's sections can be read in any order after section 7.3.

We'll start by reviewing the Amazon Products dataset from chapter 3 and introducing GeoGrid. Then, we'll discuss ways to characterize and measure scale, focusing on the three metrics. Finally, we'll go through each method in more detail and provide code where appropriate.

> **NOTE**   Code from this chapter can be found in notebook form at the GitHub repository (https://mng.bz/QDER). Colab links and data from this chapter can be accessed in the same locations.

7.1   Examples in this chapter

In this chapter, two cases are used to illustrate various concepts. We use the Amazon Products dataset from chapter 3. We'll use this dataset to demonstrate code examples, which can be found in the GitHub repository. Secondly, mini-cases featuring a fictional company called GeoGrid will be used to illuminate guidelines and the practice of using the methods presented.

7.1.1   Amazon Products dataset

This subsection will reintroduce the dataset and its training from chapter 3. First, the dataset is reviewed and then the configuration of the hardware used to train it. Finally, as a prelude to the sections that follow, we highlight a couple of methods we applied in chapter 3 to accommodate the dataset size. This dataset will be used extensively in the GitHub code examples of the sections that follow.

In chapter 3, we studied node classification problems using two convolutional GNNs: GCN and GraphSAGE. To this end, we used the Amazon Products dataset with co-purchasing information, which is popularly used to illustrate and benchmark node-classification [2]. This dataset (also referred to as *ogbn-products*) consists of a set of product nodes linked by being purchased in the same transaction, illustrated in figure 7.2. Each product node has a set of features, including its product category. The ogbn-products dataset consists of 2.5 million nodes and 61.9 million edges. More information on this dataset is summarized in table 7.1.

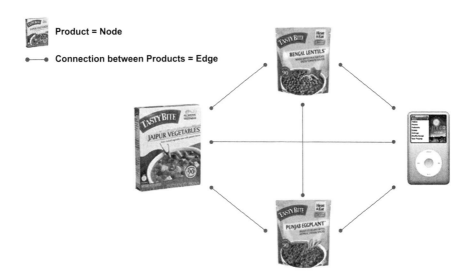

Figure 7.2 A graph representation of one of the co-purchases from the Amazon Products dataset used in chapter 3. Each product's picture is a node, and the co-purchases are the edges (shown as lines) between the products. For the four products shown here, this graph is only the co-purchasing graph of one customer. If we show the corresponding graph for all Amazon customers, the number of products and edges could feature tens of thousands of product nodes and millions of co-purchasing edges.

NOTE For more details on this dataset and its origin, as well as GCN and GraphSAGE, refer to chapter 3.

Table 7.1 Summary characteristics of the ogbn-products dataset

Nodes	Edges	Average Node Degree	Number of Class Labels	Number of Node Feature Dimensions	Size of Zipped Data (GB)
2.5 million	61.9 million	51	47	100	1.38

For the implemented code in chapter 3, we used a Colab instance with the following configuration:

- Storage: 56 GB HDD
- Two CPUs: 2-core Xeon 2.2GHz
- CPU RAM: 13 GB
- One GPU: Tesla T4
- GPU RAM: 16 GB

While we'll discuss the details later, we've already identified three factors that will affect whether we'll have trouble due to too much data. One is obviously the size of the dataset itself—not only in its raw, unzipped size in storage but also its representation, which affects working size when processing and training are applied to it (covered in detail in section 7.5). A second factor is the storage and memory capacity of the hardware (section 7.4). Finally, the choice of GNN training algorithm—such as GraphSAGE—will significantly influence the computational demands, particularly in terms of time and memory constraints (section 7.6).

As we were implementing the example in chapter 3, we indeed ran into problems whose root cause was the size of the dataset. Our focus in that chapter was on showcasing the algorithms, so we didn't point this out and silently used one of the methods to alleviate this problem. Specifically, we used an optimal representation of the dataset (sparse instead of dense).

7.1.2 GeoGrid

As you navigate through this chapter, we'll draw upon a fictional yet representative example of a tech company—GeoGrid—grappling with the challenges and opportunities in the field. GeoGrid is a geospatial data analysis and modeling company. Using advanced technologies such as GNNs, the company provides solutions for problems ranging from traffic prediction to climate change planning. As a startup in a competitive space, GeoGrid is often faced with crucial technical decisions that could make or break the company, especially as it competes for large-scale government projects.

GeoGrid will be used to explore a range of concepts and technical decisions related to scale problems. Whether the team is debating the pros and cons of different machine learning architectures, considering the use of distributed data parallel (DDP) training across multiple GPUs, or strategizing on how to scale their algorithms for massive datasets, the company's story offers a real-world context to the theories and methodologies discussed in this chapter.

In the next section, we'll provide a framework to judge and characterize scale problems. We'll then summarize the methods of solving such problems. Finally, we'll survey these methods in detail.

7.2 Framing problems of scale

Before we dive into solutions, let's define the challenge presented by scaling. This section provides an overview of the root causes of data size problems and their symptoms. Then, it highlights the essential metrics that are crucial in identifying, diagnosing, and remedying such problems [1, 3].

From the point of view of machine resources, the development process is broken down into three phases. Of the following three, in this chapter, the focus will be on preprocessing and training:

- *Preprocessing*—Transforming a raw dataset into a format suitable for training
- *Training*—Creating a GNN model by applying a training algorithm to the preprocessed dataset
- *Inference*—Creating predictions or other output from the trained model

7.2.1 Root causes

In simple terms, problems of scale arise when the training data becomes too large for our system. Determining when data size becomes problematic is complex and depends on several factors, including hardware capabilities, graph size, and constraints on time and space.

HARDWARE SPEED AND CAPACITY

A suitable system has to be able to support the preprocessing and training process via its memory capacity and processing speed. Memory should not only support the graph size itself but also accommodate the data needed for implementing the transformations and training algorithms. Processing speed should be enough to finish training in some reasonable amount of time.

We wrote this book assuming you have access to free cloud resources such as those found on Google's Colab and Kaggle, or modest local resources that host at least one GPU processor. When these resources are exceeded, upgrading the hardware setup may be an option if resources exist. For training on the largest enterprise graphs, using computing clusters is unavoidable. We'll look more closely at computing hardware in section 7.4.

GRAPH SIZE

Fundamentally, we can go by the number of nodes and edges to get a rough idea of scale and how it may affect our training solution. Understanding these characteristics gives us an idea of how long an algorithm will take to process the graph. Further, the data representation that holds the structural information will affect the size of data.

Aside from structural information, nodes and edges can contain features that encompass one or many dimensions. Often, the sizes of the node and edge features can be greater than the graph's structural information.

Defining the exact size of small, medium, and large graphs for GNNs is somewhat contextual. This depends on the specific problem domain, hardware, and computational resources available. At the time of writing, here's a general categorization:

- *Small graphs*—These may include graphs with hundreds to a few thousand nodes and edges. They can usually be processed on standard hardware without requiring specialized resources.
- *Medium graphs*—This category might encompass graphs with tens of thousands of nodes and edges. The complexity in medium-sized graphs may require more sophisticated algorithms or hardware, such as GPUs, to process efficiently.
- *Large graphs*—Large graphs can include hundreds of thousands to millions (or even billions) of nodes and edges. Handling such graphs often require distributed computing and specialized algorithms designed for scalability.
- *Time and space complexity of algorithms*—Time and space complexity point to the computational and memory resources needed to run the algorithm. These directly affect processing speed, memory usage, and efficiency. Understanding these complexities helps in making informed decisions about algorithm selection and resource allocation. High time complexity may lead to slower runtimes, affecting your model training schedule. High space complexity can limit the size of the dataset the GNN can handle, affecting your ability to process large, complex graphs. We examine this further in section 7.6.

7.2.2   Symptoms

The root causes of scalability problems manifest in several ways. One common problem is *long processing times*, which can occur when larger datasets require more computational power and time to process. Slower algorithms can increase the time required to train models, making it difficult to iterate and improve models quickly. However, the amount of time that is seen as too long will depend on the problem at hand. Several hours might be fine for results that need to be provided weekly but can be far too long if the model needs to be retrained throughout the day. Similarly, compute costs can quickly increase if processing times are long, especially if a large machine is required to run the model.

Another problem is *memory usage* at or over capacity, which can happen when large datasets consume a significant amount of memory. If the dataset is too large to fit into your system's memory, it can cause the system to slow down or even crash.

Finally, an inability to scale to larger datasets can occur when your algorithms and system setup can't handle the *increase in data size*. Ensuring efficiency in terms of time and space is critical for your system to remain effective and scalable.

7.2.3   Crucial metrics

For understanding scalability insights, running empirical analyses on key performance metrics is helpful. These metrics include memory, time per epoch, FLOPs, and convergence speed, as described here:

- *Memory usage*—Memory usage (units in gigabytes), specifically the amount of RAM or processor memory available, plays a significant role in determining the size and complexity of the models you can train [4, 5]. This is because GNNs require storing node features, edge features, and adjacency matrices in memory. If your graph is large or the node and edge features are high-dimensional, your model will require more memory.

There are several modules in PyTorch and Python that can do memory profiling. PyTorch has a built-in profiler that can be used alone or in combination with the PyTorch Profiler Tensorboard plugin [4]. There is also a `torch_geometric.profile` module. In addition, cloud notebooks hosted on Colab and Kaggle provide real-time visualizations of memory usage per processor.

In our repository's code examples, we use two libraries for monitoring system resources: `psutil` (Python system and process utilities library) and `pynvml` (Python bindings for NVIDIA Management Library). `psutil` is a cross-platform utility that provides an interface for retrieving information on system utilization (CPU, memory, disks, network, sensors), running processes, and system uptime. It's particularly useful for system monitoring, profiling, and limiting process resources in real time. Here's a snippet of how `psutil` is used in the code:

```
import psutil

def get_cpu_memory_usage():
process = psutil.Process(os.getpid())
return process.memory_info().rss
```

In this snippet, `psutil.Process(os.getpid())` is used to get the current process, and `memory_info().rss` retrieves the resident set size, or the portion of the process's memory that is held in RAM.

Alongside `psutil`, `pynvml` is a Python library for interacting with NVIDIA GPUs. It provides detailed information about GPU status, including usage, temperature, and memory. `pynvml` allows users to programmatically retrieve GPU statistics, making it an essential tool for managing and monitoring GPU resources in machine learning and other GPU-accelerated applications. Here's how `pynvml` is used in the code:

```
import pynvml

pynvml.nvmlInit()
def get_gpu_memory_usage():
    handle = pynvml.nvmlDeviceGetHandleByIndex(0)
    info = pynvml.nvmlDeviceGetMemoryInfo(handle)
    return info.used
```

Here, `pynvml.nvmlInit()` initializes the NVIDIA Management Library, `pynvml.nvmlDeviceGetHandleByIndex(0)` retrieves the handle of the GPU at index `0`, and `pynvml.nvmlDeviceGetMemoryInfo(handle)` provides detailed information about the GPU's memory usage.

Both `psutil` and `pynvml` are used in our examples for providing insights into the performance characteristics of the preprocessing and training processes, offering a detailed view of system and GPU resource utilization.

- *Time per epoch*—Time per epoch (aka "seconds per epoch" because the unit for this metric is usually in seconds) refers to the time it takes to complete one pass over the entire training dataset. This factor is influenced by the size and complexity of your GNN, the graph size, the batch size, and the computational resources at your disposal. A model with a lower time per epoch is preferable as it allows for more iterations and faster experimentation. The profilers proved by PyTorch or PyG can also be used for such measurement.

  In the provided code, the time taken for each epoch is measured by calculating the difference between the start and end times of the epoch. At the beginning of each epoch, the current time is captured using `start_time = time.time()`. The model is then trained for 1 epoch, and upon completion, the current time is again captured using `end_time = time.time()`. The epoch time, which is the time taken to complete 1 epoch of training, is then calculated as the difference between the end time and start time (`epoch_time = end_time - start_time`). This gives a precise measurement of how long it takes for the model to be trained for 1 epoch, including all the steps involved in the training process such as forward pass, loss calculation, backward pass, and model parameter updates.

- *FLOPs*—Floating point operations (not to be confused with floating point operations per second, FLOP/s [6, 7]) calculates the number of floating-point operations that are needed to train a model. This can include operations such as matrix multiplications, additions, and activations. For our purposes, the total number of FLOPs gives an estimate of the computational cost of training the GNN.

  FLOPs aren't all created equal in terms of execution time. This variability arises from several factors. First, the types of operations involved can greatly influence computational costs: simple operations such as addition and subtraction are generally faster, while more complex operations, such as division or square root calculations, typically take longer. Second, the execution time of FLOPs can vary significantly depending on the hardware being used. Some processors are optimized for specific types of operations, and specialized hardware such as GPUs may handle certain operations more efficiently than CPUs. Additionally, the structure of an algorithm affects how efficiently FLOPs are executed; operations that can be parallelized may be processed faster on multicore systems, whereas sequential operations that depend on previous results may take longer overall. Despite these variations in execution time, the total number of FLOPs required for a given algorithm remains constant.

  At the time of writing, while there are some external modules that can profile PyTorch operations, these aren't compatible with PyG models and layers. Efforts seen in the literature rely on custom programming.

In our code examples on GitHub, we often use the `thop` library to estimate the FLOPs associated with each epoch during the training of a neural network. Here's a brief snippet where FLOPs are calculated:

```
from thop import profile                    ⊲── Heterogeneous GCNs

input = torch.randn(1, 3, 224, 224)
macs, params = profile(model, inputs=(input, ))
print(f"FLOPs: {macs}")
```

The profile function from `thop` is invoked, with the model and a sample input batch passed as arguments. It returns the total FLOPs and parameters for a forward pass. In this context, FLOPs measure the total number of operations, not operations per second.

FLOP is a useful metric for a general sense of the model's computational requirements and complexity when used alongside other indicators for a comprehensive understanding of performance.

- *Convergence speed*—Convergence speed (units of seconds or minutes) is how quickly the model learns or reaches an optimal state during training. Convergence speed is influenced by factors such as the model's complexity, the learning rate, the optimizer used, and the quality of the training data. Faster convergence is often desirable as it means the model requires fewer epochs to reach its optimal state, saving time and computational resources.

  As with memory and time-per-epoch profiling, the PyTorch and PyG profilers can be used to measure time to convergence.

  In our code examples, convergence time is calculated by measuring the time interval it takes to complete the training of the model over a specified number of epochs. At the beginning of the training process, the `convergence_start_time` is recorded using `time.time()`, marking the start of training. The model then undergoes training through several epochs, with each epoch involving steps such as forward pass, loss computation, backward pass, and parameter updates. After all epochs are completed, the current time is captured again, and the `convergence_time` is calculated by subtracting `convergence_start_time` from this final timestamp. This `convergence_time` gives the total time taken for the model to complete its training over all epochs, offering insights into the model's efficiency and performance in terms of time. The shorter the convergence time, the faster the model learns and reaches a satisfactory level of performance, assuming quality of learning is maintained.

The right balance among these four factors depends on the specific project constraints such as available computational resources, project timeline, and the complexity and size of the dataset. For some real-world benchmarking of these metrics, Chiang [8] does a great job at using these metrics to do a comparative analysis between his proposed GNN, ClusterGCN, and benchmark GNNs. Given this background on what constitutes a scale problem, as well as ways to benchmark and measure such problems, we turn to methods that can alleviate these challenges.

7.3   *Techniques for tackling problems of scale*

As we outlined in the previous section, when data becomes voluminous, we must deal with problems related to memory constraints, processing time, and efficiency. To navigate these challenges, it becomes essential to have a toolkit of strategies at our disposal. In the following sections, we present an array of methods designed to provide flexibility and control over the training process. These strategies range from hardware configuration to algorithm optimization and are tailored to suit different scenarios and requirements. These methods were drawn from best practices in deep learning and graph deep learning across academia and industry.

7.3.1   *Seven techniques*

First, we start with three basic choices that can be planned for ahead of time and reconfigured during the course of a project. To prepare, choose the following for your project:

- *Hardware configuration*—These choices cover the processor type, the memory configuration of the processor, and whether to use a single machine/processor or many.
- *Dataset representation*—PyG provides support for dense and sparse tensors. Conversion from dense to sparse may significantly reduce the memory footprint when dealing with large graphs. You can convert dense adjacency matrices or node feature matrices into sparse representations using PyG's `torch_geometric.utils.to_sparse` function.
- *GNN architecture*—Certain GNN architectures are designed to be computationally efficient and scalable for large graphs. Choosing an algorithm that scales well can significantly mitigate size problems.

Given these three categories of choices, if the problem overwhelms our system, then the following are techniques we can use to alleviate the problems:

- *Sampling*—Instead of training on the entire large graph, you can sample a subset of nodes or subgraphs for each training iteration. The cost in complexity (adding sampling and batching routines) can be made up for with the gains in memory efficiency. To perform sampling of nodes or graphs, PyG provides functionalities from its `torch_geometric.sampler` and `torch_geometric.loader` modules.
- *Parallelism and distributed computing*—You can use multiple processors or clusters of machines to reduce the training time by spreading the dataset from one to many machines during training. Depending on the way you do this, some development and configuration overhead may be required.
- *Use of remote backends*—Instead of storing the training graph dataset in memory, it can be stored completely in the backend database and pull in mini-batches

when needed. The simplest case of this involves storing data on the local hard drive, and reading mini-batches iteratively from there. In PyG, this method is called a *remote backend*. This is a relatively new method in PyG, with some examples but not many. At the time of writing, two database companies have developed some support for PyG's remote backend functionality. This method requires the most development and maintenance overhead, but it's most rewarding in alleviating big data problems.

- *Graph coarsening*—Graph coarsening techniques are used to reduce the size of the graph while (hopefully) preserving its essential structure. These techniques aggregate nodes and edges, creating a coarser version of the original graph. PyG provides graph clustering and pooling operations for this purpose. The drawbacks are that you must be careful that the coarsened graph will truly represent the original, and, for supervised learning, you must make decisions about how targets will be consolidated.

The multifaceted problem of scale in training GNNs requires a thoughtful approach. Through the application of various levers such as hardware choice, optimization techniques, memory management, and architectural decisions, you can tailor the process to fit specific needs and constraints.

7.3.2 General Steps

In this section, we provide some general guidelines for planning and evaluating a project with scale in mind. The general steps are provided here:

1 *Planning stage*
 - *Anticipate hardware needs*—Familiarize yourself with available hardware options in advance. Many online and local systems have published configurations.
 - *Understand your data*—Have a clear idea of your dataset size for every phase of the machine learning lifecycle.
 - *Memory-to-data ratio*—As a rule of thumb, your memory capacity should ideally be between 4 and 10 times the size of your dataset.
2 *Benchmarking stage*
 - *Establish baselines*—Benchmark these metrics using a representative dataset. These initial figures can then serve as a foundation to predict training and experimentation timelines for your project.
 - ○ *Metrics for preprocessing*—Track memory usage and time to completion.
 - ○ *Metrics for training*—Monitor and measure key metrics such as memory utilization, time per epoch, floating point operations per second (FLOP/s), and time to convergence.
3 *Troubleshooting*—If you encounter challenges and lack the resources for a hardware upgrade, consider implementing the strategies detailed in this chapter to navigate around hardware constraints.

Now that we've learned about scale problems, the metrics to gauge them, and a set of techniques to alleviate them, let's dig into these individual methods in more detail.

7.4   *Choice of hardware configuration*

This section examines choosing and adjusting hardware configuration to solve scale problems. First, we'll review general choices for hardware configurations, followed by taking a broad overview of relevant system and processor choices. Guidelines and recommendations are given for these options. The section ends with the first GeoGrid mini-case study.

7.4.1   *Types of hardware choices*

Various hardware configurations are available for training GNNs. Each configuration is tailored to meet different needs and optimize performance:

- *Processor type*—PyTorch offers the flexibility to run on different types of processors, including central processing units (CPUs), graphics processing units (GPUs), neural processing units (NPUs), tensor processing units (TPUs), and intelligence processing units (IPUs). While CPUs are ubiquitous and can handle most general tasks, GPUs, equipped with parallel processing capabilities, are specifically designed for intensive computations, making them ideal for training large-scale neural network models. TPUs are custom accelerators for machine learning tasks. They can offer even greater computational capabilities, but their availability might be restricted. More details are given in the next subsection. Two other accelerators, NPUs (processors specially designed to run neural network workloads in phones, laptops, and edge devices) and IPUs (designed for highly parallel workloads that require large-scale data processing), are important classes of processors. PyTorch only supports Graphcore IPUs at this time.

- *Memory size*—Each processor type comes with its associated RAM. The size of this RAM plays a pivotal role in determining the scale of workload a system can handle. Adequate RAM ensures smooth model training, especially for networks that require processing large volumes of data or those with complex architectures.

- *Single versus multiple GPUs or TPUs*—For those fortunate enough to have access to multiple GPUs or TPUs, they can significantly expedite training times. PyTorch offers the `DistributedDataParallel` module, which harnesses the power of multiple GPUs or TPUs to train a model in parallel. This means you can distribute the computational load across several devices, enabling faster iteration and model convergence.

- *Single machine versus computing clusters*—Beyond just the scope of a single machine, sometimes training demands can scale up to require entire clusters. A cluster, in this context, refers to a collective of machines, each equipped with its distinct set of computational, memory, and storage resources. If you find yourself with access to such a resource, PyTorch's `DistributedDataParallel` module is again the tool of choice, at least for clustering at a small scale. In this case, it lets you span your training process across the entire cluster, which proves invaluable when working with especially large models or massive datasets.

As you scale up in terms of hardware capabilities—from individual processors to multiple devices and then to whole clusters—the complexity of planning, setup, and management also rises. Making informed decisions based on the task's requirements and available resources can make this journey smoother and more productive. As highlighted in the introduction, we'll focus on single machine optimizations in this chapter.

7.4.2   Choice of processor and memory size

As we pivot to the topic of hardware considerations, it's important to understand the primary options for training GNNs: CPUs, GPUs, NPUs, IPUs, and TPUs. In this section, we offer a concise overview of each type of hardware and present guidelines for their application. These key points are encapsulated in table 7.2.

- *Central processing units (CPUs)*—CPUs excel in general-purpose computing tasks, from data preprocessing to model training. However, they aren't optimized for specialized deep learning tasks, which can affect their speed and efficiency. On the plus side, CPUs are generally more budget-friendly compared to other hardware options, making them accessible for a broader range of users.
- *Graphics processing units (GPUs)*—GPUs are engineered for tasks requiring parallel computing capabilities. From reading this book so far, you know they frequently serve as the preferred hardware for training GNNs in a PyTorch environment, particularly when using libraries (e.g., PyG) that are designed to make the most of GPU parallelism. Most of the examples in this book have been run on NVIDIA GPUs available on the Colab platform, which include Tesla T4, A100, and V100.
- *Tensor processing units (TPUs)*—TPUs represent a specialized choice, built by Google to boost machine learning computations. They provide rapid computational speeds and can be cost-effective. However, their scope may be limited because they are a proprietary technology primarily compatible with Google Cloud and TensorFlow, and they may not offer full PyTorch compatibility.
- *Neural processing units (NPUs)*—Both AMD and Intel have NPU product lines, accompanied by an acceleration library that can be integrated with PyTorch. NPUs are dedicated hardware for parallelized processing, similar to TPUs. While GPUs were designed originally for processing graphics, they typically contain circuits that are dedicated to machine learning tasks. NPUs make a dedicated unit out of these circuits, improving efficiency and performance. Apple typically provides a similar dedicated unit (known as the Apple Neural Engine [ANE]) in most of their laptops and computers.
- *Intelligent processing units (IPUs)*—These are specialized circuit chips, designed and optimized with deep learning tasks in mind. IPUs were developed by

Graphcore and specialize in graph-based computing. These are extremely well suited for GNN-based models as they allow for independent tasks to be parallelized as needed for GNN models during message passing. IPUs are compatible with both PyTorch and PyG but require rewriting certain tasks. Other companies designing very large and powerful specialized chips include Cerebras and Groq.

- *Configuration considerations*—When selecting hardware, it's crucial to account for memory constraints, as GNNs are often data-intensive due to the unique structure of graph data. The choice of hardware can also influence the pace of both training and inference. Therefore, it's essential to weigh the tradeoffs between cost and performance, tailored to the specific demands of your project.

The principal factors to contemplate while selecting hardware for GNN training in PyTorch include the processor type (e.g., CPU, GPU, or TPU), the available memory, and your budgetary limitations. These considerations are organized for quick reference in table 7.2.

Table 7.2   Pros and cons of processor choice

Hardware	Recommended Workload	Pros	Cons
CPU	Preprocessing	Suitable for data collection and pre-processing More affordable than GPUs and TPUs	Slower for training due to lack of accelerated parallel processing
GPU	Training	Excellent for training due to parallel processing	More expensive than CPUs Surpassed by TPUs for deep learning tasks
TPU	Preprocessing and training	Faster computation time and cost-effectiveness for deep learning tasks	Requires specific software infrastructure Limited to Google platforms
NPU	Training	Optimized for deep learning and especially good for on-device AI applications, reducing reliance on cloud services	Limited to specific AI workloads, primarily neural network-based tasks
IPU	Training	Especially good for graph-based tasks such as GNNs	Can be more complex to program and optimize compared to NPUs

One last thing to consider is that certain processor types shine in particular steps in the machine learning lifecycle:

- *Data collection and preprocessing*—CPUs are typically sufficient for these steps. Often, they can handle a variety of tasks efficiently without requiring specialized hardware. However, in our experience, for some memory-intensive, long pre-processing steps, a TPU will perform better when available.

- *Model training*—Usually, this is the most compute-intensive part of the lifecycle, and GPUs are usually the best option here. They are designed for parallel processing, which accelerates the training of neural networks. GNNs, in particular, benefit from this as they often involve calculations across multiple nodes and edges in a graph. When available, TPUs may provide a performance edge.

- *Model evaluation and inference*—For evaluation and inference, the choice between CPUs and GPUs depends on the specific use case. If cost-effectiveness is more important, CPUs might be preferred. TPUs, with their high computational speed and cost-effectiveness, could be a good choice for large-scale deployments, but their usage is more limited compared to CPUs and GPUs.

Note that the best choice of processor may vary depending on the specific requirements of the project, such as the model complexity, the size of the dataset, the platform used, and the available budget. We end this section with an example from our fictional company, GeoGrid.

EXAMPLE

Dr. Smith works for GeoGrid, a leading mapping company, on a research project involving GNNs to analyze the spread of infectious diseases across different cities. Her dataset comprises data from 10,000 connected towns (nodes), with each town having approximately 1,000 node features. This dataset has a size of 10 GB. The following outlines some of the different steps required in preparing this project for analysis using a GNN:

1 *Planning stage*
   - *Anticipate hardware needs*—Dr. Smith reviews her university's computational resources and finds they have access to both GPUs and CPUs, but TPUs are currently in limited supply.
   - *Understand your data*—Dr. Smith estimates that her dataset will be about 10 GB in total. Via exploratory data analysis, she has determined that her data is sparse.
   - *Memory-to-data ratio*—Keeping the rule of thumb to reserve capacity of 4 to 10 times the data size in mind, she deduces that she'd ideally want access to a machine with at least 40 GB to 100 GB of RAM.
2 *Benchmarking stage*—Using a subset of her data, Dr. Smith benchmarks the data preprocessing time and model training time on both a GPU and CPU. She notices a significant speed-up when using the GPU for model training, as expected, but the CPU performs comparatively well for data preprocessing. She decides to use a CPU device for preprocessing and a GPU for model training.
3 *Troubleshooting*—By investigating the cause of frequent system crashes and memory errors, Dr. Smith realizes that her current GPU doesn't have sufficient memory to handle the larger graphs. Instead of requesting a machine with a device

with larger memory (in short supply at the time), she decides to use subgraph sampling methods, a technique detailed in section 7.7, to make her data more manageable for her current hardware.

Through this example, we see the importance of understanding your dataset and available resources, benchmarking to set expectations, and troubleshooting to find solutions within the constraints. Next, we examine the choice of how to represent our data.

7.5   *Choice of data representation*

Depending on the characteristics of your input graph(s), how you store and represent them in PyG will have an effect on time and space constraints. In PyG, the primary data classes, `torch_geometric.data.Data` and `torch_geometric.data.HeteroData`, can be represented in two formats to represent graphs in a sparse or dense format. In PyG, the difference between dense and sparse representation lies in how the graph's adjacency matrix and node features are stored in memory. Dense representation has the following characteristics:

- The entire adjacency matrix is stored in memory, both zero and nonzero elements, using a 2D tensor of size $N \times N$, where N is the number of nodes.
- Node features are stored in a dense 2D tensor of size $N \times F$, where F is the number of features per node.
- This representation is memory-intensive but allows for faster computation when the graph is dense, meaning most of the graph's vertices are connected to one another; that is, its adjacency matrix has a high percentage of nonzero elements, as explained in appendix A.

Sparse representation, on the other hand, has these characteristics:

- The adjacency matrix is stored in a sparse format, such as the COO (coordinate) format, which only stores the nonzero elements' indices and their values.
- Node features can be stored in a sparse 2D tensor or a dictionary mapping node with indices to their feature vectors.
- This representation is memory-efficient, especially when the graph is sparse, meaning few of the graph's vertices are connected to one another; that is, its adjacency matrix has a low percentage of nonzero elements, as explained in appendix A. However, it may result in slower computation compared to dense representation for specific tasks.

NOTE   To understand the difference between sparse or dense formats and the characteristic of a graph *being* sparse or dense, refer to appendix A, section A.2.

In PyG, two approaches that can be used to convert a dense dataset into a sparse representation are using the built-in function or performing the conversion manually:

- `torch_geometric.transforms.ToSparseTensor`—This transformation in PyG can be used to convert a dense adjacency matrix or edge index to a sparse tensor representation. It constructs a sparse adjacency matrix using the COO (Coordinate) format. You can apply this transformation to your dataset to convert the dense representation to a sparse one:

```
torch_geometric.transforms import ToSparseTensor

dataset = YourDataset(transform=ToSparseTensor())
```

- *Manual conversion*—You can manually convert a dense adjacency matrix or edge index to a sparse representation using PyTorch or SciPy sparse tensor functionalities. You can create a `torch_sparse.SparseTensor` or `scipy.sparse` matrix and construct it from the dense representation:

```
from torch_sparse import SparseTensor

dense_adj = ...                                      ◁──┐  Dense adjacency
sparse_adj = SparseTensor.from_dense(dense_adj)            matrix
```

In general, the primary motive for using sparse tensors is to save memory, especially when dealing with large-scale graphs or matrices with a high percentage of zeros. But, if your data has very few zero elements, dense tensors could provide a slight advantage in terms of memory access and computation speed, as the overhead associated with indexing and accessing sparse tensors may outweigh the space savings. Note that converting your graph dataset from one representation to another can itself tax your memory and processing power.

EXAMPLE

A school district has hired GeoGrid to study the relationships of its honor students across its many campuses. One aspect of this work is a social network where students are nodes and associations between students are edges. Dr. Barker is researching a social network graph of the students, hoping to determine patterns of friendship formation:

- *Initial analysis*—Dr. Barker finds that within this small community, almost everyone knows everyone else. In terms of raw data, there are 1,000 students (nodes) and around 450,000 friendships (edges). Dr. Barker compares the existing edges to the total possible connections: $n(n-1)/2$, where n is the number of nodes; this equals 499,500. Because the existing edges (450,000) are nearly equal to the total number of edges (499,500), he determines he is dealing with a dense graph.
- *Dense representation*—Considering the density of the graph:
  - The adjacency matrix is of size 1,000 × 1,000.
  - If each student has a feature vector capturing 10 attributes (e.g., grade, number of clubs, etc.), the node features are stored in a tensor of size 1,000 × 10.

Given the high number of nonzero elements in the adjacency matrix due to the dense nature of the graph, Dr. Barker first considers using the dense representation for more efficient computation:

- *Memory consideration*—However, as Dr. Barker's research progresses, he plans to incorporate more schools into his dataset, expecting the graph to become much larger but not necessarily denser. He anticipates that the increased size could become memory-intensive with a dense representation.

- *Sparse representation*—To handle this potential problem, he decides to experiment with sparse representation as well. He uses the `torch_geometric.transforms.ToSparseTensor` transformation to convert his current dense graph dataset into a sparse tensor representation.

- *Results*—Upon conversion, he observes memory-saving with the sparse representation that is substantial enough to choose it, especially considering his future plans. Although there's a slight increase in computation time, the memory savings make the sparse format more suitable for his expanding dataset.

7.6   *Choice of GNN algorithm*

Choosing your GNN algorithm well is essential to ensure the scalability and efficiency of your machine learning tasks, particularly when dealing with large-scale graphs and limited computational resources. Leaving aside predictive performance and task suitability, two ways to choose the GNN algorithm with scalability in mind is by considering time and space complexity and by gauging a few key metrics.

7.6.1   *Time and space complexity*

We gauge time and space complexity by using *Big O notation*, which is a kind of math shorthand used to explain how fast a function grows or declines as the input size changes. It's like a speedometer for functions or algorithms, telling you how they'll behave when the input gets really big or goes toward a specific value. It's especially useful in machine learning engineering and development to measure the efficiency of algorithms.

> **NOTE**   For a more comprehensive explanation of Big O notation, see Goodrich et al. [9]. In addition, any beginning text on algorithms should cover this topic.

We also discuss time and space complexity with respect to graphs and graph algorithms in the appendix, but here are a few examples of Big O notation for time complexity, sorted in rising order:

- *Constant time complexity, O(1)*—This is the best-case scenario, where the algorithm always takes the same amount of time, regardless of the input size. An example is accessing an array element by its index.

- *Linear time complexity, O(n)*—The running time of the algorithm increases linearly with the size of the input. An example is finding a specific value in an array.
- *Logarithmic time complexity, O(log n)*—The running time increases logarithmically with the size of the input. Algorithms with this type of time complexity are highly efficient. An example is binary search.
- *Quadratic time complexity, $O(n^2)$*—The running time of the algorithm is proportional to the square of the size of the input. An example is bubble sort.

When you understand the basics of how to assess Big O, you can use the information provided by the authors of a GNN algorithm to assess this. Often in a publication of an algorithm, the authors will provide the steps of the algorithm itself, which can be used to conduct a Big O analysis. In addition, authors will also often provide their own complexity analysis.

Now that we've covered the benefits of Big O, we'll list some of its caveats. Conducting a standalone or comparative complexity analysis of GNN algorithms can be challenging due to reasons that include the following:

- *Diverse operations*—GNN algorithms involve a variety of operations, such as matrix multiplications, nonlinear transformations, and pooling. Each operation has different complexities, making it hard to provide a singular measure. Further, not all GNNs employ the same operations, so comparing them side-by-side can be of limited use. Often, in the literature, when comparisons are made between GNNs, one major operation is compared instead of the entire algorithm.
- *Implementation specifics*—The actual implementation of the GNN algorithm such as the use of specific libraries, hardware optimization, or parallel computing strategies, also influences the complexity.

As an example, table 7.3 compares the complexity of GCN with GraphSAGE found in Bronstein et al. [10]. This comparison specifically looks at one operation (the convolution-like operation in forward propagation) on a type of input graph (sparse). Specifically, Bronstein et al. compare the time and space complexities of the operation $Y = \text{ReLU}(A \times W)$. Broken down, this operation consists of two main stages:

- *Matrix multiplication (A × W)*—This means we're multiplying matrix A (which could be our input data) by matrix X (our weights or parameters that the algorithm is trying to optimize) and then by matrix W. Matrix multiplication is a way of transforming our data.
- *Activation (ReLU)*—The rectified linear unit (ReLU) is a type of activation function that's used to introduce nonlinearity into our model. Essentially, ReLU takes the result of our matrix multiplication and, for each element, if the value is less than 0, it sets it to 0. If it's greater than 0, ReLU leaves it as is.

Table 7.3   Factors on the scalability of two graph algorithms: GCN and GraphSAGE.

Algorithm	Time Complexity	Space Complexity	Memory/Epoch Time/Convergence Speed	Notes
GCN	$O(Lnd^2)$	$O(Lnd + Ld^2)$	Memory: Bad Epoch time: Good Convergence speed: Bad	Pros: Spectral convolution: Efficient and suitable for large-scale graphs Versatility: Applicable to various graph-related problems Node feature learning: Rich feature learning that captures the topological structure of the graph Con: High memory and time complexity due to the need to store the entire adjacency matrix and node features
Graph-SAGE	$O(Lbd^2k^L)$	$O(bk^L)$	Memory: Good Epoch time: Bad Convergence speed: Good	Pro: Solves GCN's scalability problem by using neighborhood sampling and mini-batching Cons: May introduce redundant computations when sampled nodes appear multiple times in the neighborhood Keeps $O(bk^L)$ nodes in memory for each batch, but the loss is computed only on b of them

n = Number of nodes in the graph
d = Dimensions of the node feature representation
L = Number of message-passing iterations or layers in the algorithm
k = Number of neighbors sampled per hop
b = Number of nodes in a mini-batch

One takeaway from this comparison is that while GCN's complexities have a dependence on the entire node count in the input graph, GraphSAGE's complexity is independent of this, offering a great improvement in both space and time performance. GraphSAGE accomplishes this by employing neighborhood sampling and mini-batching.

EXAMPLE

GeoGrid is tasked with predicting the likelihood of an area undergoing development based on various urban factors. The nodes in the graph represent geographical areas, while the edges could represent proximity to amenities, road networks, or other areas that have undergone development:

- *Team analysis*—While the current project consists of only one metropolitan area, GeoMap hopes to gradually expand the system in the future to have nationwide coverage, including a database with millions of geographical nodes and billions of edges. Each node has a feature vector that may include attributes such as land value, proximity to public transit, and zoning regulations.

Due to the current size of the graph, the plans to expand it, and the need for timely predictions, GeoGrid's data science team must carefully select an appropriate GNN architecture.

- *GCN*—GCNs are easy to interpret, but their time complexity of $O(Lnd)$ may pose challenges as the graph scales. However, with the use of PyG's mini-batch method, the team can manage the graph without needing to store the entire adjacency matrix, making GCN a reasonable candidate.
- *GraphSAGE*—GraphSAGE offers a time complexity of $O(Lbdk)$, appealing for its memory efficiency and scalability. It allows for the adjustment of the mini-batch size b and the number of sampled neighbors k, providing flexibility in performance tuning.
- *GAT*—Graph attention networks (GATs) offer the potential for nuanced insights through attention mechanisms, but they come with added computational costs. While the Big O complexity might be similar to GCN, the attention mechanisms could introduce additional computational overhead.

ALGORITHM COMPARISON

While GCN appears simpler than GraphSAGE, its dependency on the number of nodes n can be problematic as the graph grows. GraphSAGE offers scalability due to its dependency on b and k. GAT, although potentially more accurate, comes with computational complexities due to its attention mechanism.

Using PyG for mini-batch processing makes GCN more manageable. However, the team also liked GraphSAGE for its inherent scalability advantages. GAT, despite its likely higher accuracy, could be too resource-intensive for this application.

- *Decision*—After a thorough assessment, the GeoGrid team decides that GraphSAGE offers the most balanced approach, optimizing between computational efficiency and prediction accuracy.
- *Conclusion*—They plan to trial GAT in a controlled setting later to assess whether its added computational demands genuinely yield more accurate urban development predictions. They will set out user acceptance testing with clear metrics before moving to production.

The previous three sections have covered the fundamental choices to be made when planning to train a GNN with size problems in mind. In the next five sections, we review the methods that can solve scale problems, including deep learning optimizations, sampling, distributed processing, use of remote backends, and graph coarsening.

7.7 Batching using a sampling method

In this section, we explore how to piece large data into batches chosen by a sampling method. We'll explain this in general, and then break down a few implementations from the PyG package. We close with a GeoGrid case, highlighting the practical choices and implications of using these methods.

Sampling: Literature versus implementation

In the literature, there is much discussion covering various types of sampling techniques (usually classified as node-, layer-, and graph-sampling) designed into GNN algorithms, but in this section, we'll focus on sampling implementations in the PyG package. Many of these techniques are derived from the literature, but are nonetheless meant to generalize sampling to support various GNN algorithms and training operations. For the purposes of this section, we use these sampling implementations to support mini-batching.

A GCN provides a good illustration for this. While it's true that the GCN model as conceived in its standard form doesn't involve sampling, PyG's `NeighborSampler` function can still be applied with the `GCNConv` layer. This is possible because `NeighborSampler` is essentially a dataloader that returns a batch of subgraphs from the larger graph.

In this context, the subgraphs are used to approximate the full graph convolution operation. The obvious advantage is that we can work with large graphs that may otherwise overwhelm the algorithm or our machine's memory. A drawback is that the accuracy of `GCNConv` with `NeighborSampler` might not be as high as the full batch training due to this approximation.

7.7.1   *Two concepts: Mini-batching and sampling*

Two distinct methods—batching and sampling—can often be combined into one function. *Batching* (done by *loaders* in PyG) is breaking up a large dataset into subsets of nodes or edges to be run through the training process. But how do we determine the subset of nodes or edges to include in the smaller groups? *Sampling* is the specific mechanism that we use to choose the subsets. These subsets can be in the form of connected subgraphs, but they don't necessarily have to be. Batching done in this way will alleviate the memory load. During an epoch, instead of storing the entire graph in memory, we can store smaller pieces of it at a time.

Batching with sampling can have drawbacks. One concern is the loss of essential information. For instance, if we consider the message passing process, every node and its neighborhood are critical for updating node information. Sampling could miss important nodes, thus affecting the model's performance. This can be likened to omitting crucial messages in a message-passing framework. Additionally, the sampling process may introduce bias, affecting the generalizability of the model. This is equivalent to having a biased aggregation operation in a message passing framework.

BATCHING IMPLEMENTED IN PyG

Batching methods can be found in the `loader` and `sampler` modules. Most of these combine a sampling method with functions that batch and serve the sampled data to a model training process. There are vanilla classes that allow you to write custom samplers (`baseloader`, `basesampler`) as well as loaders with predetermined sampling mechanisms [11, 12].

CHOOSING THE RIGHT SAMPLER

Choosing the ideal sampling method can be nontrivial and depends on the nature of the graph and the training objectives. Different samplers will yield a range of epoch times and convergence times. There is no general rule to determine the best sampler; it's best to experiment with limited sets of your data to see what works best. Implementing sampling adds another layer of complexity to the GNN architecture, just as message passing requires carefully orchestrated aggregation and update steps.

7.7.2 A glance at notable PyG samplers

As we've seen, GNNs work by aggregating across local neighborhoods. However, for very large graphs, it can be infeasible to consider all the nodes or edges in the aggregation operation, so samplers are typically used instead. The following lists some of the commonly used samplers that are also supported by default from the PyG libraries:

- `NeighborLoader`—Ideal for capturing local neighborhood dynamics and frequently used in social network analysis.
- `ImbalancedSampler`—Built for imbalanced datasets, such as in fraud-detection scenarios.
- `GraphSAINT Variants`—Designed to minimize the gradient noise, making them apt for large-scale training [9].
- `ShaDowKHopSampler`—Useful for sampling larger neighborhoods, capturing broader structural information.
- `DynamicBatchSampler`—Designed to group nodes by neighbor count, optimizing batch-wise computational consistency.
- `LinkNeighborLoader`—A loader that samples edges using a methodology analogous to `neighborloader`.

NOTE This overview isn't exhaustive, and functionalities may differ based on the PyG version in use. For in-depth information, consult the official PyG documentation (https://mng.bz/DMBa).

Let's look at a code snippet using the `Neighborloader` loader. The full code is in the GitHub repository, and we'll look at snippets here. The code runs a training loop for a GNN using the sampler. For each batch, it moves node features, labels, and adjacency information to the device, that is, the GPU. It then clears prior gradients, performs a forward and backward pass through the model to compute the loss, and updates the model parameters accordingly. To add neighbor batching using the `NeighborSampler` in your code, you can follow these steps:

1 Import the required modules:

```
from torch_geometric.loader import NeighborLoader
```

2 Define the mini-batch size and the number of layers to sample:

```
batch_size = 128
num_neighbors = 2
```

Sets the desired mini-batch size

Sets the number of layers to sample for each node

3 Create the `NeighborLoader` instance for sampling over a neighborhood during mini-batch training:

```
loader = NeighborLoader(data, input_nodes = train_mask,
  batch_size=batch_size\
    num_neighbors=*num_neighbors)
```

Here, `data` is the input graph, `input_nodes` contains the indices of the training nodes, and `num_neighbors` specifies the number of neighbors to sample for each layer.

4 Modify your training loop to iterate over the mini-batches using the sampler, as shown in the following listing.

Listing 7.1   Training loop using `NeighborSampler`

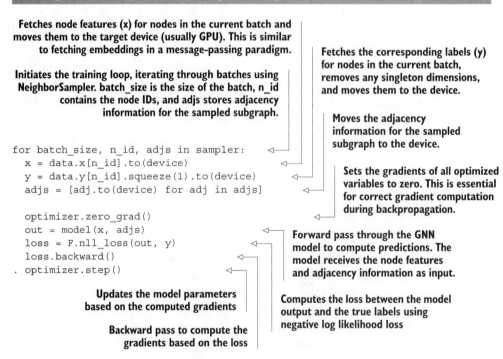

Fetches node features (x) for nodes in the current batch and moves them to the target device (usually GPU). This is similar to fetching embeddings in a message-passing paradigm.

Initiates the training loop, iterating through batches using NeighborSampler. batch_size is the size of the batch, n_id contains the node IDs, and adjs stores adjacency information for the sampled subgraph.

Fetches the corresponding labels (y) for nodes in the current batch, removes any singleton dimensions, and moves them to the device.

Moves the adjacency information for the sampled subgraph to the device.

```
for batch_size, n_id, adjs in sampler:
  x = data.x[n_id].to(device)
  y = data.y[n_id].squeeze(1).to(device)
  adjs = [adj.to(device) for adj in adjs]

  optimizer.zero_grad()
  out = model(x, adjs)
  loss = F.nll_loss(out, y)
  loss.backward()
. optimizer.step()
```

Sets the gradients of all optimized variables to zero. This is essential for correct gradient computation during backpropagation.

Forward pass through the GNN model to compute predictions. The model receives the node features and adjacency information as input.

Updates the model parameters based on the computed gradients

Backward pass to compute the gradients based on the loss

Computes the loss between the model output and the true labels using negative log likelihood loss

To round out this section, we'll look at a case where a team at GeoGrid has to decide among three batchers for a project.

EXAMPLE

Let's return to GeoGrid, a leading mapping company. A team is developing a graph-based representation of the entire US road system, with intersections as nodes and road segments as edges. The sheer scale of this project presented computational and memory challenges.

After a thorough investigation, the team shortlisted three prominent batching techniques, for which we'll assess the tradeoffs of each here:

- `GraphSAINTSampler` is advantageous for its noise-reduction capabilities, offering more accurate gradient estimates, and is scalable—ideal for expansive systems such as the US road network. However, its implementation might be complex, and there's a risk of overrepresenting highly connected nodes.
- `NeighborSampler` is memory-efficient, focusing on essential road segments, and emphasizes local neighborhood connections, offering insights into significant intersections. Yet, it might omit crucial data from less-traveled routes and potentially be biased toward densely connected nodes.
- `ShaDowKHopSampler` effectively samples k-hop subgraphs, capturing larger neighborhoods, and its depth is adjustable to accommodate various road system complexities. However, certain k values can make it computationally demanding, and the broad capture might introduce excessive and not immediately relevant data.

In the following, we demonstrate how different samplers are used in practice, with the same GeoGrid company as our case study:

- *Decision*—After extensive deliberation, the team leaned toward `ShaDowKHopSampler`. The method's ability to capture broader neighborhoods without being restricted to immediate neighbors seemed apt for the varied complexity of the US road system. They believed that with the right value of k, determined by experimentation, they could achieve a balance between depth and computational efficiency.

  To counteract potential information overload and ensure relevance, Geo-Grid planned to check the results against real-world traffic data, ensuring the sampled graph remained practical and accurate.

- *Conclusion*—GeoGrid's decision to adopt the `ShaDowKHopSampler` stemmed from an in-depth analysis of their requirements against the pros and cons of each technique. By pairing the sampling method with real-world data, they aimed to strike a balance between granularity and relevance in their graph representation.

Now that we have a grasp on batching, we can examine two techniques that work hand-in-hand with sampling: parallel processing and using a remote backend.

7.8   *Parallel and distributed processing*

Batching lends itself well to the next two methods, parallel processing and the use of remote backends, because these methods work best when data is split up. Parallel processing is a method of training machine learning models by spreading the computational tasks across multiple compute nodes or multiple machines. In this section, we focus on spreading the model training across multiple GPUs in a single machine [13–17]. We'll use PyTorch's `DistributedDataParallel` for this purpose.

DataParallel and DistributedDataParallel

In the realm of PyTorch, you'll encounter two main options for parallelizing your neural network models: `DataParallel` and `DistributedDataParallel`. Each has its merits and limitations, which are critical to making an informed decision.

`DataParallel` is tailored for multi-GPU setups on a single machine but comes with a few caveats, such as the model's replication during each forward pass incurs additional computational costs. These limitations become more pronounced as your model and data scale up.

On the other hand, `DistributedDataParallel` scales across multiple machines and GPUs. It outperforms `DataParallel` by allocating dedicated Compute Unified Device Architecture (CUDA) buffers for inter-GPU communication and by generally incurring less overhead. This makes it ideal for large-scale data and complex models.

Both `DataParallel` and `DistributedDataParallel` offer pathways to parallelize your models in PyTorch. Understanding their respective strengths and weaknesses enables you to choose the technique that best suits your specific machine learning challenges. Given its advantages in scalability and efficiency, especially for complex or large-scale projects, we've chosen `DistributedDataParallel` as our go-to option for model parallelization.

7.8.1   *Using distributed data parallel*

In plain language, distributed data parallel (DDP) is a way to train a machine learning model on multiple graphics cards (GPUs) at the same time. The idea is to split the data and the model across different GPUs, perform computations, and then bring the results back together. To make this work, you first need to set up a *process group*, which is just a way to organize the GPUs you're using. Unlike some other methods, DDP doesn't automatically split your data; you have to do that part yourself.

When you're ready to train, DDP helps by synchronizing the updates made to the model across all GPUs. This is done by sharing the gradients. Because all GPUs get these updates, they're all helping to improve the same model, even though they're working on different pieces of data.

The method is particularly fast and efficient, especially when compared to running on a single GPU or using simpler methods of parallelism. However, there are some technical details to keep in mind, such as making sure that you're loading and saving your model correctly if you're using multiple machines. The general steps to train are as follows:

- *Model instantiation*—Initialize the GNN model that will be used for training.
- *Distributed model setup*—Wrap the model in PyTorch's `DistributedDataParallel` to prepare it for distributed training.
- *Training loop*—Implement a training loop that includes forward propagation, computing the loss, backpropagation, and updating the model parameters.
- *Process synchronization*—Use PyTorch's distributed communication package to synchronize all the processes, ensuring that all processes have finished training before proceeding to the next step. This can be done using `dist.barrier()` before moving on to the next epoch. Once all epochs are done, it destroys the process group.
- *Entry point guard*—Use `if __name__ == '__main__':` to specify the dataset and start the distributed training. This ensures that the training code is executed only when the script is run directly, not when it's imported as a module.

Using distributed processing requires careful handling of synchronization points to ensure that the models are trained correctly. You must also ensure that your machine or cluster has enough resources to handle the parallel computations.

`Torch.distributed` supports various backends for distributed computing. The two most recommended are the following:

- NVIDIA Collective Communications Library (NCCL)—Nvidia's NCCL is used for GPU-based distributed training. It provides optimized primitives for collective communications.
- `Gloo`—Gloo is a collective communications library, developed by Facebook, providing various operations such as broadcast, all-reduce, and so on. This library is used for CPU training.

7.8.2 Code example for DDP

Following is an example of distributed training using PyTorch. For simplicity, we train a simple neural network using the Modified National Institute of Standards and Technology (MNIST) dataset. An example using GCN on the Amazon Products dataset can be found in the GitHub repository. In that case, instead of Google Colab to run the code, we use a Kaggle notebook, which has a dual GPU system. Another difference in the GCN example is that we use the `NeighborLoader` dataloader, which uses the `NeighborSampler` sampler.

Let's break down what's happening in this code. The GCN version essentially follows this logic as well.

SETTING UP FOR DISTRIBUTED TRAINING

The script imports necessary modules such as `torch`, `torch.distributed`, and so on. It initializes the DDP environment using `dist.init_process_group`. It sets up communication using NCCL and specifies a localhost address and port (tcp://localhost:23456) for synchronization.

PREPARING THE MODEL AND DATA

The code defines a simple `Flatten` layer, which is a part of the neural network that reshapes its input. The data transformation and loading steps are set up using PyTorch's DataLoader and torchvision datasets. The data loaded is MNIST.

TRAINING FUNCTION

`train` is the function responsible for training the model. It iterates through batches of data, performs forward and backward passes, and updates the model parameters.

MAIN FUNCTION

Within the `main()` function, each process (representing a single GPU in this example) sets its random seed and device (CUDA device based on the rank of the process). The neural network model is defined as a sequential model with the `Flatten` layer followed by a `Linear` layer. It's then wrapped with `DistributedDataParallel`. Loss function (`CrossEntropyLoss`) and optimizer (`SGD`) are defined.

MULTIPROCESSING SPAWN

Finally, the script uses the `mp.spawn` function to start the distributed training. It runs `main()` on the `world_size` number of processes (basically, two GPUs). Each process will train the model on its subset of data.

RUNNING THE TRAINING

Each process trains the model using its subset of data, but the gradients are synchronized across all processes (GPUs) to ensure that the processors are updating the same global model. This process is summarized in figure 7.3.

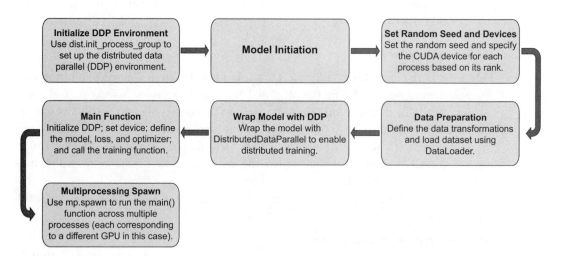

Figure 7.3   Process diagram for initiating and running a training with multiple processor devices

The following listing uses the `DistributedDataParallel` module to train a neural network.

Listing 7.2 Training using DDP

```
import torch
import torch.distributed as dist
import torch.multiprocessing as mp
import torch.nn as nn
from torch.nn.parallel import DistributedDataParallel
from torch.utils.data import DataLoader
from torchvision import datasets, transforms

class Flatten(nn.Module):
  def forward(self, input):
    return input.view(input.size(0), -1)

def train(model, trainloader,
            criterion,
            optimizer,
            device):
    model.train()
    for batch_idx, (data, target) in enumerate(trainloader):
      print(f'Process {device}, Batch {batch_idx}')
        data, target = data.to(device), target.to(device)
        optimizer.zero_grad()
        output = model(data)
        loss = criterion(output, target)
        loss.backward()
        optimizer.step()

def main(rank, world_size):
    filepath = '~/.pytorch/MNIST_data/'
    dist.init_process_group(
    backend='nccl',
    init_method='tcp://localhost:23456',
    rank=rank,
    world_size=world_size
    )

    torch.manual_seed(0)
    device = torch.device(f'cuda:{rank}')

    transform = transforms.Compose(
                    [transforms.ToTensor(),
                     transforms.Normalize((0.5,),
                     (0.5,))]
                     )

    trainset = datasets.MNIST(filepath ,
                        download=True,
                        train=True,
                        transform=transform)
```

Imports the **DistributedDataParallel** class for distributed training

Imports the **DataLoader** utility for data loading

Defines the main training function

Defines the main function for the distributed training setup

Initializes the distributed process group

Specifies the total number of participating processes

Sets a random seed for reproducibility

Sets the device based on the process rank

Loads and transforms the MNIST dataset

```
train_loader = DataLoader(trainset,
                          batch_size=64,
                          shuffle=True,
                          num_workers=2)
```
**Creates a
DataLoader for
the training data**

```
model = nn.Sequential(Flatten(), nn.Linear(784, 10)).to(device)
model = DistributedDataParallel(model, device_ids=[rank])
```
**Wraps the
model for
distributed
training**

```
criterion = nn.CrossEntropyLoss()
optimizer = torch.optim.SGD(model.parameters(), lr=0.01)
```

```
train(model, train_loader, criterion, optimizer, device)
```
**Calls the training function to
start the training process**

We end this section with another example from our friends at GeoGrid.

EXAMPLE

GeoGrid had the opportunity to submit a proof-of-concept for a government project that aimed to use GNNs for complex environmental modeling. Winning this contract could establish them as leaders in the field, but they were up against stiff competition. The government set a tight deadline to review a proof-of-concept demo, making the situation tense for GeoGrid, which was still in the early stages of development.

During a team meeting, the focus shifted to a crucial technical decision and an important dilemma: the potential use of DDP training across multiple GPUs. The lead data scientist saw the allure of DDP's capability to speed up training times, offering a potentially impressive demonstration of efficiency and readiness for the government project.

On the other hand, an experienced engineer on the team harbored concerns. DDP, despite its advantages, could introduce problems such as computational overhead from synchronizing gradients between GPUs. Another layer of complexity came from other team members who pointed out that their specialized GNN algorithms hadn't been tested with DDP. They expressed concerns over how the data would distribute across the GPUs and the potential for imbalances and inefficiencies. Other concerns centered around the time needed to develop and test the code.

The team weighed these factors carefully. Producing a demo quickly and on time would be desirable. Yet, the complexities and unknowns of applying DDP to their specific GNN model could risk unexpected delays and costs, maybe causing them to miss the submission deadline.

Further consideration was given to the iterative nature of model development. At the proof-of-concept stage, quick iterations for performance optimization were crucial. Adding DDP into the mix could complicate debugging and extend the development cycle:

- *Decision*—In the end, the team opted for a measured approach. They decided to conduct a one-week feasibility study to rigorously evaluate the effect of using

DDP on their GNN architecture. This would allow them to make an informed decision based on empirical data, which tracked convergence time and average time per epoch. IT would be consulted to ensure that the necessary computational resources were available exclusively for this critical study.

- *Conclusion*—The decision to roll out GNNs is typically highly dependent on data, timelines, and compute requirements. Feasibility studies are an important part of the decision-making progress, especially when identifying compute requirements.

In the next section, we look at another technique that rests upon sampling, training while drawing data directly from a remote storage system.

7.9 Training with remote storage

A prominent approach to data pipelining in this book is to source data from a data storage system and then preprocess this data by transforming it for use in the GNN platform. This preprocessed data is stored in memory during training.

By contrast, when data gets too big for memory, one approach is to integrate the preprocessing into the training process. Instead of preprocessing the entire dataset, placing it in memory, and then training, we can basically sample and mini-batch directly from the initial data storage system when training. Using an interface between our GNN platform and our data source, we can process each batch pulled directly from the data source [18]. In PyG, this is called *remote backend* and is designed to be agnostic of the particular backend that is used [19–22].

The benefit is that our dataset's size is now limited by the capacity of our database. The tradeoffs are as follows:

- We have to do a bit of work to set up the remote backend, as detailed in this section.
- Pulling from a remote backend will introduce I/O latency.
- Integrating a remote backend adds complexity to a training setup. Basically, more things can go wrong, and there will be more items to debug.

In PyG, remote backends are implemented by storing and sampling from two aspects of a graph: the structural information (i.e., the edges) using a `GraphStore`, and the node features using a `FeatureStore` (at the time of writing, edge features aren't yet supported). For storing graph structures, the PyG team recommends using graph databases as the backend, such as Neo4J, TigerGraph, Kùzu, and ArangoDB. Likewise for node features, the PyG team recommends using key-value databases, such as Memcached, LevelDB, and RocksDB. The key elements to implementation of a remote backend are as follows:

- *Remote data sources*—Databases that store your graph structure and node features. This choice may be simply the database system you're currently using to store your graph.

- *A graphstore object*—The `torch_geometric.data.GraphStore` object stores edge indices of a graph, enabling node sampling. Core components of your custom class must be the connection to your database, and CRUD (create, read, update, delete) functions, including `put_edge_index()`, `get_edge_index()`, and `remove_edge_index()`.
- *A featurestore object*—The `torch_geometric.data.FeatureStore` manages features for graph nodes. The size of node features is considered to be a major storage problem in graph learning applications. Like the `GraphStore`, custom implementations include connecting to the remote database and CRUD functions.
- *A sampler*—A graph sampler, linked to a `GraphStore`, uses sampling algorithms to produce subgraphs from input nodes via the `torch_geometric.sampler.BaseSampler` interface. PyG's default sampler pulls edge indices, converts them to Compressed Sparse Column (CSC) format, and uses in-memory sampling routines. Custom samplers can use specialized `GraphStore` methods by implementing `sample_from_nodes()` and `sample_from_edges()` of the `BaseSampler` class. This involves node-level and link-level sampling, respectively.
- *A dataloader*—A dataloader operates similarly to what has been presented in previous chapters. The differences here are that the dataloader uses the `GraphStore`, `FeatureStore`, and `sampler` objects created instead of the usual PyG data objects. An example from the PyG docs is shown in the next listing.

Listing 7.3   Loader object using remote backend

```
loader = NodeLoader(
    data=(feature_store, graph_store),
    node_sampler=node_sampler,
    batch_size=20,
    input_nodes='paper',
)

for batch in loader:
    <training loop>
```

While custom classes and functionalities can be developed, using tools crafted by database vendors is encouraged. Currently, KuzuDB and ArangoDB offer implementations for PyG's remote backend [14, 18–20, 23]. We close this section with another mini-case featuring GeoGrid.

7.9.1   *Example*

GeoGrid has a graph so large that it can't fit into the memory of the available hardware. They want to employ GNNs to analyze the large graph, predicting features such as traffic congestion and route popularity. But how can they train a GNN on a graph that doesn't even fit into memory? Following are some specific examples of working with large GNNs:

- *Adopting remote backend with PyG*—GeoGrid uses PyG's remote backend feature, which aligns perfectly with the company's need to handle large-scale graphs. They use Neo4J as the graph database for storing the graph structure and RocksDB for storing node features such as location type, historical traffic data, and so on.

- *Remote data sources*—GeoGrid chose Neo4J and RocksDB as their data storage systems. The first task was to write scripts that load their vast graph data into these databases. This involved data validation to ensure that the loaded data was correct and consistent.

- `GraphStore` *object*—The development team at GeoGrid spent a significant amount of time implementing the `GraphStore` object. They needed to build secure and reliable connections to the Neo4J database. Once the connections were established, they implemented CRUD operations.

- `FeatureStore` *object*—Similarly, implementing the `FeatureStore` object for RocksDB wasn't trivial. The main challenge was handling the varying sizes and types of node features, which required thorough testing to ensure efficiency and correctness.

- *Sampler*—Developing the custom sampling strategy was a project on its own. The sampler needed to be both effective and efficient, and it went through several iterations before it met the performance criteria.

- *Dataloader*—The `NodeLoader` was the final piece of the puzzle, combining all the preceding elements into a coherent pipeline for training. The development team had to ensure that the `NodeLoader` was optimized for speed to minimize I/O latency.

TESTING AND TROUBLESHOOTING

As with all software development, machine learning, or AI projects, testing is a critical part of the workflow. The following lists some of the typical testing and quality assurance (QA) steps when working on a project:

- *Unit testing*—Each component underwent rigorous unit testing. This was crucial to catch bugs early and ensure that each part of the system worked as expected in isolation.

- *Integration testing*—After unit testing, the team performed integration tests where they ran the entire pipeline from loading a batch of data to running it through the GNN model. They found a few bottlenecks and bugs, particularly with the sampler and the database connections, which took considerable time to troubleshoot and resolve.

- *I/O latency*—One significant problem the company encountered was the I/O latency when pulling data from Neo4J and RocksDB. GeoGrid optimized its queries and also used some caching mechanisms to mitigate this.

- *Debugging*—During the development and testing phases, the team encountered various bugs and errors, from data inconsistencies to unexpected behavior in the sampling process. Each problem had to be debugged meticulously, adding to the overall development time.

Despite these challenges, GeoGrid was able to successfully implement a scalable solution for training GNNs on their enormous geographical graph. The project was time-consuming and had its complexities, but the scalability and capability to train on out-of-memory graphs were invaluable benefits that justified the effort.

7.10   *Graph coarsening*

Graph coarsening is a technique used to reduce the size of a graph while preserving its essential features. This technique reduces the size and complexity of a graph by creating a coarser version of the original graph. Graph coarsening reduces the number of nodes and edges, making them more manageable and easier to analyze. It involves aggregating or merging nodes and edges to form a simplified representation of the original graph while trying to preserve its structural and relational information.

One approach to graph coarsening involves starting with an input graph G, with its labels Y, and then generating a coarsened graph G' using the following steps [23]:

1. Apply a graph coarsening algorithm on G, producing a normalized partition matrix (i.e., set of node clusters) P.
2. Use this partition matrix to do the following:
   a. Construct a course graph, G'.
   b. Compute the feature matrix of G'.
   c. Compute the labels of G'.
3. Train using the coarsened graph, producing a weight matrix that can be tested on the original graph.

While we can use graph coarsening to reduce the size of large graphs by reducing vertices and edges, it has drawbacks. It can result in information loss, as key details of the original graph may be removed, complicating subsequent analyses. It may also introduce inaccuracies, not fully representing the original graph's structure. Finally, no universal method exists for graph coarsening, leading to varied results and possible bias. In PyG, graph coarsening involves two steps:

1. *Clustering*—This involves grouping similar nodes together to form super-nodes. Each super-node represents a cluster of nodes in the original graph. The clustering algorithm determines which nodes are similar based on certain criteria. In PyG, there are various clustering algorithms available such as `graclus()` and `voxel_grid()`.
2. *Pooling*—Once the clusters or super-nodes are formed, pooling is then used to create a coarser graph from the original graph. Pooling combines the information from the nodes in each cluster into a single node in the coarser graph. The `max_pool()` and `avg_pool()` functions in PyG are pooling operations that input clusters from the first step.

If used repeatedly, the combination of clustering and pooling allows us to create a hierarchy of graphs, each one simpler than the last, as shown in figure 7.4.

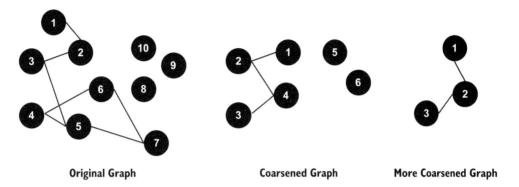

Original Graph   **Coarsened Graph**   **More Coarsened Graph**

Figure 7.4   Graph coarsening process: The original graph (left) is progressively simplified through coarsening. The first stage (middle) merges nearby nodes to create a coarsened graph, while the second stage (right) further reduces the graph's complexity, highlighting the essential structure for efficient processing.

If used in supervised or semi-supervised learning, labels have to be generated for the new set of nodes. This generation must be carefully tended to preserve the new labels as closely as possible to the originals. Simple methods for this involve using a centrality statistic for the new assigned label, such as the mode or average of the labels in the cluster.

In listing 7.4, graph coarsening is implemented through the use of the Graclus algorithm, which recursively applies a clustering procedure to the nodes of the graph, grouping them into clusters of roughly equal size. The resulting clusters are then merged into a new graph, which is coarser than the original one. This is a type of hierarchical clustering that operates on the graph's edge indices. The function graclus(edge_index) clusters the nodes of the graph together based on the structure of the graph. The resulting cluster tensor maps each node to the cluster it belongs to.

The max_pool function is then applied to this clustered data. This operation essentially coarsens the graph, reducing the number of nodes based on the clusters formed by Graclus. The most influential node (based on certain criteria, e.g., edge weight) in each cluster becomes the representative of that cluster in the coarsened graph.

Listing 7.4   Graph coarsening using graclus and Max_Pool

```
import torch
from torch_geometric.data import Data
from torch_geometric.nn import graclus, max_pool
from torch_geometric.utils import to_undirected
from torch_geometric.datasets import KarateClub
```

```
dataset = KarateClub()
data = dataset[0]   # Get the first graph

edge_index = to_undirected(data.edge_index)

batch = torch.zeros(data.num_nodes, dtype=torch.long)

cluster = graclus(edge_index)

data_coarse = max_pool(cluster, data)
```

Converts to undirected graph for the graclus function

Creates a batch vector for max_pool

Applies Graclus clustering

Sets the early stopping criteria

This code applies two major operations on the graph data, which changes its structure and properties. The result is a coarsened version of the original graph. The number of nodes decreases from 34 to 22 due to the max pooling operation. Meanwhile, the number of edges also reduces from 156 to 98 as the graph becomes more compact. This is summarized in table 7.4.

Table 7.4   Input and output graphs from listing 7.4

Input	Output
Data(x=[34, 34], edge_index=[2, 156], y=[34], train_mask=[34])	DataBatch(x=[22, 34], edge_index=[2, 98])
Nodes: 34 Edges: 156	Nodes: 22 Edges: 98

This table provides an overview of the structure and features of both the input and output graphs described in listing 7.4. The input graph is represented as data, with 34 nodes, each having 34 features, as indicated by x=[34, 34]. It contains 156 edges, described by the edge index tensor edge_index=[2, 156]. Additionally, the input graph includes a label tensor y=[34], representing one label per node, and a training mask train_mask=[34], specifying which nodes are part of the training set.

The output graph, processed and represented as DataBatch, shows a reduction in size. It now contains 22 nodes, while each node retains the original 34 features (x=[22, 34]). The number of edges is also reduced to 98, as indicated by edge_index=[2, 98]. This transformation demonstrates a typical graph reduction process, which simplifies the graph for downstream tasks.

7.10.1 *Example*

GeoGrid has a mammoth task: to analyze an extensive graph of the US road system for their ambitious traffic management solution. With an initial dataset comprising 50,000 nodes and 200,000 edges, the computational toll is daunting. In the initial exploration when GeoGrid considered the computational load, graph coarsening seemed like a tempting strategy. But apprehensions were high. Initial concerns ranged from the loss of crucial information and the introduction of inaccuracies given the complexities around label preservation and method bias.

GeoGrid decided to proceed cautiously with a trial run using the Graclus algorithm and `max_pool` for pooling on the entire graph. The trial run confirmed the company's fears. The graph's size was reduced significantly but at the cost of losing detail in high-traffic zones. Newly generated labels for clustered nodes didn't reflect the original optimally, affecting machine learning model performance.

Given the unsatisfactory trial results, GeoGrid explored alternative optimizations. GeoGrid's breakthrough idea was a multilayer analytical framework as follows:

- *National level*—A broad, high-level layer where each node signifies a state or major region
- *State level*—An intermediate layer representing cities or counties
- *City level*—The most granular layer, focusing on individual intersections and road segments

The team speculated that applying graph coarsening at an intermediate layer might alleviate some of the initial concerns. The state level became the company's target for coarsening, which promised a balance between computational efficiency and data integrity. With this new approach in mind, GeoGrid reevaluated the disadvantages of graph coarsening:

- *Loss of granular information*—While still a concern, the damage appeared to be minimized because coarsening was being applied to an intermediate layer, preserving the city level's details.
- *Introduction of inaccuracies*—GeoGrid theorized that the other layers could serve as compensatory mechanisms for any inaccuracies introduced at the state level.
- *Label preservation*—Coarsening at the state level seemed less risky regarding label reconciliation, as they could reference both the national and city levels for corrections.

They went ahead and coarsened the state level with the same Graclus algorithm and `max_pool` technique. The subsequent evaluation found that the loss of granularity was acceptable for this specific layer, and any inaccuracies introduced were mostly balanced by the city and national levels.

Though the company initially shied away from graph coarsening, GeoGrid found a way to incorporate it meaningfully into a more complex, multilayer system. The compromise allowed GeoGrid to conserve computational resources without severely compromising the model's accuracy. However, they remained cautious and committed to ongoing research to fully grasp the tradeoffs involved.

Table 7.5 summarizes the tradeoffs of graph coarsening. Graph coarsening presents a balance between computational efficiency and data fidelity. On the upside, it enables quicker real-time processing, simplifies high-level analyses, and offers scalability. Its flexibility allows selective application to specific layers of a hierarchical graph, as demonstrated when GeoGrid applied coarsening only to its state level layer.

Table 7.5   Tradeoffs of using graph coarsening, with insights from the GeoGrid case

Category	Insight	GeoGrid's Use Case
Computational efficiency	Ideal for real-time processing with limited computational resources	Enabled quicker analyses at the state level, reducing computational load
Simplified analysis	Useful for high-level overviews for initial understanding or macro-level decision-making	The national level layer provided a broad picture, serving as a basis for more detailed analyses at lower layers.
Scalability	Allows handling of larger graphs that might otherwise be computationally infeasible	Multilayer approach could be further extended to include additional hierarchical layers if needed.
Flexibility	Can be applied to selected layers or segments of a graph, rather than the entire graph	Applied coarsening only to the state level layer, mitigating some disadvantages while still gaining computational benefits
Loss of granular information	Not suitable for tasks requiring precise, detailed data	Initially avoided coarsening due to loss of critical details at the intersection level
Potential for inaccuracies	Requires validation from more detailed layers or additional data to mitigate inaccuracies	The city level and national level acted as checks against the coarsened state level.
Label preservation challenges	Requires additional steps to generate or map new labels, which could introduce errors	Found it easier to reconcile labels when coarsening was applied to an intermediate layer
Method bias	Choosing a coarsening algorithm can affect the outcome and introduce biases.	Identified as an area for ongoing research to understand its effect better

As we wrap up this section, it becomes clear that the ability to scale for expansive datasets is crucial for individuals working with GNNs. Handling large-scale data problems demands careful strategy, and this section has supplied a detailed outline of diverse methods to address such hurdles. From choosing the ideal processor to making decisions regarding sparse versus dense representations, from batch processing strategies to distributed computation—the options for scaling optimization are numerous.

As you move forward, the code provided in our repository can be used as a useful benchmark, ensuring that the methods mentioned here aren't just high-level ideas but actionable plans.

Navigating the vast landscape of GNNs requires a blend of strategic foresight and hands-on execution. Irrespective of your data's size or complexity, the trick lies in planning, optimizing, and iterating. Let our insights be your compass, guiding you confidently through challenges, no matter their scale.

Summary

- Time and scale optimization methods are critical when training on very large datasets. We can characterize a large graph by the raw number of vertices and edges, the size of their edge and node features, or the time and space complexity of the algorithms used in the processing and training of our datasets.

- A few well-known techniques exist to manage scale problems, which can be used singularly or in tandem:
  - Your choice of processor and its configuration
  - Using sparse versus dense representation of your dataset
  - Your choice of the GNN algorithm
  - Training in batches based on sampling from your data
  - Using parallel or distributed computing
  - Use of remote backends
  - Coarsening your graph

- Being selective of how graph data is represented for training can affect performance. PyTorch Geometric (PyG) provides support for sparse and dense representations.

- Choice of training algorithm can affect the time performance of training and the space requirements of memory. Using Big O notation and benchmarking key metrics can help you select the optimal GNN architecture.

- Node or graph batching can improve time and space complexity by using portions of your data instead of the full dataset in training.

- Parallelism, dividing the work of training across several processor nodes on one machine or across a cluster of machines, can improve the speed of execution but requires the overhead of setting up and configuring the additional devices.

- Remote backends pull directly from your external data source (graph database and key/value stores) to mini-batch during training. This can alleviate memory problems but requires additional work to set up and configure.

- Graph coarsening can reduce memory requirements by replacing a graph with a smaller version of itself. This smaller version is created by consolidating nodes. A drawback of this method is that the coarsened graph will deviate from the representation of the original graph. Graph coarsening is a tradeoff between computational efficiency and data fidelity. It's most effective when applied judiciously and as part of a larger, layered analytical strategy. Application to intermediate layers can mitigate some drawbacks.

Considerations
for GNN projects

This chapter covers

- Creating a graph data model from nongraph data
- Extract, transform, load and preprocessing from raw data sources
- Creating datasets and data loaders with PyTorch Geometric

In this chapter, we describe the practical aspects of working with graph data, as well as how to convert nongraph data into a graph format. We'll explain some of the considerations involved in taking data from a raw state to a preprocessed format. This includes turning tabular or other nongraph data into graphs and preprocessing them for a graph-based machine learning package. In our mental model, shown in figure 8.1, we are in the left half of the figure.

We'll proceed as follows. In section 8.1, we introduce an example problem that might require a graph neural network (GNN) and how to proceed with tackling this project. Section 8.2 goes into more detail on how to use nongraph data in graph models. We then put these ideas into action in section 8.3 by taking a dataset

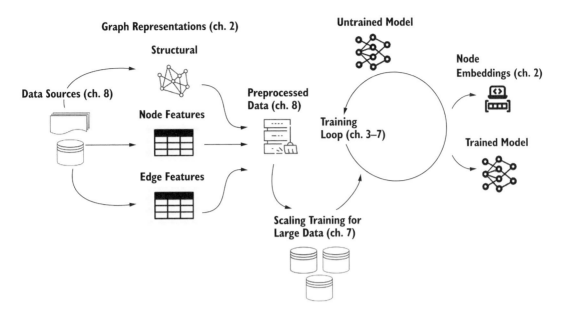

Figure 8.1   Mental model for graph training process. We're at the start of the process, where we prepare our data for training.

from a raw file to preprocessed data, ready for training. Finally, ideas for finding more graph datasets are given in section 8.4.

In this chapter, we'll consider how to apply GNNs to a social graph created by a recruiting firm. In our example, nodes are job candidates, and edges represent relationships between job candidates. We generate graph data from raw data, in the form of edge lists and adjacency lists. We then use that data in a graph processing framework (`NetworkX`) and a GNN library (PyTorch Geometric [PyG]). The nodes in this data include the candidate's *ID*, *job type* (accountant, engineer, etc.), and *industry* (banking, retail, tech, etc.).

We frame the goals of candidates as a graph-based challenge, detailing the steps to transform their data for graph learning. Our aim here is to map out the data workflow, starting with raw data, converting it into a graph format, and then preparing it for the GNN training we use in the rest of the book.

NOTE   Code from this chapter can be found in notebook form at the GitHub repository (https://mng.bz/Xxn1). Colab links and data from this chapter can be accessed in the same locations.

8.1   *Data preparation and project planning*

Consider the case of a hypothetical recruiting firm called Whole Staffing. Whole Staffing headhunts employees for a variety of industries and maintains a database of their candidate profiles, including their history of engagement with the firm and other candidates. Some candidates get introduced to the firm via referrals from other candidates.

8.1.1   *Project definition*

Whole Staffing wants to get the most value from its database. They have a few initial questions about their collection of job candidates:

1   Some profiles have missing data. Is it possible to fill in missing data without bothering the candidate?
2   History has shown that candidates who have worked on similar projects in the past can work well together in future work. Is it possible to figure out which candidates could work well together?

Whole Staffing has tasked you with exploring the data to answer these questions. Among other analytical and machine learning methods, you think there may be an opportunity to represent the data as a graph and use a GNN to answer the client's questions.

Your idea is to take the collection of referrals and convert it into a social network where the job candidates are nodes and the referrals between candidates are edges. To simplify things, you can ignore the direction of the referrals so that the graph can be undirected. You also ignore repeat referrals, so that relationships between candidates remain unweighted.

We'll walk through the steps needed to prepare the data and establish a pipeline to pass the data to a GNN model. First, let's consider the project planning stage.

8.1.2   *Project objectives and scope*

Given any problem, having clear objectives, requirements, and scope will serve as a compass that steers all subsequent actions and decisions. Every facet, from planning and schema creation to tool selection should follow the core objectives and scope. Let's consider each of these for our problem.

PROJECT OBJECTIVES

Whole Staffing wants to optimize the use of its candidate database. First, the project should enhance data quality by filling in missing information in candidate profiles, reducing the need for direct candidate engagement. Second, the work ahead should facilitate informed candidate suggestions, predicting which teams will work well using the historical success of candidates.

PROJECT REQUIREMENTS AND SCOPE

Several key requirements will directly affect your project. Let's run through a few and point out their importance to our client's industry. Then, we'll draw some conclusions about the project at hand. Requirements include the following:

- *Data size and velocity*—What is the size of the data, in terms of item counts, size in bytes, or number of nodes? How fast is new information added to the data, if at all? Is data expected to be uploaded from a real-time stream, or from a data lake that is updated daily?

The planned graph might grow with the increase in data, affecting the computational resources needed and the efficiency of algorithms. Accurately assessing data size and velocity ensures that the system can handle the expected load, can offer real-time insights, and is scalable for future growth.

- *Inference speed*—How fast are the application and the underlying machine learning models required to be? Some applications may require sub-second responses, while for others, there is no constraint on time.

  Response time is particularly vital in providing timely recommendations and insights. For a recruitment firm, matching candidates with suitable job openings is time-sensitive, with opportunities quickly becoming unavailable.

- *Data privacy*—What are the policies and regulations regarding personally identifiable information (PII), and how would this involve data transformation and preprocessing?

  Data privacy becomes a huge concern when dealing with sensitive information such as candidate profiles, contact details, and employment histories. In a graph and GNN setting, ensuring that nodes and edges don't reveal PII is essential. Compliance with regulations such as General Data Protection Regulation (GDPR) or the California Consumer Privacy Act (CCPA) is mandatory to avoid legal complications. The graph data should be handled, stored, and processed in a way that respects privacy norms. Anonymization and encryption techniques may be needed to protect individuals' privacy while still allowing for effective data analysis. Understanding these requirements early in the project planning ensures that the system architecture and data processing pipelines are designed with privacy preservation in mind.

- *Explainability*—How explainable should the responses be? Will direct answers be enough, or should there be additional data that sheds light on why a recommendation or prediction was made?

  In the recruitment sector, explainability and transparency are pivotal. They instill trust among candidates and employers by ensuring fairness and clarity in the talent-selection process. Ethical standards are upheld, and unintended biases should be mitigated. These elements aren't just ethical imperatives but often legally binding.

Given the objectives and scope, for Whole Staffing, the deliverables might be a system that does the following:

1 Fortnightly scan the candidate data for missing items. Missing items can be inferred and suggested or filled in.

2 Predict candidates that will work well together by using link prediction and/or node classification. Unlike the first deliverable, the response time here should be fast.

The following lists some of the specifications for the preceding requirements:

- *Data size*—This is conservatively set at enough capacity for 100,000 candidates and their properties, which is estimated to be 1 GB of data.
- *Inference speed*—Application will run biweekly and can be completed overnight so we don't have a considerable speed constraint.
- *Data privacy*—No personal data that directly identifies a candidate can be used. However, data known to the recruitment company, such as whether employees have been successfully placed at the same employer, can be used to improve operations of the company, provided this data isn't shared.
- *Explainability*—There must be some level of explainability for the results.

The objectives and requirements will guide the decisions regarding system design, data models, and, often, GNN architecture. The preceding gives an example for the type of considerations needed when beginning or scoping a graph-based project.

8.2   *Designing graph models*

Given an appropriate scope of work, the next step is in building the graph models. For most machine learning problems, data will be organized in a standard way. For example, when dealing with tabular data, rows are treated as observations, and columns are treated as features. We can join tables of such data by using indexes and keys. This framework is flexible and relatively unambiguous. We may quibble about which observations and features to include, but we know where to place them.

When we want to express our data with graphs, in all but the simplest scenarios, we'll have several options for what structure to use. With graphs, it's not always intuitive where to place the entities of interest. It's this ambiguity that drives the need for systemic methods in using graph data, but getting it right early on can serve as a foundation for downstream machine learning tasks [1].

In this section, we embark on a journey of transforming Whole Staffing's recruitment data into graph-based data to support our downstream pipeline. We start by considering the domain and use case, a critical step to understanding the data. Next, we create and refine a schema, pivotal for organizing and interpreting complex datasets. Through rigorous testing of the schema, we could then ensure its robustness and reliability. Any necessary refinements should be made to optimize performance and accuracy. This approach ensures that our future analytic systems, which ingest graph-based data, can answer complex queries about job candidates with precision and reliability. Here's the process to follow, and figure 8.2 provides a visual:

1 Understand the data and the use case.
2 Create a data model, schema, and instance model.
3 Test your model using the schema and instance model.
4 Refactor if necessary.

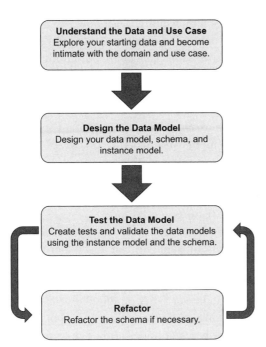

Figure 8.2   Process of creating a
robust graph data model from
nongraph data

8.2.1   *Get familiar with the domain and use case*

As with most data projects, to be effective, we have to come to grips with the dataset and the context. For our immediate goal of creating a model, understanding our referral data in its raw format and digging into the intricacies of the recruiting industry can provide critical insights. This knowledge also gives us a basis to design tests for the model during deployment. For example, preliminary analysis on the raw data gives us the information in table 8.1.

Table 8.1   Features of the dataset

Number of candidates	1,933
Number of referrals	12,239

From the raw data, it's apparent that there are many relationships, offering potential insights into candidate referrals. The large number of referrals in comparison to the number of candidates suggests an interconnected network. Our models need to be sufficiently large to translate this structure into results within the recruitment problem-space.

Turning to domain knowledge, beyond the immediate asks of the client, we should be asking questions that solidify our understanding of the industry. In setting the requirements for our data model, we should consider the key questions and challenges to the industry. For the recruitment problem, we might ask how we can optimize the referral process or what underlying structures and patterns govern candidate referrals. By addressing these types of questions, we can align our model with domain expertise, with a likely boost in both its relevance and validity.

8.2.2   *Constructing the graph dataset and schemas*

Next, we'll discuss how to design our database. The term *graph dataset* denotes a general effort to describe data using the elements and structure of a graph: nodes, edges, and node features and edge features. To achieve this, we need a *schema* and an *instance*. These specify the structure and rules of our graph explicitly and allow our graph dataset to be tested and refined. This section is drawn from several references, listed at the end of the book for further reading.

By addressing the details of our graph dataset up front, we can avoid technical debt and more easily test the integrity of our data. We can also experiment more systematically with different data structures. In addition, when the structure and rules of our graphs are designed explicitly, it increases the ease with which we can parameterize these rules and experiment with them in our GNN pipeline.

Graph datasets can be simple, consisting of one type of node and one type of edge. Or they can be complex, involving many types of nodes and edges, metadata, and, in the case of knowledge graphs, ontologies.

> **Key terms**
>
> The following are key terms used in this section (for more details on graph data models and types of graphs, see appendix A):
>
> - *Bi-graph (or bipartite graph)*—A graph with two sets of nodes. There are no edges between nodes of the same set.
> - *Entity-relationship diagram (ER diagram)*—A figure that shows the entities, relationships, and constraints of a graph.
> - *Graph dataset*—A representation of nodes, edges, and their relationships.
> - *Heterogeneous/homogeneous graphs*—A homogeneous graph has only one type of node or edge. A heterogeneous graph can have several different types of nodes or edges.
> - *Instance model*—A model based on a schema that holds a subset of the actual data.
> - *Ontology*—A way of describing the concepts and relationships in a specific domain of knowledge, for example, connections between different entities (writers) in a semantic web (of works of literature). The ontology is the structured framework that defines the roles, attributes, and interrelations of these writers and their literary works.

- *Property graph*—A model that uses metadata (labels, identifiers, attributes/properties) to define the graph's elements.
- *Resource Description Framework graph (RDF graph, aka Triple Stores)*—Model that follows a subject-predicate-object pattern, where nodes are subjects and objects, and edges are predicates.
- *Schema*—A blueprint that defines how the elements of the graph will be organized as well as which specific rules and constraints will be used for these elements.
- *Conceptual schema*—A schema not tied to any particular database or processing system.
- *System schema*—A schema designed with a specific graph database or processing system in mind.
- *Technical debt*—The consequences of prioritizing speedy delivery over quality code, which later has to be refactored.

Graph datasets are good at providing conceptual descriptions of graphs that are quick and easy to grasp by others. For example, for people who understand what a property graph or an RDF graph is, telling them that a graph is a bi-graph implemented on a property graph can reveal much about the design of your data (property graphs and RDF graphs are explained in appendix A).

A *schema* is a blueprint that defines how data is organized in a data storage system, such as a database. A graph schema is a concrete implementation of a graph dataset, explaining in detail how the data in a specific use case is to be represented in a real system. Schemas can consist of diagrams and written documentation. Schemas can be implemented in a graph database using a query language or in a processing system using a programming language. A schema should answer the following questions:

- What are the elements (nodes, edges, properties), and what real-world entities and relationships do they represent?
- Does the graph include multiple types of nodes and edges?
- What are the constraints regarding what can be represented as a node?
- What are the constraints for relationships? Do certain nodes have restrictions regarding adjacency and incidence? Are there count restrictions for certain relationships?
- How are descriptors and metadata handled? What are the constraints on this data?

Depending on the complexity of your data and the systems in use, you may use multiple but consistent schemas. A *conceptual schema* lays out the elements, rules, and constraints of the graph but isn't tied to any system. A *system schema* reflects the conceptual schema's rules but just for a specific system, such as a database of choice. A system schema could also omit unneeded elements from the conceptual schema. Here are the steps to create a schema:

1. *Identify main entities and relationships.* For instance, in our social network example, entities can be candidates, recruiters, referrals, hiring events, and relationships.

2. *Define node and edge labels.* These labels serve as identifiers for the types of entities and their interrelationships in the graph.

3. *Specify properties and constraints.* Each vertex and edge label is associated with specific properties and constraints that store and restrict information, respectively.

4. *Define indices (optional, for database-oriented schemas).* Indexes, based on properties or combinations thereof, enhance query speeds on graph data.

5. *Apply the graph schema to a database (optional, for database-oriented schemas).* Commands or codes, contingent on the specific graph database, are employed to create the graph schema, with specifications on its static or dynamic nature.

Depending on the complexity of the graph dataset and the use cases, one or several schemas could be called for. In the case of more than one schema, compatibility between the schemas via a mapping must also be included.

For a dataset with few elements, a simple diagram with notes in prose can be sufficient to convey enough information to fellow developers to be able to implement in query language or code. For more complex network designs, ER diagrams and associated grammar are useful in illustrating network schemas in a visual and human readable way.

Entity-relationship diagrams (ER diagrams)

ER diagrams have the elements to illustrate a graph's nodes, edges, and attributes and the rules and constraints governing a graph [2, 3]. The following figure (left) shows some connectors notation that can be used to illustrate edges and relationship constraints. The figure (right) shows an example of a schema diagram conveying two node types that might be represented in our recruitment example (Recruiter and Candidate), and two edge types (Knows, and Recruits/Recruited By). The diagram conveys implicit and explicit constraints.

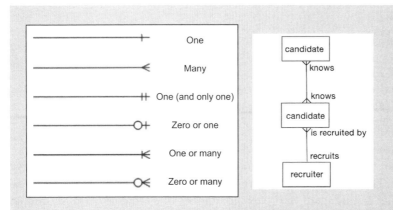

At left is the relationship nomenclature for ER diagrams. At right is an example of a conceptual schema using an ER diagram.

Some explicit constraints are that one employee can refer many other employees and that one referee can be referred by many employees. Another explicit constraint is that a person can only be employed full-time by one business, but one business might have many employees. An implicit constraint is that, for this graph model, there can be no relationship between a business and a referral.

Turning to our example, to design conceptual and system schemas for our example dataset, we should think about the following:

- The entities and relationships in our data
- Possible rules and constraints
- Operational constraints, such as the databases and libraries at our disposal
- The output we want from our application

Our data will consist of candidates and their profile data (e.g., industry, job type, company, etc.), as well as recruiters. Properties can also be treated as entities; for instance, Medical Industry could be treated as a node. Relations could be Candidate Knows Candidate, Candidate Recommended Candidate, or Recruiter Recruited Candidate. As stated previously, graph data can be extremely flexible in how entities can be represented.

Given these choices, we show a few options for the conceptual schema. Option A is shown in figure 8.3.

A.

Figure 8.3   Schema with one node type and one edge type

As you can see, example A consists of one node type (Candidate) connected by one undirected edge type (Knows). Node attributes are the candidate's Industry and their Job Type. There are no restrictions on the relationships, as any candidate can know 0 to n-1 other candidates, where n is the number of candidates. The second conceptual schema is shown in figure 8.4.

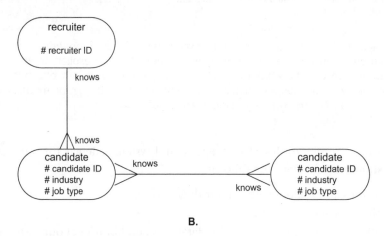

B.

Figure 8.4   Schema with two node types and one edge type

Example B consists of two node types (Candidate and Recruiter), linked by one undirected edge type (Knows). Edges between candidates have no restrictions. Edges between candidates and recruiters have a constraint: a candidate can only link to one recruiter, while a recruiter can link to many candidates.

    The third schema is shown in figure 8.5. It has multiple node and relationship types. In example C, the types are Candidate, Recruiter, and Industry. Relation types include Candidate Knows Candidate, Recruiter Recruits Candidate, Candidate Is a Member of Industry. Note, we've made Industry a separate entity, rather than an attribute of a candidate. These types of graphs are known as *heterogeneous*, as they contain many different

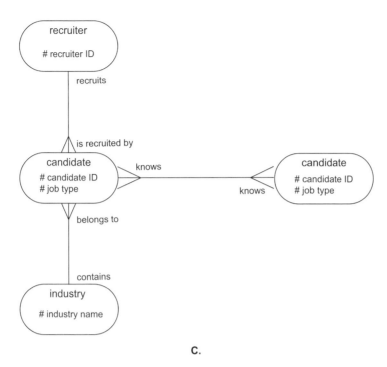

C.

Figure 8.5   Schema with three node types and three edge types

types of nodes and edges. In a way, we can imagine these as multiple graphs that are layered on top of each other. When we have only one type of nodes and edges, then graphs are known as *homogenous*. Some of the constraints for example C include the following:

- Candidates can only have one Recruiter and one Industry.
- Recruiters don't link to Industries.

Depending on the queries and the objectives of the machine learning model, we could pick one schema or experiment with all three in the course of developing our application. Let's stick with the first schema, which can serve as a simple structure for our exploration and experimentation.

8.2.3   *Creating instance models*

An *instance model* contrasts the abstract nature of the graph dataset by providing a tangible, specific example of the data, according to the schema. Such an example serves to validate and test the schema. Following are the steps to create an instance model:

1   *Identify the schema.* Begin by identifying the general model or schema that your instance will be based upon. Ensure that the class definition, attributes, and methods are well established.

2   *Select a subset of the data.* Choose a specific subset of data to represent, adhering to the established graph schema.

3   *Create nodes.* Develop nodes for each entity within your data subset, ensuring each has a label, unique identifier, and associated properties.

4   *Create edges.* Develop links for each relationship, assigning labels and properties and specifying edge directions and multiplicities.

5   *Adhere to the rules and constraints of your schema.* In constructing the instance model, make sure to follow the rules and constraints of the schema.

6   *Visualization.* Use visualization tools to represent the instance model graphically.

7   *Instantiation.* Realize the instance model using a graph database or graph processing system. This will allow for queries that can test and validate it.

Figure 8.6 shows an example of an instance model derived from the schema discussed formerly. The nodes and edges have features filled with the real data of candidates instead of placeholders.

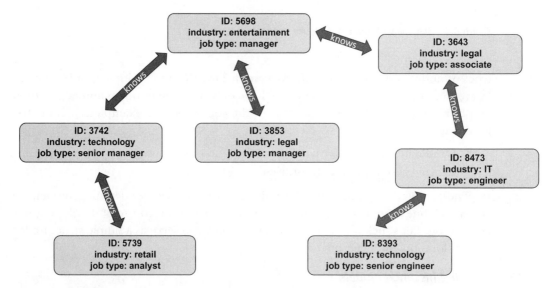

Figure 8.6   Example of an instance model with nodes filled with actual data from the recruiter example. Real instance models may have much more data.

8.2.4   Testing and refactoring

Technical debt can occur when we have to change and evolve our data or code, but we haven't yet planned for backward- or forward-compatibility in our models. It can also happen when our modeling choices aren't a good fit for our database and software choices, which may call for expensive (in time or money) workarounds or replacements.

Having well-defined rules and constraints on our data and models gives us explicit ways to test our pipeline. For example, if we know that our nodes can at most have two degrees, we can design simple functions or queries to process and test every node against this criterion.

Testing and refactoring are iterative processes and crucial in scaling an optimized graph schema and instance model [4, 5]. It will involve executing queries, analyzing results, making necessary adjustments, and validating against metrics. In the context of Whole Staffing's recruitment data, this practice would ensure the model is tailored to capture real-world relationships and robust new data streams. Following are some examples for tests and refactoring:

1 *Cast your instance model in a system.* Store the model in your graph database or processing system of choice.
2 *Create tests and run queries.* Based on the specific requirements, draft queries to test the integrity of your model. Use query languages such as Cypher or SPARQL to execute queries on a graph database. Programming languages, for example, Python, can also be used to query graphs within graph processing systems such as NetworkX.

   For our example's simple schema, here are some possible tests:
   - *Node attributes verification*—Each node should be checked to confirm that it possesses the required attributes, specifically the candidate's industry and job type, and that these attributes have non-null values.
   - *Edge type verification*—All connections between candidates should be validated to confirm that they are of the Knows type, ensuring consistency in relationship labeling.
   - *Relationship verification*—Check the average number of relationships that exist to ensure it's consistent with the average number of referrals.
   - *Unique IDs*—Every candidate node should be checked for unique identifiers to prevent data duplication and ensure data integrity.
   - *Attribute data type*—The data types of `industry` and `jobType` attributes should be validated to ensure consistency across all candidate nodes.
   - *Network structure*—The structure of the network should be validated to ensure it's undirected, confirming the bidirectional nature of the Knows relationships between candidate nodes.

 – *Edge cases*—Determine edge cases and query for those. In our case, the nodes that are unconnected may present a problem. Using queries to understand the extent of unconnected nodes and their effect on the analytics will drive decisions to refactor. Another edge case could be an isolated group of candidates whose relationships form a cycle. It would be important to ensure the data model and the analytical tools could handle such complex or unusual data patterns and still produce valid answers.

3 *Validate and evaluate performance*—Based on the results of the tests, determine if there are logical problems with your model and your use case, or problems with the data and attributes.

4 *Refactor*—Make adjustments to labels, properties, relationships, or constraints as needed to minimize errors.

5 *Repeat*—Iterate the preceding steps, refining the model based on evaluations and ensuring alignment with the project needs and constraints.

6 *Final assessment*—Evaluate the final model against criteria and best practices to ensure its readiness for complex queries and machine learning applications.

With this iterative process of testing and refactoring, we refine the dataset for Whole Staffing's recruitment data and use case. Attention to detail guarantees the model is ready to support evaluation of the complex, nuanced relationships hidden within the recruitment data.

As we transition into the next section, our focus shifts to the practical implementation of some of these concepts. We'll look at creating data pipelines in PyG, showing how to convert data from its initial raw form to a preprocessed state, ready for input into other downstream model training and testing routines.

8.3 *Data pipeline example*

With the schema decided, let's walk through an example of a data pipeline. In this section, we assume our objective is to create a simple data workflow that takes data from a raw state and ends with a preprocessed dataset that can be passed to a GNN. These steps are summarized in figure 8.7.

Note that while the overall steps shown can be consistent from one problem to another, the details of implementation for each step can be unique to the problem, its data, and the chosen data storage, processing, and model training options.

Raw Data Collection and Processing
Collect raw data from various sources, such as relational database tables or files.

ETL (Extract, Transform, Load)
Extract data from sources and transform it into a specific format that matches the predetermined schema.

Data Exploration
Use visual and statistical methods to explore and analyze the data, ensuring it aligns with assumptions and requirements.

Preprocessing
Convert the processed data into formats compatible with GNN frameworks such as PyTorch Geometric (PyG) or Deep Graph Library (DGL).

Figure 8.7   Summary of steps in the data pipeline process in this section

Key terms

The following are key terms used in this section (for more details on graph data models and types of graphs, see appendix A):

- *Adjacency list*—A basic representation of graph data. In this format, each entry contains a node with a list of its adjacent nodes.
- *Adjacency matrix*—A basic representation of graph data. In a matrix, each row and column correspond to a node. The cells, where these rows and columns intersect, signify the presence of edges between the nodes. A cell with a non-zero value indicates an edge between the nodes, while a zero value signifies no connection.
- *Degree*—The degree of a node is the count of its adjacent nodes.
- *Edge list*—A basic representation of a graph. It's an array of all the edges in a graph; each entry in the array contains a unique pair of connected nodes.
- *Mask*—A Boolean array (or tensor in the case of PyTorch) that is used to select specific subsets of data. Masks are commonly used for splitting a dataset into different parts, such as training, validation, and testing sets.

(continued)

- *Rank*—In our context, rank refers to the position of each node's degree in a sorted list. So, the node with the highest degree has rank 1, the next highest has rank 2, and so on.
- *Raw data*—Data in its most unprocessed form.
- *Serialization*—Putting data into a format that is easily stored or exported.
- *Subgraph*—A subgraph is a subset of a larger graph's nodes and edges.

8.3.1 Raw data

Raw data refers to data in its most unprocessed state; such data is the starting point for our pipeline. This data can be in various databases, serialized in some way, or generated.

In the development stage of an application, it's important to know how closely the raw data used will match the live data used in production. One way to do this is by sampling from data archives.

As mentioned in section 8.1, there are at least two sources for our example problem: relational database tables that contain recommendation logs and candidate profiles. To keep our example contained, we assume a helpful engineer has already queried the log data and transformed it into a JSON format, where keys are a recommending candidate, and the values are the recommended candidates. From our profile data, we have two other fields: *industry* and *job type*. For both data sources, our engineer has used a hash to protect PII, which we can consider a unique identifier for the candidate. In this section, we'll use the JSON data, where an example snippet is shown in figure 8.8. The data is displayed in two ways: with a hash and without a hash.

DATA ENCODING AND SERIALIZATION

One key consideration when constructing the pipeline is the choice of what data format to use when importing and exporting data from one system to another. For transferring graph data into another system or sending it over the internet, *encoding* or *serialization* is typically used. These terms refer to the process of putting data in a form that is easily transferable [6, 7]. Before choosing an encoding format, you must have decided upon the following:

- *Data model*—Simple model, property graph, or other?
- *Schema*—Which entities in your data are nodes, edges, and properties?
- *Data structure*—How is the data stored: in adjacency matrices, adjacency lists, or edge lists?
- *Receiving systems*—How does the receiving system (in our case, GNN libraries and graph-processing systems) accept data? What encodings and data structures are preferred? Is imported data automatically recognized, or is custom programming required to read in data?

```
                {                                              {
  "b39ae65ebc89363c9dce2fd3ff73f58191cb8947": [          "JohnDoe": [
    "20e53a5a9875ce3c1beaec367c52699f69772ef9",            "JaneSmith",
    "1c75ca2200efa313ff9b89195b2fb9809727e4e9"             "AliceJohnson"
    ],                                                     ],
  "131e840479c73b6835c1a97872a436972fc142e5": [          "MichaelBrown": [
    "b49b6a8f89d0737949d1eb1a19240f4938b787d8"             "EmilyDavis"
    ],                                                     ],
  "ad63f970d01947ce1b2a9a14c92103c4252a0e86": [          "WilliamWilson": [
    "03e4c9e8593fd47ca6df56bb56b3d5993ad24834",            "JessicaTaylor",
    "4e3f27e27fb1ab924a4b183e70ab7caeb9595cf5",            "SarahMoore",
    "c7962b11d0c5a52f7071bf7ed2d7c7e57b64b32f",            "NancyThomas",
    "a35b3586e5ac639c902d37ad4998b2e4604f9471",            "KarenJackson",
    "6a4914bf66aac804eb8261b1486677128e4954a2",            "SusanWhite",
    "5f31e4dbae313306f94be96f19433ae954d05fd9",            "LindaHarris",
    "8f332fcb048bf08725d22ad15752a6a46e1cd8c4"             "BarbaraClark"
    ],                                                     ],
  "90876fe6ad4269c9457e5e13ffc394964a0ea82a": [          "JamesLewis": [
    "84c71629d8e221d2203ec72cb2526272105c3ff9",            "PatriciaWalker",
    "0921a7bde1679667b64b6003c8108a093a8c11bb",            "SandraHall",
    "97d1726f12a6f1d4a067e462951b857f1ad8f962",            "MaryAllen",
    "367711fd450fdfdc1d40a6c52ccd3ac6df328cec",            "JenniferYoung",
    "14c7f7835db605f8bd1c311ef3fcb804846b62c1",            "ElizabethKing",
    "1f143c52d8e178c7b7c04adc4f68bf1d4b65d0fc",            "MargaretWright",
    "84b73cd9840aa8331159797e584f8b7dd319758a",            "SharonScott",
    "40155f5683c54e39da3e348eac81f1d2c3e336cc",            "LauraGreen",
    "0c8b68323763a684c1792b9cf7d68328a618497c",            "HelenAdams",
    "25501cd00a8e5d8195387076ff9072bcbff9c6df"             "CatherineBaker"
    ]                                                      ]
                }                                              }
```

Figure 8.8 View of raw data: JSON file. The figure on the left is in key/value format. The keys are the members, and the values are their known relationships. The figure on the right shows unhashed values, demonstrating example names for these individuals.

Here are a few encoding choices you're likely to encounter:

- *Language and system-agnostic encodings formats*—These are most popular as they are extremely flexible and work across many systems and languages. However, data arrangement can still differ from system to system. Therefore, an edge list in a CSV file, with a specific set of headers, may not be accepted or interpreted in the same way between two different systems. Following are some examples for this format:
  - *JSON*—Has advantages when reading from APIs or feeding into JavaScript applications. `Cytoscape.js`, a graph visualization library, accepts data in JSON format.
  - *CSV*—Accepted by many processing systems and databases. However, the required arrangement and labeling of the data differs from system to system.
  - *XML*—Graph Exchange XML (GEXF) format is of course an XML format.

- *Language specific*—Python, Java, and other languages have built-in encoding formats.
- *Pickle*—Python's format. Some systems accept Pickle encoded files. Despite this, unless your data pipeline or workflow is governed extensively by Python, pickles should be used lightly. The same applies for other language-specific encodings.
- *System driven*—Specific software, systems, and libraries have their own encoding formats. Though these may be limited in usability between systems, an advantage is that the schema in such formats is consistent. Software and systems that have their own encoding format include Stanford Network Analysis Platform (SNAP), NetworkX, and Gephi.
- *Big data*—Aside from the language-agnostic formats listed previously, there are other encoding formats used for larger sizes of data.
- *Avro*—This encoding is used extensively in Hadoop workflows
- *Matrix based*—Because graphs can be expressed as matrices, there are a few formats that are based on this data structure. For sparse graphs, the following formats provide substantial memory savings and computational advantages (for lookups and matrix/vector multiplication):
  - Sparse column matrix (.csc filetype)
  - Sparse row matrix (.csr filetype)
  - Matrix market format (.mtx filetype)

8.3.2 The ETL step

With the schema chosen and data sources established, the *ETL* (*extract, transform, load*) step consists of taking raw data from its sources and then producing data that fits the schema and is ready for preprocessing or training. For our data, this consists of programming a set of actions that begin with pulling the data from the various databases and then joining them as needed.

We need data that ends up in a specific format that we can input into a preprocessing step. This could be a JSON format or an edge list. For either the JSON example or edge list example, our schema is fulfilled; we'll have nodes (the individual persons) and edges (the relationships between these people).

For our recruitment example, we want to transform our raw data into a graph data structure, encoded in CSV. This was chosen for ease of manipulation with Python. This file can then be loaded into our graph-processing system, NetworkX, or a GNN package such as PyG. To summarize the next steps, we'll do the following:

1 Convert the raw data file to a graph format, following your chosen graph data model. In our case, we convert the raw data into an edge list and an adjacency list. We then saved it as a CSV file.
2 Load the CSV file into NetworkX for exploratory data analysis (EDA) and visualization.
3 Load into PyG and preprocess.

RAW DATA TO ADJACENCY LIST AND EDGE LIST

Starting with our CSV and JSON files, we next convert the data into two key data models: an edge list and an adjacency list, which we define in appendix A. Both adjacency and edge lists are two basic data representations used with graphs. An edge list is a list where every item in this structure contains a node with a list of its adjacent nodes. These representations are illustrated in figure 8.9.

A)

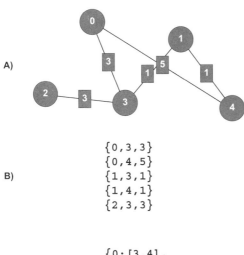

B)

{0,3,3}
{0,4,5}
{1,3,1}
{1,4,1}
{2,3,3}

C)

{0:[3,4],
1:[3,4],
2:[3],
3:[0,1,2],
4:[0,1]}

Figure 8.9   A graph with nodes and edges marked (top). An edge list representation (middle); each entry contains the edge number and the pair of nodes connected. An adjacency list representation in a dictionary (bottom); each key is a node, and the values are its adjacent nodes.

First using the `json` module, we load the data from a JSON file into a Python dictionary. The Python dictionary has the same structure as the JSON, with member hashes as keys and their relationships as values.

CREATING AN ADJACENCY LIST

Next, we create an adjacency list from this dictionary. This list will be stored as a text file. Each line of the file will contain the member hash, followed by hashes of that member's relationships. The process for creating an adjacency list is illustrated in figure 8.10.

This function transforms our raw data into an adjacency list, which we'll apply to our recruitment example. We'll have *inputs* that consist of the following:

- A dictionary of candidate referrals where the keys are members who have referred other candidates, and the values are lists of the people who were referred
- A suffix to append to the filename

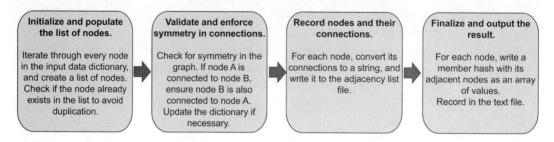

Figure 8.10 Flow diagram illustrating the process of transforming a relationship dictionary into a well-structured adjacency list, stored in a text file, while ensuring the symmetry of connections in the undirected graph.

We'll have *outputs* that consist of the following:

- An encoded adjacency list in a txt file
- A list of the node IDs found

This is shown in the following listing.

Listing 8.1   Create an adjacency list from relationship dictionary

```
def create_adjacency_list(data_dict, suffix=''):
    list_of_nodes = []

    for source_node in list(data_dict.keys()):

        if source_node not in list_of_nodes:
            list_of_nodes.append(source_node)

        for y in data_dict[source_node]:
            if y not in list_of_nodes:
                list_of_nodes.append(y)
            if y not in data_dict.keys():
                data_dict[y]=[source_node]
            Else:
                if source_node not in data_dict[y]:
                    data_dict[y].append(source_node)
                else: continue

    g= open("adjacency_list_{}.txt".format(suffix),"w+")
    for source_node in list(data_dict.keys()):
        dt = ' '.join(data_dict[source_node])
        print("{} {}".format(source_node, dt))
        g.write("{} {} \n".format(source_node, dt))

    g.close
    return list_of_nodes
```

Runs through every node in the input data dictionary → (points to `for source_node in list(data_dict.keys()):`)

Because this is an undirected graph, there must be a symmetry in the values; that is, every value in a key must contain that key in its own entry. As an example, for entry F, if G is a value, then for entry G, F must be a value. These lines check for that and fix the dictionary if these conditions don't exist.

Creates a text file that will store the adjacency list

For every key in the dictionary

Creates a string from the list of dictionary values. This value is a string of member IDs separated by empty spaces.

Writes a line to the text file. This line will contain the member hash, and then a string of relationship hashes.

Optional print

CREATING AN EDGE LIST

Next, we show the process to create an edge list. As with the adjacency list, we transform the data to account for node pair symmetry. Note that either format could work for this project. For your own project, another format could also be warranted. Figure 8.11 illustrates the process.

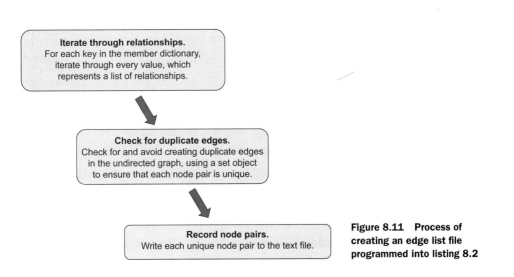

Iterate through relationships.
For each key in the member dictionary, iterate through every value, which represents a list of relationships.

Check for duplicate edges.
Check for and avoid creating duplicate edges in the undirected graph, using a set object to ensure that each node pair is unique.

Record node pairs.
Write each unique node pair to the text file.

Figure 8.11 Process of creating an edge list file programmed into listing 8.2

As with the adjacency list function, the edge list function illustrates the transformation of raw data into an edge list and has the same inputs as the previous function. The outputs consist of the following:

- An edge list in a .txt file
- Lists of the node IDs found and the edges generated

By definition, every entry of an edge list must be unique, so we must ensure that our produced edge list is the same. Here's the code to create an edge list from a relationship dictionary.

Listing 8.2   Create an edge list from relationship dictionary

```
def create_edge_list(data_dict, suffix=''):
    edge_list_file = open("edge_list_{}.txt".format(suffix),"w+")
    edges = []
    nodes_all = []

    for source in list(data_dict.keys()):
        if source not in list_of_nodes_all:
            nodes_all.append(source)
        connections = data_dict[source]
```

```
for destination in connections:
    if destination not in nodes_all:
        nodes_all.append(destination)
```

Each member dictionary value is a list of relationships. For every key, we iterate through every value.

```
    if {source, destination} not in edges:
        print(f"{source} {destination}")
        out_string =  f"{source} {destination}\n"
        edge_list_file.write(out_string)
        edges.append({source, destination })

    else: continue

edge_list_file.close
return list_of_edges, list_of_nodes_all
```

Because this graph is undirected, we don't want to create duplicate edges. For example, because {F,G} is the same as {G,F}, we only need one of these. This line checks if a node pair exists already. We use a set object because the node order doesn't matter.

Writes the line to the text file. This line will consist of the node pair.

In the next sections, we'll use the adjacency list to load our graph into NetworkX. One thing to note about the differences between loading a graph using the adjacency list versus the edge list is that edge lists can't account for single, unlinked nodes. It turns out that quite a few of the candidates at Whole Staffing haven't recommended anyone, and don't have edges associated with them. These nodes would be invisible to an edge list representation of the data.

8.3.3   *Data exploration and visualization*

Next, we want to load our network data into a graph processing framework. We chose NetworkX, but there are many other choices available, depending on your task and language preferences. We chose NetworkX because we have a small graph, and we also want to do some light EDA and visualization.

With our newly created adjacency list, we can create a NetworkX graph object by calling the `read_edgelist` or `read_adjlist` methods. Next, we can load in the attributes `industry` and `job type`. In this example, these attributes are loaded in as a dictionary, where the node IDs serve as keys.

With our graph loaded, we can explore and inspect our data to ensure that it aligns with our assumptions. First, the count of nodes and edges should match our member count, and the number of edges created in our edge list, respectively, as shown in the following listing.

Listing 8.3   Create an edge list from the relationship dictionary

```
social_graph = nx.read_adjlist('adjacency_list_candidates.txt')
nx.set_node_attributes(social_graph, attribute_dict)
print(social_graph.number_of_nodes(), social_graph.number_of_edges())
>> 1933 12239
```

We want to check how many connected components our graph has:

```
len(list((c for c in nx.connected_components(social_graph))))
>>> 219
```

The `connected_components` method generates the connected components of a graph; a visualization is shown in figure 8.12 and generated using NetworkX. There are hundreds of components, but when we inspect this data, we find that there is one large component of 1,698 nodes, and the rest are composed of less than 4 nodes. Most of the disconnected components are singleton nodes (the candidates that never refer anyone). For more information about components of a graph, we give definitions and details in appendix A.

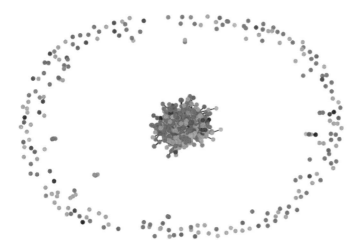

Figure 8.12　The full graph, with its large connected component in the middle, surrounded by many smaller components. For our example, we'll use only the nodes in the large connected component.

We're interested in this large connected component and will work with that going forward. The `subgraph` method can help us to isolate this large component.

Finally, we use NetworkX to visualize our graph. For this, we'll use a standard recipe for analyzing graphs which can also be found in the NetworkX documentation.

Let's go through the different steps (the full code sample for each step is also in the repository, labeled "Function that visualizes the social graph and shows degree statistics"):

1　*Create the graph object.* Generate a distinct graph object, selecting the largest connected component from the given graph. In cases where there's only one connected component, this step might be unnecessary but ensures the selection of the major component.

```
connected_component = nx.connected_components(social_graph
Gcc = social_graph.subgraph(sorted(connected ),
                            key=len,
                            reverse=True)[0]
                            )
```

2 *Determine the layout.* Decide the positioning of nodes and edges for visualization. Choose an appropriate layout algorithm; for example, the Spring Layout models the edges as springs and nodes as repelling masses:

```
pos = nx.spring_layout(Gcc, seed=10396953)
```

3 *Draw nodes and edges.* Use the chosen layout to draw nodes on the visualization. Adjust visual parameters such as node size to enhance the clarity of the figure. Based on the selected layout, draw the edges. Modify appearance settings such as transparency to achieve the desired visual effect.

```
nx.draw_networkx_nodes(Gcc, pos, ax=ax0, node_size=20)
nx.draw_networkx_edges(Gcc, pos, ax=ax0, alpha=0.4)
ax0.set_title("Connected component of Social Graph")
ax0.set_axis_off()
```

4 *Generate and plot node degrees.* Employ the degree method on the graph object to create an iterable of nodes with their respective degrees, and sort them from highest to lowest. Visualize the sorted list of node degrees on a plot to analyze the distribution and prominence of various nodes. Use NumPy's `unique` method with the `return_counts` parameter to plot a histogram showing the degrees of nodes and their counts, providing insights into the graph's structure and complexity:

```
degree_sequence = sorted([d for n, d in social_graph.degree()],
    reverse=True)

ax1 = fig.add_subplot(axgrid[3:, :2])
ax1.plot(degree_sequence, "b-", marker="o")
ax1.set_title("Degree Rank Plot")
ax1.set_ylabel("Degree")
ax1.set_xlabel("Rank")

ax2 = fig.add_subplot(axgrid[3:, 2:])
ax2.bar(*np.unique(degree_sequence, return_counts=True))
ax2.set_title("Degree histogram")
ax2.set_xlabel("Degree")
ax2.set_ylabel("# of Nodes")
```

These plots are shown in figure 8.13.

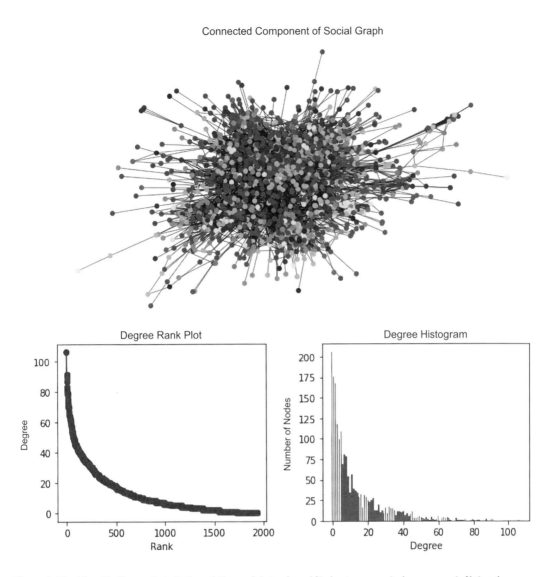

Figure 8.13 **Visualization and statistics of the social graph and its large connected component. Network visualization using NetworkX default settings (top). A rank plot of node degree of the entire graph (bottom left). We see that about three-fourths of nodes have less than 20 adjacent nodes. A histogram of degree (bottom right).**

Lastly, we can visualize an adjacency matrix of our graph, shown in figure 8.14, using the following command:

```
plt.imshow(nx.to_numpy_matrix(social_graph), aspect='equal',cmap='twilight')
```

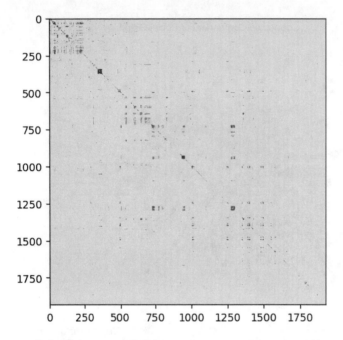

Figure 8.14   A visualized adjacency matrix of our social graph. Vertical and horizontal values refer to respective nodes.

As with the numerical adjacency matrix, for our undirected graph, this visual adjacency matrix has symmetry down the diagonal. All undirected graphs will have symmetric adjacency matrices. For directed graphs, this can happen but isn't guaranteed.

8.3.4   *Preprocessing and loading data into PyG*

For this book, *preprocessing* consists of putting our data, including its properties, labels, or other metadata, in a format suitable for downstream machine learning models. Feature engineering can also be a step in this process. For feature engineering, we'll often use graph algorithms to calculate the properties of nodes, edges, or subgraphs.

An example for node features is betweenness centrality. If our schema allows, we can calculate and attach such properties to the node entities of our data. To perform this, we take the output of the ETL step, say an edge list, and import this into a graph processing framework to calculate betweenness centrality for each node. Once this quantity is obtained, we can store it using a dictionary with the node ID as keys, then use this as a node feature later on.

Betweenness centrality

Betweenness centrality is a critical measure of node importance that quantifies the tendency of a node to lie in the shortest paths from source to destination nodes. Given a graph with *n* nodes, you could determine the shortest path between every unique pair of nodes in this graph. We could take this set of shortest paths and look for the presence of a particular node. If the node appears in all or most of these paths, it has a high betweenness centrality and would be considered to be highly influential. Conversely, if the node appears a few times (or only once) in the set of shortest paths, it will have a low betweenness centrality, and a low influence.

Now that we have our data, we want to make it ready for use in our selected GNN framework. In this book, we use PyG, due to its robust suite of tools and flexibility in handling complex graph data. However, most standard GNN packages have mechanisms to import custom data into their frameworks. For this section, we'll focus on three modules within PyG:

- `Data` *module* (`torch_geometric.data`)—Allows inspection, manipulation, and creation of data objects that are used by the PyG environment.
- `Utils` *module* (`torch_geometric.utils`)—Many useful methods. Helpful in this section are methods that allow the quick import and export of graph data.
- `Datasets` *module* (`torch_geometric.datasets`)—Preloaded datasets, including benchmark datasets, and datasets from influential papers in the field.

Let's begin with the `Datasets` module. This module contains datasets that have already been preprocessed and can readily be used by PyG's methods. When starting with PyG, having these datasets allows for easy experimentation without worrying about creating a data pipeline. Similarly, by studying the codebase underlying these datasets, we can also learn how to create our own custom datasets.

At the end of the previous section, we converted our raw data into a standard format and loaded our new graphs into a graph-processing framework. Now, we want to load our data into the PyG environment. Preprocessing in PyG has a few objectives:

- Creating data objects with multiple attributes from the level of nodes and edges to the subgraph and graph level
- Combining different data sources into one object or set of related objects
- Converting data into objects that can be processed using GPUs
- Allowing splitting of training/testing/validation data
- Enabling batching of data for training

These objectives are fulfilled by a hierarchy of classes within the `Data` module:

- `Data` *class*—Creates graph objects. These objects can have optional built-in and custom-made attributes.

- `Dataset` *and* `InMemoryDataset` *classes*—Creates a repeatable data preprocessing pipeline. You can start from raw data files and add custom filters and transformations to achieve your preprocessed *data* objects. `Dataset` objects are larger than memory, while `InMemoryDataset` objects fit in memory.
- `Dataloader` *class*—Batches data objects for model training.

This is shown in figure 8.15, including how different data and dataset classes connect to the dataloader.

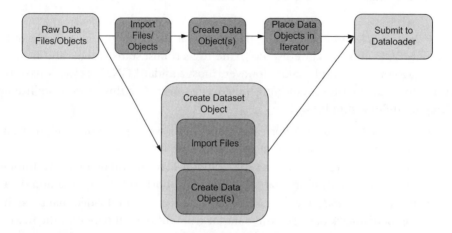

Figure 8.15   Steps to preprocess data in PyG. From raw files, there are essentially two paths to prep data for ingestion by a PyG algorithm. The first path, shown here, directly creates an iterator of data instances, which is used by the dataloader. The second path mimics the first but performs this process within the dataloader class.

There are two paths to preprocess data, one uses a `dataset` class and the other goes without it. The advantage of using the `dataset` class is that it allows us to save the generated datasets and also preserve filtering and transformation details. Dataset objects are flexible and can be modified to output variations of a dataset. On the other hand, if your custom dataset is simple or generated on the fly, and you have no use for saving the data or process long term, bypassing dataset objects may serve you well. So, in summary, we have the following different data-related classes:

- `Datasets` *objects*—Preprocessed datasets for benchmarking or testing an algorithm or architecture (not to be confused with `Dataset`—no "s" at the end— objects).
- `Data` *objects into iterator*—Graph objects that are generated on the fly or for whom there is no need to save.
- `Dataset` *object*—For graph objects that should be preserved, including the data pipeline, filtering and transformations, input raw data files, and output

processed data files. Not to be confused with `Datasets` (with "s" at the end) objects.

With those basics, let's preprocess our social graph data. We'll cover the following cases:

- *Convert into a* `data` *instance using NetworkX.* For quick conversion from NetworkX to PyG, ideal for ad hoc processing or when using NetworkX's functionalities.
- *Convert into a* `data` *instance using input files.* Offers control over the data import process, which is ideal for raw data and custom preprocessing requirements.
- *Convert to* `dataset` *instance.* For systematic, scalable, and reproducible data preprocessing and management, especially for complex or reusable datasets.
- *Convert* `data` *objects for use in* `dataloader` *without the* `dataset` *class.* For scenarios where simplicity and speed are prioritized over systematic data management and preprocessing, or for on-the-fly and synthetic data.

First, we'll import the needed modules from PyG in the following listing.

Listing 8.4   Required imports, covering data object creation

```
import torch
from torch_geometric.data import Data
from torch_geometric.data import InMemoryDataset
from torch_geometric import utils
```

CASE A: CREATE PyG DATA OBJECT USING THE NETWORKX OBJECT

In the previous sections, we've explored a graph expressed as a NetworkX `graph` object. PyG's `util` module has a method that can directly create a PyG `data` object from a NetworkX `graph` object:

```
data = utils.from_networkx(social_graph)
```

The `from_networkx` method preserves nodes, edges, and their attributes, but it should be checked to ensure the translation from one module to another went smoothly.

CASE B: CREATE PyG DATA OBJECT USING RAW FILES

For greater control over data import into PyG, we can start with raw files or files from any stage of the ETL process. In our social graph case, we can begin with the edge list file created earlier.

Now, let's review an example where we use code to process and convert our social graph from an edge list text file into a format suitable for training a GNN model in PyG. We prepare node features, labels, edges, and training/testing sets for use in the PyG environment.

PART 1: IMPORT AND PREPARE GRAPH DATA

This part includes reading an edge list from a file to create a NetworkX graph, extracting the list of nodes, creating mappings from node names to indices, and vice versa:

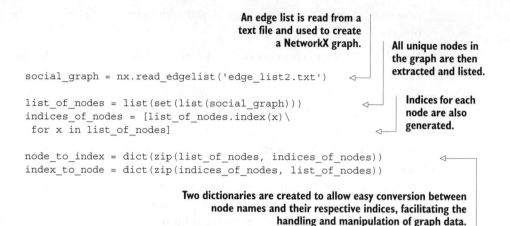

An edge list is read from a text file and used to create a NetworkX graph.

All unique nodes in the graph are then extracted and listed.

```
social_graph = nx.read_edgelist('edge_list2.txt')
```

```
list_of_nodes = list(set(list(social_graph)))
indices_of_nodes = [list_of_nodes.index(x)\
 for x in list_of_nodes]
```

Indices for each node are also generated.

```
node_to_index = dict(zip(list_of_nodes, indices_of_nodes))
index_to_node = dict(zip(indices_of_nodes, list_of_nodes))
```

Two dictionaries are created to allow easy conversion between node names and their respective indices, facilitating the handling and manipulation of graph data.

PART 2: PROCESS EDGES AND NODE FEATURES

This part focuses on converting the edges and node attributes into a format that can be easily used with PyTorch for machine learning tasks:

A NetworkX edge list object is created.

It's then transformed into two separate lists representing the source and destination nodes of each edge.

```
list_edges = nx.convert.to_edgelist(social_graph)
list_edges = list(list_edges)
named_edge_list_0 = [x[0] for x in list_edges]
named_edge_list_1 = [x[1] for x in list_edges]

indexed_edge_list_0 = [node_to_index[x]\
 for x in named_edge_list_0]
indexed_edge_list_1 = [node_to_index[x] for x in named_edge_list_1]

x = torch.FloatTensor([[1] for x in\
range(len(list_of_nodes))])
y = torch.FloatTensor([1]*974 + [0]*973)
y = y.long()
```

These lists are then indexed using the previously created node-to-index mapping.

The node features and labels are prepared using PyTorch tensor objects, assuming a simple scenario where all nodes have the same single feature.

The node features and labels are prepared using PyTorch tensor objects, assuming a simple scenario where all nodes have the same single feature.

PART 3: PREPARE DATA FOR TRAINING AND TESTING

In this part, the dataset is prepared for training and testing by creating masks for data splitting and combining all the processed data into a single PyTorch data object:

```
edge_index = torch.tensor([indexed_edge_list_0,\
 indexed_edge_list_1])
```

The edge indices created in part 2 are converted into a PyTorch tensor.

```
train_mask = torch.zeros(len(list_of_nodes),\
 dtype=torch.uint8)
train_mask[:int(0.8 * len(list_of_nodes))] = 1 #train only on the 80% nodes
test_mask = torch.zeros(len(list_of_nodes),\
 dtype=torch.uint8) #test on 20 % nodes
test_mask[- int(0.2 * len(list_of_nodes)):] = 1
train_mask = train_mask.bool()
test_mask = test_mask.bool()

data = Data(x=x, y=y, edge_index=edge_index,\
 train_mask=train_mask, test_mask=test_mask)
```

Masks for training and testing datasets are created by splitting the nodes into two separate groups, ensuring that specific portions of the data are used for training and testing.

All the processed components, including node features, labels, edge indices, and data masks, are then combined into a single PyTorch Data object, preparing the data for subsequent machine learning tasks.

We've created a `data` object from an `edgelist` file. Such an object can be inspected with PyG commands, though the set of commands is limited compared to a graph processing library. Such a `data` object can also be further prepared so that it can be accessed by a `dataloader`, which we'll cover next.

CASE C: CREATE PyG DATASET OBJECT USING CUSTOM CLASS AND INPUT FILES

If the previous listing is suitable for our purposes, and we want to use it repeatedly, a preferable option is to create a permanent class that we can include for our pipeline. This is what the `dataset` class does.

Let's next create a `dataset` object, shown in listing 8.5. In this example, we name our `dataset` `MyOwnDataset` and have it inherit from `InMemoryDataset` because our social graph is small enough to sit in memory. As discussed earlier, for larger graphs, data can be accessed from disk by having the `dataset` object inherit from `Dataset` instead of `InMemoryDataset`.

This first part of the code initiates the custom `dataset` class, inheriting properties from the `InMemoryDataset` class. The constructor initializes the dataset, loads processed data, and defines the properties for raw and processed filenames. The raw files are kept empty as this example doesn't require them, and the processed data is fetched from a specified path.

Listing 8.5 Class to create a dataset object (part 1)

```
class MyOwnDataset(InMemoryDataset):
    def __init__(self, root, \
    transform=None, pre_transform=None):\
        super(MyOwnDataset, self).__init__(root,
    @property transform, pre_transform)
        self.data, self.slices = torch.load(self.processed_paths[0])

    def raw_file_names(self):
        return []
    @property
```

Initializes the dataset class. This class inherits from the InMemoryDataset class. This init method creates data and slices objects to be updated in the process method.

An optional method that specifies the location of the raw files required for processing. For our more rudimentary example, we don't make use of this but have included it for completeness. In later chapters, we'll make use of this as our dataset becomes a bit more complex.

```
def processed_file_names(self):
    return ['../test.dataset']
```

This method saves our generated dataset to disk.

This segment of the code is for data downloading and processing. It reads an edge list from a text file and converts it into a NetworkX graph. The nodes and edges of the graph are then indexed and converted into tensors suitable for machine learning tasks. The method downloaded is kept as a placeholder in case there's a need to download raw data in the future.

Listing 8.6   Class to create a dataset object (part 2)

```
def download(self):
    # Download to `self.raw_dir`.
    pass
```

Allows raw data to be downloaded to a local disk.

```
def process(self):
    # Read data into `Data` list.
    data_list = []

    eg = nx.read_edgelist('edge_list2.txt')

    list_of_nodes = list(set(list(eg)))
    indices_of_nodes = [list_of_nodes.index(x) for x in list_of_nodes]

    node_to_index = dict(zip(list_of_nodes, indices_of_nodes))
    index_to_node = dict(zip(indices_of_nodes, list_of_nodes))

    list_edges = nx.convert.to_edgelist(eg)
    list_edges = list(list_edges)
    named_edge_list_0 = [x[0] for x in list_edges]
    named_edge_list_1 = [x[1] for x in list_edges]

    indexed_edge_list_0 = [node_to_index[x] for x in named_edge_list_0]
    indexed_edge_list_1 = [node_to_index[x] for x in named_edge_list_1]
```

The process method contains the preprocessing steps to create our data object, and then makes additional steps to partition our data for loading.

This final part of the code is focused on preparing and saving the data for machine learning models. It creates feature and label tensors, prepares the edge index, and generates training and testing masks to split the dataset. The data is then collated and saved in the processed path for easy retrieval during model training.

Listing 8.7   Class to create a dataset object (part 3)

```
        x = torch.FloatTensor([[1] for x in range(len(list_of_nodes))])#
 [[] for x in xrange(n)]
        y = torch.FloatTensor([1]*974 + [0]*973)
        y = y.long()

        edge_index = torch.tensor([indexed_edge_list_0, indexed_edge_list_1])

        train_mask = torch.zeros(len(list_of_nodes), dtype=torch.uint8)
        train_mask[:int(0.8 * len(list_of_nodes))]\
 = 1 #train only on the 80% nodes
```

```
        test_mask = torch.zeros(len(list_of_nodes), \
dtype=torch.uint8) #test on 20 % nodes
        test_mask[- int(0.2 * len(list_of_nodes)):] = 1

        train_mask = train_mask.bool()
        test_mask = test_mask.bool()

        data_example = Data(x=x, y=y, edge_index=edge_index, \
train_mask=train_mask, test_mask=test_mask)

        data_list.append(data_example)

        data, slices = self.collate(data_list)
        torch.save((data, slices),\
 self.processed_paths[0])
```

← In this first simple use of a dataset class, we use a small dataset. In practice, we'll process much larger datasets and wouldn't do this all at once. We'd create examples of our data, then append them to a list. For our purposes (training on this data), pulling from a list object would be slow, so we take this iterable, and use collate to combine the data examples into one data object. The collate method also creates a dictionary named slices that is used to pull single samples from this data object.

Saves our preprocessed data to disk

CASE D: CREATE PYG DATA OBJECTS FOR USE IN DATALOADER WITHOUT USE OF A DATASET OBJECT
Lastly, we explain how to bypass `dataset` object creation and have the `dataloader` work directly with your `data` object, as illustrated in figure 8.15. In the PyG documentation, there is a section that outlines how to do this.

Just as in regular PyTorch, you don't have to use datasets, for example, when you want to create synthetic data on the fly without saving them explicitly to disk. In this case, simply pass a regular Python list holding `torch_geometric.data.Data` objects and pass them to `torch_geometric.data.DataLoader`:

```
from torch_geometric.data import Data, DataLoader

data_list = [Data(...), ..., Data(...)]
loader = DataLoader(data_list, batch_size=32)
```

In this chapter, we've covered the steps that go from project outline, through to converting raw data into a format ready for GNNs. As we conclude this section, it's worth noting that every dataset is different. The procedures outlined in this discussion provide a structural framework that serves as a starting point, not a one-size-fits-all solution. In the final section, we turn to the subject of sourcing data to support data projects.

8.4   Where to find graph data

To not start from scratch in developing a graph data model and schema for your problem, there are several sources of published models and schemas. They include industry standard data models, published datasets, published semantic models (including knowledge graphs), and academic papers. A set of example sources is provided in table 8.2.

Sourcing graph data

Details of different sources for graph-based data that can be used for GNN projects.

- *From nongraph data*—In this chapter, we assumed that the data lies in non-graph sources and must be transformed into a graph format using ETL and preprocessing. Having a schema can help guide such a transformation and keep it ready for further analysis.
- *Existing graph datasets*—The number of freely available graph datasets is growing. Two GNN libraries we use in this book, Deep Graph Library (DGL) and PyG, come with a number of benchmark datasets installed. Many such datasets are from influential academic papers. However, such datasets are small scale, which limits reproducibility of results, and whose performance don't necessarily scale for large datasets.

  A source of data that seeks to mitigate the problems of earlier benchmark datasets in this space is Open Graph Benchmark (OGB). This initiative provides access to a variety of real-world datasets, of varying scales. OGB also publishes performance benchmarks by learning task. Table 8.2 lists a few repositories of graph datasets.
- *From generation*—Many graph processing frameworks and graph databases allow the generation of random graphs using a number of algorithms. Though random, depending on the generating algorithm, the resulting graph will have characteristics that are predictable.

Table 8.2   Graph datasets and semantic models

Source	Type	Problem Domains	URL
Open Graph Benchmark (OGB)	Graph datasets and benchmarks	Social networks, drug discovery	https://ogb.stanford.edu/
GraphChallenge Datasets	Graph datasets	Network science, biology	https://graphchallenge.mit.edu/data-sets
Network Repository	Graph datasets	Network science, bioinformatics, machine learning, data mining, physics, and social science	http://networkrepository.com/
SNAP Datasets	Graph datasets	Social networks, network science, road networks, commercial networks, finance	http://snap.stanford.edu/data/
Schema.org	Semantic data model	Internet web pages	https://schema.org/
Wikidata	Semantic data model	Wikipedia pages	www.wikidata.org/

Table 8.2 Graph datasets and semantic models *(continued)*

Source	Type	Problem Domains	URL
Financial Industry Business Ontology	Semantic data model	Finance	https://github.com/ edmcouncil/fibo
Bioportal	List of medical semantic models	Medical	https://bioportal.bioontology .org/ontologies/

Public graph datasets also exist in several places. Published datasets have accessible data, with summary statistics. Often, however, they lack explicit schemas, conceptual or otherwise. To derive the dataset's entities, relations, rules, and constraints, querying the data becomes necessary.

For semantic models based on property, RDF, and other data models, there are some general datasets, and others are targeted to particular industries and verticals. Such references seldom use graph-centric terms (e.g., *node, vertex,* and *edge*) but will use terms related to semantics and ontologies (e.g., *entity, relationship, links*). Unlike the graph datasets, the semantic models offer data frameworks, not the data itself.

Reference papers and published schemas can provide ideas and templates that can help in developing your schema. There are a few use cases targeted toward industry verticals that both represent a situation using graphs and use graph algorithms, including GNNs, to solve a relevant problem. Transaction fraud in financial institutions, molecular fingerprinting in chemical engineering, and page rank in social networks are a few examples. Perusing such existing work can provide a boost to development efforts. On the other hand, often such published work is done for academic, not industry goals. A network that is developed to prove an academic point or make empirical observations may not have qualities amenable to an enterprise system that must be maintained and be used on dirty and dynamic data.

Summary

- Planning for a graph learning project involves more steps than in traditional machine learning projects. The objectives and requirements will influence the design of the system, data models, and GNN architecture. The project includes creating robust graph data models, understanding and transforming raw data, and ensuring that the models effectively represent the complex relationships within the recruitment landscape.
- One important step is creating the data model and schema for your data. These processes are essential to avoid technical debt. This involves designing the elements, relationships, and constraints; running queries; analyzing results; making adjustments; and validating against criteria to ensure the model's readiness for complex queries and machine learning applications. A graph data model will be refined through iterative testing and refactoring to ensure it effectively supports the analysis of complex relationships within the recruitment data.

- There are many encoding and serialization options for keeping data in memory or in raw files, including language and system-agnostic formats such as JSON, CSV, and XML. Language-specific formats, such as Python's Pickle, and system-driven formats from specific software and libraries such as SNAP, NetworkX, and Gephi, are also mentioned. For big data, Avro and matrix-based formats (sparse column matrix, sparse row matrix, and matrix market format) are high-lighted as efficient options for handling large datasets.

- A data pipeline can start with raw data that undergoes exploratory analysis and preprocessing to be usable by GNN libraries such as PyG. The raw data is transformed into standard formats such as edge lists or adjacency matrices, ensuring consistency and usability for different problems.

- Graph processing frameworks such as NetworkX are used for light exploratory data analysis (EDA) and visualization. Graph objects, such as adjacency and edge lists, are loaded into NetworkX. The visual representation and statistical analysis, such as the number of nodes, edges, and connected components, are derived to understand the graph's structure and complexity.

- The PyG library is used for preprocessing, involving the conversion of data into formats that can be easily manipulated and trained with. Data objects are created with multiple attributes at various levels, enabling GPU processing and facilitating the splitting of training, testing, and validation data. The choice between using dataset objects or bypassing them depends on the need for saving data and the complexity of the dataset.

- There are numerous repositories of ready-to-use graph datasets and semantic models covering various domains, such as social networks and drug discovery. However, while these datasets are useful for learning and benchmarking, they are often small-scale and may not be directly applicable for large, real-world problems.

- While public graph datasets and semantic models provide a starting point, they often lack explicit schemas requiring additional work to derive entities, relations, and constraints. Additionally, while academic papers offer templates for developing schemas, they are typically designed for academic purposes and may not be directly transferable to real-world, industry-specific applications with dynamic and dirty data.

appendix A
Discovering graphs

In this appendix, we explore the theory and implementations of graphs that are most pertinent to using the GNNs covered in the rest of the book. The goal is to help those of you who are less familiar with graphs learn enough to follow the book (if you're familiar with graphs, you can skip this appendix). We establish basic definitions, concepts, and nomenclature, and then survey how the theory is realized in real systems. This foundation is not only necessary to follow the material in this book but also for building the insights that make architecting custom systems and troubleshooting errors easier.

Additionally, in a rapidly evolving field, the ability to quickly absorb new academic and technical literature is crucial for staying up to date with the state of the art. We also provide the basic background to pick up the essence of relevant published papers. In this appendix, we'll use a running example of a social networking dataset to demonstrate the concepts. This is a dataset of more than 1,900 professionals and their industry relationships. Figure A.1 visualizes this graph (generated using Graphistry).

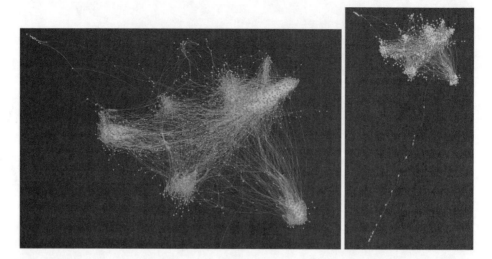

Figure A.1   A stylized visualization of the example social network, consisting of industry professionals and their relationships. The nodes (dots) are the professionals, and the edges (lines) denote a relationship between people. In this visualization, created using Graphistry, the left image shows an edge diverge out of the frame (bottom right). The right image is the entire graph, showing the cut-off edges and nodes.

A.1   Graph fundamentals

Let's start with some definitions, and then we'll see how the concepts work.

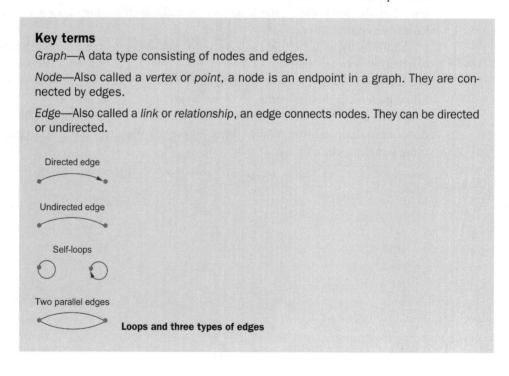

Key terms

Graph—A data type consisting of nodes and edges.

Node—Also called a *vertex* or *point*, a node is an endpoint in a graph. They are connected by edges.

Edge—Also called a *link* or *relationship*, an edge connects nodes. They can be directed or undirected.

Directed edge

Undirected edge

Self-loops

Two parallel edges   **Loops and three types of edges**

Directed edge—A directed edge, usually represented by an arrow, denotes a one-way relationship or flow from one node to another.

Undirected edge—An undirected edge has no direction. In such an edge, a relationship or flow can go in either direction.

Adjacent—The property that two nodes are directly connected via an edge. Such nodes are said to be *joined*.

Self-loop—An edge that connects a node to itself. Such edges can be directed or undirected.

Parallel edges—Multiple edges that connect the same two nodes.

Weights—One important attribute of an edge is weight, which is a numerical value assigned to an edge. Such an attribute can describe the intensity of the connection, or some other real-world value, such as length (if a graph modeled cities on a road map).

These concepts give us the tools to create the simplest graphs. With a simple graph created from these concepts, we could derive network properties explained in the following section.

While real-world graphs are complex, simple graphs can often effectively represent them for various purposes. For example, though our social graph data contains node features (covered in section A.1.2), to create the visualization in figure A.1, we only used node and edge information.

A.1.1   Graph properties

In the following subsections, we discuss some of the more important properties of graphs. Many of the software programs and databases in the graph ecosystem (described in section A.3) should have the capability to compute some or all of these properties.

SIZE/ORDER

We're often interested in the overall number of nodes and edges in a graph. Formal names for these properties are *size* (the number of edges) and *order* (the number of nodes). In our social graph, the number of nodes is 1,933, and the number of edges is 12,239.

DEGREE DISTRIBUTION

A degree distribution is simply the distribution of the degrees of all the nodes in a graph. This can be shown as a histogram, as in figure A.2.

The *degree* of a node is the number of adjacent nodes in an undirected graph. For directed graphs, there are two types of degrees a node can have: an *in-degree* for edges directed to the node and an *out-degree* for edges directed outward from the node. Self-loops often are given a count of 2 when calculating degree. If edges are given weights, a *weighted degree* can also account for these weights.

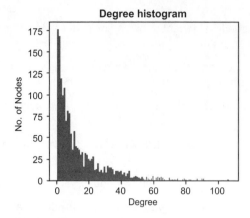

Figure A.2   **A histogram showing the degree distribution of our social graph**

Related to the concept of a degree is that of a node's neighborhood. For a given node, its adjacent nodes are also called its *neighbors*. The set of all its neighbors is called its *neighborhood*. The number of vertices in a node's neighborhood is equal to that node's degree.

CONNECTEDNESS

A graph is a set of nodes and edges. In general, however, there is no condition that says for an undirected graph, every node can be reached by any other node within the same network. It can happen that within the same graph, sets of nodes are utterly separated from one another; that is, no edge links them.

An undirected graph where any node can reach any other node is called a *connected graph*. It may seem obvious that all graphs must be connected, but this is often not the case. Graphs that have discontinuities (where a node or set of nodes are unlinked to the rest of the graph) are *disconnected graphs*. Another way to think about this is that in a connected graph, there is a path or walk whereby every node can reach every other node in the graph. For a disconnected graph, each disconnected piece is called a *component*. For a directed graph, where it's not always possible to reach any node from any other node, a *strongly connected graph* is one where every node can reach every other node.

As an example, the human population can be considered a disconnected social graph if we consider every individual human as a node and our communication channels as edges. While most of the population can be said to be connected by modern communication channels, there are hermits who chose to live off the grid and isolated hunter-gatherer tribes that reject contact with the rest of the world. In other use cases, there are often discontinuities in the network and its data.

Examining our social graph, we see it's disconnected with a large component that contains most of the nodes. Figures A.3 and A.4 show the entire graph, and the large connected component. If we focus on the large connected component, we find that the number of nodes is 1,698 and the number of edges is 12,222.

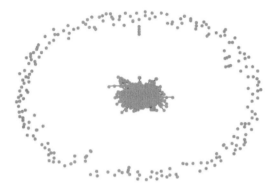

Figure A.3 Our entire social graph, which is disconnected. (`NetworkX` was used to generate this figure.) We observe a large connected component at the center, surrounded by disconnected nodes and small components consisting of two to three nodes.

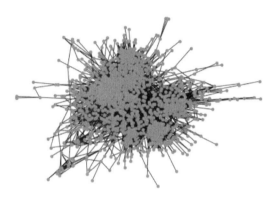

Figure A.4 The connected component of the social graph. (NetworkX was used to generate this figure.) Compare this to figure A.1, which is the same graph visualized using Graphistry. Differences in the parameters used in the algorithms, as well as visual features, account for the distinctiveness of the two figures.

GRAPH TRAVERSALS

In a graph, we can imagine traveling from a given node *a* to a second node *b*. Such a trip may require passing only one edge or passing several edges and nodes. Such a trip is called a *traversal*, or a *walk*, among other names. A traversal from one node to another is sometimes called a *hop*. Traversing a series of nodes is said to be done in *n* hops. A walk can be *open* or *closed*. Open walks have an ending node that is different from the starting node. A closed walk starts and ends with the same node.

A *path* is a walk where no node is encountered more than once. A *cycle* is a closed path (with the exception of the starting node, which is also the ending node, no node is encountered twice). A *trail* is a walk where no edge is encountered more than once, and a *circuit* is a closed trail. Examples of these different types of paths are given in figure A.5. Note how the number of steps (or hops) changes between different types of paths.

Imagine that for a given pair of nodes, we could find walks and paths between them. Of the paths we could navigate, there will be the shortest one (or maybe more than one path will tie for shortest). The length of this path is called the *distance* or *shortest path length*.

Walk: Traversal along any set of nodes and edges

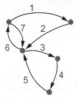

Path: Traversal with no repeated nodes

Cycle: A closed path

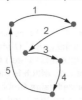

Trail: Traversal with no repeated edges

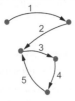

Circuit: A closed trail

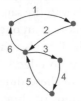

Figure A.5   Five types of paths

If we zoom out and examine the entire graph and its node pairs, we can list all the shortest path lengths. One of these distances will be the longest (or more than one may tie for longest). The largest distance is the *diameter* of the graph. The diameter is often used to characterize and compare graphs.

If we take our list of distances and average them, we'll generate the *average path length* of the graph. Average path length is another important measure for graphs. Both average path length and diameter give an indication of the density of the graph. Higher values for these metrics imply more connections, which in turn allow a greater variety of paths, both longer and shorter.

For our social graph, the diameter of our largest component is 10. The diameter is undefined for the entire graph, as it's unconnected.

SUBGRAPHS

Consider a graph of nodes and edges. A *subgraph* is a subset of these nodes and edges. Subgraphs are of importance when these neighborhoods in the graph have properties that are distinct from other locations in the graph. Subgraphs occur in connected and disconnected graphs. A component of a disconnected graph is a subgraph.

CLUSTERING COEFFICIENT

A node may have a high degree, but how well connected is its neighborhood? We can imagine an apartment building where everyone knows the landlord, but no one knows their neighbors (what a sad place!). The landlord would have a clustering coefficient of 0. At the other extreme, we could have an apartment where the landlord knows all the tenants, and every tenant knows every other tenant. Then, the landlord would have a clustering coefficient of 1 (such a situation, where all the nodes in a network are connected to every other node is called a *complete graph* or *fully connected graph*). Of course, there will be intermediate cases where only some of the tenants know one another, and these situations will have coefficients between 0 and 1.

The dimension of a graph

In machine learning and engineering in general, *dimension* is used in several ways. This term can be confusing as a result.

Even within the topic of graphs, the term is used in a few ways in articles and academic literature. However, the term is often not explicitly defined or clarified. Thus, in the following list, we attempt to deconstruct the meaning of this term:

- *Size/shape of datasets*—In this case, dimension refers to the number of features in a dataset. Low-dimensional datasets are implied to be small enough to visualize (i.e., two or three features) or small enough to be computationally viable.
- *Mathematical definitions*—In math, the dimension of a graph has more strict definitions. In linear algebra, graphs can be represented in vector spaces, and the dimension is an attribute of these vector spaces [1].
- *Geometric definition*—There is also a geometric definition of a graph's dimension. This definition relates a graph's dimension to the least number of Euclidean dimensions that will allow a graph's edges to be of unit size 1 [1].

A.1.2   *Characteristics of nodes and edges*

In the most basic type of graph, we have a collection of nodes and edges, without parallel edges or self-loops. For this basic graph, we have a geometric structure only. While even this basic graph structure is useful, often more complexity is desired to properly model a situation for real-world problems and use cases. For example, we can do the following:

1 Reduce the geometric restrictions discussed earlier. Explicitly, these restrictions are as follows:
   – Each edge is incident to two nodes, one on each end of the edge.
   – Between two nodes, only one edge can exist.
   – No self-loops are used.

   With these restrictions relaxed, we're able to model more situations at the cost of more complex graphs.

2 Add *properties* to our graph elements (nodes, edges, the graph itself). A property or feature is data tied to a specific element. Depending on the context, terms such as *labels*, *attributes*, and *decorators* are used in place of *properties*.

In this section and the next, we'll discuss the characteristics and variants of nodes, edges, and entire graphs.

NODE PROPERTIES

In the following list, we outline some of the different properties that nodes might contain. These become features in many data science or GNN tasks:

- *Names, IDs, and unique identifiers*—A name or an ID is a unique identifier. Many graph systems will either assign an identifier such as an index to a node, or allow the user to specify an ID. In our social graph, each node has a unique alphanumeric ID.

- *Labels*—Within a graph, nodes may fall within certain classes or groups. For example, a graph modeling a social network may group people by their country of residence (USA, PRC, Nigeria) or their level of activity within the network (frequent user, occasional user). In this way, in contrast to the unique identifiers explained earlier, we'd expect several nodes to share the same label.

- *Properties/attributes/features*—Properties that aren't IDs or labels are usually called attributes or features. While such properties don't have to be unique to a node, they don't describe a node class either. Properties can be based on structural or nonstructural qualities.

- *Structural/topological properties*—Intrinsic characteristics of a node are related to the node's topological properties and the geometrical structure of the graph in proximity to the node. Two examples are listed here:
   – A node's degree, which, as we learned, is the number of incident edges it has.
   – A node's centrality, which is a measure of how important a node is relative to the nodes in its neighborhood.

   By employing graph analytical methods (described in section A.4) characteristics of nodes, relative to their local environment, can be identified. These can be incorporated into certain GNN problems as features. Node embeddings such as those generated by transductive methods (chapter 2) are another example of a property based on the graph's local structure.

- *Nonstructural properties*—These are often based on real-world attributes. Taking the example of our social graph, we have two categorical properties: a person's job category (e.g., scientist, marketer, administrator) and the type of company they work for (e.g., medical, transportation, consulting). These examples are categorical attributes. It's possible to have numerical attributes, such as *years of experience* or *average number of direct reports* in all current and past roles.

- *Edge properties*—Properties for edges mirror those for nodes. The most often used and important edge property is that of the edge weight, described earlier.

EDGE VARIATIONS

Unlike nodes, there are a few geometric variants of edges that can be used to make a graph model more descriptive.

- *Parallel edges*—Meaning more than one edge between two nodes u and v.

- *Directionality*—Edges can have no direction or one direction. Because nodes u and v can have parallel edges connecting them, it's possible to have two edges with opposite directionality or multiple edges with some combination of directions or undirectionality.

- *Bidirectionality*—The case where between two nodes, both directions are represented in the respective edges. In practice, this term is used in a few ways:
  - To describe nondirected edges, or simple edges.
  - To describe two edges that have opposite directions (shown in figure A.6).

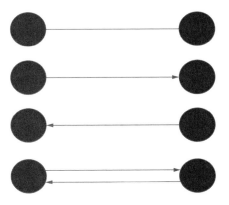

Figure A.6 From top to bottom, between two nodes, an example of an undirected edge, a directed edge from left to right, a directed edge from right to left, and two directed edges traversing both directions (bidirectionality)

  - To describe an edge that has a direction at each end. This usage, while popular in the literature, is fairly rare in practical systems at the time of writing.

- *Self-loops*—Discussed previously, a self-loop, or loop, is the case where both ends of an edge connect to the same node. Where would one encounter a self-loop in the real world? For our social graph, let's keep all the nodes, and consider a case where an edge would be an email sent from one professional to another. Sometimes, people send emails to themselves (for reminders). For such a scenario, an email to oneself could be modeled as a self-loop.

A.1.3   *Categories of graphs*

Different categories of graphs depend on the node and edge characteristics we've just described. Following are the graph categories:

- *Simple graph*—A graph whose edges can't be parallel edges or self-loops. Simple graphs can be connected or disconnected, as well as directed.
- *Weighted graph*—A graph that uses weights. Our social graph has no weights; another way to express having no weights is to set all weights to 1 or 0.
- *Multigraphs*—A graph that is permitted to have multiple edges between any two nodes and multiple self-loops for any one node. A simple graph could be a special case of a multigraph if we're working within a problem where we could add more edges and self-loops to it.
- *Di-graphs*—Another term for a directed graph.
- *K-partite graphs*—In many graphs, we may have a situation where we have two or more groups of nodes, where edges are only allowed between groups and not between nodes of the same group. "Partite" refers to the partitions of node groups, and "k" refers to the number of those partitions.
- *Monopartite graph*—A graph in which there is only one group of nodes and one group of edges. A monopartite social graph could consist of only "Texan" nodes connected with "work colleague" edges. For example, in a social graph, nodes can belong to "New Yorkers" or "Texans" groups, and relationships can belong to "friend" or "work colleague" groups.
- *Bipartite (or bi-graph) graph*—A graph that has two node partitions within a graph. Nodes of one group can only connect to nodes of a second type and not to nodes within their own group. In our social graph example, nodes can belong to "New Yorkers" or "Texans" groups, and relationships can belong to "friend" or "work colleague" groups. In this graph, no New Yorkers would be adjacent to other New Yorkers, and the same for Texans. This is shown in figure A.7.

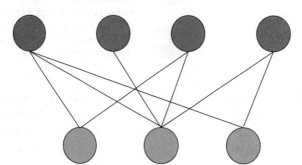

Figure A.7   A bipartite graph. There are two types of nodes (upper and lower row of circles). In a bipartite graph, nodes can't be connected to nodes of the same type (those in the same row). This is also an example of a heterogeneous graph.

For more than three partitions, the requirement that adjacent nodes can't be the same type still holds. In practice, k can be a large number.

- *Trees*—A tree is a well-studied data structure in machine learning and is a special case of a graph. It's a connected graph without cycles. Another way to describe a graph without cycles is *acyclic*. In the data science and deep learning worlds, a well-known example is the directed acyclic graph (DAG), used in designing and governing data workflows.

- *Hypergraphs*—Up to now, our graphs have consisted of edges that connect to two nodes or one node (a self-loop). For a hypergraph, an edge can be incident to more than two nodes. These data structures have a range of applications, including ones that involve the use of GNNs. This is shown in figure A.8.

- *Heterogeneous graphs*—A heterogeneous graph has multiple node and edge types, while a multirelational graph has multiple edge types.

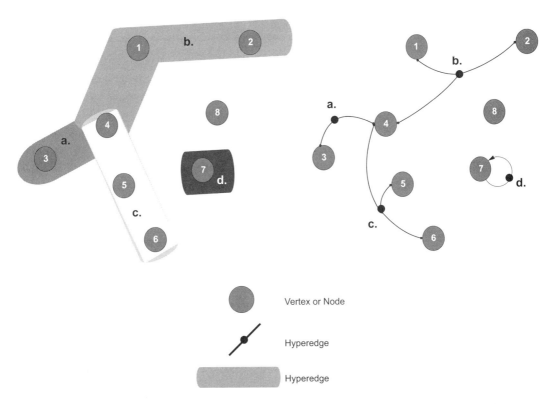

Figure A.8   One undirected hypergraph, illustrated in two ways. On the left, we have a graph whose edges are represented by shaded areas and marked by letters, and whose vertices are dots, marked by numbers. On the right, we have a graph whose edge lines (marked by letters) connect up to three nodes (circles marked by numbers). Node 8 has no edge. Node 7 has a self-loop.

A.2   *Graph representations*

Now that we have a conceptual idea of what graphs are, we move on to how to work with them. First, we focus on data structures most relevant to building graph algorithms and storing graph data. We'll see that some of these structures, particularly the adjacency matrix, play a prominent role in the GNN algorithms we study in the bulk of this book.

Next, we'll examine a few graph data models. These are important in designing and managing how databases and other data systems deal with network data. Lastly, we'll briefly take a look at how graph data is exposed to analysts and engineers via APIs and query languages.

A.2.1   *Basic graph data structures*

There are a few important ways to represent graphs that can be ported to a computational environment:

- *Adjacency matrix*—A node-to-node matrix.
- *Incidence matrix*—An edge-to-node matrix.
- *Edge lists*—A list of edges by their nodes.
- *Adjacency lists*—Lists of each node's adjacent nodes.
- *Degree matrix*—Node-to-node matrix of degree values.
- *Laplacian matrix*—The degree matrix minus the adjacency matrix (**D-A**). This is useful in spectral theory.

These are by no means the only ways to represent a graph, but from a survey of the literature, software, storage formats, and libraries, these are the most prevalent. In practice, a graph may not be permanently stored as one of these structures, but to execute a needed operation, a graph or subgraph may be transformed from one representation to another.

What representations are used depends on many factors that should be weighed in planning. These factors include the following:

- *Size of graph*—How many vertices and edges does the graph contain, and how much are these expected to scale?
- *Density of graph*—Is the graph sparse or dense? We'll touch on these terms in the next subsection.
- *Complexity of the graph's structure*—Is the graph closer to a simple graph, or one that uses one or more of the variations discussed previously?
- *Algorithms to be used*—For a given algorithm, a given data structure may perform relatively weakly or strongly compared to others. In the following subsections, for each structure, we'll touch on two simple algorithms to compare.
- *Costs to do CRUD (create, read, updated, delete) operations*—How will you modify your graph (including creating, reading, updating, or deleting nodes, edges, and their attributes) over the course of your operations and how frequently will you do so?

In many data projects, transformation from one data structure to another is common to accommodate particular operations. So, it's normal to employ two or more of the previously mentioned data structures in a project. In this case, understanding the compute effort to execute the transformation is key. For the most popular structures, graph libraries allow methods that allow seamless transformations, but given the considerations listed previously, executing these transformations could take unexpected time or cost.

For the following discussion, we'll talk about how these data structures are used to store topological information about graphs. The only attributes we'll consider are node IDs and edge weights. To illustrate these concepts, let's use the weighted graph, consisting of five nodes, as shown in figure A.9. Circles indicate nodes with their IDs; rectangles are the edge weights.

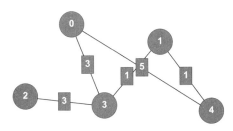

Figure A.9   An example graph with different weighted edges and labeled nodes from 0 to 4

Let's now dive into those six popular ways of representing graphs so they can be used computationally.

ADJACENCY MATRIX
For a graph with *n* nodes, an *adjacency matrix* represents the graph as an $N \times N$ matrix format, where each row or column describes the edge between two nodes. For our example graph, shown previously in figure A.9, we have five columns and five rows. These rows and columns are labeled for each node. Cells of the matrix denote adjacency.

Adjacency matrices can be used for simple directed and undirected graphs. They can also be used for graphs with self-loops. In an unweighted graph, each cell is either 0 (no adjacency) or 1 (adjacency). For a weighted graph, the values in the cells are the edge weights. For unweighted parallel edges, the values of the cells are the number of edges.

For our example, a weighted, undirected graph, the corresponding adjacency matrix is shown in table A.1. Because our graph is undirected, the adjacency matrix is symmetric. For directed graphs, symmetry is possible but not guaranteed.

Table A.1   An adjacency matrix for the graph in figure A.9

	0	1	2	3	4
0	0	0	0	3	5
1	0	0	0	1	1
2	0	0	0	3	0
3	3	1	3	0	0
4	5	1	0	0	0

By inspecting this matrix, we can get a quick visual understanding of the characteristics of the matrix. We can see, for example, how many degrees node 1 has and get a general idea of the distribution of the degrees. We also see that there are more empty spaces (cells with a 0 value) than edges. This ease of using the matrix to draw quick insights for small graphs is one advantage of adjacency matrices. Even for large graphs, plotting the adjacency matrix can indicate certain subgraph structures.

Adjacency matrices, and matrix representations in general, allow you to analyze graphs by using linear algebra. One relevant example is spectral graph theory (which underlies a few GNN algorithms).

Adjacency matrices are straightforward to implement in Python. The matrix in our example can be created using a list of lists, or a NumPy array:

```
>>import numpy as np
>>arr = np.array([[0, 0, 0, 3, 3],
                  [0, 0, 0, 1, 1],
                  [0, 0, 0, 3, 0],
                  [3, 1, 3, 0, 0],
                  [5, 1, 0, 0, 0]])
```

With our adjacency matrix as a NumPy array, let's explore another property of our graph. From our visual inspection of our matrix, we noticed many more zero values than nonzero values. This makes it a sparse matrix. *Sparse matrices*, that is, matrices with a large proportion of zero values, can take up unnecessary storage or memory space and increase calculation times. *Dense matrices*, contrarily, contain a large proportion of nonzero matrices. The following determines the sparsity of our matrix:

```
>>sparsity = 1.0 - ( np.count_nonzero(arr) / arr.size )
>>print(sparsity)
>> 0.6
```

So, our matrix has a sparsity of 0.6, meaning 60% of the values in this matrix are zeros.

Sparsity using node degree

Another way to think about sparsity is in terms of node degree. Let's derive the sparsity value just shown from the perspective of the node degree.

For a simple, undirected graph of *n* nodes, each node can make at most *n-1* connections, and thus have a maximum degree of *n-1*. The maximum number of edges can be calculated using combinatorics: because each edge represents a pair of nodes, for a set of *n* nodes, the maximum number of edges is "*n* choose 2", that is, *(n C 2)* or $n(n-1)/2$. However, for our small matrix, we have a directed graph, which is clear because the adjacency matrix isn't symmetric. This means that both directions count separately and need to times by 2. Hence, for our small matrix, the maximum number of possible edges is $5(5-1) = 20$. The density of a graph is defined as the actual number of edges, *e*, over all possible edges, and sparsity can then be defined as 1 – density. In our example, this leads to a quantity that disagrees with what was calculated using the matrix alone, namely $(1 - 10/20) = 0.5$, which is not equal to 0.6 in the preceding code snippet. This is because we haven't considered self-loops, which is standard practice for graph theory. If we included self-loops, we would have five additional possible edges (or 5^2), resulting in $(1 - 10/25)$, or 0.6, matching the value in the earlier code. This highlights that care needs to be taken when reporting on the sparsity of a graph.

Now, think of a graph that has not five, but millions or billions of nodes. Such graphs exist in the real world, and quite often the sparsity can be orders of magnitudes less than 0.6. For undirected simple graphs, the adjacency matrix is symmetric, so only half the storage is needed. Most of the memory or storage containing the adjacency matrix would be devoted to zero values. Thus, the high sparsity of this data structure leads to memory inefficiencies.

In terms of complexity, for a simple graph, the space complexity would be $\mathbf{O}(n^2)$, for undirected simple graphs. For an undirected graph, due to the symmetry, the space complexity would be $\mathbf{O}(n(n-1)/2)$.

For time complexity, this of course depends on the task or the algorithm. Let's look at two rudimentary tasks that we'll also address for adjacency list and edge lists:

- Checking the existence of an edge between a particular pair of nodes
- Finding the neighbors of a node

For the first task, we simply check the row and column corresponding to those nodes. This would take $\mathbf{O}(1)$ time. For the second, we need to check every item in that node's row; this would take $\mathbf{O}(\deg(n))$ time, where $\deg(n)$ is the degree of the node.

To summarize, the advantages of adjacency matrices are that they can quickly check connections between nodes and are easy to visually interpret. The downsides are that they are less space-efficient for sparse matrices. The computational tradeoffs depend on your algorithm. They shine in cases where we have small and dense graphs.

INCIDENCE MATRIX

While the adjacency matrix has a row and column for every node, an *incidence matrix* represents every edge as a column and every node as a row. Using the same graph shown earlier in figure A.9, we can construct an incidence matrix, which we show in table A.2.

Table A.2   Incidence matrix for the example graph in figure A.9

	0	1	2	3	4
0	0	3	5	0	0
1	0	0	0	1	1
2	3	0	0	0	0
3	3	3	0	1	0
4	0	0	5	0	1

An incidence matrix can represent wider variations of graph types than an adjacency matrix. Multigraphs and hypergraphs are straightforward to express with this data structure.

How does the incidence matrix perform with respect to space and time? To store the data of a simple graph, the incidence matrix has a space complexity of $O(|E| * |V|)$, where $|V|$ is the number of nodes (V for vertices), and $|E|$ is the number of edges. Thus, it's superior to the adjacency matrix for graphs with fewer edges than nodes, including sparse matrices.

To get an idea of time complexity, we turn to our two simple tasks: checking for an edge, and finding a node's neighbors. To check the existence of an edge, an incidence matrix has a time complexity of $O(|E| * |V|)$, far slower than the adjacency matrix, which does this in constant time. To find the neighbors of a node, an incidence matrix also takes $O(|E| * |V|)$.

Overall, incidence matrices have space advantages when used with sparse matrices. For time performance, they have slow performance on the simple tasks we covered. The overall advantage of using incidence matrices is for unambiguously representing complex graphs, such as multigraphs and hypergraphs.

ADJACENCY LISTS

In an *adjacency list*, the aim is to show which vertices each node is adjacent to. So, for *n* nodes, we have *n* lists of neighbors corresponding to each node. Depending on what data structures are used for the lists, properties may also be included in the summary. For our example, a simple adjacency list is shown in figure A.10.

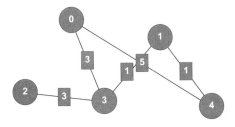

Node 0: Node 3, Node 4
Node 1: Node 3, Node 4
Node 2: Node 3
Node 3: Node 0, Node 1, Node 2   **Figure A.10   Our example graph and**
Node 4: Node 0, Node 1   **its adjacency list**

Such an adjacency list can be accomplished in python using a dictionary with each node as the keys, and lists of the adjacent nodes as values:

```
{ 0 : [ 3, 4],
1 : [3, 4],
2 : [3],
3 : [0, 1, 2],
4 : [0, 1] }
```

We can improve on the dictionary values to allow for the inclusion of the weights of the neighbors:

```
{ 0 : [ (3, 3), (4, 5)],
1 : [(3, 1), (4, 1)],
2 : [(3, 3)],
3 : [(0, 3), (1, 1), (2, 3)],
4 : [(0, 5) , (1, 1)] }
```

For undirected graphs, the set of nodes doesn't have to be ordered. Because the adjacency list doesn't devote space to node pairs that aren't neighbors, we see that adjacency lists lack the sparsity problems of adjacency matrices. So, to store this data structure, we have a space complexity of $\mathbf{O}(n + v)$, where n is the number of nodes, and v is the number of edges.

Going back to the two computational tasks, checking the existence of an edge (task 1) would take $\mathbf{O}(\deg(node))$ time, where deg(node) is the degree of either node. For this, we simply check every item in that node's list, where for the worst case, we'd have to check them all. For task 2, finding a node's neighbors would also take $\mathbf{O}(\deg(node))$ time, because we have to inspect every item in that node's list whose length is the node's degree.

Let's summarize the tradeoffs of an adjacency list. The advantages are that they are relatively efficient in terms of storage because only edge relationships are stored. This means a sparse matrix would take up less space stored as an adjacency list than as an adjacency matrix. Computationally, the tradeoffs depend on the algorithm you're running and the type of graph you're using as input data.

EDGE LISTS

Compared to the preceding two representations, *edge lists* are relatively simple. They consist of a set of doubles (two nodes) or triples (two nodes and an edge weight). These identify a unique edge thusly:

- Node, node (edge weight), for an undirected graph
- Source node, destination node (edge weight), for a directed graph

Edge lists can represent single, unconnected nodes. For our example graph, the edge list would be the following:

```
{ 0, 3, 3 }
{ 0, 4, 5 }
{ 1, 3, 1 }
{ 1, 4, 1 }
{ 2, 3, 3 }
```

In Python, we can create this as a set of tuples:

```
>> edge_list = {( 0, 3, 3 ), ( 0, 4, 5 ), \
( 1, 3, 1 ), ( 1, 4, 1 ), ( 2, 3, 3 ) }
```

On performance, for storage, the space complexity of an edge list is $O(e)$, where e is the number of edges. Regarding our two tasks shown previously, to establish the existence of a particular edge will have a time complexity of $O(e)$, assuming an unordered edge list. To discover all the neighbors of a node, $O(e)$ is the space complexity. In each case, we have to go through the edges in the list one by one to check for the edge or the node's neighbor. So, from a compute performance point of view, edge lists have a disadvantage compared to the other two data structures, especially for executing more complex algorithms.

However, another advantage of edge lists is that they are more compact than adjacency lists or adjacency matrices. Additionally, they are simple to both create and interpret. For example, we could store an edge list as a text file where each line only consists of two identifiers separated by a space. For many systems and databases, edge lists in CSV or text files are the default option to serialize data.

The Laplacian matrix

One data representation of a graph that is highly valuable in analyzing graphs is the Laplacian matrix, as mentioned earlier. This matrix is key to the development of graph spectral theory, which is in turn critical to the development of spectral-based GNN methods.

To produce the Laplacian matrix, we subtract the adjacency matrix from the degree matrix (D – A). The degree matrix is a node-to-node matrix whose values are the degree of a particular node. The degree matrix for our example graph is given in the first table and the Laplacian matrix follows.

Degree matrix for our example graph

	0	1	2	3	4
0	2	0	0	0	0
1	0	2	0	0	0
2	0	0	1	0	0
3	0	0	0	3	0
4	0	0	0	0	2

Laplacian matrix for our example graph

	0	1	2	3	4
0	2	0	0	–3	–5
1	0	2	0	–1	–1
2	0	0	1	–3	0
3	–3	–1	–3	3	0
4	–5	–1	0	0	2

In practice, Laplacian matrices aren't used for storage or as a basis for graph operations like the other data structures covered in this section. Their advantages lie in spectral analysis. We discuss spectral graph analysis in chapter 3.

A.2.2   Relational databases

We're steadily marching from theory to implementation. In the previous section, we reviewed common data structures used to represent graphs and their tradeoffs. Graphs can be implemented in these structures from scratch in your preferred programming language and are also implemented in popular graph processing libraries.

With the listed data structures, we have a variety of ways to implement the structural information in graphs. But graphs and their elements often come with useful attributes and metadata.

A *relational database* is an organized way to represent the structural information, attributes, and metadata of a graph. Very much related to this is the notion of a *schema*, which is a framework that explicitly defines the elements that make up a graph (i.e., varieties of nodes and edges, attributes, etc.), and explicitly defines how these elements work together.

Data models and schemas are critical parts of the scaffolding used to design graph systems such as graph databases and graph processing systems, and they often build on the data structures reviewed in the previous section. We'll review three such models and provide examples of real systems where they are used.

MINIMALIST GRAPH DATA MODEL

The simplest relational database uses only nodes, edges, and weights. It can be used on directed or undirected graphs. If weights are used, they can be retrieved using a lookup table.

Pregel, Google's graph processing framework, which other popular frameworks are based on (including Apache Giraph used by Facebook, and Apache Spark GraphX), relies on such a directed graph. There, both edges and nodes have an identifier and a single numerical value, which can be interpreted as a weight or attribute.

RDF GRAPH DATA MODEL

Resource Description Framework (RDF; aka Triple Stores) models follow a subject-predicate-object pattern, where nodes are subjects and objects, and edges are predicates. Nodes and edges have one main attribute, which can be a unique resource identifier (URI) or a literal. URIs, in essence, identify the type of node or edge being described. Examples of literals can be specific timestamps or dates. Predicates represent relationships. Such triples (subject-predicate-object) represent what are called *facts* in this context. Usually, facts are directed and flow in the direction from subject to object.

Popular graph databases that use the RDF model include Amazon's Neptune (Neptune also allows the use of labeled property graphs [LPGs]), Virtuoso, and Stardog.

PROPERTY GRAPH DATA MODEL

In property graphs (aka LPGs), allowances are made to confer various metadata to nodes and edges. Such metadata include the following:

- *Identifiers*—Distinguish individual nodes and edges.
- *Labels*—Describe classes (or subsets) of nodes or edges.
- *Attributes or properties*—Describe individual nodes or edges.

Nodes have an ID and a set of key/value pairs that can be used to supply additional attributes (also called properties). Similarly, edges have an ID and a set of key/value pairs for attributes.

You can think of the property graph as the minimalist graph extended by adding labels and removing the restrictions on the types and number of attributes. Figure A.11 provides a look at a property graph and its equivalent RDF graph. Popular graph databases that use models based on the property graph include Neo4j, Azure Cosmos, and TigerGraph.

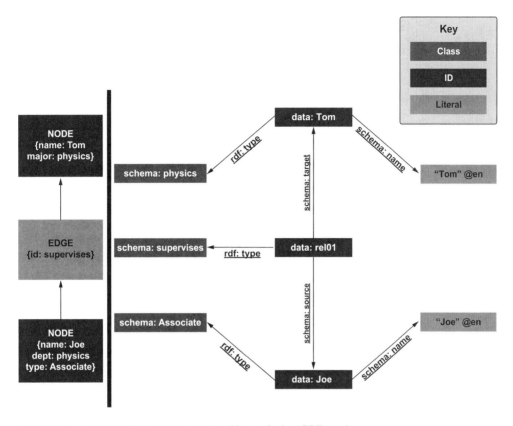

Figure A.11   Example of a property graph and its equivalent RDF graph

NONGRAPH DATA MODEL

There are a variety of databases and systems that use neither RDF nor LPG. These databases and systems store or express nodes, edges, and attributes within other storage frameworks, such as document stores, key value stores, and even within a relational database framework.

KNOWLEDGE GRAPHS

Although the term is used widely in academic, commercial, and practitioner circles, there is no unifying definition of a knowledge graph. Most relevant to GNNs, we define a *knowledge graph* as a representation of knowledge discretized into facts, as defined earlier. In other words, a knowledge graph is a multigraph set onto a specific *subject-relationship-object* schema.

Knowledge graphs may be represented with RDF schemas, but there are other data models and graph models that can accommodate knowledge graphs. GNN methods are used to embed the data in the nodes and edges, establish the quality of facts, and discover new entities and relations. An example of a knowledge graph is shown in figure A.12.

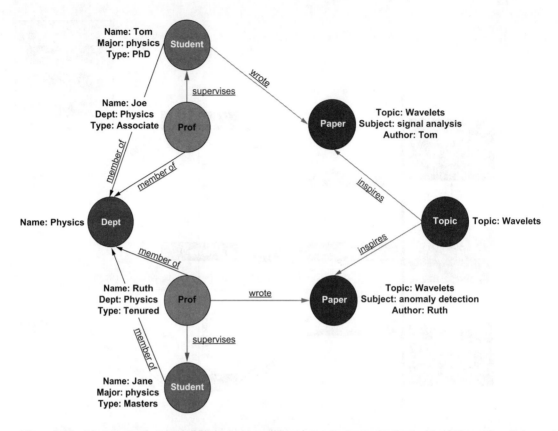

Figure A.12   An example of a knowledge graph representing an academic research network within a university's physics department. The graph illustrates both hierarchical relationships, such as professors and students being members of the department, and behavioral relationships, such as professors supervising students and authoring papers. Entities such as Prof, Student, Paper, and Topic are connected through semantically meaningful relationships (e.g., Supervises, Wrote, and Inspires). Entities also have detailed features (e.g., Name, Department, and Type) to provide further context. The semantic connections and features enable advanced querying and analysis of complex academic interactions.

NODE AND EDGE TYPES

In graphs that have a schema, including knowledge graphs, the edges and nodes can be assigned a *type*. *Types* are part of a defined schema, and as such, govern how data elements interact with each other. They also often have a descriptive aspect. To distinguish *types* from *properties*, consider that while types help define the rules of how data elements work together and how they are interpreted by the data system, properties are descriptive only.

To illustrate types, we can use a road map analogy, where towns are nodes, and passages between them are edges. Our edges may include highways, footpaths, canals, or bike paths. Each one is a type. Due to geography, towns can be surrounded by swamps, sit atop mountain peaks, or have other obstacles and impediments to one versus another passage. For towns separated by a desert, passage is only possible by a highway.

For other towns, passages can be by multiple passage types. In building this analogy, we see that our town nodes also have types defined by their proximate geography: swamp town, desert town, island town, valley town.

A.2.3   *How graphs are exposed*

We've talked about relational data structures and relational databases to understand how graphs are constructed and stored. In real life, however, most of us won't build graphs from scratch or from the bottom up. When constructing and analyzing graphs, there will be a layer of abstraction between us and the primitive data. In what ways, then, is a graph exposed to the data scientist or engineer? Next, we'll briefly explain the following two ways and then discuss the graph ecosystem:

- *APIs*—Using graph libraries or data processing systems
- *Query languages*—Querying graph databases via specialized query languages

APIs: GRAPH OBJECTS IN GRAPH SYSTEMS

When using a graph library or processing software, usually we want the graph we work with to have certain properties and to be able to execute operations on the graph. From this lens, it's helpful to think of graphs as software objects that can be operated on by software functions.

In Python, an effective way to implement these is to have a graph class, with some operations implemented as methods of the graph class or as standalone functions. Nodes and edges can be attributes of the graph class, or they can have their own node and edge classes. Properties of graphs implemented in this way can be attributes of the respective classes.

An example of this is `NetworkX`, a Python-based graph processing library. `NetworkX` implements a graph class. Nodes can be any hashable object; examples of node objects are integers, strings, files, and even functions. Edges are tuple objects of their respective nodes. Both nodes and edges can have properties implemented as Python dictionaries. Following are two short lists of typical methods and attributes of graph classes found in libraries and processing systems.

Basic methods of graph objects

In the following list, we outline some of the methods that can be applied to graph objects:

- `Graph_Creation`—A constructor that creates a new graph object
- `Add_Node`, `Add_Edge`—Adds nodes or edges, and their attributes and labels, if any
- `Get_Node`, `Get_Edge`—Retrieves stored nodes or edges, with specified attributes and labels
- `Update_Node`, `Updage_Edge`, `Update_Graph`—Updates properties and attributes of nodes, edges, and graph objects
- `Delete_Node`, `Delete_Edge`—Deletes a specified node or edge

> ### Basic attributes of graph objects
>
> In the following list, we outline some of the attributes for graph objects:
>
> - `Number_of_Nodes, Number_of_Edges`—A constructor that creates a new graph object
> - `Node_Neighbors`—Retrieves the adjacent nodes or incident edges of a node
> - `Node_List, Edge_List`—Adds nodes or edges and their attributes and labels, if any
> - `Connected_Graph`—Retrieves stored nodes or edges, with specified attributes and labels
> - `Graph_State`—Retrieves global attributes, labels, and properties of the graph
> - `Directed_Graph`—Deletes a specified node or edge

GRAPH QUERY LANGUAGES

When working with a graph in a graph database, a query language is used. For most relational databases, some variant of SQL is used as the standard language. In the graph database space, there is no standard query language. Following are the languages that currently stand out:

- *Gremlin*—A language that can be written declaratively or imperatively, which is designed for database or processing system queries. Developed by the Apache TinkerPop project, Gremlin is used in several databases (Titan, OrientDB) and processing systems (Giraph, Hadoop, Spark).
- *Cypher*—A declarative language for property graph–based database queries. Developed by Neo4j, Cypher is used by Neo4j and several other databases.
- *SPARQL*—A declarative query language for RDF-based database queries. SPARQL is used by Amazon Neptune, AllegroGraph, and others.

A.3 Graph systems

We've covered the basic building blocks that allow us to implement graphs in a programming language. In practice, you'll seldom create a graph from scratch because you'll load data into memory or a database using a library or API. The field of graph libraries, databases, and commercial software is broad and growing rapidly. A good way to determine what to use is to start with your use case and requirements, and then choose your development and deployment architecture from there. This section will briefly give an overview of this landscape to help you. The taxonomy we develop here is by no means absolute but should serve as a useful guideline.

At the time of writing, commercial and open source tools for graph analysis, machine learning modeling, visualization, and storage are expanding relatively rapidly. With a lot of overlap between tools and functions, as well as many hybrid tools that don't neatly fit into any category, there is no clean delineation of segments. Given this, we just highlight basic methods and focus on the most popular tools in the following segments:

- Graph databases
- Graph compute engines (or graph frameworks)
- Visualization libraries
- GNN libraries

A.3.1   *Graph databases*

Graph databases are the graph analogues of traditional relational databases from a functional standpoint. Such databases were devised to handle transactions focused on Online Transaction Processing (OLTP). They allow CRUD transactions and also tend to follow ACID (atomicity, consistency, isolation, and durability) principles regarding the integrity of the data. Graph databases of this type differ from relational databases in that they store data using graph data models and schemas. At the time of writing, the most popular graph databases are Neo4j, Microsoft Cosmos DB, OrientDB, and ArangoDB. Except for Neo4j, these databases support multiple models, including property graphs. Neo4j supports property graphs only. The most popular databases that support RDF models are Virtuoso and Amazon Neptune.

In addition to property graphs and RDF databases, other types of nongraph databases are used to store graph data. Document stores, relational databases, and key-value stores are examples. To use such nongraph databases with graph data models, you must carefully define how the existing schema maps to the graph elements and their attributes.

A.3.2   *Graph compute engines (or graph frameworks)*

Graph compute engines are designed to make queries using batches of data. Such queries can output aggregate statistics or output graph-specific items, such as cluster identification and find shortest paths. These data systems tend to follow the Online Application Processing (OLAP) model. It's not unusual for such systems to work closely with a graph database, which serves the input data batches needed for the analytic queries. Examples of such systems include Apache Spark's GraphX, Giraph, and Stanford Network Analysis Platform (SNAP).

A.3.3   *Visualization libraries*

Graph visualization tools share characteristics with graph compute engines, as they are geared toward analytics versus transactional queries and computations. However, such tools are designed to create aesthetic and useful images of the networks under analysis. In the best visualization tools, these images are interactive and dynamic. Outputs of visualization systems can be optimized for presentation on the web, or in printed format with high definition. Examples of such tools are Gephi, Cytoscape, and Tulip.

A.3.4   *GNN libraries*

The last segment of graph tools is the central subject of this book. Here, we're grouping software tools that create graph embeddings with tools that train the models using graph data. At the time of writing, there are many solutions available. Graph representation tools range from dedicated, standalone libraries (PyTorch BigGraph [PBG]) to graph systems that have embedding as a feature (Neo4j as a database and SNAP as a compute framework).

GNN libraries come as standalone libraries, and as libraries that use TensorFlow or PyTorch as a backend. In this text, the focus will be on PyTorch Geometric (PyG). Other popular libraries include Deep Graph Library (DGL; a standalone library) and Spektral, which uses Kera and TensorFlow as a backend. The best libraries implement not only a range of deep learning layers but also the available benchmark datasets.

A.4   *Graph algorithms*

As the field of graphs has been around for a while, the number of different graph algorithms is vast. Understanding well-used graph algorithms can provide valuable context with which to think about the algorithms used in neural networks. Graph algorithms can also serve as sources of node, edge, or graph features for GNNs. Finally, as with all machine learning methods, sometimes a statistical model isn't the best solution. Understanding the analytical landscape can help when deciding whether or not to use a GNN solution.

In this section, we review two types of graph algorithms, *search algorithms* and *shortest path*. We provide a general description, explaining why they are important. For an in-depth treatment on this topic, review the references for this appendix at the end of the book, particularly [1–3].

A.4.1   *Traversal and search algorithms*

In section A.1.1, we discussed the concept of a walk and a path. In these fundamental concepts, we get from one node in a graph to another by traversing a set of nodes and edges between them.

For large graphs with many nonunique walks and paths between node pairs, how do we decide which path to take? Similarly, for graphs we haven't explored and don't have a map of, what is the best way to create that map? Wrapped into these questions is the problem of what direction to take when traversing a graph at a particular node. For a node of degree 1, this answer is trivial; for a node with degree 100, the answer is less so.

Traversal algorithms offer systematic ways to walk a graph. For such algorithms, we start at a node, and following a set of rules, we decide on the next node to hop to. Often, as we conduct the walk, we keep track of nodes and edges that have been encountered. For certain algorithms, if we outline the path taken, we can end up with a tree structure. Three well known strategies for traversal are given here:

- *Breadth first*—A breadth-first traversal prefers to explore all of the immediate neighbors of a node before going further away. This is also known as breadth-first search (BFS).
- *Depth first*—With depth-first search (DFS), rather than explore every immediate neighbor first, we follow each new node without regard to its relationship to the current node. This is done in such a way that every node is encountered *at least* once, and every edge is encountered *exactly* once.

  There are versions of DFS and BFS for directed graphs as well.
- *Random*—In random traversals, in contrast to BFS and DFS, where traversal is governed by a set of rules, traversal to the next node is done randomly. For a starting node of degree 4 in a random traversal with a uniform distribution, each neighboring node would have a 25% chance of being chosen. Such methods are used in algorithms such as DeepWalk and Node2Vec (covered in chapter 2).

A.4.2 *Shortest path*

An enduring problem highly related to graphs is that of the shortest path. Interest in solving this problem has existed for decades (a great survey paper of shortest path methods was published as far back as 1969 [4]), with several distinct algorithms existing. Modern applications of shortest path methods are used in navigation applications, such as finding the fastest route to a destination. Variations of such algorithms include the following:

- Shortest path between
  - Two nodes
  - Two nodes on a path that includes specified nodes
  - All nodes
  - One node to all others
- Ranked shortest paths (i.e., second shortest path, third shortest, etc.)

Such algorithms can also take into account weights in graphs. In these cases, shortest path algorithms are also called least-cost algorithms.

A highly lauded algorithm for least-cost determination is Dijkstra's algorithm. Given a node, it finds the shortest path to every other node or to a specified node. As this algorithm progresses, it traverses the graph while keeping track of the distance and connecting nodes (to the start node) of each node it encounters. It prioritizes the nodes encountered by their shortest (or least-cost) path to the start node. As the algorithm traverses, it prioritizes low-cost paths.

A.5   *How to read GNN literature*

GNNs are a rapidly proliferating topic. New methods and techniques have been proposed in a short span of time. Though this book focuses on practical and commercial applications of graphs, much of the state of the art in this field is disclosed in academic journals and conferences. Knowing how to effectively study publications from these sources is essential to keep up to speed with the field and to encounter valuable ideas that can be implemented in code.

In this short section, we list some commonly used notations to describe graphs in technical publications as well as a few tips on reading academic literature for the practitioner. These tips are especially for those interested in using the methodology in a paper but are working under time constraints:

- To efficiently extract value from a paper, be selective on which sections of the publication to focus on. It's important to clearly understand the problem statement and the solution to translate this into code. This might sound obvious, but many papers include sections that, for a practitioner, can be distracting at best. Mathematical proofs and long historical notes are good examples.
- A positive trend is the increasing inclusion of code and data in research papers to enhance reproducibility. However, replicating results may still be challenging due to factors like model-specific optimizations or hardware constraints. If you encounter difficulties, reaching out to the authors can often provide valuable clarification.
- Look closely at indicators of the application scope of the problem and solution. An exciting development may not be applicable to your problem, and it may not be immediately obvious. Similarly, don't take all claims for state-of-the-art results at face value. The academic world is extremely competitive and claimed state-of-the-art results may not hold, especially if a paper isn't yet peer-reviewed.

A.5.1   *Common graph notations*

In mathematical notation, a graph is described as a set of nodes and edges:

$$G = (V, E) \tag{A.1}$$

where V and E are collections or sets of vertices (nodes) and edges, respectively. When we want to express the count of elements in these collections, we use $|V|$ and $|E|$. In the following list, we outline some of the typical nomenclature for the mathematics of graphs:

- For directed graphs, an accented G ($\vec{G}$) is sometimes, but not always used.
- Individual nodes and edges are denoted by lowercase letters, v and e, respectively.
- When referring to a pair of adjacent nodes, we use u and v. Thus, an edge can also be expressed as $\{u, v\}$, or uv.

- When dealing with weighted graphs, a weight for a particular edge is expressed as $w(e)$. In terms of an edge's nodes, we can include the weight as $\{u, v, w\}$.

- To express the features of a graph or its elements, we use the notation x or $\mathbf{x}$ when the features are expressed as a vector or matrix, respectively.

- For graph representations, because many such representations are matrices, bold letters are used to express them: $\mathbf{A}$ for the adjacency matrix, $\mathbf{L}$ for the Laplacian matrix, and so on.

appendix B
Installing and configuring
PyTorch Geometric

B.1 Installing PyTorch Geometric

PyTorch Geometric (PyG) is a library built on top of PyTorch for working with graph neural networks (GNNs). The newest pytorch geometric versions can be installed with: pip install torch_geometric. Only PyTorch is needed as a dependency. To install PyG with its extensions, you need to ensure that you have the correct versions of Compute Unified Device Architecture (CUDA), PyTorch, and PyG installed and compatible with each other.

B.1.1 On Windows/Linux

If you're on a Windows or Linux system, follow these steps:

- *Install PyTorch.* First, install the appropriate version of PyTorch for your system. You can find the instructions on the official PyTorch website (https://pytorch.org/get-started/locally/). Make sure to select the correct CUDA version if you have an NVIDIA GPU.

- *Find the PyTorch CUDA version.* After installing PyTorch, check its version and the CUDA version it was built with by running the following from Python:

```
import torch
print(torch.__version__)
print(torch.version.cuda)
```

This can also be run from the command line as follows:

```
!python -c "import torch; print(torch.__version__)"
!python -c "import torch; print(torch.version.cuda)"
```

The outputs from this code will be used in the next step.

- *Install PyG dependencies.* Install the PyG dependencies (`torch-scatter`, `torch-sparse`, `torch-cluster`, `torch-spline-conv`) from the PyG repository, specifying the correct CUDA version:

  ```
  pip install torch-scatter torch-sparse torch-cluster torch-spline-conv -f
  https://data.pyg.org/whl/torch-${PYTORCH}+${CUDA}.html
  ```

  In this code, replace `${PYTORCH}` with your PyTorch version (e.g., 1.13.1) and `${CUDA}` with the CUDA version from the previous step (e.g., cu117).

- *Install PyG.* Finally, install the PyG library itself:

  ```
  pip install torch-geometric
  ```

B.1.2   *On MacOS*

Since Macs don't come with Nvidia GPUs, you can install the `cpu` version of PyG by following the same steps as in the previous section, but using `cpu` instead of a CUDA version when installing the dependencies.

B.1.3   *Compatibility issues*

For installing the extensions, it's crucial to match the versions of CUDA, PyTorch, and PyG to avoid compatibility issues. Using mismatched versions can lead to errors during installation or runtime. Always refer to the official documentation for the latest installation instructions and version compatibility information. When writing this book, we encountered a few frustrating errors that were solved only by installing the correct combination of CUDA, PyTorch, and PyG.

One particular insight we gained from dealing with tools designed to work with PyG, such as Open Graph Benchmark (OGB) and DistributedDataParallel (DDP), is that they may only work with specific versions of PyTorch. In chapter 7, the distributed computing example would only work with PyTorch v2.0.1 and CUDA v11.8.

further reading

Chapter 1

Chen, F., Wang, Y-C., Wang, B., and Kuo, C-C. Jay. (2020). Graph representation learning: A survey. *APSIPA Transactions on Signal and Information Processing, 9,* e15.

Elinas, P. (2019, June 5). Knowing your neighbours: Machine learning on graphs. https://mng.bz/1XBQ

Hua, C., Rabusseau, G., and Tang, J. (2022). High-order pooling for graph neural networks with tensor decomposition. *Advances in Neural Information Processing Systems, 35,* 6021-6033.

Liu, Z., and Zhou, J. (2020). *Introduction to Graph Neural Networks,* Morgan & Claypool.

Sanchez-Gonzalez, A., Heess, N., Springenberg, J. T., et al. (2018). Graph networks as learnable physics engines for inference and control. In *An International Conference on Machine Learning* (pp. 4470–4479). PMLR.

Chapter 2

DIMACS. (2011). Tenth DIMACS Implementation Challenge. Georgia Institute of Technology. https://sites.cc.gatech.edu/dimacs10/archive/clustering.shtml

Duong, C. T., Hoang, T. D., Dang, H. T. H., Nguyen, Q. V. H., and Aberer, K. (2019). On node features for graph neural networks. arXiv preprint arXiv:1911.08795.

Krebs, V. (2003, January). Divided we stand??? Orgnet.com. www.orgnet.com/divided1.html

Chapter 4

Cai, T., Shengjie L., Keyulu X., et al. (2021). GraphNorm: A principled approach to accelerating graph neural network training. In *Proceedings of the 38th International Conference on Machine Learning* (pp. 1204–1215). PMLR.

Iacurci, G. (2022, February 22). Consumers lost $5.8 billion to fraud last year—up 70% over 2020. CNBC.com. https://mng.bz/2yG9

Li, F., Huang, M., Yang, Y., and Zhu, X. (2011). Learning to identify review spam. In *Twenty-Second International Joint Conference on Artificial Intelligence* (pp. 2489–2493). IJCAI.

Ma, Y., and Tang, J. (2021). *Deep Learning on Graphs.* Cambridge University Press.

Wang, Y., Zhao, Y., Shah, N., and Derr, T. (2022). Imbalanced graph classification via graph-of-graph neural networks. In *Proceedings of the 31st ACM International Conference on Information & Knowledge Management* (pp. 2067–2076). ACM.

Yelp Multirelational Review Dataset. (n.d.). GitHub. https://mng.bz/RVaD

Zhang, L., and Sun, H. (2024). ESA-GCN: An enhanced graph-based node classification method for class imbalance using ENN-SMOTE sampling and an attention mechanism. *Applied Sciences, 14,* 111.

Chapter 5

Kingma, D. P., and Welling, M. (2013). Auto-encoding variational Bayes. arXiv preprint arXiv:1312.6114.

Langr, J., and Bok, V. (2019). *GANs in Action.* Manning.

RDKit. (n.d.). The RDKit documentation. www.rdkit.org/docs/index.html

Topping, J., Di Giovanni, F., Chamberlain, Dong, X., and Bronstein, M.M. (2021). Understanding over-squashing and bottlenecks on graphs via curvature. arXiv preprint arXiv:2111.14522.

Chapter 7

AMD. (n.d.). Ryzen AI software. https://mng.bz/0QOl

Goodrich, M. T., Tamassia, R., and Goldwasser, M. H. (2013). *Data Structures and Algorithms in Python.* Wiley.

Higham, N. J. (2023, September 5). What is a flop? [blogpost]. https://nhigham.com/2023/09/05/what-is-a-flop/

Intel. (n.d.). Intel NPU Acceleration Library. https://mng.bz/zZeX

Kingma, D. P., and Welling, M. (2013). Auto-encoding variational Bayes. arXiv preprint arXiv:1312.6114.

PyTorch. (n.d.). How to adjust learning rate. https://mng.bz/lY8B

Zeng, H., Zhou, H., Srivastava, A., Kannan, R., and Prasanna, V. (2019). GraphSAINT: Graph sampling based inductive learning method. arXiv preprint arXiv:1907.04931.

Chapter 8

Bechberger, D., and Perryman, J. (2020). *Graph Databases in Action.* Manning.

Appendix A

Besta, M., Peter, E., Gerstenberger, R., et al. (2019). Demystifying graph databases: Analysis and taxonomy of data organization, system designs, and graph queries. ArXiv abs/1910.09017.

Duong, V. M., Nguyen, Q. V. H., Yin, H., Weidlich, M., and Aberer, K. (2019). On node features for graph neural networks. arXiv preprint arXiv:1911.08795.

Fensel, D., Şimşek, U., Angele, K., et al. (2020). *Knowledge Graphs: Methodology, Tools, and Selected Use Cases.* Springer.

Goodrich, M. T., and Tamassia, R. (2015). *Algorithm Design and Applications.* Wiley.

Hamilton, W. L. (2020). *Graph Representation Learning.* Springer.

Nickel, M., Murphy, K., Tresp, V., and Gabrilovich, E. (2015). A review of relational machine learning for knowledge graphs. arXiv preprint arXiv:1503.00759v3.

Resource Description Framework Working Group. (2004, February 10). Resource description framework (RDF): Concepts and abstract syntax. W3C Recommendation. www.w3.org/TR/rdf-concepts/

references

Chapter 1

1 Bronstein, M. M., Bruna, J., LeCun, Y., Szlam, A., and Vandergheynst, P. (2017). Geometric deep learning: Going Beyond Euclidean data. *IEEE Signal Processing Magazine, 34*(4), 18–42.

2 Wu, Z., Shirui, P., Chen, F., et al. (2020). A comprehensive survey on graph neural networks. *IEEE Transactions on Neural Networks and Learning Systems, 32,* 4–24.

3 Deo, N. (1974). *Graph Theory with Applications to Engineering and Computer Science*, Prentice-Hall of India.

4 Luce, D., and Perry, A. D. (1949). A method of matrix analysis of group structure. *Psychometrika, 14,* 95–116.

5 Jia, J., Baykal, C., Potluru, V. K., and Benson, A. R. (2021). Graph belief propagation networks. arXiv preprint arXiv:2106.03033.

6 Gärtner, T., Le, Q. V., and Smola, A. (2005). A short tour of kernel methods for graphs. https://api.semanticscholar.org/CorpusID:4854202

7 Zhukov, L. (2015, May 19). Network analysis: Lecture 17 (part 1). Label propagation on graphs [video]. https://youtu.be/hmashUPJwSQ

8 Keen, B. A. (2017, May 9). Isomap for dimensionality reduction in Python [blogpost]. https://mng.bz/ey8P.

9 Ying, R., He, R., Chen, K., et al. (2018). Graph convolutional neural networks for web-scale recommender systems. In *Proceedings of the 24th ACM SIGKDD International Conference on Knowledge Discovery & Data Mining*. ACM.

10 Sanchez-Lengeling, B., Wei, J. N., Lee, B. K., et al. (2019). Machine learning for scent: Learning generalizable perceptual representations of small molecules. arXiv preprint arXiv:1910.10685.

11 Rigoni, D., Navarin, N., and Sperduti, A. (2020). Conditional constrained graph variational autoencoders for molecule design. *2020 IEEE Symposium Series on Computational Intelligence (SSCI)*. IEEE.

12 Jiang, W., Luo, J., He, M., et al. (2023). Graph neural network for traffic forecasting: The research progress. *ISPRS International Journal of Geo-Information, 12*(3), 100. https://doi.org/10.3390/ijgi12030100

13 Sanchez-Gonzalez, A., Heess, N., Springenberg, J. T., et al. (2018). Graph networks as learnable physics engines for inference and control. In *International Conference on Machine Learning*. PMLR.

14 Rampášek, L., and Wolf, G. (2021). Hierarchical graph neural nets can capture long-range interactions." In *2021 IEEE 31st International Workshop on Machine Learning for Signal Processing* (pp. 1–6). IEEE.

15 Hamilton, W. (2020). *Graph Representational Learning*. Morgan & Claypool.

Chapter 2

1   Hamilton, W. L. (2020). Graph representation learning. *Synthesis Lectures on Artificial Intelligence and Machine Learning, 14*(3), 1–159.

2   Grover, A., and Leskovec, J. (2016). Node2Vec: Scalable feature learning for networks. In *Proceedings of the 22nd ACM SIGKDD International Conference on Knowledge Discovery and Data Mining* (pp. 855–864). ACM.

3   Krebs, V. (n.d.). Pol Books Dataset. www.orgnet.com

4   Krebs, V. (n.d.). Books about US politics. www.orgnet.com/divided.html

5   McInnes, L., Healy, J., and Melville, J. (2018). UMAP: Uniform manifold approximation and projection for dimension reduction. arXiv preprint arXiv:1802.03426.

6   Rossi, A., Tiezzi, M., Dimitri, G. M., et al. (2018). Inductive–transductive learning with graph neural networks. In *Artificial Neural Networks in Pattern Recognition* (pp. 201–212). Springer-Verlag.

7   Perozzi, B., Al-Rfou, R., and Skiena, S. (2014). DeepWalk: Online learning of social representations. In *Proceedings of the 20th ACM SIGKDD International Conference on Knowledge Discovery and Data Mining* (pp. 701–710). ACM.

Chapter 3

1   Kipf, T. N., and Welling, M. (2016). Semi-supervised classification with graph convolutional networks. arXiv preprint arXiv:1609.02907.

2   Hamilton, W. L., Ying, R., and Leskovec, J. (2017). Inductive representation learning on large graphs. In *Proceedings of the 31st International Conference on Neural Information Processing Systems* (pp. 1025–1035). Springer.

3   Li, G. (2022, November). A principled approach to aggregations. *PyTorch Geometric*. https://mng.bz/ga8x

4   Xu, K., Li, C., Tian, Y., et al. (2018). Representation learning on graphs with jumping knowledge networks. In *International Conference on Machine Learning* (pp. 5453–5462). PMLR.

5   Niepert, M., Ahmed, M., and Kutzkov, K. (2016). Learning convolutional neural networks for graphs. In *International Conference on Machine Learning* (pp. 2014–2023). PMLR.

6   Shuman, D. I., Narang, S. K., Frossard, P., et al. (2012). The emerging field of signal processing on graphs: Extending high-dimensional data analysis to networks and other irregular domains. *IEEE Signal Processing Magazine, 30*(3), 83–98.

7   Hamilton, W. L. (2020). Graph representation learning. *Synthesis Lectures on Artificial Intelligence and Machine Learning, 14*(3), 51–89.

8 Gao, H., and Ji, S. (2019). Graph U-nets. In *International Conference on Machine Learning* (pp. 2083–2092). PMLR.

9 McAuley, J., Pandey, R., and Leskovec, J. (2015). Inferring networks of substitutable and complementary products. In *Proceedings of the 21st ACM SIGKDD International Conference on Knowledge Discovery and Data Mining* (pp. 785–794). AMC.

Chapter 4

1 Veličković, P., Cucurull, G., Casanova, A., et al. (2017). Graph attention networks. arXiv preprint arXiv:1710.10903.

2 Brody, S., Alon, U., and Yahav, E. (2021). How attentive are graph attention networks? arXiv preprint arXiv:2105.14491.

3 Alliance to Counter Crime Online. (2020). Fake review fraud. www.counteringcrime.org/review-fraud.

4 Howarth, Josh. 2023. "81 Online Review Statistics." ExplodingTopics. https://explodingtopics.com/blog/online-review-stats

5 Fake Review Statistics. (2024, September 26). CapitalOne Shopping. https://mng.bz/ga0x

6 YelpChi Dataset. GitHub. https://mng.bz/aveo

7 Rayana, S., and Akoglu, L. (2015). Collective opinion spam detection: bridging review networks and metadata. In *Proceedings of the 21st ACM SIGKDD International Conference on Knowledge Discovery and Data Mining* (pp. 985–994). ACM.

8 Dou, Y., Liu, Z., Sun, L., et al. (2020). Enhancing graph neural network-based fraud detectors against camouflaged fraudsters." In *Proceedings of the 29th ACM International Conference on Information & Knowledge Management* (pp. 315–324). ACM.

9 GATConv costs huge GPU memory: Issue #527. (2019). GitHub. https://mng.bz/Zl05

10 Hamilton, W. L., Ying, R., and Leskovec, J. (2017). Inductive representation learning on large graphs. In *Advances in Neural Information Processing Systems* (pp. 1025–1035). ACM.

11 Ma, Y., Tian, Y., Moniz, N., and Chawla, N. V. (2023). Class-imbalanced learning on graphs: A survey. arXiv preprint arXiv:2304.04300.

12 Zhao, T., Zhang, X., and Wang, S. (2021). GraphSMOTE: Imbalanced node classification on graphs with graph neural networks. In *Proceedings of the 14th ACM International Conference on Web Search and Data Mining* (pp. 833–841). ACM.

13 Cristina, S., and Saeed, M. (2022). *Building Transformer Models with Attention.* Machine Learning Mastery.

14 Allamar, J. The illustrated transformer. http://jalammar.github.io/illustrated-transformer/

15 Rusch, T. K., Bronstein, M. M., and Mishra, S. (2023). A survey on over-smoothing in graph neural networks. arXiv preprint arXiv:2303.10993.

Chapter 5

1 Karras, T., Laine, S., and Aila, T. (2019). A style-based generator architecture for generative adversarial networks." In *Proceedings of the IEEE/CVF Conference on Computer Vision and Pattern Recognition* (pp. 4217–4228). IEEE.

2   McAuley, J., Pandey, R., and Leskovec, J. (2015). Inferring networks of substitutable and complementary products. In *Proceedings of the 21st ACM SIGKDD International Conference on Knowledge Discovery and Data Mining* (pp. 785–794). ACM.

3   Kipf, T. N., and Welling, M. (2016). Variational graph auto-encoders. arXiv preprint arXiv:1611.07308.

4   De Cao, N., and Kipf, T. (2018). MolGAN: An implicit generative model for small molecular graphs. arXiv preprint arXiv:1805.11973.

5   Gómez-Bombarelli, R., Wei, J. N., Duvenaud, D., et al. (2018). Automatic chemical design using a data-driven continuous representation of molecules. *ACS Central Science, 4,* 268–276.

6   Basu, V. (2024, December 17). Drug molecule generation with VAE. Keras. https://mng.bz/rKve

7   Alon, U., and Yahav, E. (2020). On the bottleneck of graph neural networks and its practical implications. arXiv preprint arXiv:2006.05205.

Chapter 6

1   Carnegie Mellon University. (n.d.). CMU Graphics Lab Motion Capture Database. http://mocap.cs.cmu.edu/

2   Kipf, T., Fetaya, E., Wang, K-C., Welling, M., and Zemel, R. (2018). Neural relational inference for interacting systems. In *International Conference on Machine Learning* (pp. 2688–2697). PMLR.

3   Raff, E. (2022). *Inside Deep Learning.* Manning.

4   Xu, D., Ruan, C., Korpeoglu, E., Kumar, S., and Achan, K. (2020). Inductive representation learning on temporal graphs. arXiv preprint arXiv:2002.07962.

5   Rossi, E., Chamberlain, B., Frasca, F., et al. (2020). Temporal graph networks for deep learning on dynamic graphs. arXiv preprint arXiv:2006.10637.

6   Zheng, Y., Yi, L., and Wei, Z. (2024). A survey of dynamic graph neural networks. arXiv preprint arXiv:2404.18211.

7   Veličković, P., Cucurull, G., Casanova, A., et al. (2017). Graph attention networks. arXiv preprint arXiv:1710.10903.

Chapter 7

1   Khatua, A., Mailthody, V. S., Taleka, B., et al. (2023). IGB: Addressing the gaps in labeling, features, heterogeneity, and size of public graph datasets for deep learning research. arXiv preprint arXiv:2302.13522.

2   McAuley, J., Pandey, R., and Leskovec, J. (2015). Inferring networks of substitutable and complementary products. In *Proceedings of the 21st ACM SIGKDD International Conference on Knowledge Discovery and Data Mining* (pp. 785–794). ACM.

3   Bronstein, M., Frasca, F., and Rossi, E. (2020, August 8). Simple scalable graph neural networks. Towards Data Science. https://mng.bz/N1Q7

4   Chiang, W-L., Liu, X., Xiaoqing, S., et al. (2019). Cluster-GCN: An efficient algorithm for training deep and large graph convolutional networks. In *Proceedings of the 25th ACM SIGKDD International Conference on Knowledge Discovery and Data Mining* (pp. 257–266). ACM.

5   PyTorch. (n.d.). PyTorch Profiler with TensorBoard. https://mng.bz/EaAj

6 PyTorch. (n.d.). PyTorch Profiler. https://mng.bz/8OBB

7 Heim, L. (2023, September 11). FLOP for quantity, FLOP/s for performance [blogpost]. https://mng.bz/KGnZ

8 Wu, Z., Pan, S., Chen, F., et al. (2020). A comprehensive survey on graph neural networks. *IEEE Transactions on Neural Networks and Learning Systems, 32,* 4–24.

9 PyTorch Geometric. (n.d.). Torch_Geometric.Loader. https://mng.bz/BXBr

10 PyTorch Geometric. (n.d.). Torch_Geometric.Sampler. https://mng.bz/dX8v

11 Kipf, T. N., and Welling, M. (2016). Variational graph auto-encoders. arXiv preprint arXiv:1611.07308.

12 PyTorch Geometric. (n.d.). Memory-efficient aggregations. https://mng.bz/9Ymo

13 namespace-PT. (2021, August 15). A comprehensive tutorial to PyTorch DistributedDataParallel. https://mng.bz/YDzK

14 PyTorch Geometric. (n.d.). Distributed batching. GitHub. https://mng.bz/GeBR

15 Lin, H., Yan, M., Yang, X., et al. (2022). Characterizing and understanding distributed GNN training on GPUs." *IEEE Computer Architecture Letters, 21,* 21–24.

16 Defferrard, M., Bresson, X., and Vandergheynst, P. (2016). Convolutional neural networks on graphs with fast localized spectral filtering. In *Advances in Neural Information Processing Systems* (pp. 3844–3852). ACM.

17 PyTorch Geometric. (n.d.) Scaling up GNNs via remote backends. https://mng.bz/jpdp

18 PyTorch Geometric. (n.d.) Graph_store.py. GitHub. https://mng.bz/W2Yw

19 KuzuDB. (n.d.). KuzuDB Graphstore implementation. GitHub. https://mng.bz/OBXo

20 ArangoDB. (n.d.). ArangoDB remote backend module, FastGraphML. GitHub. https://github .com/arangoml/fastgraphml#fastgraphml

21 Huang, Z., Zhang, S., Xi, C., Liu, T., and Zhou, M. (2021). Scaling up graph neural networks via graph coarsening. In *Proceedings of the 27th ACM SIGKDD Conference on Knowledge Discovery and Data Mining* (pp. 675–684). ACM.

Chapter 8

1 Alexopoulos, P. (2020). *Semantic Modeling for Data.* O'Reilly Media.

2 Barker, R. (1990). *CaseMethod: Entity Relationship Modelling.* Addison-Wesley.

3 Pokorný, J. (2016). Conceptual and database modelling of graph databases. In *Proceedings of the 20th International Database Engineering & Applications Symposium (IDEAS '16)* (pp. 370–377). ACM.

4 Gosnell, D., and Broecheler, M. (2020). *The Practitioners Guide to Graph Data.* O'Reilly Media.

5 Pokorný, J., and Kovačič, J. (2017). Integrity constraints in graph databases. *Procedia Computer Science, 109,* 975–981.

6 Nego, A. (2021). *Graph Powered Machine Learning.* Manning.

7 Neo4j GraphAcademy. (n.d.). Graph data modeling fundamentals. https://mng.bz/pKo2

Appendix A

1 Deo, N. (2017). *Graph Theory with Applications to Engineering and Computer Science.* Dover.

2 Cormen, T. H., Leiserson, C. E., Rivest, R. L., and Stein, C. (2009). *Introduction to Algorithms.* 3rd ed. MIT Press.

3 Skiena, S. (1997). *The Algorithm Design Manual.* Springer-Verlag.

4 Dreyfus, S. E. (1969). An appraisal of some shortest path algorithms. *Operations Research, 17,* 395–412.

index